Political ideology tod

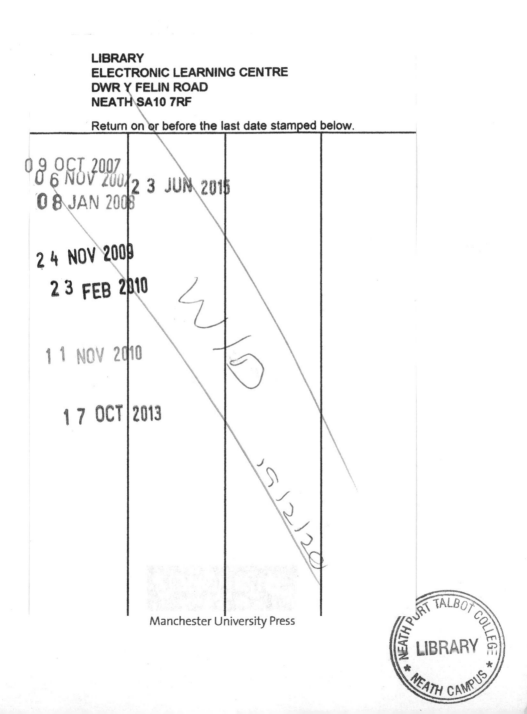

Manchester University Press

Politics Today

series editor: Bill Jones

Political ideology today

Second edition

Ian Adams

Manchester University Press

Manchester and New York
distributed exclusively in the USA by Palgrave

First edition published in 1993 by Manchester University Press
Reprinted 1995

This edition published 2001 by
Manchester University Press
Oxford Road, Manchester M13 9NR, UK
and Room 400, 175 Fifth Avenue, New York, NY 10010, USA
http:///www.manchesteruniversitypress.co.uk

Distributed exclusively in the USA by
Palgrave, 175 Fifth Avenue, New York.
NY 10010, USA

Distributed exclusively in Canada by
UBC Press, University of British Columbia, 2029 West Mall
Vancouver BC, Canada V6T 1Z2

British Library Cataloguing-in-Publication Data
A catalogue record for this book is available from the British Library

Library of Congress Cataloging-in-Publication Data applied for

ISBN 0 7190 6019 2 *hardback*
      0 7190 6020 6 *paperback*

This edition first published 2001

10 09 08 07 06 05   10 9 8 7 6 5 4 3

Typeset
by Helen Skelton, Brighton, UK
Printed in Great Britain
by Biddles Ltd, King's Lynn, Norfolk

To Syd and Muriel

True political science is the science not of what is,
but of what ought to be.

The Abbé Siéyès, *Economie politique* (MS), 1772

Contents

1

Introduction

As recently as the mid-1980s, the pattern of world politics seemed indefinitely fixed. There were two dominant 'blocs' of countries, each bound together by similar beliefs. The Western bloc believed in liberal democracy and a government-managed welfare capitalism, while the Eastern bloc believed in a version of Marxism called communism.

Since then, much has changed. Most spectacular has been the collapse of communist regimes of the Soviet Union and its satellites beginning in 1989. Some argue that the West has simply won the Cold War, and we look forward to an era of ideological uniformity. But this is perhaps wishful thinking. For one thing, the ending of old rigidities in itself implies the possibility of greater variety. There are still communist regimes and former communist regimes that may yet evolve in any number of directions. There has been a striking revival of nationalism in many areas, while religious fundamentalism, particularly anti-Western Islamic fundamentalism, has made a considerable impact on world affairs in recent years which is unlikely to diminish. Within liberal democracies there are new ideological developments, including feminism and sexual politics and green politics. Some argue that the great ideological traditions are dead or dying, yet new varieties of socialism, liberalism and other ideologies continue to evolve.

The world today is a fast-changing place ideologically. If we are to understand the modern world as we embark on the twenty-first century we must know something about the nature and influence of these developments.

What is ideology?

Beyond the idea of a political doctrine, there is little agreement about the nature of ideology. Its essential elements; whether all political doctrines are ideological or only some, and if so which; how we decide whether doctrines are true or false, good or bad, are all questions that have generated many opinions and much heated debate.

Concepts of ideology

For most of its controversial career as a concept, the word 'ideology' has implied some kind of false thinking, something we could all well do without. As a consequence, most theories of ideology have been partisan, where theorists and followers of one political doctrine have tried to characterise other people's ideas as ideological.

Thus, Marx saw ideology as distortions of reality ('false consciousness') in the interests of a particular social class, usually the ruling class. For example, liberalism was the ideology of the bourgeoisie, which masked its exploitation and oppression of other classes. Marx deemed his own theories scientific and therefore not ideological.

Liberals, on the other hand, usually associate ideology with what they call 'closed' systems of thought which purport to be absolute truth. Such thinking leads to the view that those people possessed of the truth must have power and that other people must not be allowed to stand in the way of truth and progress, which then leads directly to totalitarianism. This is seen as contrasting with liberalism itself, which is open and tolerant and rational. Liberalism claims to be a set of sound philosophical principles, while doctrines like Marxism and fascism are seen as ideological.

Traditional conservatism (which liberals tend to regard as lacking in principle and only interested in power, rather than as ideological) tends to see ideology as any kind of politics driven by theory. That is, a politics based on some vision of how society ought to be and pursuing policies designed to make the vision a reality. This they believe to be a futile and dangerous way of approaching politics, and a way to which all doctrines, except conservatism, are prone. Conservative ideas, by contrast, are conceived of as being based upon experience and common sense and judicious caution; in other words, pragmatic rather than ideological.

One of the problems with these partisan views of ideology is that, apart from being manifestly self-serving, they each form part of a wider set of beliefs; so that it is difficult, for example, to subscribe to the Marxist view of ideology without being committed to the rest of Marxism as well.

Sociologists and other academics have tried to be more objective about the question, but they too tend to see ideology as a false kind of thinking from which we need to rid ourselves. However, recent years have seen a change of attitude. Increasingly scholars, as well as politicians and journalists, have taken to using the word in a non-partisan, non-pejorative way, so that it means simply a set of political beliefs about how society ought to be and how to improve it, irrespective of whether those ideas are true or false or good or bad. This neutral concept also makes it easier to discuss the role of ideology in politics, and analyse its elements, without becoming involved in partisan disputes.

Ideology and politics

Politics is largely about reconciling conflicting views in order to come to collective decisions over what to do. Conflicting views arise because people's interests differ. People's values differ as well, and conflicts over values are just as important because we are not only concerned to do what will be effective, but also to do what is right. Individual values may be involved in particular issues, such as the rights and wrongs of abortion, or nuclear weapons; but there are also broader systems of ideas about how society should be run, what values – such as justice or equality or freedom – it should embody, and these broader systems are ideologies.

Although ideologies are concerned with large and distant questions about the best kind of society and the ideal way to live, they are also closely bound up with practical political activity. For example, some politicians may oppose a government proposal to privatise some aspect of the social services because, quite apart from technical considerations of efficiency or cost, they do not wish to see a society where people's welfare becomes a matter of private profit, with the danger that the worse off will end up with a poorer service or none at all. Other politicians may support the same proposal because they want to see a society where as much as possible is left to the free market, which they believe is a society that brings the greatest individual freedom, and therefore is a morally superior society to one where the state provides such things. It is with these fundamental differences of what is morally right and what kind of society we should live in that ideology is concerned above all.

Values and the ideal society

Ideology is first of all concerned with values: that is, how we ought to treat each other and live together in society. Ideologies offer rival visions of the 'good society', the morally best kind of society for human beings to live in. This is true of doctrines we may despise as morally contemptible. The Nazis, for example, saw a world in which the superior races ruled over the inferior as a just world, the right way for human beings to live, and saw racial mixing as immoral.

All ideologies have a conception of an ideal society which embodies the values that the ideology believes in. And for the major ideologies this is not just what is best society for some people in a particular time or place, but what is best for humanity as a whole. To have a view like this involves having a belief about human nature, such that only if human beings live in a certain way will they fulfil their true potential and humanity flourish.

Thus, one ideology, *laissez-faire* liberalism, may see human nature as essentially selfish but rational and therefore see the ideal society as one where individuals have maximum freedom to pursue their own interests in competition with everyone else. Another ideology, a version of classical socialism, may see people as essentially equal and co-operative, where selfishness and competition leads to a class-divided society which distorts human nature and prevents it flourishing. Yet another ideology, ecologism, may see human nature as properly fulfilled only in harmony with nature as a whole, a relationship which modern industrial society distorts. Perhaps only in certain forms of conservatism is the ideal associated with the present or past world, although usually idealised and cleansed of corrupting tendencies and false ideas.

If we have a picture of how the world ought to be then we have a means of evaluating our present world. We can measure it against the ideal and see how far it falls short. We can judge to what extent equality or freedom or justice or the right order of things is missing or denied or threatened.

Furthermore, if the world is not as the ideology would have it be, then there must be some reason why it is not so. Each ideology has its theory about why there is a difference between what is and what ought to be. Liberals tend to blame ignorance, irrational ideas and unchecked power. Socialists blame capitalism, while for anarchists the source of evil is the state.

Finally, if we have a conception of the ideal way to live, the 'good society', and we have an evaluation of our present state, then we need a programme for getting from our present state to the ideal (or for defending the ideal we have). For some the need is to abolish capitalism, or abolish government, or create a society where everybody is in free competition with everyone else, or re-establish monarchy, or free the nation from foreign domination, or regain a lost harmony with nature, or whatever it might be.

Thus, rather like religions, the major ideologies have a certain comprehensiveness about their conception of the human condition. They offer all-embracing theories about human nature and the ideal society best suited to that nature, and why our present world falls short and how the better world can be created, or the present good defended. These elements all connect together to present a more-or-less coherent vision of social reality.

Belief, action and tradition

Ideologies, then, are guides to political action. They give us ideals to believe in, tell us for what goals to strive and for what causes to fight. They thereby give the individual believer a sense of identity and a sense of purpose. One can see oneself as a liberal working for human rights, a nationalist working for one's country's freedom, a revolutionary socialist working to overthrow the capitalist system, or a woman challenging the power of patriarchy, all on behalf of some part of humanity, yet thereby working for the ultimate good of humanity as such.

Ideologies can tell us what policies to pursue, who are our friends and enemies, and why rival beliefs are at best wrong and dangerous. Ideologies can, therefore, inspire common action and satisfy our aspiration to create or preserve the best possible world in which all, or at least those most worthy, can find fulfilment.

However, an important point must be made here. The various elements of ideology only fit neatly together in the way just described when we look at particular versions of ideology. When we speak of socialism or conservatism or any of the major ideologies, we are speaking of broad traditions of thought made up of many such versions. These versions frequently conflict with each other and give rise to disputes about which is the true or authentic version, such as whether, for example, communism was 'true' Marxism or a distortion of it, or if anarcho-capitalism is authentic anarchism. To understand ideologies we need to see each tradition developed individually over time.

An historical approach

Readers of this book might reasonably complain that it could just as well have been called 'Political ideology yesterday'. There is certainly much in it about the past. But there are good reasons for this. In the first place, the ideological beliefs that prevail today are the outcomes of often long and complicated developments, which need to be understood to some extent if we are to make sense of present complexities. For example, in Britain it could be argued that the Conservative Party is to a considerable degree no longer inspired by conservatism; that pure liberalism is no longer the doctrine of the Liberal Party; and that the Labour Party has finally given up socialism. Unravelling confusing truths such as these requires a certain amount of historical perspective.

Second, while it is true that there have been recent developments in ideology, it is nevertheless still the case that the political beliefs of most people today were developed a century or more ago. The great creative phase of ideological construction was roughly the century following the outbreak of the French Revolution, and we are still to a large extent living off the intellectual capital of that period when the foundations of much of our present thinking were laid.

Thirdly, it is a mistake to regard ideological thinking as a body of accumulating knowledge or wisdom in the manner of science. In science for the most part, present theories have replaced older ones because they were demonstrably superior, and it is not really necessary to be a good scientist to know what those discarded theories were. But political ideologies are not like this. They are broad traditions of thought, often with co-existing contradictory strands, that evolve and grow more according to what people find plausible at any one time, rather than in conformity to any set of rules determining truth or falsity. Consequently, ideas that are convincing at one time may come to seem outmoded and useless at another; but then may be revived with new vigour at yet another time. This is easy enough to illustrate with an example.

One of the most dynamic and successful ideological positions in recent times has been New Right free-market capitalism, of the kind with which Margaret Thatcher and Ronald Reagan were associated. This view is also sometimes called 'neo-liberalism' because it is essentially a revival of early nineteenth-century liberal thought, a version of liberalism that as late as the 1960s seemed obsolete to most people interested in political ideas. Furthermore, the most distinguished philosopher connected with this movement, Robert Nozick, took his inspiration from the ideas the seventeenth-century thinker, John Locke.

Therefore, to make sense of our present ideological preoccupations we need to look back. We need to be aware of the evolution of ideas in order to comprehend the full range of the familiar, the new and the exotic species of ideology that inhabit the political world today. In this book, therefore, the various ideologies are presented in the order of their appearance on the political stage. Each ideology is described as a tradition of thought evolving over time, from origins to present influence.

The crucible of modernity

Ideological thinking is at least as old as the Ancient Greeks. But if our concern is with the ideologies of today's world, then we must focus on those doctrines that have inspired modern political movements. In this sense the modern age has been very much the age of the French Revolution, for as the historian, Simon Schama, has put it:

> the Revolution had indeed been the crucible of modernity; the vessel in which all the characteristics of the modern world had been distilled.
>
> (1989, Preface, p.xiv)

Before looking at individual ideologies we need to see why the French Revolution is so critical an event in the development of today's ideologies.

The French Revolution was a mighty cataclysm that changed the history of modern times as has no other single event. It came as one of a spate of revolutions which helped to create the modern world. There was the American Revolution and the Industrial Revolution, and even an intellectual revolution in the rise of Romanticism, but it is the French Revolution that is important politically. It is the point when politics is recreated and redefined and given a new vocabulary, the point when modern politics comes into being.

It was the most self-conscious of revolutions. Unlike the Renaissance or Industrial Revolution, everyone knew it was a great revolution from the start, and especially those engaged in it. They knew that they were taking part in momentous events, that they were changing the world, and that Europe could not be the same again. Everyone in the Western world, even the least educated, was transfixed by the turmoil in France.

There had of course been political revolutions before, most notably in England in the previous century and more recently in America. But England in the seventeenth century had been on the fringe of Europe, a great European war was going on at the same time in Germany, and in any case much of the old order was restored. The American rebellion was closer in time and politics, but America was perceived as a distant wilderness on the other side of the world.

In contrast to both of these, France was in many ways the leading country of Europe, the centre of European culture, and possessed of the most majestic of monarchies. Paris was widely regarded as the leader of arts and of fashion, as well as the intellectual capital of Europe. It is against this background of eminence and splendour that the violence and fanaticism of the revolution was so extraordinary and startling. There had been nothing like it in European history.

It was because France was seen as the very heart of European civilisation, the very home of reason, that the political and psychological shock and significance was so immediate and profound for everyone. At one blow it destroyed the magic of, and the sanctity of, the time immemorial, taken-for-granted, established order of Europe that had prevailed hitherto, the order which had been regarded as natural and inevitable, God-given and ultimately indestructible. The demolition of the political order, the massacre of the ruling aristocracy and the power of the Paris mob were almost beyond belief.

More important than the destruction of the old was the possibility of making the world anew, of making a fresh start based on reason and justice. It was a frightening time, but also a time of great hope, particularly before the Terror; the end of civilisation or the beginning of civilisation, according to your point of view. The hope of a new age was expressed by the young Wordsworth in the famous lines:

> Bliss was it in that dawn to be alive,
> But to be young was very heaven!
>
> ... 'twas a time when Europe was rejoiced,
> France standing on the top of golden hours,
> And human nature seeming born again.
>
> (William Wordsworth, *The Prelude*)

When society and the frame of human existence no longer seemed divinely ordained or eternal, all things seemed possible. To the revolutionaries everything could be changed, everything remade along rational lines.

The very measurement of space and time was refashioned with the metric system and the ten-month year (dividing things by ten was taken as self-evidently more rational than by any other number). Even a new religion of the Supreme Being, to be worshipped as the fount of reason, was inaugurated. This was claimed to be a rational religion, traditional Christianity being deemed to be based on myth and superstition. But perhaps most startling of all was the notion of remaking human nature, of reshaping humanity by political means.

Symbolising this seeming capacity to change the whole of life at will, the making and remaking of the French state went on with bewildering frequency. There was an extraordinary parade of political forms – from absolute to constitutional monarchy, to totalitarian democracy to military dictatorship – all telescoped into a few years. At the same time, we were given a new vocabulary with which to understand the world politically, including 'left and right', 'popular sovereignty' and 'national self-determination'. In such an atmosphere, ideas of how society ought to be organised abounded. The ferment of ideas of the revolutionary period generated almost the whole range of modern ideologies: nationalism, socialism, conservatism, anarchism and feminism, as well as new versions of the liberalism that helped to inspire the revolution itself. Later ideologies such as Marxism and fascism built upon these revolutionary themes.

A new postmodern world?

The French Revolution thus inaugurated an age of ideologies all of which might be said to have initially developed as either extensions of liberalism or as reactions against it, and all reflected the liberal aspiration to comprehend the whole of humanity and solve its fundamental social problems. It was an age of universal ideologies, all in conflict and competition with each other.

However, it could be argued that this 'age of the French Revolution' is now over, and that such have been the massive changes in the world's political and ideological landscape recently that we can now see the emergence of a new era of ideology, with new ideologies and new types of ideology replacing the old. This may be just a passing phase, a temporary period of turbulence and uncertainty, but it could be that the change in the nature and pattern of ideology reflects a much more general and permanent change in society and politics, economy and culture.

Some people see these trends as symptomatic of the end of modern history, symbolised by the collapse of Soviet communism, and the beginning of an entirely new era in human history, which they provisionally title 'postmodernity'. This is a controversial claim and many disagree. But certainly there have been major changes, and it will be convenient to sum them up with the term 'postmodern', which has become widely used among social thinkers and commentators. Whether these changes really do amount to a new age of human history is a matter that will be discussed later. For the moment it is sufficient to mention a few of the features of the present 'postmodern' world that are relevant to ideological beliefs today.

A changed and changing world

Perhaps the most obvious way our present world is changing is in globalisation, the process of creating a world economy and system of world communications that develops and evolves quite independently of any state or other kind of control. In consequence national boundaries are less important and national sovereignty less of a reality. At the same time, cultural globalisation has, paradoxically, called forth an opposite force asserting local difference in small-scale nationalisms, religious revivals and other expressions of identity and particularity.

These wider changes are related to, and interact with, changes within individual societies. The mass-production economy, where mass workforces produced standardised goods for societies divided into social classes with attendant lifestyles and class identities, has been largely left behind. It has been superseded by a postindustrial economy driven by consumer choice, advertising and television and based on services as much as physical goods. The resultant society is much more individualist and pluralist and multi-cultural, where class and region no longer determine people's lifestyle and outlook. Other forms of identity – national, ethnic, religious, sexual and others – are more important. We now choose our own lifestyles and to a considerable degree choose who we are.

The mass parties of the industrial era, that broadly reflected class interests, still compete for government, but with the decline of class they can no longer rely on automatic mass support as once they did. Politics has become more complicated. The electorate is more volatile and there are more parties. There are also what are called 'new social movements' outside the traditional political structures that attract support for all kinds of issues, such as minority rights, protecting the environment, women's issues and so on. They have their own political agendas, as well as ideologies tailored to their particular preoccupation that are less universal and exclusive than the major ideologies, which seem to be in relative decline.

We now live, therefore, in a much more fluid and changeable world, where traditional landmarks are fading. Some thinkers, known as 'postmodernists', argue that we a witnessing a corresponding decline in intellectual certainties. They claim that we no longer believe in progress or any grand theories for the improvement of mankind, that we have lost our faith in absolute truth. Instead, in this multicultural and pluralist world we only have multiple points of view with no certain way of establishing who is right or wrong. This is a controversial theory that has large implications for the future politics and ideology that will be discussed in the closing chapter. In the meanwhile we need to analyse where we are and how we came here, which is the main purpose of the rest of this book.

2

Liberalism and democracy

Liberalism has been the most successful ideology of the modern world. The ideals of the Western world are largely liberal ideals. Indeed, with the collapse of communist regimes in Europe since 1989 it has been argued that there is no serious rival for the adherence of the majority of humankind in sight. However, it is only possible to make such a sweeping generalisation by interpreting the term 'liberalism' very broadly. For liberalism is not a single set of fixed beliefs, but a broad tradition of thought that has been evolving over more than three centuries in several different directions.

There are a number of things for which most liberals would agree that liberalism stands. Above all there is individual freedom or liberty. This in turn implies those things that will secure and enhance that liberty, including equality of rights, constitutional government, the rule of law and toleration. However, different versions of liberalism interpret freedom and its attendant values in different and sometimes conflicting ways, and also differ as to how these ideals are best pursued. To understand these differences we need to go back to liberalism's English roots.

Whigs and republicans

The end of the Middle Ages was marked by a series of overlapping and interacting revolutions and other developments that challenged and eventually overthrew the mediaeval outlook. These included the Renaissance and Reformation, the discovery of the New World, the rise of capitalist enterprise and the consolidation of the centralised nation-state, along with revolutions in philosophy and science. It was the rise of liberalism that was the equivalent in social and political thought. It offered an alternative conception of humanity as essentially rational and capable of running its own affairs without the tutelage of church and king. Instead of the old natural hierarchy with everyone fixed in their God-given place, people were conceived of as being essentially equal, possessed of equal rights and equally capable of liberty and making up their own minds. At the same time, liberalism was also a response to the more recent development of the centralised state.

England was among the countries most affected by the social and intellectual changes of the time, and it was mainly here, assisted by the catalyst of civil war, that liberal ideas gradually developed. It was later, in the eighteenth century, that these ideas reached a wider European and American audience, when they were assisted (especially in America and France) by notions of reviving and adapting ancient forms of government and citizenship.

The English Civil Wars

The English Civil Wars of the mid-seventeenth century were a conflict for supremacy between king and parliament, although complicated and exacerbated by religious differences. Parliament won, but the victory had to be consolidated a generation later by the Glorious Revolution of 1688. However, behind the struggle between ancient institutions and ancient claims to rights and privileges were new ideas. On the one hand, there were royalist claims to the divine right of kings, which was in fact a recent theory asserting absolute royal power; while on the other hand, there were liberal ideas of freedom, rationality and individuality that would come to challenge the authority of tradition as such. The traditional mediaeval outlook tended to see people in terms of their social position and the community they belonged to. Claims to freedom and toleration challenged traditional authority of the king who knew what was best for his subjects, and of the church which told them what to think. Liberalism developed as a rejection of tradition in the name of reason.

The Civil Wars were as much wars of words as of killing and destruction. The nature of society and how it should be organised and run was at the heart of the conflict and it was accompanied by a flood of books and pamphlets about how these things ought to be. They ranged from advocating absolute power by anyone who could maintain it, to various kinds of theocracy (rule by the church), to a variety of democratic solutions, and even to forgetting about politics altogether to prepare for the Second Coming.

Among the more cogent were the Levellers, a group in Cromwell's army who advocated limited democracy, demanding the vote for all men who were not servants, and claiming freedom and a degree of equality for all (what contemporaries called 'social levelling', hence their name). However, with the restoration of the monarchy in 1660 came the restoration of the old social order and such ideas soon appeared unrealistic and obscure. Nevertheless, Civil War divisions to some extent remained, especially since the king still harboured ambitions of absolute royal power. Political opinion divided between royal supporters (Tories) and those who upheld parliamentary authority (Whigs). The upshot was the driving out of King James II in 1688 for attempting to impose a Catholic absolutism upon an unwilling nation. This 'Glorious

Revolution' permanently established parliamentary supremacy. The Whig writer whose work provided the justification for the Revolution was John Locke.

John Locke

Locke's ideas owed a certain amount to the Civil War radicals, but in his *Two Treatise of Government* (1690) he created a more coherent and less iconoclastic theory. All individuals, he argued, are endowed by God with reason, by means of which each can discern what is right and wrong and how they should live. This was the old mediaeval theory of Natural Law, which stressed everyone's social obligations. What was new was Locke's individualist interpretation of it. His central idea was that God endowed every man with certain natural rights, most importantly the rights to life and liberty and property. Locke also maintained that, even without God, Natural Law and natural rights would still be true (although this is very doubtful).

Initially, Locke argued, men lived a perfectly adequate social life without any government in a 'state of nature', guided only by their reason. However, this presented certain difficulties in dealing with criminals, serious disputes and other problems. To overcome these difficulties men agree to a 'social contract' to create government as a trust, for the sole purpose of protecting their pre-existing rights. Government must, therefore, be based upon the consent of the governed, expressed in representative institutions. If government does not fulfil its trust, by, for example, attacking property (such as confiscation or taxing without consent), the people are free to remove the government and replace it with one that will do its job properly. In a separate work, *A Letter Concerning Toleration* (1689), Locke supplemented these ideas by advocating religious tolerance (although somewhat limited by our standards).

Locke is generally regarded as the first major Liberal thinker. He expounded most of the main themes of subsequent theorists: human rights, individual liberty, minimal government, constitutional government, the executive subject to the people's representatives, sanctity of property, civil liberties and toleration. On the other hand, he was no democrat. What he wanted above all was to have the king's government permanently subject to the control of parliament. He thought that the franchise should be confined to those of substantial property, and only to men (women were rational but less so than men, by whom they should be ruled). He had no desire to change existing society in any way. The Glorious Revolution was essentially a defensive revolution, to preserve traditional English liberties against authoritarian innovation based on a continental model. It was his way of defending those liberties that was new. Locke represents the socially conservative or Whig wing of liberalism, while the Levellers and related groups, who did want social change, represent the radical democratic wing.

The Glorious Revolution established the Whigs as the dominant force in British politics for most of the next century. The system Locke defended became progressively more corrupt, with the landed aristocracy controlling the House of Commons more and more. The Whig party was dominated by a number of great aristocratic families who regarded their own rights and freedoms as the bulwark of the rights and freedoms of all Englishmen. Locke and his ideas of universal rights and the right of the people to rebel if necessary, were largely ignored by the establishment Whigs. His thought had more impact in America and France.

The American Revolution

In the course of the eighteenth century, Britain's thirteen American colonies became embroiled in a fierce conflict with the mother country. When it came to a final break, the Americans turned to Locke to justify their rebellion. *The Declaration of Independence* (1776) reads:

> We hold these truths to be self-evident: that all men are created equal; that they are endowed by their Creator with certain inalienable rights; that among these are life, liberty and the pursuit of happiness; that to secure these rights governments are instituted among men, deriving their just powers from the consent of the governed; that whenever any form of government becomes destructive of these ends it is the right of the people to alter or abolish it.
>
> (quoted in Jefferson, 1999, p.102)

This is pure Locke, with one exception. 'Property' was left out (it was taken for granted as being part of liberty anyway) and replaced by 'the pursuit of happiness', a fashionable notion of the French Enlightenment.

As to the American Constitution of 1787, it is not in fact the pure democratic document it is often assumed to be. It is remarkably Whiggish. Its framers did not want a democracy but a republic, as advocated by many Ancient authors, particularly Cicero and Polybius, who attributed Ancient Rome's early greatness to her republican constitution and the civic virtue (public spiritedness) that went with it. They made a clear distinction, as we tend not to do today, between liberty and democracy, and a republic was thought the best way to secure liberty.

By a republic was meant a mixed constitution like Ancient Rome, with its combination of rule of the one, the few and the many; with each limiting and balancing the others so that no one class or group or individual would dominate, and the common good would prevail. Britain, with its king, Lords and Commons, was a republic in this sense – that is, with a monarchic element, an aristocratic element and a democratic element – and the Americans accepted it as such (Alexander Hamilton, another of the American leaders, called the British system of government 'the best in the world'). The republican idea also implied the absence of hereditary office, but it was not this or any other aspect of Britain's government that the Americans initially objected to, but to the fact that Britain had treated them badly according to Britain's own principles of government.

Of the American leaders, the most sympathetic to democracy was Thomas Jefferson (1743–1826), who had drafted the *Declaration of Independence*, and who was influenced by French radical ideas as well as by Locke. He had an optimistic view of human nature, and had a profound faith in the decency and wisdom of ordinary people, who he believed were best guardians of their own liberties. But he was not a great lover of the city, and his ideal of democracy was of a rural world of independent, educated citizen-farmers. He did not think democracy was suitable to a society of large cities and advanced manufacture, and did not want America to move in this direction.

However, when the US Constitution was being drawn up at the Constitutional Convention in Philadelphia in 1787, Jefferson was in Paris representing his country as ambassador to France, and the Convention's proceedings were dominated by those with a more conservative outlook, who were largely responsible for the elaborate system of checks and balances which characterise the constitution – the separation of powers, the federal system, the President, Senate and House of Representatives voted for in different ways and for different periods, and so on – and which were meant to fragment and frustrate the majority. Different interests would cancel each other out and no group could dominate. The ideal was a balanced constitution, combining the best elements of different forms. Only one element, the House of Representatives, was to be democratically elected, although not by all citizens, since there were property qualifications attached to the right to vote.

Thus, the Constitution was republican, in the sense of all society being represented, but it did not become genuinely democratic until later. On the other hand, great store was set by the rights of all citizens. These are laid down in the first ten amendments, or Bill of Rights, which came into force with the rest of the Constitution in 1791.

Montesquieu

The one Whiggish feature of the US Constitution which did not come mainly from British thought and practice, is the principle of the separation of powers. This came from the French Enlightenment thinker, the Baron de Montesquieu. If the essence of Whiggism is the protection of liberty through constitutionalism without trying to change society, then Montesquieu is the French Whig. He argued that tyranny consisted in all the branches of government, the executive, legislative and judicial, being concentrated in the same hands. This was true of royal government in his native France and in continental Europe generally, where kings had done away with mediaeval parliaments and made all decisions and laws themselves, backed up by the theory of divine right of kings.

It had been resistance to this development in England that had led to the

Civil Wars. To many at that time, royal absolutism was modern and efficient. However, the thinkers of the Enlightenment changed this perception. Britain was seen by them as ahead of its time in reducing the authority of priest and king and giving more liberty to the people.

Radicals and revolutionaries

While Whig liberalism prevailed in the Anglo-Saxon world, continental Europe developed its own tradition of liberal thought, especially in France. Locke was also the key figure here, but because there was no tradition of individual liberty or of parliamentary representation, his ideas were much more radical and liberalism developed more as a revolutionary doctrine that was concerned to change society.

The Enlightenment

The Enlightenment was the major intellectual movement of the eighteenth century. The idea of the Enlightenment was of the condition of mankind being improved by the light of reason. It involved a conscious rejection of tradition, including traditional authority in religion, government, science, the arts, and in all forms of human understanding. The starting point was that human beings are essentially rational, and as such are capable of pursuing their own interests and running their own affairs, and therefore should be free to do so.

Such a view of human nature conflicted with the traditional religious conception of man as tainted with original sin and therefore in need of guidance, discipline and firm rule. The theory of original sin was used to explain the crime and violence and misery in the world. Enlightenment thinkers argued that these things existed not because man was naturally bad, but because man had been kept in the darkness of ignorance and superstition and not allowed to develop his reason; and the main responsibility for this had been the kings and priests who had a vested interest in keeping the population in ignorance. Mankind would only make progress if it learnt to use its reason (above all in philosophy and science) and applied it to its circumstances. The ills of mankind could be cured and all could be happy and fulfilled if they lived a rational life and society was reorganised along rational lines, based upon a genuine science of human nature.

The main centre of Enlightenment thinking was France, although it was to Britain that the French thinkers looked for inspiration. In particular they regarded the two greatest contributors to human reason as Isaac Newton and John Locke. They took Locke's ideas as providing the basis of the rational society, once the centuries of prejudice and superstition that clouded people's minds had been removed. Only then would there be a new age of reason and unlimited human progress. The idea of progress was in fact an invention of the Enlightenment.

These ideas were extremely radical in authoritarian France, although less so by the standards of Britain and America. Only one of the Enlightenment thinkers was a democrat. Rousseau was the least typical and most original of them, and he demanded a form of democracy that no modern thinker has advocated before or since.

Rousseau

Jean-Jacques Rousseau (1712–78) was Swiss, although he spent most of his adult life in France. His writings gained an enormous following all over Europe. In his main political work, *The Social Contract* (1762), Rousseau argued that all men had an absolute right to be free. His argument was that what distinguishes the human from the animal was not that humans have reason, but the fact that human beings are capable of moral choice, and therefore man must be free in order to exercise that choice. (It is worth noting that, like Locke, Rousseau tended to see women as lesser beings who were not entitled to the same rights as men.) If people are not free, or if their freedom is restricted, then their humanity is being denied and they are being treated as sub-human, as slaves or animals.

Rousseau then went on to insist that if people had to live according to laws they did not make themselves then they are not free, they are slaves. It made little difference if a law-making body had been elected by the people, since it was still other people making the laws; and those subject to them were still denied the freedom which was their natural right as human beings. On Rousseau's theory, the vast majority of us living in today's liberal democracies are 'slaves'.

The problem Rousseau's theory led him to was this: how was it possible for people to live in society and yet still be free. It was only possible, he said, if people lived by only those laws they had made themselves, and not by anyone on their behalf. This in turn was only possible if the entire citizen body gathered in one place and voted spontaneously upon proposals for new laws (he did not want political parties or any discussion). If everyone voted according to what they knew was the common good, and not their own interests, then the laws passed would be valid and binding; and in obeying them everyone would be free because they would be obeying themselves. These laws would be, as he put it, an expression of the General Will.

Rousseau's idea of the General Will may sound straightforward enough but in fact it bristles with difficulties. Only laws based on the General Will are valid and binding. But it is never entirely clear which laws are and which are not – for when people vote some, or even all of them, may be voting out of selfish interests, which does not count. It is possible that in fact only one person voting represents the General Will. But Rousseau never gives us a sure way of telling.

He only insists that the General Will is always right and that 'the voice of the people is the voice of God'. But apart from these theoretical difficulties, Rousseau's notion of an assembly of all citizens is clearly not possible in modern states.

His ideal was the city states of Ancient Greece (notably the austere and puritanical Sparta). Like Ancient city states he wanted a civic religion to which all citizens must conform and which would inculcate patriotism and other civic virtues. But unlike the city states, he wanted a citizenry of equals. His ideal seems to have been a community of artisans and small farmers, each with just sufficient property to be independent. Such a society could hardly exist in his day, let alone ours. What the practical implications of his ideas for the modern world might be, Rousseau does not tell us.

Rousseau is the most exasperating of political thinkers. He is the first modern democratic theorist, and yet he believed in a form of direct democracy that is impossible; he did not believe in parties or pressure groups; and believed we are only bound by laws unanimously consented to, even if people did not vote for them (though they apparently would have done had they been thinking unselfishly). He is insistent on popular sovereignty and the necessary equality of all citizens, yet some writers on Rousseau have attributed to him the intellectual parenthood of modern totalitarianism (most notably J.L.Talmon in *The Origins of Totalitarian Democracy*, 1952). Robespierre claimed to be representing the General Will when he inaugurated the Terror, although some think it grossly unfair to saddle Rousseau with responsibility for later regimes that at best only used his ideas selectively. But either way, Rousseau is an important thinker, if a difficult one. In some ways he is as controversial now as he ever was.

If Rousseau belongs in the liberal tradition, and there are some who insist he does not, he is a very different kind of liberal from John Locke. He certainly did not advocate the kind of liberal democracy we know today, and repudiates many aspects of modern democracy that we take for granted. The main reason why some dispute his liberal credentials is that his ideal appears to be social unity and uniformity; there seems to be no room for the individual who wishes to be different. On the other hand, he believed in freedom, equality, the rights of citizens and popular sovereignty against the claims of traditional authority; all characteristic of the liberal outlook.

The French Revolution

What happened in France began as a civilised affair. The authority of the monarchy collapsed and the king called the Estates General (the ancient parliament that had not met for several hundred years) to sort out the mess. This led to a conflict where the section representing the common people declared itself the National Assembly, committed itself to human rights in its *Declaration of the Rights of Man*, and demanded a government that would protect them. What they had in mind was a constitutional monarchy subject to an assembly elected by a limited franchise, which was the basis of the Constitution of 1791.

However, the tide of events grew faster and favoured the more radical Jacobins, who brushed the moderates aside and introduced the Terror to stiffen the population in the face of possible invasion and destruction of the Revolution. The king and a large part of the aristocracy were guillotined. The bloodshed and anarchy were horrific, and even when it ceased government remained a shambles. However, the Jacobins did not represent different beliefs so much as the beliefs that inspired the first phase pushed to their logical conclusion.

Neither John Locke and the men of the Glorious Revolution of 1688, nor the American Revolutionaries of 1776, had any idea of changing society. Indeed, they thought of themselves as preserving their society from alien imposition. Their ideas of constitutionalism and individual rights were meant to defend the social order they knew. They thought in terms of equality of rights; any egalitarian or democratic implications their ideas might have had were ignored.

The French Revolution was different. Notions of egalitarianism and democracy were there from the start. They are there in the revolutionary cry for 'Liberty, Equality, Fraternity', and in the *Declaration of the Rights of Man*. While individual rights are important, the real starting point is the sovereignty and authority of the people, as against their usurpation by King and nobility. The French Revolution was inevitably, therefore, a social revolution. Liberty, Equality and Fraternity implied that the citizen body is a brotherhood of social equals, bound together by a civic virtue that gives priority to the common good.

The Jacobins merely made the egalitarian and democratic content of the revolutionary thinking explicit and acted upon it. As Robespierre put it:

> Democracy is the only form of state which all the individuals composing it can truly call their country ... the French are the first people in the world to establish a true democracy, by calling all men to enjoy equality and fullness of civil rights ... Now what is the principle of popular or democratic rule, I mean the fundamental motive which sustains and impels it? It is virtue. I refer to the public Virtue which accomplished so many marvellous things in Greece and Rome, and which should create even more wondrous things in our Republican France – that Virtue which is nothing more than love of the Nation and its laws
>
> (quoted in Vansittart, 1989, pp.272–3)

Civic virtue was promoted by the new religion of the Supreme Being (following Rousseau's belief in the need for a civic religion) to replace Christianity.

All supporters of the Revolution accepted Rousseau's idea of the sovereignty of the people. Only the Jacobins took his radical democratic ideas seriously. Their constitution of 1793 guaranteed universal manhood suffrage, annual parliaments, referenda, the 'sacred right' of the people to revolt if government was violating their rights, work for each individual or else support by the state, education for all, and other measures, all in the name of the happiness of the people.

The Jacobins wrote little, but from notes left by Robespierre's closest associate, Saint-Just, it seems that their ideal was a society of small farmers and craftsmen, each with sufficient property for a livelihood, to be achieved through confiscation of aristocratic land. It needs to be remembered that until the vast private wealth created by the industrial revolution, virtually all radicals saw property as a great bulwark of freedom

When the Jacobins were overthrown and executed, a more moderate constitution was restored, but instability continued. In fact despite interludes of strong government, the French did not achieve a fully stable system during the next century. There were a series of revolutions and new constitutions as France struggled to come to terms with its own revolutionary legacy.

Contemporary influence of the French Revolution

In Germany, the most important influence of the early Revolution was upon the great philosopher, Immanuel Kant. He was inspired by the ideals of the Revolution, while being horrified by the course of events. As an admirer of Rousseau, he believed that the essence of freedom lay in moral autonomy, in people's capacity to live according to rules they have made themselves. To be genuinely free, therefore, was not to simply pursue one's self-interest, but to act according to one's self-defined moral duty in spite of one's self-interest.

Kant believed that this very capacity alone gave human beings a moral stature that entitled all individuals to be as free as was consistent with maximum freedom for all. The good society therefore was one that was consistent with this principle. That, in Kant's view, meant a constitutional monarchy answerable to a representative assembly elected on a property franchise and guaranteeing civil rights for all. (He did not follow Rousseau in dismissing representative government as a sham.) However, it was a long time before Kant's ideas became influential in Europe, and even longer in his native Germany. In the meanwhile, liberalism was divided between its more radical and more Whiggish proponents.

The leading radical in Britain during the 1790s was Tom Paine who, remarkably, also played a significant role in both the American and French Revolutions. His main book, *The Rights of Man* (1791–92), advocated radical democracy, the abolition of the monarchy and all social privilege. Like the radicals of Paris he was also concerned with equality and advocated what we would call welfare state measures. He could not, however, be called a socialist. Like almost all radicals of the time he saw property as among the most fundamental of natural rights, and essential to the defence of freedom.

The British establishment was badly shaken by the French Revolution and repressed all agitation for reform, banned trade unions and turned a deaf ear to appeals to deal with the appalling social problems thrown up by the

Industrial Revolution. When political and social reform did really begin, with the Great Reform Act of 1832, the outcome was decidedly Whiggish and far removed from any radicalism. However, by this time a new dimension of liberalism had developed, and was making an impact on the thinking and actions of governments. This was economic liberalism.

Classical liberalism

Liberal ideas were behind both of the great political revolutions of the late eighteenth century, and were principally concerned with matters of civil rights and constitutions. The other great revolution of the age, which was even more central to the creation of the modern world than those of America and France, was the Industrial Revolution; liberal ideas were important here as well.

The break-up of the mediaeval world, with its feudal system and guilds, allowed people more economic freedom and made possible the early growth of capitalism. Nevertheless, governments still had a great deal of control over economic activity in manufacturing and trade. When the case for economic liberalism began to be argued in the eighteenth century, the startling claim was made that if everyone was simply left to their own economic devices, then the result would not be chaos but a harmonious society of ever-growing prosperity. The fusion of this economic liberalism with political liberalism produced one of the most powerful and influential doctrines of modern times, known as classical or *laissez-faire* liberalism.

Adam Smith

The Enlightenment aspiration to create a rational science of man did not have much success, except in the one area of economics. In 1776, the Scottish philosopher Adam Smith (1723–90) published his great work, *The Wealth of Nations*, which laid the foundations of modern economic theory. Above all, it revealed the wonders of the free market and demonstrated the overall benefits of the unrestricted movement of goods, capital and labour. It argued that the free market, free of all government interference, would produce maximum prosperity for the whole nation. Everyone pursuing their own selfish self-interest would in fact be for the maximum benefit of all (see Chapter 9.).

The government policy of non-intervention, or *laissez-faire*, that Smith was advocating was at odds with the economic practice of most governments of his day, who sought to control economic activity in great detail. They protected home industry by high import duties, granted legal monopolies and allowed a multitude of internal barriers to trade between regions. It took time, therefore, for his ideas to influence government. But such influence was inevitable in the long run, since they chimed so well with the wishes of the new class of industrialists who were creating Britain's industrial revolution. To a great degree, it was the adherence of this group to liberal ideas that eventually gave a more radical liberalism (though not of the revolutionary kind) a certain respectability in the early nineteenth century.

It was the coming together of the ideas of Adam Smith and his followers (known as the 'classical economists') with the ideas of Locke, and other advocates of civil rights and limited government, that created classical or *laissez-faire* liberalism, based on the principles of the free market, minimal government and individual freedom and responsibility. It produced a picture of an ideal society of free, self-reliant, responsible, productive individuals, possessed of equal rights, creating a prosperous economy with the minimum of government involvement. Such a government would be representative of, and responsible to, the people, according to a constitution.

Although the term 'liberalism' has been used freely up to now, it was not until the early nineteenth century that the word began to be used to denote a political doctrine. The name came to be adopted by some of the more progressive members of the Whig Party, and by the followers of Jeremy Bentham (1748–1832).

Utilitarianism

Bentham founded a system of ideas known as utilitarianism. This was based on the idea that all human psychology could be reduced to the pursuit of pleasure and the avoidance of pain, from which it followed, according to Bentham, that all good was essentially pleasure and all bad was pain; from which it was further supposed to follow that the ultimate good for which we can strive is the greatest happiness of the greatest number. Bentham appeared to think that we all go about our lives making little calculations that set so many units of pleasure against so many of pain in deciding all that we do. People only behave badly, he thought, because they made bad calculations: they thought in the short instead of the long term.

The importance of all this for government, Bentham believed, was that it provided a means of evaluating good and bad laws, and good and bad institutions. The good government, armed with this knowledge, could make calculations of the amount of pleasure or pain caused according to what Bentham called the 'felicific calculus' (felicity = happiness) and could then pass laws and create institutions that could shape and mould human behaviour for the common good. He believed that all existing laws, institutions and practices could be assessed according to his principles and, if found wanting, could immediately be replaced by better ones. The good society could therefore be set up very easily by using his ideas.

To begin with, Bentham's ideal form of government was benevolent autocracy, simply on grounds of greater efficiency. But when governments ignored his ideas he changed his mind. Influenced by his friend James Mill, around 1808 Bentham became converted to popular government virtually overnight.

Each individual, Bentham and Mill insisted, was the best judge of their own happiness. They should be as free as possible to pursue their own interests, which meant minimal government and minimal legislation (Bentham believed that fewer laws automatically meant greater freedom). This included economic freedom, for they were devoted to Adam Smith's free-market economics. People should vote on a wide, though not universal, franchise, for their representatives, who would then be mandated delegates, there to express the people's wishes. There would be no monarchy or House of Lords. Many working men would have the vote, although Mill believed that they would vote for middle-class representatives, the professional and business middle classes being the most intelligent and competent section of society.

Bentham and James Mill, therefore, developed a distinct version of liberalism that was radical and democratic (although not in the French sense of deliberately changing society in order to make it more equal). It also differed from previous versions of liberalism in dismissing the idea of natural rights, which Bentham thought was not only nonsense, but 'nonsense upon stilts'.

The ideas of Bentham and James Mill were disseminated by a body of disciples, including several influential MPs, who called themselves 'philosophical radicals'. But *laissez-faire* liberal ideas in general were also influencing the main parties, especially the Whigs, who eventually became the Liberal Party. However, the party's leadership was still dominated by Whig aristocrats who were suspicious of democracy, even though as the century proceeded it was increasingly believed that Britain, and indeed the rest of Europe, would eventually go the way of America and introduce democracy. For this reason, America was regarded by Europeans with intense fascination.

American democracy

It was the presidency of Andrew Jackson, from 1828 to 1836, that saw the final extension of the franchise to all adult males, and the end of the monopoly of old East Coast families over American government. It was the land not only of free government but also of free enterprise, without any prompting from the classical economists. It was far easier there to start a business and prosper than it was in Europe. In a very real sense, America began as a liberal paradise and has remained so ever since. Neither socialism nor any other ideology has had much impact there, only different varieties of liberalism.

The European fascination led to a number of writers travelling to America and reporting on the new democratic civilisation they found there. Much the most thorough and perceptive was that of a French aristocrat, Alexis de Tocqueville (1805–59). His *Democracy in America* (1835–40) suggested, among many other things, that in a society in which everyone had maximum freedom to do as they please there was in fact a very strong tendency to conform, reinforced by a strong social pressure of public opinion. This was one of the conclusions that most influenced John Stuart Mill, the son of James Mill and the most distinguished liberal philosopher of the nineteenth century. J.S. Mill was also influenced by Romanticism.

Romantic liberalism

Liberal movements developed in most of continental Europe in the nineteenth century, although with rather mixed success. While liberalism flourished unchecked in America and infused itself into all the national parties in Britain, continental liberalism tended to confine itself to specific parties and have specific enemies.

European liberalism has a number of distinctive features that distinguish it from the liberalisms of Britain and America, such as anti-clericalism. But Europe has also contributed a number of features to the broad tradition of liberal thinking. Apart from Kant, there had been two major theoretical developments. There was the liberal nationalism of such as Mazzini (see Chapter 4) and there was the development of the concept of individuality that came from the Romantic Movement.

Romanticism was a Europe-wide intellectual movement that was a direct reaction to Enlightenment rationalism and its consequences. Where the Enlightenment stressed reason and universality, Romantics emphasised feeling and particularity. Each individual and each nation had its own uniqueness.

The Romantic Movement influenced all the major ideologies of the time, especially nationalism and conservatism (see Chapter 3). But liberalism also felt the impact, although for the most part the influence was slow to develop. One early thinker who sensed the political implications of an enhanced concept of individualism was the Prussian aristocrat and educational reformer, Karl Wilhelm von Humboldt. As a young man, fired with enthusiasm both for the French Revolution and the new Romantic ideas, he wrote an essay entitled *The Limits of State Action* in 1792. Humboldt stressed human individual uniqueness that must be allowed to develop naturally from inner promptings. The more the state interfered in and directed society the less this was possible. He wrote (in a passage later used by J.S. Mill as the epigraph for his own most famous essay *On Liberty*):

> The grand, leading principle, towards which every argument unfolded in these pages directly converges, is the absolute and essential importance of human development in its richest variety.
>
> (in Mill, 1910)

Thus, minimal constitutional government was essential for human development and happiness.

This conception of human nature is very far from the conceptions prevailing in earlier versions of liberalism. They are all universalistic notions that emphasise how all individuals are the same: that they are rational, possessed of natural rights, have a capacity for moral self-direction, all seek their self-interest; or are all pleasure–pain machines. The Romantic view stresses their uniqueness, and the preciousness of that uniqueness, and the limitation of government in the name of that uniqueness. Freedom is demanded not only so that individuals may pursue their own selfish interests, but primarily so that each individual may develop to their full potential and thereby contribute to the development of mankind.

However, Humboldt's essay was not properly published until 1850, long after his death. Like the works of Kant, and the general Romantic notion of individuality, it did not have influence on political ideas until the second half of the nineteenth century. It was part of the intellectual background to social liberalism.

Liberalism and progress

The idea of progress goes back essentially to the eighteenth-century Enlightenment. The development of reason in general and science in particular, together with the replacement of superstition and ignorance and the overcoming of tyrannies of priest and king, were combining, it was thought, to lead mankind towards ever greater perfection. The French Enlightenment thinker, the Marquis de Condorcet (1743–94) was the great exponent of this view. In his book *Sketch for a Historical Picture of the Progress of the Human Mind* (1795) he argued that:

> nature has set no term to the perfection of human faculties; that the perfectibility of man is truly indefinite; and that the progress of this perfectibility, from now onwards independent of any power that might wish to halt it, has no other limit than the duration of the globe upon which nature has cast us.

It shows an extraordinary optimism, especially as the author was living in the shadow of the guillotine, which shortly after claimed him.

In the eighteenth century the idea of progress developed among Enlightenment thinkers; but during the nineteenth century it became a commonplace. In the Victorian period everyone believed in progress, although different versions of the concept emerged, including those of Herbert Spencer (1820–1903) and John Stuart Mill (1806–73). The idea of progress became a central feature of the liberal outlook, at least until the horrors of the twentieth century undermined liberal confidence.

Herbert Spencer

Spencer linked liberalism to the theory of evolution as developed by Charles Darwin in his *The Origin of Species* (1859). That theory suggested that species evolved in circumstances of competition between individuals, and between different kinds of animals, for food and other necessaries of existence. Those individuals and types best adapted to their environment would tend to survive and increase at the expense of the less well adapted. It did not follow from this that the 'best adapted' were either necessarily the strongest or were 'superior' to the less well adapted. But these were precisely the conclusions that Spencer drew, and which he applied to society.

The ideal society was one characterised by maximum competition and the 'survival of the fittest' (Spencer's phrase, not Darwin's), which meant the strongest and the best. The result was progress, which Spencer saw in terms of ever-greater social complexity and integration, and an ever-diminishing role for the state. These ideas are set out in his voluminous writings on biology, sociology and psychology. Their implications for government, as seen in his *Man versus the State* (1884), were exceptionally harsh. He systematically opposed any extension of government activity, and particularly any policies to deal with social problems such as poverty or the exploitation of women and children in factories and mines. That the weak should go to the wall was part of the natural evolutionary process, and so helping the poor and exploited merely interfered with the proper order of things and held back progress.

Spencer was influential in late Victorian Britain although his views became increasingly out of step with the main trend of liberal thinking. He was a man of delicate constitution and claimed that he never read views contrary to his own because that made him physically ill. He died in 1903 not having changed his ideas for half a century. In the same period, he was much more popular and influential in the US among those who wished to justify American business. It was the age when giant business empires were being built and there were complaints of ruthlessness and exploitation and the corruption of the political system. Spencer's work appeared to justify this 'age of the robber barons' as natural and right and essential to human progress.

John Stuart Mill

J.S. Mill was Spencer's contemporary. He was the son of James Mill, who subjected him to the most extraordinary education (he began to learn Greek at three and was reading Plato at eight) in order to groom him to be the philosopher of the philosophical radicals. However, this narrow Gradgrindian education seems to have induced some kind of mental breakdown in his early twenties. As a result, he came to the conclusion that utilitarianism had thus far neglected the spiritual, aesthetic and emotional side of the human being. He was influenced by Romantic notions of individuality, which saw each human being as a complex whole, and each precious in their uniqueness.

In working out the political implications of this new sense of individuality, Mill was influenced by two sources. The first was von Humboldt's belief that the state was intrinsically inimical to the flourishing of individuality. This view lies behind Mill's difficult distinction between 'self-regarding' and 'other-regarding' actions. He argued that:

> the only purpose for which power can be rightfully exercised over any member of a civilised community against his will is to prevent harm to others.
>
> (*On Liberty*, 1859, in Mill, 1910)

Only where an individual's actions affect the lives of others – that is, other-regarding actions – can there be a case for state regulation in order to prevent harm. Where an individual's actions are self-regarding – that is, affecting no one but themselves – then the state has no right to interfere.

Mill went on to defend more specific freedoms of speech and thought, all on the grounds that they are conducive to progress. In open competition, he believed, truth will always drive out falsity. But he was particularly interested in beliefs and lifestyles which must be allowed to flourish since they are the source of creativity and therefore also progressive.

The other influence on Mill was de Tocqueville's analysis of American democracy. Its tendency to elevate public opinion as some kind of authority, and the consequent social pressure to conform, horrified him. This created something of a dilemma in Mill's attitude to democratic government. He thought in general that the coming of democracy was inevitable and right, and yet he feared what he called the 'tyranny of the majority' (a view that would have been incomprehensible to Bentham or his father, who saw nothing wrong with social pressure or conformity). Liberals had long fought against the tyranny of priest and king, but none had anticipated further problems once everyone was free of these.

J.S. Mill was, in consequence, a somewhat reluctant democrat. He believed in representative democracy as an educative force, since participation would, he believed, make for responsible citizenship and therefore was progressive. On the other hand, his Whiggish fear of democracy led him to all kinds of devices to prevent government expressing the direct will of the majority. Thus, he argued that while every adult should vote, those with education should have more votes. Again, while parliament should represent all the people and have a final say on legislation, it should be devised up by a legislative commission drawn from the intellectual elite. In ways such as these, Mill sought to protect the individualistic, creative intellectuals he so much admired and upon whom future progress, he believed, ultimately depended.

It may seem surprising that the greatest liberal thinker of the age should be so cautious about democracy. But in fact many leading liberal thinkers and politicians at that time were hostile to extending the franchise to the working masses who were the bulk of the population. They held to the traditional Whig ideal of a mixed constitution with a 'democratic element' as the best guarantee of civil rights and constitutional government. It is only in the twentieth century, after experience has shown that mass democracy is not a threat to rights and property and the individualism that Mill treasured so much, that we automatically identify democracy with liberalism.

However, while passionate in his belief in individualism, Mill was among the first liberal thinkers to advocate state intervention in areas such as education and factory acts. In this we can see the beginnings of a new version of liberalism, social liberalism, which will be considered later in this chapter. In the meanwhile we need to look at a modern phenomenon that is the very epitome of all that Mill hated and feared.

Totalitarianism

The nineteenth century's confident belief in progress was rudely shattered by the events of the twentieth century. In Europe, seen as the very heart of Western civilisation and progress, a single generation witnessed two of the most appalling wars in human history that sucked in much of the rest of the world, along with totalitarian regimes that perpetrated crimes against humanity on a colossal scale. People could not believe, until the evidence appeared at the end of the war, the evil of the Nazi extermination camps, and other atrocities occurring in what was supposed to be one of the most civilised and cultured countries in Europe (see Chapter 8). Finally, the Cold War and the threat of nuclear annihilation seemed again to reach the very depths of irrationality and perversity.

Most of these events have resulted from a new form of government called totalitarianism. The term 'totalitarian' was coined in the 1920s to characterise Mussolini's regime, and it was meant to imply a total control of every aspect of Italian life. This in fact exaggerated Mussolini's power, although it was what he aspired to, and he embraced the word with enthusiasm. While authoritarian regimes in the past had sought merely a monopoly of power over people's actions, the totalitarian regimes of Mussolini, Hitler and Stalin sought complete power over people's minds. A one-party state, with everyone believing in the party's ideology was the ideal, with terror used to enforce conformity.

Totalitarianism is the very antithesis of everything that liberals value. Under totalitarian regimes the individual is merged into the mass and is denied basic freedoms. The government knows no restraint, and in its doctrine claims a monopoly of truth from which dissent is punished. Totalitarianism has come to be seen as the greatest of threats to liberal values. While totalitarian regimes are less common today, we still have China and other communist states, Iraq, Syria and, some would add, a number of Islamic fundamentalist states such as Iran and Afghanistan.

With the decline of the belief in progress under the impact of totalitarianism, liberals have looked to institutional and legal means to prevent future wars and atrocities, but this time on an international scale. Hence the creation of organisations like the United Nations (UN), and the development of the theory of human rights.

Human rights

The concept of human rights is the idea that people have basic rights merely by virtue of being human, and irrespective of what the laws of their particular state may say. The idea is in fact a modern version of the natural rights theories of John Locke and the American *Declaration of Independence*, or, as the French revolutionaries called them, the rights of man.

The idea of God-given natural rights had gone out of fashion in the nineteenth century, partly because of its unfortunate association with the French Revolution and partly because of its religious associations. The theory had come in for very powerful criticisms in the eighteenth and nineteenth centuries, and leading liberal thinkers such as Bentham, Spencer and J.S. Mill had rejected the idea altogether. However, with the wars and the atrocities of twentieth-century totalitarian regimes, the need was felt for a modernised version of such a theory, but without the old religious metaphysics.

When the Nazi leaders were tried at Nuremburg (1945–46), they were accused of 'crimes against humanity' that had been virtually invented for the occasion and embodied in international law. The UN's founding charter of 1946 (Article 1) pledges all members to achieve:

> universal respect for, and observance of, human rights and fundamental freedoms for all without distinction as to race, sex, language or religion.

Subsequently, in 1948, the UN issued the Universal Declaration of Human Rights setting out these rights in great detail, and there are now many international organisations with the purpose of protecting human rights. Unfortunately, we live in a world where there is still much war, suffering and oppression. Nevertheless, there are some that see the end of the Cold War as a turning point, after which we can again look to the future with optimism. We will consider the future in the final chapter. In the meanwhile, we need to discuss the new form of liberalism that was developed in the late nineteenth century and came to dominate most of the twentieth, namely social liberalism.

Social liberalism and European politics

In the second half of the nineteenth century it became increasingly apparent that giving free reign to the unregulated free market was not producing the society of independent, free, self-reliant individuals that the theory had promised. Instead, the few were mightily rich while many suffered poverty, squalor, ignorance, exploitation and deprivation. Clearly something had gone wrong. Furthermore, the central liberal doctrine of minimal government, the 'night watchman state', was being ignored by governments, liberal ones as well as others, in order to cope with the social problems thrown up by industrialisation and urbanisation, problems so dire that they had to be dealt with no matter what the theory said. Consequently, there was legislation in the fields of public health and sanitation, factory conditions, education, child and women's employment and other matters. In other words, there was pragmatic state intervention instead of leaving everything to the free market.

A new concept of liberty

Eventually theory began to catch up with practice. The mainstream of liberal thinking began to shift in the direction of abandoning the minimal state in favour of justifying state intervention. A series of liberal thinkers, including J.S. Mill (who combined elements of the old liberalism and the new), T.H. Green (1836–82) in his *Lectures on the Principles of Political Obligation* (1882), Leonard Hobhouse (1864–1929) in *The Labour Movement* (1893), *Liberalism* (1911) and other writings, and J.A. Hobson (1858–1940) in *The Crisis of Liberalism* (1909) and other works, all argued for more and more state intervention with collectivist social policies to make up for the deficiencies of the capitalist system. Some, especially Hobhouse and Hobson, came close to some of the forms of socialism that were developing at the time. For example, Hobhouse was opposed to capitalism as such, believing that a society based on competition ought to be replaced by one based on co-operation. What kept them within the liberal fold was their central commitment to individual liberty.

The argument was essentially this. A person may appear to be free, with a whole array of civil liberties, but if they are uneducated, live in squalor and are overworked for starvation wages, in what real sense are they free? People can only truly be said to be free when they have a genuine opportunity to participate fully in the life of their society. Therefore, collectivist intervention is justified in liberal terms if it enables people to so participate; or, to put it another way, if it removes obstacles to people's freedom to fully develop their individuality. It is a 'positive' freedom linked to Romantic notions of individual uniqueness. In practical terms, the argument points towards a programme of welfare legislation, providing such things as education, decent housing and a system of social security. And this indeed is what it led to.

It was a liberal government that laid the foundations of the welfare state in Britain in the years before the First World War. The comprehensive welfare state we have had since the Second World War, although created by the Labour Party, was in fact largely designed by two liberals, John Maynard Keynes (1883–1946), who laid the economic foundations, and William Beveridge (1879–1963), who designed the welfare system itself.

The Keynesian revolution

Keynes was the economist who challenged the orthodoxy of classical economics which had dominated the economic thinking and policies of Britain and the other major powers for more than a hundred years. That orthodoxy assumed that the free market always solved its own problems so long as it was not interfered with by government. Thus, when Europe suffered a decade of economic recession after the First World War, governments did nothing; and when the American economy collapsed after the Wall Street Crash of 1929 and recession turned into a massive slump, the orthodox policy was still to do nothing. But Keynes, in his great work *The General Theory of Employment, Interest and Money* (1936), demonstrated that it is not in fact the case that the free-market economy is always a self-righting mechanism and that in certain conditions (such as those prevailing) it was quite possible for slump to go on indefinitely.

The answer, Keynes argued, was not to get into a slump in the first place. Governments could break out of the pattern of boom and slump by actively managing the economy. This could be done by the management of demand (the amount people have to spend), by such means as taxation, government spending and credit control. If the economy is growing too fast, then the total amount of people's spending can be reduced by higher taxes, cutting public spending and making it harder to borrow money, thereby slowing the boom down. If there is recession, with goods unsold, factories closing and people losing the jobs, then the answer is to cut taxes, increase government spending (by borrowing the money if necessary) and by making credit easier. This will increase demand for goods, needing more factories and workers to make them.

By these means, it was argued, it would be possible to break out of the cycle of boom and slump and replace it with a steady economic growth and permanent full employment. In putting forward his theory, Keynes was undoubtedly seeking to save capitalism from itself. For him it meant preserving the free market by civilising it and making it more humane.

The modern welfare state

Keynes's formula appeared to solve one of the most central and intractable of social problems, unemployment, which was a key to poverty and its attendant social problems. However, it was another liberal, William Beveridge, who was to make this the basis of a comprehensive welfare state, set out in his report, *Social Insurance and Allied Services* (1942). Taking full employment as a basic assumption, Beveridge designed a system of social security that would protect every citizen 'from the cradle to the grave'. His vision was of a civilised society in which none would be denied the necessities of education, health, work, decent housing or general way of life because of poverty. That is, a society without fear in which all had the opportunity to develop to their full potential.

It was only after the Second World War that these ideas were put into practice, but not by the Liberal Party which had gone into terminal decline after the First World War. The post-war Labour government (1945–51) introduced the welfare state, which fitted in well with its socialist ideals, and was soon converted to Keynesian economic management. It also nationalised a number of key industries, thereby creating the 'mixed economy'.

These policies became accepted by all parties and this general agreement on policy, known as the 'consensus', dominated British politics until the mid-1970s. It was also known as social democracy, since it was also a kind of mild version of socialism, a compromise between socialism and capitalism, that had been introduced by a socialist government (see Chapter 5). These policies also came to dominate post-war Europe, where, as in Britain, a triumph of liberal ideas was accompanied by a strange failure of liberal parties.

Liberalism in twentieth-century Europe

While liberalism had been permanently secured in Britain and America in the nineteenth century, this was not so of continental Europe, where totalitarianism of both left and right for a time virtually wiped out liberal forms of government on the European mainland.

Liberalism, however, survived and eventually triumphed in Western Europe, with the rest of Europe following later. Furthermore, the post-war governments of Western Europe pursued social liberal policies. However, what is curious, and needs some explaining, is that for all this intellectual success, political parties that are avowedly liberal have hardly benefited. The social liberal policies of the post-war world were not put into effect by governments controlled by Liberal parties, despite the major role played by liberal thinkers in devising them. In Britain, Sweden and a number of other countries it was social democratic governments that were responsible, while in West Germany, Italy and elsewhere it was Christian Democrats (that is, centre-right parties). As in Britain, there were strong Liberal parties all over Western Europe in the late nineteenth century, whereas today Liberal parties tend to be weak centre parties, such as the Free Democrats in West Germany and the Liberal, Republican and Radical parties of Italy (in Denmark the Liberals are rather confusingly called the Left Party). It seems that the moderate parties of the left and the right that have in some way managed to divide the liberal inheritance between them.

The failure of Liberal politics

For most of the nineteenth century in representative systems like Britain, the main political divide was between two forms of property, with Conservative parties representing the aristocracy and landed interest, and Liberal parties representing the commercial middle classes. But when, towards the end of the century, the working classes gained greater representation a realignment began. Politics was re-polarised into a conflict between those with and those without property. As the propertied classes closed ranks they tended to look to the Conservatives to represent them, while the Liberals tried to appeal to both sides. The socialists and conservatives absorbed liberal ideas, and from time to time adopted liberal policies; but it was these parties that were able to command large sections of the electorate, which the Liberals failed to do.

The adoption of liberal ideas by other parties was easiest in Britain, where both conservative and socialist thought already had strong liberal elements (see Chapters 3 and 5). Continental conservatives and socialists tended to be more extreme and anti-liberal, so that the absorption took longer. Since 1945, it has been the Christian Democrats and Social Democrats that have been the standard bearers of liberal values, while Liberal parties have dwindled. Even the West European Communist parties came to accept the necessity of liberal democracy. In one way or another, therefore, liberal ideas have come to thoroughly infuse European politics today.

Liberal parties in Europe now find their niche at the centre of the political spectrum. Often, as in Britain, they seek a middle way, rejecting the left's dislike of free enterprise and the right's dislike of social provision.

American liberalism

In North America things are a little different, the most general difference being the absence of socialism as a serious political movement. There is, in consequence, a major Liberal party in Canada, where the main contest for power there is between Liberals and Conservatives. The USA itself is different again, since unlike Canada and Europe it did not develop a party system as firmly based on ideological difference.

Left and Right in the US

The US has national parties in only a partial sense. Traditionally, the parties that fight Presidential elections every four years are coalitions of state parties that come together to fight for the highest office and then revert back to their previous condition. For example, the Democrats of the South have traditionally been right wing, while northern Democrats are traditionally left wing. Similarly the Republicans have their right and left wings, although particularly since the 1970s the Democrats in general have tended more to the left and Republicans to the right. There is some national organisation in Congress, but not the tight disciplined parties of Europe and elsewhere.

Ideologically, all US parties are liberal and always have been. Essentially they espouse classical liberalism, that is a form of democratised Whig constitutionalism plus the free market. The point of difference comes with the influence of social liberalism. How far should the free market be left alone; how far should the state regulate or manage; and how far should government at federal or local level provide social security and welfare services?

The American right has nothing to do with maintaining the traditional social order, as in Europe. What it believes in is extreme individualism and *laissez-faire*: that is, individuals should be left to sink or swim on their own and big business can do no wrong. Left-wingers are social liberals, believing in greater state intervention in the economy and welfare (although few today would want this on a European scale). In American political parlance, right-wingers are 'conservatives', while left-wingers are rather confusingly called 'liberals'. Thus, to an American conservative 'liberal' is a term of abuse and means virtually the same as 'socialist'.

The American right has tended towards the extreme version of classical liberalism associated with social Darwinism, which insisted on the virtues of competition and the evil consequences of state interference in economic or social matters. The late nineteenth century in America became known as the age of the 'robber barons' or of the 'anarchy of the millionaires' when big business exploited people and corrupted politics with no apparent accountability. The attitude was summed up by the railway tycoon, William Vanderbilt. When asked if he ran his railroads to benefit the public, he replied 'The public be damned ... I don't take any stock of this silly nonsense about working for anybody's good but our own ...' This kind of attitude was justified by the social Darwinism of Herbert Spencer and his American follower, William Graham Sumner, for whom the strong succeeding at the expense of the weak was natural and healthy and was a sign of progress and civilisation.

Populists and Progressives

The rapacity of big business and corruption of politics resulted in a considerable degree of disillusionment with *laissez-faire* towards the end of the nineteenth century. It first found expression in the Populist movement which flared up in the South and Mid-West in the late 1880s. It was essentially a movement of farmers exploited and threatened by big business, financiers and transport companies, to whose dealings the politicians turned a blind eye. The farmers demanded financial relief and graduated income tax, and even nationalisation of transport and communications. But greatest faith was put in more democracy. Hence demands for direct election of the Senate, local 'primaries' (popular election of party candidates instead of nomination by party 'bosses'), 'recall' (popular removal of elected representatives who do not do their job), initiative referenda and other measures. However, despite becoming a major political force, with the failure of the Populist bid to win the presidency in 1896 the two main parties reasserted themselves.

However, Populism's democratic demands were taken up by the Progressive movement of the next two decades. This was a more middle-class, intellectual movement that embraced all parties and most parts of the country. Whereas the Populists were suspicious of government in general, Progressives were influenced by social liberal ideas and saw the state as potentially a positive instrument for social justice. Presidents Theodore Roosevelt and Woodrow Wilson were Progressives and the movement's successes included direct elections for the Senate after 1913, votes for women, and the introduction of referenda and primaries in many states. This was in addition to a good deal of welfare legislation in individual states, as well as state and federal 'anti-trust' laws and other measures to curb the abuse of power by big business.

John Dewey and social liberalism

Despite these developments, disillusionment with unbridled free enterprise was still strong in the 1920s; and it rose sharply following the Wall Street Crash of 1929 and the mass unemployment and social distress that followed for a decade.

The most forceful theoretical expression of this disillusionment with American capitalism came in the writings of John Dewey (1859–1952) in such works as *Individualism Old and New* (1931) and *Liberalism and Social Action* (1935). Dewey is better known as a philosopher and educationist than a political theorist, but his ideas on all three fit together. As a philosopher he was a pragmatist, which meant that he thought that what was true was what was useful to us and not what corresponded to some alleged world of objective facts. We best found out what was useful by experiment and discussion, a process that produced science and progress and should be the basis of education. It was also both essentially democratic and collectivist, relying on people working together to find common solutions. This was what democracy was really about: a way of life rather as merely a system of government, with ordinary people participating and working together in all aspects of social activity.

Dewey proclaimed a 'new individualism' that was collective and co-operative and progressive, and which enabled all to grow and fully develop their potential. This would replace the old, selfish, *laissez-faire* individualism that was anti-social and ultimately destructive. He called for extensive state intervention in the economy and society in order to provide all individuals with the security and the opportunity to participate in society and fully develop themselves. This involved planning and social engineering based on the fullest social research and consultation, together with severe curtailment of corporate capitalism. However, Dewey was less concerned with legal or institutional arrangements, since the key to progress was a properly educated citizenry committed to democracy as a way of life.

The New Deal and after

Dewey's influence was largely confined to education. It was events that dictated the extension of a degree of social liberalism. The Great Crash of 1929 and the subsequent depression were a serious blow to the 'American way'. For several years American government did nothing, believing in the accepted wisdom of classical economics which said that the free market was a self-righting vessel and the more government left it alone, the more quickly it would right itself and recover. Eventually America lost patience and President F.D. Roosevelt launched the 'New Deal' in 1933, which meant extensive intervention by government in the economy to create work, combined with welfare measures. The New Deal did not end the Depression (the Second World War did that) but it did alleviate it, and it began an era of 'big government' that culminated in the 'New Frontier' and 'Great Society' programmes of Presidents Kennedy and Johnson in the 1960s.

There was a great deal of hostility from the right to the social liberalism of the New Deal and the later Kennedy-Johnson programmes, but they were too popular for there to be any impact. However, the 1970s were a period of economic difficulties and retrenchment, which led to a revival of right-wing politics in the 1980s with the era of Reagan and the New Right.

Rawls and social justice

The New Deal and the programmes of the 1960s represent the high point of social liberalism in practice in America, and the period also produced the most significant social liberal theorist after John Dewey. This was John Rawls, whose *A Theory of Justice* was published in 1971. In this he attempted to determine the basic principles of social justice. To do so he made use of an old device of political theorists (such as Locke and Rousseau), the social contract, where people are imagined to come to some sort of agreement to set up a good society they were going to live in.

Rawls imagines a group of people charged with drawing up a social contract that lays down the rules of how society will be run in such a way as to ensure that all their interests will be protected. The people concerned do not know what their interests would be, because they are behind a 'veil of ignorance' which does not allow them to know whether in society they will be male of female, young or old, from rich backgrounds or poor, disabled or not, talented or not, and so on. This may seem rather far-fetched, but the point is to ensure that the society to be decided upon does not disadvantage any group, because the participants may find themselves belonging to that group.

Rawls believes that such a group would inevitably settle on two principles of justice upon which their society would be based. The first principle is an equality of freedom. That is, that everyone should have as much freedom as possible provided everyone can have the same amount. The second principle is equality of opportunity. This implies, Rawls argues, an equal distribution of power and wealth; unless, that is, some unequal distribution benefits everybody, and particularly the worst-off. Thus, entrepreneurs may earn more because of the jobs they create, the doctor because of the time spent in training.

Against the objection that the more talented and energetic deserve to earn more, Rawls argues that such talents and endowments are gifts of nature or upbringing which are not earned and therefore do not inevitably justify extra reward. It follows that if the wealth and power of those at the top of society does not truly work for the benefit of those at the bottom, then wealth and power must be redistributed. Neither genuine liberty nor genuine equality of opportunity are possible, Rawls believes, if society is characterised by great and unjustified inequalities of wealth.

Rawls is very firmly in the social liberal camp, but his theory is thoroughly individualist. The right of the individual to choose the kind of life he or she wants to live is absolute.

Nozick and the minimal state

Rawls's book was soon followed by a rejoinder from the conservative wing of American liberalism. Robert Nozick's *Anarchy, State and Utopia* appeared three years later in 1974. Where Rawls was concerned with the claims of society, Nozick asserts a pure individualism. In many ways he goes back to John Locke and insists that individuals have certain natural rights: most importantly, Locke's 'life, liberty and property'. Consequently, when considering how someone exercising their abilities should be rewarded, while Rawls asks 'how does this benefit society?', Nozick asks 'by what right does society deprive them of whatever they can earn in the market place?'. Nozick is only prepared to concede that government can tax in order to provide for the protection of the individual's rights, but nothing more. To tax for roads, street lighting, social services or anything else, Nozick insists, is a violation of the individual's rights.

Nozick's book represents the 'conservative' side of American liberalism, which was reviving itself in the 1970s with the New Right movement that culminated in the presidency of Ronald Reagan (see Chapter 10).

Problems, criticisms and recent developments

Liberal democracy is standard and taken for granted in the West and may ultimately triumph in most of the rest of the world in the foreseeable future. It is closely connected with liberal ideals such as freedom, equality and tolerance. Yet none of these concepts is unproblematic. Furthermore, liberalism does have its critics. Rival ideologies each have criticisms from their own particular point of view. But apart from these there are more general criticisms that come from across the spectrum, including from liberals themselves, and which have led to further developments in liberal thought. We will look at some of the conceptual difficulties first.

Freedom and equality

There is arguably a fundamental conflict at the heart of liberal theory. Individual freedom is the great liberal value, and yet equality in some form is inherent in all liberal thinking. For the American revolutionaries the very first thing they believed to be self-evident was that 'all men are created equal'. And for all liberals it seems that equality should at least mean that people should be equally free and have equal rights; that every individual is of equal worth; that every individual equally has the capacity to reason and make moral choices; that everyone should have an equal opportunity to develop their talents; and that everyone should be equal before the law. Yet, for all this, freedom and equality do not seem to fit together very well.

Crudely put, if you let people be completely free, especially economically free, they will end up being unequal. But if you keep people equal, especially economically equal, you will end up denying their freedom. There are quite different versions of liberalism according to which value is stressed. In consequence, right from the very beginning of liberalism there have been different movements stressing the different sides: Whigs and Radicals, Spencarians and social liberals, and so on. Today this is expressed in European politics in parties of left and right: Labour and Conservative; Christian Democrat and Social Democrat; while in American politics it is expressed as 'conservative' and 'liberal'.

One could say, then, that the Liberal inheritance has been divided between left and right, with both claiming that liberalism alone is an inadequate vehicle for its own ideals. In British terms the Conservative Party has always had a liberal dimension to its doctrine (distinguishing it from continental versions of conservatism in the past), while to British Conservatives and their present-day continental equivalents (such as the Christian Democrats) the defence of property is central to the defence of liberty and Christian values. Yet, at the same time, the mainstream of traditional British socialism (and post-war Social Democrats elsewhere) has always maintained that only socialism could genuinely fulfil the ideals of liberalism, and that if liberal ideals are pursued consistently, liberal society will inevitably evolve into socialist society.

Defining democracy

Few people today would challenge the legitimacy of democracy as the appropriate form of government for the modern world. But precisely because it is so universally approved, virtually every form of government and every modern ideology lays claim to it. Considerable ingenuity is shown providing justifications for the most unlikely regimes on democratic lines, while recent history has shown the relative ease with which popular enthusiasm for a regime can be manufactured.

This tends to muddy the discussion of what democracy actually is. After the Second World War, the United Nations agency UNESCO, seeking to clarify the ideals of democracy, set a body of scholars the task of reaching a definition upon which all could agree. In their report, *Democracy in a World of Tensions* (1951), they had to admit failure. There were so many conflicting definitions and theories that it was impossible to reach agreement.

The word and the concept go back to Ancient Greece, and it is worth reflecting on the fact that what we understand as democracy today would not have been recognised as such by an Ancient Greek. The democracy of fifth-century Athens, for example, involved all citizens. Women, slaves and foreigners could not hold citizenship. Nevertheless, all citizens, whether rich or poor, could participate equally in the law-making process, and also had an equal chance to participate in the day-to-day government through a system of election by lot. Thus, by Ancient Greek standards our modern representative democracy is not a democracy at all, because the ordinary citizens do not participate but elect people to go away and decide things on their behalf; indeed, some modern thinkers, most notably Rousseau, have agreed with them.

It has long been argued that this 'direct democracy' of the Greeks is not possible in the modern world, and clearly it would hardly be possible to cram all the citizens of the United Kingdom into Trafalgar Square every time a law needed to be passed. On the other hand, it is now technically possible for all households to be 'cabled up' to give all television sets a 'voting button', so that a decision of the nation could be called for and instantly given. In principle, all government decisions could be based on such votes. This would surely be more democratic than our present representative system. But whether we would necessarily want it as our form of government is another matter.

However, even if we take representative democracy to be authentic democracy and the only possible kind for modern world, there are still problems. In the first place, democracy is supposed to be based on the sovereignty of the people and therefore government should be an expression of the people's will. The French Revolutionaries claimed to represent the true will of the French people, and since that will must be a single will, then those who disagreed with them must at least be putting their selfish interests above those of the people, and at worst must in some way be enemies of the people. However that may be, divining the will of the people is no easy business, since people appear to have genuine disagreements of what the good of the community really is. The usual way around this is to say: the will of the people is the will of the majority. The question then is, just how much authority does the will of the majority then have? Does it mean that fifty per cent plus one has an absolute right to do what it wants? Does it have the right to ignore dissent, or to force the minority to conform? Does it have the right to persecute a minority, especially if that minority is permanent?

Modern liberal democracies insist on the protection of minority rights, but is this a diminution of democracy or an essential part of it? Pluralism is certainly an essential part of liberal democracy, but some would say that it is more *liberal* than it is democratic. It could be said to represent an endorsement of self-interestedness as against public spiritedness and care for the common good. Again, the radical might argue that the pluralism the liberal sets so much store by really masks the way the system protects the interests of the privileged classes. The logical conclusion of this is the socialist case against liberalism, which is that genuine liberty is impossible without genuine equality. That is, that true liberty and true democracy are only possible in a society where no one is markedly better off than anyone else. Then we are also back to the counter-argument that a society where equality has to be enforced cannot be a free one.

In addition, there are endless disputes over which system of representation, or which voting system, is more or less democratic than another, and seemingly no way of coming to a definitive conclusion.

These difficulties apart, there are other criticisms of liberalism of a more wide-ranging sort. Many are specifically targeted at the New Right, which will be dealt with in a later chapter, but others are more general.

The moral weakness of liberalism

One of these general charges against liberalism alleges that it is morally vacuous. If freedom and toleration rule, then what moral values should people have beyond not interfering with others? The answer is that this is a private matter. People can believe in what they like, or in nothing at all. At least ancient republicanism demanded civic virtue and attention to the public good. But modern liberal democracy demands nothing beyond conformity to the law. Human nature is presumed to be rational and individuals will pursue their own interests, and no one is justified in stopping anyone doing just what they like, so long as they stay within legal bounds.

On these grounds some argue that liberal democracy is materialistic, self-indulgent and decadent and breeds a meaningless, mindless, alienated individualism. This is little more than a brute selfishness that is devoid of higher values, or any sense of community, or any need to consider one's fellow human beings. People turn to all kinds of strange beliefs to give some degree of emotional and spiritual satisfaction to fill the spiritual emptiness that modern free-market consumer society leaves.

These criticisms come from a variety of quarters, from religious fundamentalists to liberals themselves. Among the latter would be many communitarians.

Communitarian critics

Communitarianism is a body of thought that developed in the 1980s. Communitarians argue that, with very few exceptions, throughout the history of liberalism, from Locke to Rawls and Nozick, the emphasis has been upon individuals and their need for freedom, autonomy and the protection of their rights. This tends to ignore the fact that our individual identity, values and aspirations all come from the community that nurtured us: from family and friends and colleagues and neighbours, to whom we owe duties and responsibilities. The ideal of the free individual, devoid of all such ties and relationships, is both unrealistic and destructive. It results in a one-sided view of the human good and human happiness, and in distorted theories such as that the market will provide for everything and so long as people have civil liberties they will be happy and fulfilled. The moral vacuousness and social disintegration suggested in the previous section is the result.

In addition to the misunderstanding of how the individual becomes an individual, liberal theory is also mistaken, so communitarians argue, in seeing all individuals as essentially the same, with the same needs and entitled to the same rights. But if values grow out of communities and they differ, then it is absurd to say that what is right for one individual must be right for all humanity. There are different notions of right and good and justice among different communities and these should be respected and not have Western liberals imposing a culturally specific uniformity on the whole world.

These ideas are not in themselves entirely new – some go back to Hegel and Burke, and can be found in some social liberal thinkers like T.H. Green – but the advent of the New Right and globalisation and the threat of greater social disintegration prompted a revival. In books such as Sandal's *Liberalism and the Limits of Justice* (1979) and Charles Taylor's *Sources of the Self* (1980) the communitarian case has been set out. Most of these would subscribe to most liberals values and some would call themselves liberals, but think that liberalism should take community and cultural difference much more seriously. There is also a political movement, centred on America and inspired by the writings of Amatrai Etzione, devoted to promoting community values and policies that embody them in books such as *The Spirit of Community* (1995). Tony Blair and other politicians have been influenced by these ideas.

Postmodern critics

Postmodern theory developed among French intellectuals and was a somewhat esoteric line of analysis, but one which gradually spread and developed different varieties and, especially since the end of the Cold War, has seeped into the intellectual mainstream. It has wide implications for ideology generally, which will be discussed in the final chapter, but it also has specific implications for liberal thought that makes a brief discussion here necessary.

Very crudely, postmodernists argue that the modern age of human history is over and that we now live, even if we do not all recognise it, in a new age, a postmodern age. Modernity for the postmodernists begins with the eighteenth-century Enlightenment and it is the intellectual aspirations of that movement that are thought to give the whole of modernity its shape and character. The Enlightenment faith was in reason, science, rational organisation and progress that would provide for all mankind a future of peace, freedom, prosperity and happiness. Liberalism is central to this picture, seeing the rational individual left to pursue his rational self-interest and possessed of rights as the instrument and beneficiary of rational progress.

Twentieth-century horrors of war and genocide, along with the mass poverty and pollution and threat of nuclear war, have all tended to disillusion us about progress. Postmodernist thinkers, like Foucault and Lyotard and Baudrillard and their associates, have questioned Western science and rationality and rejected their claims to universal validity. What postmodernism has against liberalism is its claim to be part of this universal rationalism. To some degree this is true of all ideologies, but liberalism always puts a special emphasis on universal rationality and besides it is the key ideology of modernity and the most successful. It is argued that, however benign the intention, the attempt to impose liberal values upon non-liberal communities, to demand that they recognise human rights as the West understands them or adopt liberal democracy or tolerate what they deem intolerable, when this is against their established culture, is oppressive and potentially totalitarian. It is also argued that this is equally true of the situation within modern Western societies. Virtually all Western advanced societies, especially in North America and Europe, are multicultural societies. The argument is that it is oppressive to impose the dominant culture upon minorities in the form of, for example, pressure to assimilate. All are entitled to respect, although this can lead to clashes between conflicting values (for example, in the treatment of women).

Once regarded as peculiarly French, postmodern theory has entered the mainstream through thinkers like Richard Rorty and John Gray. Rorty is an American philosopher in the tradition of pragmatism, where truth is understood in terms of usefulness. He calls himself a 'postmodern bourgeois liberal', the postmodern element coming from his rejection of all metaphysics, theories of human nature or notions of universal rationality. Liberalism, he argues, is a doctrine that grows out of the traditions of Western thought and practice and is not necessarily suitable for anyone else. John Gray, a British political theorist who has in the past been a supporter of the New Right and still claims to adhere to liberal values, none the less argues (in *Enlightenment's Wake* and elsewhere) that the age of liberalism is finished and that we have to work out a new politics for a post-liberal, postmodern age that respects other cultures and points of view.

There is an obvious link between the criticisms of communitarians and postmodernism, although they start from very different premises. And it could be argued that there is a link with liberalism itself. Both demand greater tolerance and greater respect for others and their differences, and the essential wrongness of imposing our own views upon them, asserting their right to be distinct, all of which could be said to embody liberal values and principles. In his later writings, John Rawls (especially his *Political Liberalism*, 1996) has been saying something similar: that his theory of liberalism is merely working out the implications of a particular Western political tradition, and that within a modern state there must be respect for differing moral traditions.

The future of liberalism

The end of the Cold War in 1989 seemed to mark the final triumph of Western liberalism over all rivals (Fukuyama, 1989). But as this chapter has shown, liberalism is not one unified doctrine but a complex tradition with many differing and sometimes contradictory strands. Indeed, it has been suggested that its deepest divisions are no nearer being resolved at the beginning of the twenty-first century than they were at the beginning of the twentieth (Gaus, 2000). Furthermore, liberal theory has been under attack by new strands of thought powerful enough to put liberal theorists on the defensive. Rawls has modified his views in the light of postmodern criticisms and the reality of the multicultural society, while Robert Nozick came to modify his earlier views in favour of greater emphasis on community (Nozick, 1989, pp.286–7). Rawls, Rorty, Gray and others have given up the claims of universality.

If liberalism is not in serious decline, as is the case of many other major ideologies, it has certainly become even more fragmented then in the past. It has lost much of its erstwhile confidence among its most distinguished proponents, who no longer present it as universal truth. It is, at least in some respects, out of keeping with the spirit of the age. But this is a topic we will return to in the final chapter.

3

Conservatism and the right

Many of the ideas, attitudes and arguments that we associate with conservatism go back many centuries, if not millennia. And yet conservatism, as a coherent political doctrine, is really a modern phenomenon that developed in response to the French Revolution. This curious disparity between antiquity of outlook and modernity of articulation is so because central values of at least European conservatism, such as tradition, established authority, customary practice and time-honoured hierarchy, were long sanctified by religion and taken for granted by most people, for whom their value went without saying. For the greater part of human history the life of the majority was precarious in a way that today we find difficult to conceive, and these values were deemed essential to the order and stability and security upon which civilised life depended. They hardly needed defending, for longevity alone guaranteed worth.

In the eighteenth century, when educated people were aware of these things being questioned, the debate was still peripheral to most of the population. The French Revolution changed all this. Unlike previous upheavals (such as religious wars in France and Germany and the English Civil Wars) the French Revolution was pursued in the name of the people. That is, all of the people, and just about every person in France was caught up in it. More importantly, it was a revolution against tradition, against the *ancien regime*, the established order. Tradition, prejudice, established authority, customary ceremony and all similar fixed points of society were despised and reviled. It was this radical challenge to people's habitual ways of thinking and believing that called forth attempts to turn what had hitherto been instinctively accepted into a reasoned doctrine designed to have wide appeal. Those with wealth and privilege and position believed that they had these things as of right, a right that had to be defended against those with untried ideas and with interests to further and axes to grind. However, defence of the status quo inevitably took different forms according to the different traditions and societies being defended. Thus, we have different versions of conservatism developed in different countries either experiencing the Revolution or threatened by it, especially in France, Germany and Britain.

French reactionary conservatism

The French Revolution divided French society much more deeply than the English Civil Wars divided Britain. In consequence, French politics in the nineteenth and much of the twentieth centuries has been more polarised, and more bitter and uncompromising than British politics. The same ideas did not infuse different parties as they did in Britain, and parties tended to take up more rigid positions. French opposition to the Revolution, especially among émigré aristocrats, took the form of a reactionary demand for a return to the pre-revolutionary world. The restored Bourbon monarchy of 1815 was a constitutional monarchy and not the absolute monarchy that preceded it. On the face of it, this seemed a fair compromise, but it satisfied nobody.

De Maistre and de Bonald

The right wanted a full restoration of Bourbon absolutism. This seemed implausible after France had changed so much in a quarter of a century, and it needed a theory to justify it. The chief theorists of the reactionary outlook were Joseph de Maistre (1753–1821) and Louis de Bonald (1754–1840). They wished to portray the Revolution and all it stood for as a disaster for France and the world. This necessitated the complete rejection of Enlightenment thinking, which they blamed for causing the Revolution in the first place.

They argued for a unified Christendom under the absolute rule of church and state: that is, the rule of kings and the Pope. Society should reflect the God-given order, with everyone assigned their place. De Maistre insisted that contrary to Enlightenment thinking, human reason could create nothing of any worth. The social order of the old regime had been created, like the family, from the instincts which God had implanted in man. Those same instincts led men towards obedience to their church and their social superiors, and only when men fully returned to their true natural obedience would God's harmony be restored. De Maistre and de Bonald looked to a return to a pre-Revolution unified Christendom that in fact did not exist, and had never really existed.

Everything was attributed to God, including the Revolution, which was the expression of divine wrath. The so-called Enlightenment had set human reason above God's wisdom and the Revolution was both the punishment for, and the demonstration of, the anarchic consequences of denying God's work.

Democracy, however limited, was an abomination. For democracy institutionalised a society permanently divided in its beliefs and values, which allowed a legitimate place for error and evil at the expense of morality and truth. And because an ideologically divided society could not survive, its ultimate consequence was anarchy, as the Jacobin Terror demonstrated. People had to accept the authority of church and state which God has placed over them. Politics were subordinate to religion: kings were the servants of the Pope, who embodied the will of God on earth.

Today these seem rather obscure points, but royalism, including the idea of restoring the pre-revolutionary monarchy, recognising the authority of the Catholic church and blaming all France's troubles on the French Revolution, was a significant political outlook right up to the 1940s. This points to a more general fact about French politics throughout the period since the Revolution, which has been the chronic problem of legitimacy. Essentially it was a conflict between the sovereignty of the king, sanctified by time and the church, versus the sovereignty of the people based upon theory. France has never quite solved the question to the satisfaction of all the French. Since 1789 France has had two monarchies, two Napoleonic empires and five republics; and in all there has been fifteen constitutions.

Not all of the French right were dedicated to reaction. There developed a more pragmatic conservatism. The most common form of this is perhaps best described as conservative liberalism, a kind of cautious, pragmatic, elitist liberalism that distanced itself from the Revolution and from egalitarianism. It was concerned with property rights and the maintenance of order. Although recognising the inevitability of democratisation, liberal conservatives wanted it to come slowly; they did not look forward to it; and they did not count its advent as in any sense progress. Holders of this view included Benjamin Constant and Alexis de Tocqueville. This liberal conservatism is much closer to British conservatism.

Reaction elsewhere

Other continental countries in post-revolutionary Europe tended to reaction, although for the most part it required no theorising but a continuation of the status quo and a determination to stamp out any manifestations of liberalism. This was true of Spain, Austria and Russia. In the case of Austria and Russia, a major consideration was the association of liberalism with nationalism. A growth of nationalist movements with a French-style emphasis on popular sovereignty would threaten to disrupt and destroy their multinational empires. A further factor was the hostility of the papacy to liberalism throughout the nineteenth century, though this had no significance in much of northern Europe. Germany was in some ways a special case in the sense that its traditionalism took on a distinctly German form. It developed its own form of conservatism, which although it was nationalistic was not based on popular sovereignty or unified government, and although backward looking and reactionary had its own distinctive features, based on its connection with Romantic thinking.

German Romantic conservatism

During the French Revolutionary period a profound intellectual revolution was occurring in various parts of Europe, which influenced the work of thinkers and especially artists of all kinds. This was the Romantic Movement, which was to have an important impact on political thinking in Britain and to a lesser extent in France; but its greatest influence was in Germany. Here Romanticism influenced liberal and socialist thinking, but the greatest impact of all was on conservatism and nationalism. In Germany nationalism and conservatism were closely connected, in contrast to France where nationalism was associated with liberalism and the Revolution.

Romanticism

Romanticism in general is best understood, at least initially, as a reaction against the Enlightenment. The Enlightenment stood for universalism, particularly in the interconnected forms of reason and science and human rights, as against tradition, emotion, prejudice, particularity, individual and regional differences, established authority, habitual attitudes and customary practices. Reason was the standard of knowledge and truth, tradition the source of ignorance and error. Romantic thinking turned all this upside down. The uniqueness of the particular, whether it be an individual or an experience or a nation, was what was emphasised and celebrated. What was common and what was the subject of science was a poor and narrow version of anything and no guide to its true nature. The reason which the Enlightenment glorified was a shallow and therefore misleading guide to reality. Man was an emotional and spiritual being whose true essence was revealed in art far more than in science. Individuals as well as societies had to be understood as concrete wholes, not as a collection of universally shared attributes.

In political terms these ideas had a number of implications, some of which the German Romantic conservatives, such as Freidrich Schlegel, Novalis and Adam Müller, shared with other conservative thinkers elsewhere (notably Edmund Burke in Britain), while others were particular to themselves. The French Revolution was regarded as an outcome of Enlightenment thinking and a demonstration of its simplistic inadequacy. Universal rights of man, freedom and equality all ignored the diversity and wholeness of people and peoples. It was a shallow freedom and meaningless equality. Defining people in terms of the common human rights denied their individuality, their so-called liberty and equality were a fraud.

All that the liberty and equality that the liberals demanded amounted to was the freedom of individuals to be selfish, to pursue their own interests at the expense of their neighbours and the community in general. The community, the family and all personal obligation were sacrificed for the sake of the pursuit of wealth in a war of all against all. Shorn of their social connections individuals become isolated and rootless and vulnerable to exploitation. Traditional society, with its nobility, clergy, guildsmen, merchants and peasants, was one in which everyone knew their place and their duties, but within which all had security and protection within a community which was part of a wider community, the greater family, of which the monarch was the head. Liberal freedom would destroy all this for the sake of a freedom that meant no more than a selfish freedom for the few at the expense of the many.

The Romantic state

The Romantics insisted that genuine liberty was only possible when human nature was fully expressed in all its variety, and no individual could achieve this alone. Only a state could do this because only the state could stand for the whole. No other body or class could do this, and certainly not individuals. It would be like saying the arm could represent the whole person, when only the mind could do this, and the state was the mind's equivalent for society. It was therefore morally superior to any of its parts or to the individuals that made up its population. The individual could achieve his greatest degree of fulfilment and freedom only through the greater whole. By means of this kind of reasoning the Romantics came to the rather chilling conclusion that the state was more real than the individuals who composed it (a contrast with most British political thought which is traditionally wary of the state).

However, the kind of state the Romantics had in mind was not the modern legal state, but rather the mediaeval feudal state of the distant past. It was not based on universal laws but on personal arrangements between each individual and his lord, and constituting an organic unity. This Romantic nationalism was not, therefore, about creating a modern united Germany, but more about preserving a politically fragmented feudal Germany. Being admirers of feudalism, the Romantics looked to the social leadership of the aristocracy. Unfortunately, it was to be an enlightened aristocracy devoted to arts and sciences, not the rather ill-educated aristocracy of their own day (or indeed any time in the past). Moreover, political leadership should be in the hands of poets and scholars who had the necessary insight and understanding to rule their ideal society wisely.

At the time the Romantics were writing, Germany was a patchwork (although much simplified by Napoleon) of independent feudal territories, mostly characterised by reactionary absolutism. There was a relatively small middle class, from which most of the Romantic thinkers were drawn. It had little political influence and rulers were certainly not interested in rule by poets and scholars. But liberalism was suppressed in most areas and the Romantics helped to minimise its influence, and therefore contributed to its failure in 1848 in both Germany and Austria. As against the constitutionalism and individual rights of the liberals, the Romantics stood for state worship, extreme cultural nationalism and Germany's mission to civilise the world. They did not stand either for German unification or aggressive militaristic nationalism.

It was the liberals who stood for German unification. But with the failure of 1848 the policy came to be adopted by the right as part of the 'new conservatism' that developed in Europe in the second half of the century.

Radical conservatism

Early nineteenth-century continental conservatism, in its various forms, was largely nostalgic and backward looking, hankering after a past world that at best had been idealised to the point of fiction. But in the late nineteenth century a new kind of conservative thinking developed. Old right traditionalism came to be supplemented by new ideas and attitudes that eventually came to be dominant. This radical or 'new conservatism', as it was known at the time, sought to come to terms with the modern world and be more realistic. It can be seen as a reaction to the growing influence of liberalism in Europe from mid-century, when the old simple hankering after a lost age with its traditional social hierarchy no longer seemed an adequate alternative.

New conservative themes

The new conservatism had all the authoritarianism of the old, but was more stridently nationalistic. It was more militaristic and imperialistic, glorifying war to such an extent that populations went to war with enthusiasm in 1914. It was racist in general and anti-Semitic in particular. Modern science and technology were embraced, especially for military purposes; the importance of economic strength was recognised; and to some extent it came to terms with representation. It remained firmly anti-democratic, although was aware of how right-wing causes could be popular.

Several factors contributed to this change of mood. One of these was realism, in that it was recognised that governments and peoples could not live in the past and a new world was being created by industrialisation and urbanisation. In other words, change was coming anyway and it was better to understand and control it than just ignore it and eventually be swept away by it.

Ideas like nationalism were too popular to be ignored. Hitherto it had been associated with liberalism and such concepts as popular sovereignty, but the right discovered that nationalism could appeal to the masses in a more aggressive and xenophobic form. National self-assertion could excite popular enthusiasm and military power was its obvious expression, especially in terms of territorial expansion and the acquisition of colonies abroad. This was in turn associated with the conviction that a strong state must be economically independent and self-sufficient (in contrast to the liberal emphasis on free trade and a more integrated world). The Prussians were by no means alone in glorifying war, but it was they who above all realised the importance of industrial might for success and power in the world. Finally, a major influence on the new conservative thinking was social Darwinism.

Social Darwinism

Darwin's theory of evolution (set out in *The Origin of Species*, 1859) was the intellectual sensation of the age. It appeared to undermine those religious truths that people had taken for granted for centuries as the very foundation of European civilisation, and in doing so dealt a great blow to traditional conservative thinking. On the other hand, it appeared to offer a new foundation for truth. As a consequence, right across the ideological spectrum theorists looked to evolutionary theory to provide a foundation for their own political values. Herbert Spencer's liberalism was one example and Prince Peter Kropotkin's anarchism another. Right-wing thinking was considerably influenced.

The right-wing interpretation of Darwin was far from subtle. It portrayed life as a struggle for dominance among individuals, nations and races in which the strongest, and therefore 'superior', came to dominate the weak and therefore 'inferior'. This seemed to justify ruling elites in society, wars of national expansion and the seizing of colonies as both natural and right. Social Darwinism was an important development in the new conservative thinking which developed in many countries, but especially in Germany and France.

German conservative nationalism

German conservatives were the first on the right to grasp the possibilities of nationalism. German liberalism had continued to grow in the second half of the century, despite the failure of 1848, partly due to its popular policy of German unification. However, it was not liberals who brought about German unification (as was the case in Italy) but, in Bismark's phrase, the 'blood and iron' of Prussian force of arms. Bismark, the Prussian Chancellor, in effect stole the policy and made German unity and greatness, together with aggressive imperialism, a conservative cause which even the liberals supported.

Bismark thus developed a new conservatism which united authoritarian, hierarchic, aristocratic absolutism, with a tamed parliament and even welfare state policies of a paternalistic form, to head off the growing support for the socialists. Although authoritarian, it was not reactionary and backward-looking, but embraced industrialisation as a means to national greatness. It was modernisation from above (as also happened in Japan). Austria, by contrast, resisted any social or political change and sank ever deeper into reactionary traditionalism, becoming a fossil of pre-1789 Europe. It had opposed German unification, but could not resist the Prussian war machine.

The earlier German conservatives, the Romantics, had not in fact been admirers of such bellicosity. Their glorification of the nation was cultural and not a glorification of brute power. This dimension was added in the second half of the nineteenth century and given intellectual support in the writings of the historian Heinrich von Treitschke (1834–96), who insisted that politics was about power and that states were not bound by ordinary morality (a concept known as *Realpolitik*). Proudly calling himself a 'radical reactionary', he glorified Prussian militarism and believed everything should be subordinated to German unity and expansion under Prussian leadership.

Germany had a divine mission to civilise the world, Treitschke believed, and he resented the power and dominance of the British Empire. He despised the British preoccupation with individual rights and minimal government, and the idea that the state only gained its power at the expense of its citizens. The British could afford these delusions being an island people and ruling over a distant empire of uncivilised natives. Germany understood the true necessity of power and of subordinating individuals to the greater good of the state. Civilised life was not possible without the protection of the state, for which individuals must be prepared to die if necessary, despite any so-called rights to life, liberty and the pursuit of happiness.

Treitschke was contemptuous of democracy and believed that socialism should be suppressed by force. He also wanted sociology suppressed as an academic subject, considering its class analysis to be divisive, subversive and dangerous. The explanation of history and society lay in the unfolding of God's will, of which Prussian institutions were the highest expression (an idea derived from Hegel – see Chapter 7). Any concessions to mass opinion would lead to a decline of discipline and traditional moral standards upon which Prussian greatness depended.

War was glorified because it purified the nation of corrupting individualism and self-indulgence. Treitschke saw history in terms of a struggle between the races, of which the Germanic peoples were superior because they were born warriors and state-builders, and state-building was the highest function of man, the condition of civilisation (see Chapter 9). The German people therefore had a world-historical destiny. He was fiercely anti-Semitic. The world would eventually be dominated by German and Anglo-Saxon peoples, and if necessary by Germans alone.

Treitschke was an extremely influential teacher and his ideas of *Realpolitik* were to dominate German political thinking until the defeat of 1918. Thereafter, Germany had a liberal democracy thrust upon her by the victorious allies. It was a failure for many reasons, unable to cope with the problems, especially economic problems, that faced it. Its collapse signalled the rise of Hitler's national socialists, who were able to draw on the traditions of state-worship and authoritarianism of past German history. The Nazis made Treitschke required reading.

Roman Catholicism and the new conservatism

Some radical conservative ideas found favour in Austria. Its harsher authoritarian and racist doctrines suited an imperial power trying to hold down a multinational and multiracial empire. The right in Austria, as well as in France and elsewhere, gained considerable support from the Ultramontane movement that was coming to dominate the Catholic church in the nineteenth century.

Ultramontanism was the doctrine of Papal supremacy, as against the authority of the national churches. 'Ultramontane' literally means 'beyond the mountains' and implies churches north of the Alps looking to Rome for authority and guidance. That authority was at a particularly low ebb in the eighteenth century, but attacks on the church during the French Revolution – when many priests were executed, churches closed and Notre Dame cathedral was 'dechristianised' and turned into a 'Temple of Reason' – led to a revival of Ultramontanism in France and the rest of Catholic Europe. The movement's greatest triumph was the adoption by the Vatican Council of 1870 of the doctrine of Papal infallibility in matters of faith and morality.

Morality was here deemed to include politics, and Ultramontanism tended to accompany extreme traditionalism in the political sphere. The church in the past had always tended to favour pragmatism in its dealings with states, but in 1864 the Pope declared liberalism, nationalism and socialism to be 'false doctrines of our most unhappy age' and 'incompatible with Catholic truth'.

Later a series of Papal encyclicals spelt out the position in more detail. While not condemning any system of government if properly subject to church guidance, unrestrained capitalism, individualism, popular sovereignty, free speech and toleration were all specifically condemned, together with socialist ideas *in toto*. The ideal was a Christian commonwealth under church guidance, with estates and corporations and other social bodies, each with its proper sphere of authority, all joined together in an organic harmony. It is essentially a mediaeval picture, in which government is deemed to be an expression of the whole social organism, and is underpinned by the church. Short of this ideal, the Catholic church generally tended to support the right in Catholic countries up to the 1940s. It signed agreements with both Hitler and Mussolini, both of whom suppressed moderate Catholic parties without there being any serious protest from the church hierarchy.

The radical right in France

French conservatism in the late nineteenth century was also influenced by the ideas of the radical right, especially after the crushing and humiliating defeat by Prussia in the Franco-Prussian War of 1870. After being the most powerful nation in the world a century earlier, France, it was argued, had sunk into decadence. The reason for this was obviously the Revolution with its ideas of freedom and equality and democracy. Nationalism became the most important right-wing cause, together with glorification of militarism. Military strength and unity of purpose were essential for a revival of French greatness. This is the period of the cult of Joan of Arc, with the erection of countless statues and festivals held in her honour, as the symbol of French valour and resistance to foreign aggression.

Nevertheless, despite similarities with the radical right of Germany and elsewhere, French radical conservatism remained distinctive. For one thing it retained much of the traditionalism and veneration for the Catholic church of earlier writers such as de Maistre and de Bonald. But whereas they had looked to a return to the unified Christendom of the Middle Ages that in fact had never really existed, the radicals of the late nineteenth and early twentieth centuries sought other sources of inspiration to justify their elitism, rejection of democracy and insistence on national uniformity of values. Radical conservative thinkers, such as the novelist and MP, Maurice Barres (1862–1923), and the journalist and political organiser, Charles Maurras (1867–1952), were much more narrowly nationalistic. What mattered to them was French civilisation and French greatness. Catholicism happened to be part of this, while the shallow rationalism of the Enlightenment and the Revolution was not. The Frenchman, they believed, thought with his instincts, which told him what was good for France, whatever his reason dictated.

Charles Maurras

Maurras was the leader of the Action Français movement from 1899 until 1944, which, although not an effective political party, was an important influence on French politics during this time. He believed that the 'real' France, pre-Revolutionary France, had been the true heir of Ancient Greece and Rome and the most perfect expression of subsequent European civilisation, the model of order and beauty. But France had been ruined by the Revolution and its consequences, and had become corrupt, decadent and weak in relation to inferior peoples like the Germans and the British.

For this decline he chiefly blamed the Enlightenment ideas that had inspired the Revolution: that is, liberalism, individualism, liberty, democracy and equality. His particular *bête noire* was Rousseau, with his ideas of popular sovereignty and the authority of the individual conscience. Maurras attacked all of these things with great vehemence in his writings, along with socialism, communism and anarchism. His chief charge was that these were not French but foreign, usually Germanic or Jewish (or, in the case of Rousseau, Swiss). The chief object of his attacks was democracy.

Maurras regarded democracy as a terrible wasting disease from which France was suffering. Democratic government is government by windbags, who have to pander to the ignorant masses and base their policies on vacillating and uninformed public opinion. It had reduced France from being the leading world power in the eighteenth century to being a second-rate one in the twentieth. Democracy was, he argued, not a form of government so much as a form of anarchy, with endless, debilitating discussion and with the pressure of private interests forcing out the national interest. Nothing is ever certain, nothing is under control, and the state is the constant victim of the greed of individuals, classes and organisations.

Maurras's alternative was the full restoration of the Bourbon monarchy that would alone have the necessary legitimacy and therefore the authority to do what was needed to restore France to greatness. There would be no question of a constitution, for nothing must diminish royal absolutism. All traces of democracy or any other such representation would be abolished. The monarchy was the living embodiment of French history and stood for order and discipline in society and in art. It stood for the permanent interests of the nation as against the selfishness of individuals and groups. There would be a restored aristocracy and guild system.

Maurras regarded the Catholic church as essential to the very essence of the 'true France', even though he was not a religious believer. The Catholic church, he argued, had taken a foreign and alien religion (Judaic Christianity) and Latinised it, making it a society of order and hierarchy to mediate between God and man and in the process turned it into something precise and beautiful. The German Reformation had been an attempt to return the church to its primitive, and therefore Jewish, beginnings. Protestantism was therefore alien and must be resisted.

Maurras was happy to have the church teach the God-given order where everything had its place with good reason, but this was not in fact his own view. He appeared to regard the universe as a hostile and anarchic place although the conditions for creating order and beauty could occasionally be thrown up. But when it happened, as pre-eminently it had in France, then the result was fragile and easily lost and immense efforts were needed to preserve it.

Action Français was not a political party in the usual sense of standing for elections, although it had a substantial membership and its daily paper, *L'Action Français*, was widely read. However, Maurras was so violent in his hatreds and in his attacks on politicians and prominent people that he became an embarrassment, and was disowned by both the Pope and the Bourbon Pretender to the throne. He also had violent young followers who beat up opponents, broke up meetings, and threatened anyone who disagreed. Some classify Maurras and Action Français as fascist, and certainly there are fascist features that grew stronger as time went on. His ideal monarchy increasingly appeared more as a figurehead in an essentially military state. On the other hand, the movement looked to the past rather than the future and it was not populist. Maurras had only contempt for the masses. There was no call for mobilising the people, as there was among the more obviously fascist organisation that developed in France on the 1930s.

Vichy France and after

The nearest Maurras came to seeing his ideal government was between 1940 and 1944, when that part of France that the Germans had chose not to conquer was run from Vichy by an extreme right-wing government under Marshal Pétain. The government shared theoretical sympathies with German fascism, was a virtual dictatorship and was avowedly authoritarian, paternalistic, anti-Semitic and much admiring of Maurras, who enthusiastically supported it. It was close to Germany in terms of its thinking and collaborationist in practice.

Although he detested the Germans, Maurras none the less rejoiced that they had destroyed the French Republic (for whose inadequacies the defeat had been a punishment) and were anti-Semitic. The Pétain government declared an end to the cosmopolitan, masonic, capitalist state, to class war and demagogy and the cult of pleasure, and a return to the principles of religion, patriotism and the family. Trade unions were abolished and replaced by professional corporations, to put an end to strikes and industrial unrest. The aim was a corporatist system where the interests of workers, employers and the state would be reconciled. Jews were excluded from government, teaching and a host of other professional jobs and eventually deported.

In 1945 Maurras was imprisoned for collaboration, though when he died in 1952 he was entirely unrepentant. And although his extreme reactionary, authoritarian conservatism continued to have its admirers, its closeness to fascism and the Vichy experience discredited the far right in France for a very long time.

Right-wing dictatorship

In many parts of the world, for example in some South American and Asian states, the far right has been represented by military dictatorships. In modern states the military is frequently a bastion of right-wing views. As perhaps befits their profession, the military tends to stand for order, discipline and national unity, and is inclined to see itself as the guardian of the nation; whereas democracy may seem to represent chaos and disunity. When disunity and political conflict appear to threaten the national interest the military may intervene, claiming to save the nation. Such *coup d'etat* are rare in Europe, although one occurred in Greece in 1968 and more recently in Turkey. They have been much more common, for example, in South America where the justification of saving the nation from left-wing insurgency has been used.

British conservatism

Traditional British conservatism (as distinct from the Thatcherite conservatism of the 1980s) has an altogether different character to the various continental conservatisms. If conservatism is about preserving a pre-existing way of life, then what was to be preserved in Britain was very different from continental practice. British politics and government were already deeply permeated with liberal ideas and values before British conservatism crystallised as a conscious political doctrine; a parliament and a strong tradition of civil liberties were already in existence. The chief exponent of conservative ideas, Edmund Burke (1729–97), was in fact a Whig and devoted to liberty and representative government; and consequently these things were part of the British conservative tradition from the beginning, in marked contrast to the thinking that prevailed in Europe.

Burkean foundations

Burke's conservatism is most fully and eloquently set out in his *Reflections on the Revolution in France* of 1792, in which he fiercely attacked the revolutionaries of Paris for mindless destruction of what they did not understand for the sake of an abstract theory which was for all practical purposes useless and dangerous. An extremely complex social organism was being obliterated in the name of some vague idea that human beings had certain natural rights whose existence nobody could prove. The result could only be bloodshed and chaos (Burke wrote before the deposing of the king and the Terror). These origins are significant. Traditional conservatism is, broadly, a defence of the status quo, of the established order of things, against radical or revolutionary change. It is a sophisticated defence that traditional conservatives today still express in essentially Burkean terms.

Traditional conservatives reject the idea that society is like some sort of machine that can be taken to pieces and reassembled at will. It is much more like a living creature, which cannot just be cut up and rearranged to suit a theory. Society is infinitely complex and interconnected, so that changing one part of it effects every other part and may do so in any number of unforeseen ways, probably most of them bad. Sudden or radical change is therefore bound to lead to disaster and chaos because its consequences cannot be controlled. Conservatives are always suspicious of change, while at the same time recognising that changing things is from time to time necessary to adapt to new circumstances. The organism must be allowed to evolve at its own pace. The politician can assist this process with reform, though this must always be piecemeal and pragmatic in order to minimise any ill effects.

For conservatives, a stable and well-organised society is the work of centuries. It is built out of institutions, such as the family, church, private property and local communities. Through these institutions individuals have rights, and also obligations, while others hold office and have authority. All are bound together in an established pattern of living that embodies long-held values and is sustained by custom and tradition. Custom and tradition, and even prejudice, are the best guides to action, since these represent the stored-up wisdom of the past. Relying on theory or 'pure reason' is a very poor guide.

This is a very different picture from the standard liberal view of the ideal society which is based upon contracts between free individuals that in principle can be changed at any time. Authority arises from such contracts. Above all the social contract, which, in its simplest version, involves an agreement by citizens to obey the law in exchange for the protection of the state. If the government does not do its job, then the contract is broken and the people can change it. For traditional conservatives, however, society is more than just a collection of individuals making contracts with each other, but a community bound together by a multitude of ties of loyalty and affection. Like other critics of liberalism, traditional conservatives see liberals as having no sense of community, of what it is that binds human beings together.

Every long-established and well-ordered society is a unique achievement, and makes a unique contribution to civilisation. But this achievement is vulnerable to breakdown and destruction if subject to drastic change. Politics is the art of preserving what is best (that is, conservation, hence 'conservatism') and adapting it to new circumstances. This cannot be done by following some blueprint or plan giving a picture of the ideal society to be achieved. Politics is a matter of experience and judgement, not the application of a doctrine as Jacobins, radicals, communists, fascists, and umpteen varieties of socialist have believed. Conservatives reject abstract theory in politics, which they call 'ideology'. Conservative principles, they argue, are not ideological but pragmatic, being derived from history and tradition, which is the guarantee of what does and does not work.

The preservation of the established order implies inequality. Conservatives believe all should have the opportunity to better themselves, but the idea that everyone should be equal is anathema. Since people are unequal in talent and energy, society has to reflect this. Besides, without differences of wealth and status there would be no incentive for people to work and strive. The fact that there are different stations in life, and different social classes, is not something to be lamented; it is a functional necessity. Different people need to do different kinds of jobs, and be rewarded according to their contribution. Social class is essentially an integrative feature of society, not a divisive one as the socialists think. As with any living organism, all the parts must work together in harmony if the organism is to be healthy. The task of government is to maintain that harmony.

Conservatives place special value on order and stability, along with the social hierarchy and discipline that are necessary to maintain them. They put little faith in unrestrained human nature or entertain much hope that it can be improved. Human nature has an evil streak in it, which no amount of social tinkering will eliminate. The best that can be done is to have a society that, as far as possible, encourages the good and minimises the bad. Rational schemes to fundamentally improve the human condition (that is, ideas for a better organised society that will solve all social problems) are viewed with suspicion.

Greater faith is placed in established ways of doing things and in traditional values. Patriotism is important, as is respect for authority and law, while good government and strong leadership are admired. Leadership is a key conservative concept; it is a skill which can be fostered and developed, but resides most naturally in the traditional ruling elite who can command authority without engendering hostility.

These attitudes have been characteristic of a traditional conservative outlook since Burke. However, a number of other themes have become part of conservative thinking since then.

Later development of British conservatism

Burke's views very much reflected the outlook of the landed aristocracy who ruled Britain in his day, but as the nineteenth century progressed others ideas were added as the Conservative Party sought to widen its appeal.

The Conservative prime minister, Benjamin Disraeli (1804–81) gave the party a new vision as the party of national unity. This involves a care for the whole of society, including the problems of ordinary people, as well as those of high position who have a duty to rule. The idea was to form an alliance between the old ruling class and the working classes, to some of whom Disraeli extended the franchise in 1867. Conservative reforms to help alleviate social problems would be in sharp contrast to the destructiveness and divisiveness of *laissez-faire* capitalism, which was associated with the Liberals. This was Disraeli's conception of Tory democracy; that is, of 'one nation' instead of the 'two nations' of rich and poor that he claimed unbridled free enterprise was creating at that time. On this basis, Disraeli was able to claim that the Conservatives were the party of the national unity which, unlike other parties, represented the whole nation rather than one particular class.

One further dimension Disraeli added was that of empire. Britain was portrayed as having an imperial mission to bring peace and civilisation to distant lands. Burke had little concern with the 'condition of the people' and still less with empire, while the Liberals had little interests in colonies since they conflicted with their notions of free trade. Disraeli's imperialism was immensely popular, and the theme of empire along with Tory democracy and one nation could appeal to all classes and conditions. It was a conservatism redolent with aristocratic paternalism and the values of the landowning class (in sharp contrast with liberal *laissez-faire* individualism) and yet designed for a new age of democracy, seeking a mass appeal.

Nevertheless, by the end of the century the Conservatives were increasingly seen as the party of free enterprise. Hitherto, the Liberals had been the pre-eminent party of capitalism and business, and the Conservatives the party of the landed interest, but social and political changes were moving towards a realignment. The increasing number of working-class voters, and the revival of socialism from the 1880s onwards, suggested that the political future lay in a conflict between those representing the propertied and those representing the propertyless. It was the Conservatives who most successfully represented themselves as the defenders of all property, both landed and commercial, while the Liberals made greater efforts to capture the new working-class vote. They were left in the middle, trying to appeal to both sides with a more collectivist social liberalism. The Liberal Party was increasingly unable to retain the support of businessmen, while failing to capture the working classes. Once the Labour Party became successfully established the Liberal Party was doomed.

With the recruitment of more middle-class members, especially from the world of business, the Conservatives increasingly adopted and defended classical liberal values and preached the virtues of free enterprise and individualism, and the horrors of state intervention and collectivism. The superiority of a capitalist society over a socialist one became a major theme; although these principles were held within a framework of traditional conservatism.

The Conservative leader in the closing years of the century, Lord Salisbury, was a partisan figure in this new polarisation. He was in a sense, a class warrior: elitist, anti-democratic, defending property, trying to slow down democracy, and having little Disraelian concern for the 'condition of the people'. In consequence the Conservatives were much closer to the continental right than they had been previously, or indeed have been since.

In the twentieth century the Conservative Party returned to being a pragmatic and moderate party of reform. After 1945 it accepted the 'consensus' policies of Keynesian economic management, the mixed economy and the welfare state (see Chapter 2), although it sought to interpret these in terms of traditional conservative principles that stressed individual enterprise and responsibility. However, the economic difficulties of the 1970s opened the way for the 'Thatcher revolution' (discussed in Chapter 10) that introduced a radical free-market conservatism which was in many ways a contradiction of traditional conservative ideas and related to American conservatism .

The electoral success of Margaret Thatcher ensured the eclipse of traditional conservatism within the Conservative Party to such an extent that its future is very much in doubt. The massive defeat the party suffered in 1997 left the Thatcherites firmly in charge. Some argue that traditional conservatism is dead beyond recall, for example John Gray in *Is Conservatism Dead?* (1997). On the other hand, Ian Gilmour (former cabinet minister under Margaret Thatcher and distinguished conservative thinker) has argued (Gilmour, 1997) that the Conservative Party will only recover when it goes back to its traditional values.

The European centre-right since 1945

In the post-war period, British conservatism was sufficiently flexible and pragmatic to accommodate the dominant social democratic ideas (the mixed and managed economy and the welfare state) and the policies that went with them. Continental conservatism also took these ideas on board, but had to make much larger adjustments. The radical right, with its authoritarianism, racism and hostility to democracy, had been entirely discredited by the fascist experience. In many countries the dominant position on the right of liberal democratic politics was taken by Christian democracy.

Catholicism and liberalism

Christian democracy came into its own after 1945, but its origins are much older. In its early development, the 'Christian' in Christian democracy was Catholic Christianity. Ideas of reconciling Catholic teaching with democracy go back to the French Revolution. However, for most of the nineteenth century, French republicanism and the Catholic church were deeply hostile. The Revolutionary government had attacked the church, confiscated its lands, persecuted its priests and even attempted to create a new religion of Reason and the Supreme Being.

After the revolutionary period, the church had other reasons for regarding liberalism as a threat to Catholic values. Modern industrialisation and urbanisation, the result of capitalist development, were destroying traditional communal and family life, while the policy of *laissez-faire* threatened a war of all against all. Liberal economic theory sanctified selfishness and promoted materialist values. At the same time, liberal stress on individualism, tolerance and free expression allowed all kinds of self-indulgence and permissiveness to flourish.

The hostility of the traditionalist Catholic church was not therefore surprising. Nevertheless, there were some who thought a Catholicism reconciled to some degree with liberalism was a possibility, although not until the 1830s that it was a significant political position in France. Elsewhere, such as Ireland, Belgium and the USA, the church's experience suggested that in the right circumstances it could at least live with democracy. On the other hand, towards the end of the century democracy became not only associated with liberalism but with socialism (both explicitly condemned by the Pope in 1864), which in continental Europe meant atheistic Marxism. Few thought in terms of a genuine synthesis of liberalism and Catholicism. One of these few was the British historian Lord Acton (1834–1902), who said that he rejected everything in Catholicism that was incompatible with liberty and everything in politics that was incompatible with Catholicism.

From about the 1870s political Catholicism, based on the idea that it was to the Church's advantage to participate in the modern political process, became a significant political force in Germany, Switzerland, Belgium and Austria. These movements tended to have similar programmes of opposition to liberal secularism, civil marriage, state control of education, and other policies. They were closely connected with the church and confined to the faithful. They implied no commitment to democracy, merely making use of the system to the advantage of what they believed to be right. Their ideal was the church having a privileged position in the state, able to influence policy, as against the standard view across all forms of liberalism that church and state must be clearly separated.

Initially, these Catholic movements tended to oppose capitalism and social-ism equally, as both based on materialism and productive of social conflict, preferring the ideal of self-sufficient peasants and the guild-organised craftsmen that the Catholic encyclicals (especially *Rerum Novarum* of 1892) advocated. However, many such movements had reconciled themselves to capitalism by 1914 as the prevailing economic system (socialism had come to seem the greater threat), while at the same time helping to organise Catholic peasants and workers to defend their interests within that system.

The Christian democracy movement

Between the wars, political Catholicism flourished in Italy and gave rise to Christian democracy as we know it today. The first such party was founded in 1919 by Luigi Sturzo, a priest who believed that Catholicism and democracy could be positively reconciled to the advantage of both. His party was inde-pendent of the church and advocated social reform, based on Catholic social teaching. Similar parties were established in other parts of Europe and in South America. However, political Catholicism generally had little success in stopping fascism, and even helped it in some cases. In Italy, Sturzo's party was suppressed by the fascists and he went into exile in France in 1924. In Paris he founded an international movement among whose aims were the establish-ment of a common market and European integration to prevent wars. Among those active in this group were Alcide De Gasperi, Konrad Adenauer and Robert Schuman, each of whom became leading figures in their respective countries (Italy, West Germany and France) and were major contributors to the setting up of the European Community in the 1950s.

Furthermore, until the Second World War Christian Democratic parties were essentially for the faithful and therefore lacked a certain general appeal. When parties were re-founded after the war they had a much wider appeal, and with the discrediting of the far right, had a much clearer field. They were especially strong and electorally successful in former Nazi-dominated areas, and areas where there was a strong Communist Party; that is, where traditional Catholic values had been under threat. This included most of continental Western Europe, but especially Germany, Italy, Austria and the Benelux countries. There was a French Christian Democratic Party after the war, which was absorbed by the Gaullists, while Spain and Portugal acquired modest parties after the end of their dictatorships in the 1970s. However, post-war Christian Democratic parties have not been exclusively Catholic. In West Germany's Christian Democratic Union around 40 per cent of the membership is Protestant, while the Dutch and Scandinavian parties are mostly Protestant.

Christian democratic ideas

Christian democratic ideas have, however, been largely based on Catholic social teaching. That is, while supporting the rights of property and the traditional social order, society is seen as an organic whole where all the parts must work together. There is a paternalistic concern for the less well-off, expressed in policies of social reform to improve their conditions and protect their rights. This involves a recognition of the role of trade unions, and all the major Christian democratic parties (with the exception of the German) have strong trade union wings. Opposed to notions of class consciousness and class conflict, Christian democratic parties claim to represent all sections of society (although they tend to get proportionally fewer votes among the industrial working class) and tend to look upon themselves as centrist rather than right-wing parties. The Christian democratic block in the European Union, which calls itself collectively 'The European People's Party', is a strong supporter of the European Union's social programme (for this reason the British conservatives in the European Parliament have sometimes associated themselves with this grouping, but more often they have not).

The French Catholic thinker, Jacques Maritain (1882–1973), gave the movement the principle of 'personalism' which claimed to be a third way between liberal individualism and socialist collectivism. Personalism is the idea that the individual can only fully develop through responsibility to other people, especially to the family and the community.

Christian democrats have always been strong advocates of European economic and political union. The point is to foster co-operation and prevent war. This reflects a certain distrust of the power of the sovereign state that is answerable to no one. Another aspect of this is the advocacy of federalism as a check on centralised national power. They have been strongly anti-communist.

These social and political principles have not, however, been accompanied by any distinctive economic theory. Christian Democratic parties adopted Keynesian economics after the war, which, along with the mixed economy and the welfare state, fitted very well with their outlook. West Germany's Christian Democratic finance minister in the 1950s, Ludwig Erhard, introduced a particular version of this known as the 'social market', the idea being of a free market with a social conscience. (This in fact has been the one significant Protestant contribution to Christian democratic theory.) The decline in the authority of Keynesian economics since the late 1970s has given Christian democracy something of a problem concerning what their values and economic policies are.

Post-war Christian democracy has had a much wider appeal beyond the Catholic faithful than it had previously, and as a result it has been, since 1945, Europe's most successful political movement. Christian Democratic parties have had the lion's share of power in Austria, Belgium, Holland, Italy, Luxembourg, Germany and Switzerland. However, the more general appeal of these parties has tended to dilute their doctrine, so that now there are worries that these parties have lost their distinctive identities, and in particular their Christian inspiration, becoming merely another centre-right party representing the interests of the better-off. Such fears have been exacerbated by the advent of New Right neo-liberalism which puts so much stress on the market at the expense of social policy.

Apart from Christian democracy, there are other moderate conservative parties and outlooks. One of the best known and most successful has been the Gaullist movement in France.

The right in post-war France and Italy

Charles de Gaulle (1890–1970) was a senior French army officer who came to England when France fell to the Germans in 1940. While the Vichy government collaborated with the Germans, de Gaulle raised the standard of resistance. After the Liberation he became increasingly disillusioned with post-war politics and he retired in 1952. However, the Fourth Republic ran into increasing difficulties and de Gaulle was asked to draw up a new constitution, ushering in the Fifth Republic in 1958, which de Gaulle himself dominated as president until his retirement in 1969.

'Gaullism' stands for strong leadership and centralised republican government, strong nationalism (insisting on French sovereignty within the European Community), traditional (that is, Catholic) values, and a capitalist economy. National security, political stability and economic growth are all emphasised. The party survives, but in many factions, all claiming the authority of de Gaulle's name. It has been held together since 1974 by the dynamic leadership of Jacques Chirac, and is still the most important party on the rather fragmented French right.

Post-war Italian politics were dominated by the Christian Democratic Party, taking the lead in numerous coalition governments up to the 1990s. Its popularity (and strong support from outside Italy) was to a large extent due to Italy having the largest Communist Party in Western Europe. But with the ending of the Cold War the party began to break up and finally collapsed in a welter of scandals concerning corruption and Mafia connections around 1992. The vacuum was filled by Forza Italia, a remarkable political party created from nothing by the media tycoon Silvio Berlusconi, who rapidly became prime minister. He achieved power through a coalition between his own party and other new forces in Italian politics. One of these was the former fascist party, which had recently reinvented itself as a party of democracy; the other was the Northern League, a regional party advocating independence for Northern Italy.

The coalition government did not last long and Berlusconi himself became embroiled in corruption scandals. The late 1990s were dominated by the Italian left.

4

Nationalism and internationalism

Among modern ideologies, nationalism is the simplest, the clearest and the least theoretically sophisticated; but it is also the most widespread and the one with the strongest grip on popular feeling. It has successfully demanded of people their highest loyalties and greatest sacrifices, and as a result has been among the most powerful agents of political change in the last two hundred years.

At its simplest, nationalism is the belief that humanity is divided up into nations and that all nations have the right to self-government and to determine their own destiny. Multinational states and nations divided between states are inherently wrong. It is the nation-state, therefore, that is the one legitimate political unit and the creation and preservation of national identity and national unity are primary objects of political action. Nationalism is a political doctrine, an ideology, because it insists that one particular political form is natural and therefore right.

What is perhaps surprising is just how recent this idea is. Of all modern ideologies nationalism is the most unequivocally a product of the French Revolution. This is despite the fact that a sense of national identity and national loyalty can be found as far back as the ancient world, while nation-states had existed for at least several hundred years. What the French Revolution did was to fuse together these older phenomena with a notion of 'the people' as the ultimate source of legitimacy and authority. This was in contrast with traditional and religiously sanctioned notions of the dynastic claims of princes to sovereign rule over any territories which they inherited, irrespective of the wishes of the people who lived there. For example, in the three centuries prior to the French Revolution what we now call Belgium was successively ruled by the Duke of Burgundy, the King of Spain and the Emperor of Austria, and nobody thought this was odd or illegitimate.

In the hands of the Jacobins, nationalism was a revolutionary idea which they sought to export to neighbouring peoples, which in turn called forth other forms of nationalist thought informed by quite different principles. When the dust of the revolutionary period had settled, the revolutionary and counter-revolutionary strands were integrated to produce the nineteenth-century concept of nationalism which, despite its difficulties, is still broadly with us today.

Revolutionary and Romantic nationalism

The French Revolutionaries invented nationalism almost by accident. It was a by-product of their attempts to put their Enlightenment ideas into effect. Like the revolutionaries of America, they were inspired by John Locke's ideas of natural rights, government by the consent of the governed, and the right of the people to overthrow a tyranny. They were also more directly inspired by Rousseau's ideas of popular sovereignty and the General Will. However, these ideas said little about who exactly were 'the governed' or 'the people' who possessed these rights and in whom sovereignty resided. Enlightenment theory tended to see society as a collection of individuals with natural rights, bound together by a contract entered into for the protection of those rights. This treated the state like a voluntary association of the like-minded, which ignored those things that bound societies together, such as ties of community and common culture, a sense of common history, purpose or destiny.

When the French Revolutionaries attempted to turn the Enlightenment abstractions of popular sovereignty, social contract and the assertion of individual rights into political reality, it was natural for them to assume 'the people' to be the French nation, which for centuries had been one of the most distinct and united peoples of Europe. It was the nation that was sovereign and not the king, and the nation that was the politically significant unit, not the nobility.

The Abbé Siéyès

The most important French theorist of nationalism at this time was the Abbé Siéyès (1748–1836). He was a cleric who identified himself with the ordinary people and was elected to the Third Estate of the Estates General in 1789. He wrote that: 'The nation is prior to everything. Its will is always legal: indeed it is the law itself' (Siéyès, 1963). The nation is the fundamental unit and it has a will that is the basis of all legitimate authority. The nation has a right to express its will, and consequently has the right to self-determination. Furthermore, by using a somewhat doctored version of Rousseau's general will, Siéyès was able to maintain that the Third Estate expressed the will of France. The other two Estates (the Nobility and the Clergy) represented those who gave nothing to the nation and were parasitic upon it. They could only redeem themselves by identifying with the Third Estate and therefore the nation. The Third Estate turned itself into the National Assembly in 1789 and laid down the basic principles of the Revolution in the *Declaration of the Rights of Man*, Clause III of which declared: 'The Nation is essentially the source of all sovereignty; nor can any individual, or any body of men, be entitled to any authority which is not expressly derived from it.' This laid the foundation of nationalist theory.

It became characteristic of all subsequent revolutionary leaders to identify themselves with the will of the French nation. The nation was seen as a single person with a single will and a single common purpose. And those who opposed the will of the people in some sense betrayed the nation and were outside it. The Revolutionaries in general wanted to use this new conception of the nation to overcome the provincial and feudal loyalties of the old system, and replace them with the single loyalty to the nation of free and equal citizens, having a common identity and common destiny.

This conception was successfully used to mobilise the French people in defence of the Revolution, especially when France was attacked from outside. When defence eventually turned into attack and French armies under Napoleon began conquering Western Europe, these ideas provided the French with a sense of mission, to bring freedom and self-determination to the nations of Europe.

Romantic nationalism

The French Revolutionaries' concept of nationalism was an outgrowth of Enlightenment thinking. The rights of man, national self-determination and the sovereignty of the people were the kind of rational and universal ideals that were characteristic of Enlightenment thought. However, there is no reason why national unity should not be developed around quite different principles.

The French Revolutionary armies, who saw themselves as liberating Europe, provoked nationalist reaction in Germany, Spain and elsewhere that was more to do with pride in a traditional way of life and cultural uniqueness than notions of popular government or individual rights. These very different principles were connected with the movement of ideas that was a reaction to the Enlightenment that we know as the Romantic Movement.

In many ways nationalism had more of a natural affinity with Romantic than with Enlightenment thought. The Romantic outlook (discussed in Chapter 3) insisted on the uniqueness of every nation: its history, language and culture. Romanticism inspired much historical research into national origins, folklore, traditional customs, music and other manifestations of culture that develop a sense of national identity. These ideas developed first and most strongly in Germany, which was at that time a somewhat backward region of Europe and a patchwork of small independent states.

Among the earliest of Romantic thinkers was Johann Gottfried von Herder (1744–1803). He believed that God had divided mankind into different nations so that each, through its distinctive language and culture, could make its unique contribution to civilisation. The adoption of other people's cultures was an interference with the plan, and Herder was particularly exercised by the German upper classes adopting French culture and language. At the Court of Frederick the Great of Prussia, for example, German was forbidden. Herder thought this was a spurious attempt at sophistication, to the detriment of native German thought and art and custom. His belief that a nation's spirit or soul is embodied in its language and cultural life, and needed to be preserved and celebrated, became an important feature of subsequent nationalist thinking, when scholars and artists were important figures in preserving and promoting national culture.

When the French Revolutionary armies occupied Germany in the name of German liberation, the Germans reacted against the French and developed their own version of nationalism. It was Johann Fichte (1763–1814) who converted Herder's ideas into a political programme. In his *Addresses to the German Nation* of 1807–8, Fichte exhorted the German people to unify and defeat the occupying French. The German nation should not only rid itself of foreign political influence, but also purify itself of all foreign intellectual and cultural influences.

Nineteenth-century nationalism

If we add this Romantic notion of national uniqueness to French ideas of nation and self-determination, as represented by Siéyès, we have the nine-teenth-century notion of the national state. The attendant nationalist outlook may be summarised as follows:

- Humanity is naturally divided into nations.
- The nation is more than just a political association. It is a community and is a social and economic unit.
- Membership of the nation implies more than pursuing one's own private purposes. It involves not just rights, but a duty to contribute to the good of the whole, and to be a patriot.
- The nation is a unity because its members have, in some sense, a common will. This implies a common culture and territory, and a common purpose. The nation is an agent with a history and a destiny.
- If the nation is an agent with a will and destiny then it must be free to exercise that will to pursue that destiny.
- It is the first duty of political leaders to foster national unity and identity and to lead the nation towards its common goals.

It follows from this conception that every nation must have its own state and not be under the domination of any other state. Multinational states and nations divided between states are wrong on principle. It is precisely these circumstances that have inspired the growth of nationalist sentiment and writing. Two of the most significant nationalist theorists wrote in situations where their nations were fragmented in a patchwork of small states. Fichte in Germany has already been mentioned; the other was the Italian, Joseph Mazzini (1805–72).

Joseph Mazzini

Mazzini perhaps more than anyone else personified the fusion of Enlightenment and Romantic nationalism. He argued that God had divided humanity into natural nations, with natural territories and frontiers. It is evil governments, based on barbaric feudal notions of territories as the personal possessions of their ruling families that have subverted this plan and are the cause of oppression and war. Self-determination, where nations could live according to their true identities within their natural boundaries, would enable the people of Europe to co-operate with each other in mutual respect. Proper national governments would provide liberty and care for the welfare of the people and ensure international peace and progress.

Mazzini believed it was Italy's destiny to lead mankind towards a new era of peace and harmony. He took it for granted that all national claims to territory were compatible and that only sincere goodwill was necessary to solve disputes permanently. These ideas may seem naive, but they were influential and inspired nationalists across Europe (although it must be said that the unification of Italy was more a matter of power politics than idealism).

Nineteenth-century Europe was littered with nationalist causes and conflicts. As well as Italian unification, there were the causes of the Greeks and other Balkan peoples wanting to escape Turkish rule. The rash of revolutions across Europe in 1848 were mostly inspired by liberal nationalism, with associated notions of modernising society and the economy and the end of feudal loyalties. They followed Mazzini's belief that personal liberty and national self-determination were inseparable. Such revolutions were seen as a particular threat to the Austro-Hungarian Empire, and to the ruling dynasties of fragmented Germany. In 1848 German unification was seen as very much a liberal cause; but, as we saw in the last chapter, the German aristocracy astutely turned it into a popular right-wing cause.

Right-wing nationalism

The late nineteenth century saw the development of a more aggressive, xenophobic, right-wing nationalism in Germany and elsewhere. It emphasised national self-assertion, and national economic self-sufficiency, expressed in wars for territorial expansion and the development of overseas empires. It also became bound up with notions of racial superiority which appeared to find justification in Darwinian theories of evolution, the argument being that the principle of 'survival of the fittest' applied to nations and races (see Chapter 9).

The creation of empire and the subjection of 'lesser peoples' was thus a mark of superiority. Not all justifications of empire were so crude, and not all who believed in empire did so on grounds of inherent racial superiority. It was taken for granted, however, that European peoples (including their outstations in North America and elsewhere) were more 'advanced' than the non-European world. For some, therefore, it was a moral duty to bring a higher civilisation to non-Europeans who were not already subject to colonial rule of the older European empires. Thus, the late nineteenth century was characterised by a new round of imperial expansion, where the European states sought to divide up what was left of the world not already under European control among colonies or spheres of influence.

It was a combination of the aspiration of European peoples still ruled by foreign states, and the aggressive national rivalry of the major European states that created the conditions for the First World War and which exploded in 1914. National self-determination was a major principle of the victorious powers, but it was not the basis of the lasting peace that was hoped for. For one thing, there seemed to be too many peoples to be accommodated as separate nations; and so some peoples had to be bound together in artificial fusions, such as Czechoslovakia and Yugoslavia. Second, although this principle of self-determination was supposed to be universal, it was only applied to the empires of defeated countries: Germany, Austria, Turkey and Russia. It was not applied to the victorious powers (such as Britain in Ireland) or their overseas empires. The settlement left plenty of scope for future conflict over various national questions. These have expressed themselves in the conflicts of the Second World War and since.

Anti-colonial nationalism

In the nineteenth century, nationalism began to develop beyond Europe, beginning in the old empires of the European powers, where generations of settlers had created their own way of life and aspired to free themselves from the tutelage of the 'mother country' and create a new nation. Sometimes this was done by agreement, as with Australia and Canada, but sometimes it involved 'wars of liberation', as with the Spanish colonies of South and Central America.

Anti-Europeanism

However, in the Western world the 'right of self determination' was only considered appropriate for those of European stock. It was not for non-Europeans, no matter how ancient and venerable their civilisations were. Those parts of the world not already under the control of Europeans were to be divided up among the European powers as either new colonies or spheres of influence. Ancient civilisations like China and Japan were humiliated and forced to cede trading rights and in some cases territories (Hong Kong was the last remnant of this). Anti-colonialist nationalism of the twentieth century was, as a consequence, anti-European nationalism.

The first non-European people to develop a nationalism in both reaction to, and imitation of, the European model were the Japanese. They developed a particularly right-wing and aggressive variety in the late nineteenth century, as many were to find to their cost in the course of the twentieth. But Japan was a somewhat unusual case in that it was a united, proud and warlike people affronted by foreign arrogance. It imported Western technology and Western ideas in order to preserve its identity, and in so doing became the first non-Western nation-state. This was achieved by the existing feudal aristocracy, which thereby retained its dominance in Japanese society. In China, however, foreign humiliations led to the collapse of the old Chinese Empire and its replacement by a new nationalist government, led by Sun Yat Sen in 1911.

However, the more usual pattern has been one of reaction to European colonisation, where the colonists were a small elite. In the case of much of Africa and the Middle East, the pattern of political boundaries was entirely arbitrary, bearing little relation to the indigenous population, and often making traditional enemies part of the same political unit. Nigeria, for example, was made up of over 200 linguistic groups, with several religions and other differences. Sometimes these led eventually to civil war, as happened in Sudan, Nigeria and what is now Zaire. What was to unite all the indigenous groups in such situations was resentment of the common European enemy. At the same time, it was the Europeans who were to provide the local nationalists with all the tools for their eventual overthrow.

In the first place, there was the modernisation that could make a post-colonial state viable: centralised administration, communications, industry, an education system, and so on. Second, there were European ideas of nationalism and human rights, as well as theories of imperialism and exploitation, that could be turned against the Europeans.

It was in the more developed parts of Asia, such as Japan, India and China, where nationalist movements developed first. India was different from Japan or China, in that its nationalism grew up not amongst the traditional ruling class, still less the ordinary people, but among the Europeanised middle class that had grown up under European rule and had benefited most from it.

Indian nationalism

Indian nationalism saw its early development in the late nineteenth century, but grew into a significant political movement in the years following the First World War. One of its most striking features was its pacifism. Traditional pacifist influences included Buddhism and Janism, as well as the example of the great emperor Ashoka of the third century BC, who abjured war and violence as instruments of policy. This strand of Indian tradition was brought out by the movement's remarkable leader Mohandas Ghandi (1869–1948) (although he was also influenced by Western pacifists like Thoreau and Tolstoy). Known as 'the Mahatma' because of his saintliness, Ghandi refused to countenance the terrorist methods some nationalists urged upon him. Non-violent civil disobedience was preferred, emphasising the moral strength of the cause in contrast to those who opposed it (which influenced later leaders like Martin Luther King).

In nationalism in general there is often a conflict between tradition and modernisation. Ghandi was predominantly a traditionalist. He did not want India to industrialise, but wanted an India based on the traditional village with its agriculture and craft industries. On the other hand, he also believed that independence must be linked with social reform to overcome inter-communal conflict and the problem of the 'untouchables' (that is, the despised outcasts of the caste system). Others, especially Jawaharlal Nehru (1889–1964) who was to become India's first prime minister and founder of a ruling dynasty (his daughter and grandson were both future prime ministers), was a moderniser and a socialist who wanted industrialisation and a planned economy.

Indian nationalists did not exploit Britain's weakened position during the war, but when it was over nationalism had become so strong that it could no longer be controlled. Independence came in 1947, although the new India could not hold together. It split amidst horrifying communal violence, of which Ghandi himself was a victim. The main conflict was between Hindus and Muslims, resulting in the setting up of the states of India (predominantly Hindu but with substantial Muslim and other minorities), and the Muslim state of Pakistan.

African nationalism

The new European colonial empires of the late nineteenth century in Africa saw their first stirrings of nationalist feeling around the beginning of the twentieth in the west and south (what became the African National Congress or ANC, for example, was founded in South Africa in 1912). To begin with they were often concerned with a greater say and better conditions for indigenous peoples within the colonial regimes. Later, mostly after the First World War, they became dedicated to independence. During these years pan-Africanism was influential, and the notion of 'negritude', an early version of Black Consciousness, was developed (see Chapter 9).

It was only after the Second World War that nationalism became a major force in most of these countries. It was then that new nationalist parties were founded or re-founded. They were usually led by Western-educated elites, often with little commitment to traditional culture. They were bent on modernisation and were often influenced by socialist ideas, which they sought to adapt to African conditions. Britain, France, Holland, Belgium, and eventually

Portugal, all gave independence to millions of square miles of colonial territory, with greater or lesser degrees of agreement or violence.

Anti-imperialism

Often these liberation struggles, both in Africa and Asia, were caught up in the wider conflicts of the Cold War and many of the new regimes were communist, although wedded to nationalist aspirations and modernisation rather than to the world proletarian cause.

Communists promoted the view that formal independence did not mean genuine freedom or self-determination. Imperialism, it was argued, was more subtle and operated through trade agreements and aid, which exploited the former colonial world just as effectively as under direct rule. This theory drew on Lenin's analysis of imperialism as a global extension of the capitalist system (see Chapter 8), which sees the problems of new nations in terms of capitalist exploitation and the determination of Western capitalism to keep the rest of the world in thrall. Whatever the merits of this theory, many of these new states are now poverty stricken and hopelessly dependent on the West.

Most of these successful independence movements aspired to create new states on the European model, with all the symbols of such status: flags and anthems, a modern administration, modern armed services, a national airline and a seat at the United Nations. However, in some cases modernisation has created a Westernised middle class and a large urban population that is dependent on imports of both consumer goods and food supplies, with old tribal loyalties and ways of life broken up and unable to sustain the country in food. This was true of many former colonial territories in black Africa and the Arab north. The situation was sustainable so long as aid flowed in and international trade was buoyant. But economic problems in the West during the 1970s and early 1980s left such countries stranded in a no man's land between traditional cultures that were no longer viable and an equally nonviable modern state.

Such countries were encouraged to borrow from the West, but huge rises in interest rates during the series of economic recessions since the 1970s left many of them with mountainous debts that they cannot possibly repay. India was more fortunate. After an initial drive to industrialisation which, like many newly independent states attempting to follow the Western path to prosperity, failed to come up to expectations, India switched resources into improving agriculture in the late 1950s. This has helped to make India self-sufficient and relatively prosperous, although with some ups and downs, while many countries are beset with insoluble economic problems. It is one of the reasons for the rise of anti-Western religious fundamentalism in some Third World countries.

Pan-nationalism

The idea of pan-nationalism is that nation-states may participate or even be subsumed under a higher unity based upon ethnic, religious, geographical or other common features. Pan-nationalism today is very much part of anti-colonial nationalist ideas. However, the first pan-nationalist movements grew within the context of nineteenth-century European nationalism.

Pan movements in Europe

Pan-Slavism was the earliest of these movements, developing among various Slav nations within the Austro-Hungarian and Turkish empires during the 1830s and 1840s. Among its theorists was a Slovak Protestant minister, Jan Koller (1793–1852), who saw the Slavs as fundamentally a single people with a common cultural heritage. He thought, therefore, that Slavs should strive to end their fragmentation and seek spiritual and political unity, which was the key to the Slavs achieving their potential greatness.

The first All-Slav Congress was held in 1848. However, the movement was soon taken over by Russians, becoming an expression of Russian imperialist ambitions to extend their empire to Constantinople and the Balkans, in the name of Slav freedom. The movement died out towards the end of the century, although much later the USSR revived ideas of this kind to help the communists justify their empire in Eastern Europe.

Pan-German thought was somewhat similar. In the late nineteenth century it saw German unification as merely a step in the creation of a greater Germany, to include the Austrians and all other German speakers. However, in the pan-Germanic case there was much more an element of dominating neighbouring peoples among whom ethnic Germans had settled, and thus partook of the aggressive nationalist and racist ideas of the period (see Chapter 9). Pan-German ideas have been discredited by German expansionism in two world wars.

'Scandinavianism' was initially a cultural movement inspired by Romantic ideas in the early nineteenth century, but the military defeat of Denmark by Prussia and Austria in 1864 led to calls for a political union of Norway, Sweden and Denmark. Although this did not happen, various Scandinavian organisations of economic and political co-operation have developed during the twentieth century.

In 1923 a Pan-European Union was founded in Vienna by private initiative. The idea was that Europe had been fragmented after the First World War and that it needed unity in the face of the Bolshevic threat. The movement aimed to bring together the states of Europe in ever greater economic and political co-operation with the ultimate aim of creating a United States of Europe. The movement faded away in the 1930s, but was clearly a precursor of the post-war European movement.

Pan-African and Arab movements

Arab and African pan-nationalism grew out of anti-colonial nationalism after the Second World War. A growing nationalism in Africa and in the Arab north were both accompanied by the feeling that the territories into which such nationalisms were channelled, and which formed the basis of the new states, were entirely artificial and alien impositions by colonial powers, which in fact hampered the development of the peoples which such boundaries divided. It was felt that the populations of the whole of Africa or of the whole of the Arab world had more in common than the populations within particular states. The hope was that increasing co-operation among African or among Arab states would eventually lead to a dissolving of colonial boundaries to create a new and stronger unity.

Ideas of pan-Africanism were in fact first put forward by former slaves in America and the Caribbean at the end of the nineteenth century. The movement held its first congress in 1900 in London. However, these ideas were more important in their areas of origin than in Africa itself until after 1945. The idea was that all the indigenous peoples, including the Arabs in the north, had a common heritage and therefore a common political identity and destiny. It was taken up by nationalist politicians seeking independence for their colonies, who saw opportunities for forging common links and mutual support among groups otherwise divided by race or religion or by the culture of the different colonial powers (that is, there was a certain commonality among English-speaking colonies, French-speaking and so on).

In 1963 the Organisation of African Unity (OAU) was founded in Addis Ababa. However, despite the efforts of some enthusiasts its role and aims were modest. It was and remains a forum for discussion and co-operation among African states (excluding such states as South Africa until majority rule). The impulse to create a genuine pan-African integration diminished as more and more states became independent.

Pan-Arabism had better chances of succeeding in creating significant political structures than pan-Africanism, if only because the Arab people had greater homogeneity and sense of common heritage. The movement had an organisation and also a cause in the destruction of Israel and restoration of the Palestinian homeland. The organisation was the Arab League, founded in 1945 and imposing upon its members the duty of integrating foreign policy and settling disputes between them by reference to the League.

Furthermore, the movement for some time had a charismatic leader in Gamal Abdel Nasser, president of Egypt, victor of the Suez conflict with Britain, and symbol of Arab unity from Morocco to the Persian Gulf. Since Egypt has a stronger sense of national identity than most Arab states, Nasser was inclined to see the future of the Arabs as a series of independent socialist states working closely together under Egyptian leadership. The alternative vision, of a single socialist state embracing all Arabs was put forward by the Ba'ath parties, found in most of the other Middle Eastern states.

Islamic fundamentalism always offered an alternative to pan-Arabism and was often in conflict with it. Islamic fundamentalism tends to be traditionalist, while the pan-nationalists tended to be modernising, Westernising and secular (see Chapter 11). In the 1950s and 1960s the centre of Islam was Saudi Arabia and in 1962 its religious leaders proclaimed socialism to be incompatible with Islam. This condemned both Nasser and the Ba'ath, who in turn condemned the conservative Saudi regime as corrupt and reactionary.

Ba'athism

One of the most dynamic expressions of pan-Arabism has been the Ba'ath movement, founded after the Second World War when most of the Arab lands (except for Saudi Arabia) were either European colonies or under some other form of European tutelage. 'Ba'ath' in Arabic means 'renaissance', and the movement sought a rebirth of the Arabs as a single modern nation. Ba'athism essentially combined pan-Arabism and a socialism that borrowed and adapted a number of theoretical and organisational elements from communism.

The Ba'ath slogan is 'Unity, Freedom and Socialism'. Unity is conceived in terms of uniformity of outlook and purpose, the melding of all individuality into a single united mass with a single national will. That will is represented by the party, which thereby has the right to control everything: government, the economy, education, the media and all other aspects of national life. This is the socialist element of Ba'athism, although the Ba'ath Party represents no particular social class, in the sense of proletarian or peasant. The ordinary masses are nearer the heart of the Arab nation because of their experience of oppression and suffering. It is their interests that the Ba'ath Party alone can represent.

As to freedom, the Western sense of the term is rejected as being connected with capitalist selfishness and exploitation. The individual finds fulfilment and self-realisation, and therefore true freedom, by identifying with the mass. The mass finds self-realisation and true freedom in the self-determination of the nation. To achieve this the masses, led by the Ba'ath Party, must overthrow the enemies of the nation – imperialism, Zionism, and reactionary traditionalist Arab ruling elites – and overcome the divisions of the Arab nation they have imposed or perpetuated.

Ba'athism grew in the 1950s and early 1960s and had parties in the various countries of the Middle East. Today there are only two countries with signifi-cant Ba'ath parties, Syria and Iraq, and in both cases they are the instruments of totalitarian tyrannies of great ruthlessness. That Ba'athism has lost its initial idealism is clear from the fact that President Assad of Syria and Saddam Hussein were long-time enemies (Assad joined the coalition against Iraq in the 1991 Gulf War). Insofar as Ba'athism still has a connection with pan-Arabism it is as providing the ideological underpinnings of Assad and Hussein's imperial ambitions. The Gulf War of 1991 put a stop to Hussein, although despite a crushing defeat he remained in power in Iraq. In the 1980 and 1990s, pan-Arabism has become less significant in the Arab world than Islamic fundamentalism.

Internationalism, federalism and conflict

The twentieth century was an extraordinarily violent one, with its world wars and multitude of lesser conflicts, its terrorism and its threat of nuclear annihilation. The greatest single cause of all this violence has been nationalism in various forms. It is not surprising, therefore, if some have come to see nationalism as a curse of mankind, and sought to develop an antidote to it in various kinds of internationalism. The first priority of the advocates of internationalism is the prevention of war. There is wide agreement of the need for some international body that can ensure this, although the practical difficulties are immense. The much larger issue of the possibility of a world government is a very different matter, which many regard as a mere fantasy.

International organisations

The First World War was called 'the war to end all war', and in its aftermath it was hoped that institutions would be set up to prevent future wars through international agreement, co-operation and mediation. The peace conference at Versailles duly created the League of Nations, but this was a failure.

After the Second World War there was initially more hope. The United Nations (UN) was established in 1945, but the hopes and ideals which attended its creation were defeated by the coming of the Cold War. It became a battleground for super-power rivalry, and could do little unless both were in accord. Consequently, it failed to stop major conflicts like the Korean and Vietnam wars. On the other hand, it has proved a useful forum for debate, a sometimes powerful instrument of international co-operation in areas like health, and an extremely useful neutral broker and arbitrator on lesser disputes.

The collapse of European communism and the end of the Cold War in 1989–91 seemed to offer the opportunity for the UN finally to fulfil its potential. The Gulf War of 1991 was an extraordinary display of international co-operation to reverse the conquest of a tiny nation. President Bush spoke of a 'new world order', of peace and co-operation, but the picture since has been very mixed. Certainly the prospects of world peace enforced by an international body seem no nearer than in the past.

Liberals in particular have always set great store by the idea of world organisation. The German philosopher Kant was among the first to suggest such a scheme in the eighteenth century. Nineteenth-century liberals believed passionately that free trade would bring people together and be a great force for peace. However, that hope proved a false one, and the prospect of world government still looks distinctly unlikely. The problem is the enforcement of international law. At present there are world courts which make judgements against states; but if a state chooses to ignore this, then there is not much anyone can do about it, unless major powers see it as in their strategic interest to intervene (as in the Gulf War). Any world government would have to have some kind of police and armed forces to enforce its decrees, and existing states would have to submit to them or suffer the consequences. There seems little likelihood of that. For one thing, the notion of the state and its sovereignty, bound up as it is with notions of national independence, is an extremely power-ful one that will only be given up with the greatest reluctance.

Regional integration

If there are moves towards world government it seems highly unlikely that they will come from above, but from groups of countries working together and building up links and networks of co-operation out of which the need for supra-national government will grow naturally. There are various co-operative groupings in different regions of the world, but by far the most important development in this direction is the European Union.

Our present world of independent nation states, jealously guarding their sovereignty and answerable to no one, is very much a product of European thought and political development. There is, therefore, a certain appropriate-ness in Europe leading the way in exploring the possibilities of transcending the modern state. Two world wars, while they dragged in much of the rest of the world, were essentially European wars and were a culmination of centuries of warfare between nation-states. The escalating horror and destructiveness of modern warfare has alone made the possibility of bringing together the states of Europe together in a union strong enough to prevent war, a persistent dream of statesmen and thinkers for two hundred years or more. But various factors conspired after 1945 to make the attempt viable. Europe had to be rebuilt, old hatreds buried and an integrated Europe needed as a defence of freedom against the threat from the East. Because the community was an economic success, the original six countries who signed the Treaty of Rome in 1956 attracted new members. They now stand at fifteen, but with a queue of poten-tial members at the door.

Although long known as the European Common Market, the ambitions of its founders and advocates have never been confined to creating a free trade area and this is clear from the institutions of Commission, Parliament and Council of Ministers. There have always been those whose ideal has been a United States of Europe with a federal government. During the 1960s and 1970s new members were absorbed into an established system, while the 1980s were characterised by a fresh impetus towards greater integration, culminating in the project of a single European currency which began in 1999, with Britain having the option of joining later. The new currency is seen by some as a major step towards political integration and a federal government.

Such a step has its sceptics and the debate over a common currency has sharply divided federalists from those who want essentially just a free trade area and greater co-operation between members of a club of forever-sovereign states. The British Conservative Party is among the most sceptical about the currency and further integration. At the 1999 European election, the UK Independence Party, committed to total withdrawal, won three seats. The future development of the EU is therefore very much bound up with nationalism. There are those with objections to closer political union on the one hand, but on the other, some see EU federalism as a counter to a future resurgence of German nationalism. Recent evidence of federalism being an effective check on upon nationalism, however, is not encouraging.

Federalism

Federalism is a form of government where a great deal of power, including legislative power, is devolved to the federated units in a way that is guaranteed by the constitution. Legal sovereignty is divided so that neither the centre or the units can unilaterally change the relationship. This is in contrast to, say, local government in Britain or devolution to Scotland and Wales, where the British Parliament in London can change powers and structure at any time. The powers of the federated units in a federal system may be set out in detail (for example, the right to control education), but in cases such as the USA the powers of the federal government are specified and the states have a right to everything else.

Federal systems have been introduced to limit the power of central government (the USA and Germany) and to deal with great distances (Australia), but federalism has also been seen as a way of overcoming problems of nationality within states. We tend to think of the nation-state as the norm, and certainly the overwhelming majority of nationalities, however small, want and feel entitled to run their own affairs. However, for a multiplicity of historical and other reasons virtually all modern states contain one or more minority nationalities. A great many of these states would disintegrate if all nationalities had their own state, many of which would simply not be viable. Besides, some territories may be disputed between one or more nationalities, and there may be differences between members of the same nationality.

Federalism can be seen as a partial answer to some of these problems. A national minority may be accorded a degree of independence within a federal system that may satisfy national aspirations and give greater security. Or a group of nationalities may each be too small to be the basis of a viable nation-state and may join together in federal system that does constitute a viable state, while at the same time respecting the individuality of the constituent nations.

However, federal states created to give autonomy to national groups have not been entirely successful. Least successful have been the communist federal systems. There has been the almost tidal wave of nationalism generated by the collapse of European communism. Not only has there been the reassertion of national independence of Eastern Europe and within states such as Czechoslovakia (which have split into Slovakia and the Czech Republic), but the Soviet Union itself has disintegrated and may fragment further into a host of mini and micro-nationalisms. The result may be bloodshed, as in parts of the former Soviet Union and in Yugoslavia where a series of brutal civil wars through the 1990s have been the dreadful consequence of the collapse of the communist regime. In all these cases nationalism had been suppressed by a totalitarian communist regime. With the weakening of that harsh grip, nationalism has re-emerged, and with all the ethnic rivalries, hatreds and conflicts that go with it.

Federal systems involving national differences have not been totally successful in the West either. The largest example is India. Here there is a multitude of nationalities, and India has been a relatively successful state. But there are now great strains. The Sikhs are only one of several nationalities who want their own independent state, and there is growing violence. Even Canada, one of the most peaceful and prosperous states of the modern world, is in immanent danger of breaking up because of the demands of the French Canadians for their own state, despite a considerable degree of autonomy under the present federal system.

It would seem that federalism can be a successful device for limiting central government, although in many cases power has gravitated towards the centre over time (the USA, Australia, although not Canada or Switzerland). It would appear to be much less successful in coping with the strains of nationalism.

Nationalism and conflict

This question has a bearing on the European Union beyond the present issue of governmental integration. Even while the European Community was developing in the 1960s, there was a resurgence of nationalism in the settled states of Western Europe. From 1968 we saw the violent emergence of small ethnic communities in several countries determined upon independence or unification: Basques in Spain, the Republicans in Northern Ireland, the Corsicans in France. Other nationalities began to assert themselves by more conventional and constitutional means: including the Scots and Welsh in the UK, Bretons in France, and Catalans in Spain. The existence of an EC framework has encouraged such national minorities to seek independence within the EC. It could be that if the EC strengthens its centre, the nation-state could weaken.

Nationalism has an almost endless capacity to generate conflict and violence, as is apparent from any survey of the world's violent trouble spots. The present and former communist world apart, we might consider the Middle East, the Punjab and Sri Lanka, Northern Ireland, Iraq, Northern Spain, and others, to see nationalism creating conflict. It is nationalism (whether mixed with religion or other political ideology or not) that is the most potent source of terrorism in the world today.

There are hopeful signs that internationalism and regional integration will lessen the prospect of wars, but nobody can say that these will not be undermined by the power of nationalism. Nationalism is indeed one of the forces of fragmentation at work in the world today. How it will interact with the contrary force of globalisation may determine much about the future of politics in many parts of the world. But before discussing this we need to look more at the nature of the concept itself.

The coherence and autonomy of nationalism

Nationalism is the simplest and most powerful of ideologies, but intellectually the weakest. This is because the central concept upon which the ideology is based is quite remarkably vague and difficult to pin down.

What is a nation?

The question is, what exactly constitutes a nation? By what criteria can we unambiguously identify a candidate for nation-statehood? It might be thought that a certain ethnic homogeneity would be a necessary condition. After all, we think of such as Chinese and Poles and Egyptians as definite ethnic entities that form 'natural' states. But then, many nations are ethnically mixed (in fact no country is totally ethnically uniform, not even France). Indeed, the USA, which on some reckonings is the most successful of modern nation-states, has the most mongrel of populations and has seen this as a source of strength.

Another candidate, that seems to be stronger, is language. But again, there are too many counter-examples. The case usually cited is Switzerland, where the Swiss most definitely regard themselves as a distinct nation of long standing, and yet they speak four separate languages: French, German, Italian and Romansch. Several hundred languages are spoken in India, yet most Indians see themselves as one people.

What, then, makes a nation a nation? The answer would seem to be that a people sees itself, or feels itself, to be a nation, because of shared history or language or whatever other reason. Theoretically this is not very precise or satisfactory. It cannot, for example, decide questions where it is a matter of dispute as to who does and who does not belong to the nation, or (as with Northern Irish Protestants) where one part of the nation refuses to identify with another part. Nevertheless, the highly subjective criterion of what a body of people perceive themselves to be is about the best defining characteristic of nationhood we have.

The viability of states

However, even if we were able to identify unambiguously 'natural' national units, there is no guarantee that they will be suitable for states. A United Nations International Covenant on Human Rights (1966) declares that 'All peoples have the right to self-determination'. But if a people or its territory are too small for a state to be viable, what then? And if the right of nations to self-determination is enshrined in international law, then who has the right to deny any group feeling itself to be a nation, however small? Given that all states today have ethnic minorities, this could be a recipe for chaos, particularly in circumstances of economic distress. The Russian Federation (the core of the former Soviet Union) may yet shatter into literally hundreds of national fragments. At the other, pan-national end of the scale, it is not clear that, say, the Slav or Arabic speaking peoples do not form a more natural political unit than the many states between which they are currently divided.

The autonomy of nationalism

A further problem is illustrated by the Arabs. Pan-Arab nationalism was seen as a secular modernising force by most of its proponents, wanting to see the Arabs as a major force in the modern world. But there were also those who saw modernity in terms of alien Westernisation that was destroying the essence of Arab culture and identity, a view strengthened by the rise of Islamic fundamentalism (see Chapter 11). The often acute conflict between tradition and modernisation has been a common feature of nationalist conflicts since the nineteenth century.

The question is, of course, bound up with what kind of society nationalists in any given situation want their nation to have. This in turn leads to questions concerning the relationship between nationalism and other systems of belief that are more concerned with these matters. At various times and places nationalism has been associated with liberalism, conservatism, socialism and even Marxism, which on the face of it is an anti-nationalist doctrine. The reason for this is that the core ideas of nationalism as such say nothing about how society ought to be organised, what kind of economy and similar questions that other ideologies try to answer. Because there must be answers of some sort, nationalism needs to be supplemented by other ideologies that provide them.

The question may therefore be asked as to whether nationalism is a complete and autonomous ideology. Certainly it is different from the other great ideological traditions of the 'age of the French Revolution' in its lack of interest in questions of internal social organisation, a difference that makes nationalism unusual in its capacity to combine readily with other ideologies. There is another sense in which nationalism might be said to be 'incomplete' in that these other ideologies are universalist, and deal with the whole of humanity. Some version of nationalism are universal, for example those that insist upon the same rights for all peoples. But other nationalisms are simply aggressive and xenophobic, and are purely concerned with national self-assertion with little or no concern for anyone else.

Liberal nationalism has been continuously asserted in one form or another since the French Revolution. Essentially, liberal nationalists see nations as individuals and accord them rights similar to those they accord to the individual person: freedom, autonomy and equality within the community (in this case the community of nations), with the assurance that if all enjoy equal rights then a natural harmony will prevail. On the other hand, liberals are never wholehearted in their nationalism in that they do not allow the rights of the individual to be sacrificed for the sake of the nation.

On the whole, ideologies on the left of the spectrum do not fit too well with nationalism. Anarchism is just about impossible to reconcile since anarchists reject the state as such, whether based upon the nation or not. Marxists have tended to stress class solidarity across national boundaries, and to see nationalism as a dimension of bourgeois ideology that facilitated the creation of national markets and distracted the workers from class struggle. Orthodox theory insisted that workers had a higher loyalty to class than to nation, a view that spectacularly broke down in 1914 when worker's parties all over Europe voted to support their national governments in preparing for war. Nevertheless, there are plenty of examples of Marxists making use of nationalism at a practical level. The Soviet Union, China, Viet Nam and other communist regimes have often put great stress on the patriotism of workers, especially in times of war.

A stronger fusion of nationalism and socialism was achieved among a number of post-colonial nationalisms after 1945 when socialism was fashionable in the West. Post-colonial leaders like Pandit Nehru in India and Julius Neyrere in Tanganyika (now Tanzania) attempted to interpret socialism in terms of the communal traditions of their respective nations. Nevertheless, it is fair to say that in general most fusions of nationalism and socialism have been in the form of pragmatic accommodations rather than genuine cases of theoretical synthesis.

There is undoubtedly a greater natural affinity between nationalism and the ideologies of the right. Where liberalism and socialism were very much products of Enlightenment rationalism, various forms of conservatism and its derivatives could be said to be derived, or at least touched by, Romanticism, which stressed emotion, instinct and will as against reason, and celebrated the particular as against the universal. These features are characteristic of various kinds of conservatism from the mildly liberal Burkian conservatism traditional in Britain to the more radical and aggressive conservatisms of late-nineteenth-century Europe which were to culminate in the fascism of the twentieth century. Today, nationalism is most firmly associated with the right (British Conservatives, American Republicans and so on). On the other hand, today nationalism is everywhere, contrary to expectations in the past, and often in ways that seem to have little to do with the left/right spectrum.

The survival and future of nationalism

The demise of nationalism as a major political force has frequently been predicted by both opponents and supporters alike. Marxists have believed that nationalism would disappear with the fall of capitalism. Liberals, including different kinds of liberal nationalists, have tended to see nationalism as a doctrine inspiring strong passions but temporary ones. Once all the nations had their homeland and all the border disputes sorted out through some rational procedure, then nationalist passions would inevitably subside.

The advent of 'political science' in America following the Second World War reinforced the liberal view by giving it an aura of scientific certitude. The theory was that all non-Westernised societies were destined to follow the path of the West from backwardness through industrialisation and urbanisation to a condition of 'modernity' when their society and politics would approximate that of the West, and particularly the USA. Nationalism was seen as a feature of an earlier stage in this development which, like religion, was destined to die out as a political force once the European empires had given way to new states. These would in due course cease to be concerned with nation-building and settle down to interest politics on the American model. Nationalism was a form of political primitivism appropriate to an early stage of nation-building and out of place in the later stages of 'modernisation'.

Such views of the demise of nationalism were commonplace in the 1950s and 1960s; thereafter they simply evaporated in the heat of experience. The 1970s and 1980s saw a growth of small-scale regional nationalism in Europe and elsewhere many other parts of the world, while the ending of the Cold War has stimulated a massive resurgence of nationalism and nationalist conflicts in the former communist world.

Whether we choose to call the present post-Cold War period 'postmodernity' or not, we are clearly living in some new phase of history, which is in some ways less stable and predictable than the Cold War period. It is a phase characterised by globalisation, but also by the assertion of particularity and difference, and by the politics of identity. The assertion of particular identities of all forms (sex, gender, age, region, religion, ethnicity and so on) is partly at least a reaction against the homogenising and also destructive effects of globalisation. Nationality is perhaps the most important of these, particularly in an age of disillusionment with grand theoretical ideologies. Consequently, those who predicted the end of nationalism (along with that of religion and ideology) were badly wrong. Nationalism seems destined to continue to be a major shaping force in world politics for the foreseeable future.

5

Varieties of socialism

Of all ideologies socialism is perhaps the most difficult to pin down. Debates among socialists about what constitutes 'true socialism' are notoriously indecisive, long-lasting and bitter. We are well advised to take the view that there is no such essential socialism but many socialisms.

Primitive and classical socialisms

Trying to classify the different types of socialism is a difficult exercise and what follows does involve some groupings and labels not usually made, but none should be taken entirely seriously. For clarity's sake Marxist theory is dealt with separately in a later chapter, as are various versions of socialistic anarchism. These aside, it will be convenient to group the many forms of socialism into three broad types.

From time to time in human thought – usually in periods of upheaval and social distress – there have been those who have offered the view that mankind's problems could be solved if only great personal wealth and poverty were eliminated and the goods of the world more fairly shared amongst all. Ideas of this kind appeared, for instance, during the period of the Reformation, the English Civil War and the French Revolution. They are mostly just pictures of an ideal with no means of achievement. Sir Thomas More's *Utopia* is a prime example. We might call this kind of socialism 'primitive socialism' ('utopian socialism' might have been a more fitting title, but historically this has always been applied, not very appropriately, to a specific group of thinkers, as we shall see below).

From the early nineteenth century to the Second World War the term 'socialism' signified various forms of doctrine that sought the elimination of capitalism, or capitalist domination of society, by various rapid or gradual means, and their replacement by an egalitarian socialist society. We might call this form of socialism 'classical' since it was the form of socialism that flourished when socialism first became a modern doctrine and for long after. It is what many still feel to be genuine socialism, even among those who would accept that it is no longer appropriate to today's world.

However, after the Second World War new forms of socialism developed which did not require the elimination of capitalism but in fact embraced it. These forms of socialism, which may be conveniently called 'liberal socialism' became widely popular and successful, although criticised by some as not genuine socialism at all. These criticisms have increased in recent years because, it is argued, the desire to ensure capitalism works well has squeezed out any real socialist content. Some insist that as an influential modern ideology, socialism is effectively dead. These issues will be discussed later.

Socialism and the French Revolution

It is entirely appropriate that socialism should make an appearance on the stage of the French Revolution, along with all the others that were to dominate the nineteenth century, even though its contribution to the ideas of the time was brief and insubstantial.

Socialism made its appearance shortly after the Jacobins had fallen from power and their radical democratic constitution replaced by one that gave power to the better-off. Francois-Noel 'Gracchus' Babeuf was a Jacobin sympathiser who had escaped the purge that followed their fall. He concluded that the radical Jacobin programme to make all Frenchmen free and equal could only be accomplished by an abolition of property. To this end, he planned a seizure of power by himself and his followers, who called themselves the 'Conspiracy of the Equals'. They would then set up a dictatorship for the purpose of seizing all wealth and redistributing it on an equal basis. It would be a policy enforced by a reign of terror even more ferocious than that of Robespierre.

However, Babeuf revealed little as to how his ideal society would be organised, or how long the revolutionary dictatorship might be necessary, or what freedom individuals would have, or a host of other matters. The aspect of Babeuf's thinking that was to be influential was his notions of how to seize power and then use it. He had very modern ideas as to how to stage a coup in a planned and professional way, much copied up to our own time; while his notions of a revolutionary dictatorship influenced Marx, Lenin and others. But as a theorist of socialism, Babeuf really belongs among the primitives. He has no worked-out theory of the nature and necessity of a socialist society. Modern socialism, as a fully developed ideology, is better understood as a product of that other great revolution of the age, the Industrial Revolution.

Classical socialism

Modern socialism developed in the early nineteenth century largely as a response to the social impact of industrialisation. The factories destroyed many people's livelihoods, forced them to work immensely long hours, often for star-vation wages, and live in the vilest conditions in the new industrial towns. At the same time, the attempts of working people to organise in order to improve their conditions were made illegal and brutally suppressed. In Britain particu-larly, where industrial development was far ahead of the rest of the world, there were strikes and violence of various kinds and much nostalgia for a disappear-ing world. Working-class discontent was used to press for parliamentary reform, widely offered by radicals as the solution to all ills.

The authentic socialist note was struck by those who argued that what people were really suffering from was not the greed of individual employers, nor a conspiracy of the ruling class, but the nature of the capitalist system itself. It was, they argued, a system that had exploitation built into it, and a system which could be replaced by a better one in which the evils of capitalism would be ended for good and a new system of co-operation, harmony and justice put in its place.

The evils of capitalism

There are many varieties of this kind of socialist thinking. The easiest and clearest way to give an initial characterisation of classical socialism as such, that can embrace different varieties, is to say what socialism is against, and consequently what, in broad terms, a socialist society would be without. What links all classical socialists is the belief that capitalism is bad, and necessarily produces certain evil social consequences (for liberal socialists it is *unrestrained* capitalism that tends to produce such evils). These include the following:

* an unfair, exploitative and class-divided society
* a distorted human nature that emphasises greed and competitiveness instead of compassion and sociability
* an inefficient and disorganised economic system prone to dislocation and breakdown.

These criticisms of capitalism are a combination of the ethical and the practi-cal. Capitalism is bad because it is unjust and divisive: people are robbed of the proper reward for their work because it is appropriated as profit. The few, therefore, appropriate the wealth that others produce and live in luxury, while the many live poor and diminished lives. The system is simply unfair. And if it be argued that it is perfectly fair that the success and its rewards should properly go to those with energy and talent, it rapidly becomes unfair once the first generation pass on their wealth and privileges to their heirs.

The moral case against capitalism continues with a different set of argu-ments to do with the impact of capitalism upon human nature. Capitalism is powered by a selfish individualism. It is the law of the jungle, a war of all against all. This brings out the worst in people and suppresses the best. One might even say that, because it is so at odds with human nature, capitalism is 'unnatural' and therefore wrong.

Third, capitalism is wrong on practical grounds. It is wasteful and inefficient: it cannot effectively do what an economy properly exists to do. The waste of capitalism is most strikingly seen in the slumps to which the free market is periodically subject. Goods go unsold, people are out of work, factories and machinery lie idle. Nobody wants any of this and yet it is apparently unavoidable. The trouble is that goods are only produced for profit, instead of in a properly planned manner to cater for people's real needs.

In modern society we are endlessly encouraged to spend money on an endless array of objects that we do not really want and certainly do not need. At the same time many people's genuine needs (for better houses, clothes and so forth) are ignored because supplying them cheaply cannot be done profitably.

The socialist alternative

The only real alternative to a capitalist society, in this view, is a fully socialist one, which would have the following features:

- There would be common ownership of the economy, with little or no private property. There would therefore be no class system and no one would have the means to exploit anyone else.
- There would be equality of wealth, and therefore of power and opportunity.
- Production would be for use and not for profit, while competition would be replaced by co-operation. The competitive free-for-all is replaced by planning.
- Everyone would work for the community and contribute to the common good, and society would be based on the principle, in Marx's words, 'from each according to his ability, to each according to his need'.
- Human nature would flourish, no longer distorted by poverty or greed, and a society would develop where the goods of the world would be freely shared and all would care for each other.

It should be noticed that the picture rests on certain assumptions that are not always made explicit and may be difficult to accept. It assumes that human character is essentially good and that the evils of the world – such as poverty, crime, cruelty, ignorance and war – are not due to any evil inherent in human nature, but to the workings of the system in which human beings find themselves. Change the system in the right way and human nature as we know it will improve. There is the further assumption that famine and scarcity are also the result of the 'system' and not in the nature of things. If only the economy were properly organised and planned there would be abundance with plenty for all.

These complimentary accounts of capitalism and socialism are of course only skeletal and can be filled out in an infinity of ways, many of which may contradict. This criticism of capitalism, and this vision of the ideal society that would follow its elimination, was shared by virtually all varieties of socialists until at least the 1940s (although for some of them it was a very long-term ideal). Thereafter it was rivalled and ultimately eclipsed by versions of liberal socialism (most notably social democracy) which did not see the elimination of capitalism and its replacement by a fully socialist society as essential. However, prior to the Second World War classical socialism had developed many forms.

The utopian socialists

Socialism as a modern political doctrine began to develop in the early nine-teenth century, mainly in Britain and France, as a response to social and economic consequences of industrialisation, and the social upheaval of the Revolutionary period. There were various movements and thinkers struggling to find a new alternative to free-market capitalism and to the traditional struc-tures of society that had failed to protect people from it. Three thinkers stand out because of the range and coherence of their thought. They are known collectively (and somewhat unfairly) as the 'utopian socialists'.

Utopian socialism sprang to life in three different forms at the same time, but quite independently of each other, in the works of Saint-Simon, Fourier and Owen. Though very different characters with different schemes, they had much in common. They all believed that humanity was at a critical crossroads when it must make a choice about its future. They each believed, with total confidence, that their own system was the future, one way or another – either mankind would accept this and act accordingly, or else there would be blood-shed and social chaos before the new world was born in struggle. All three had witnessed the twenty-six years of war and social conflict following 1789, so that all three totally rejected violence. They hoped to persuade by example and by the sheer rationality and common sense of their proposals.

After the Napoleonic Wars there was a widespread recognition that the old world was beyond recall, but there was confusion and apprehension about what might come in its place. The utopian socialists shared with the Romantics a sense of the fragmentation and lost harmony of a society that was turning against itself. The result was a growing isolation of the individual. Things could only be repaired with a new sense of community, some new communal system. One of the interesting features of these utopians is that, despite the wars and revolutions they experienced, they ignored the political system. Human relationships were more important, and this required an under-standing of human nature – of human reason, needs, instincts, desires and capacities – from which could be built a new, satisfying and permanent social structure. In the past, states and constitutions had changed but people's lives had not. The central questions were moral, social and religious, not political.

Saint-Simon and his followers

The first of these thinkers to develop his ideas was Henri de Saint-Simon (1760–1825). He had been born into a poorer branch of one of the most distinguished aristocratic families in France. He had fought in the American War of Independence, travelled the world as an engineer and returned to France for the Revolution. He became staggeringly rich through property speculation, only to lose it all and be rescued starving from the streets by a former servant. Eventually, his family found him a post as a librarian, upon which he settled down to pursue his ideas for improving society. He tended neither to the left nor to the right, but worked out his own unique conception of an ideal future. His ideas might be described as 'socialistic' (that is, having socialist features) rather than purely socialist, but he had a number of able followers who pursued his ideas in that direction.

What caught Saint-Simon's imagination had been the potential of industrialisation, and the possibilities this held out of a new civilisation based on harmony and abundance. He conceived of human history in terms of alternating periods of integration and change. The first he called 'organic periods' in which society and technology were matched and there was social peace. In between were revolutionary periods of technical change when change is resisted by the old order and society becomes unbalanced and prone to conflict. The Middle Ages was an organic period, while from the Renaissance to the French Revolution was a revolutionary period. Saint-Simon looked forward to a new organic age based on industry and science, and a more united and better-organised society.

In such a society there would be no politics but only administration in the interests of the whole of society but especially the poorest and most numerous. It would be in the hands of the three types of elite group: one group would be administrators and businessmen; a second would be engineers and scientists; and a third would be priests (of his new religion) and artists. This was based upon a psychological theory that suggested that people were predominantly doers, thinkers or those of sensitivity and feeling. The task of these elites would be to ensure that everyone had fulfilling and useful work and made the maximum contribution to society as a whole and everyone had at least an adequate standard of living. The elite would also control the compulsory educational system, which would inculcate the principles of a scientific industrial civilisation into everyone.

Saint-Simon's socialism was, therefore, limited. It was elitist and paternalistic. He thought people should have wealth and privilege if it was proper reward for hard work and service to the community. He did not in fact object to individuals creating great wealth for themselves, so long as everyone was properly cared for and equal opportunity was not impaired. Wealth had to be recognised as having social obligations attached. He also foresaw a time when the economy would be taken out of politics and run by experts in a rational manner. He wanted to replace orthodox Christianity with a new religion of universal brotherhood. He was the first to insist that it is the duty of the state to care for the welfare of all its citizens.

Although Saint-Simon was only, as it were, a semi-socialist, his followers went further. They advocated state ownership of land and factories to ensure Saint-Simon's ideals were fulfilled.

Charles Fourier

Charles Fourier (1772–1837) was the son of a successful cloth merchant family from Besançon, which had lost its fortune in the Revolution. Fourier earned his living as a travelling salesman, but detested commerce, believing it to be fundamentally dishonest. He settled in Paris and had a modest education. He never read books, which he thought mostly full of nonsense, but was an avid reader of newspapers. From these and his own experience he spun all his theories and projects. He was a lifelong bachelor. In 1808 he published *The Theory of the Four Movements and the General Destinies*, which set out his vision of the universe, man and history. He never changed his basic ideas thereafter, although he elaborated them obsessively.

Fourier had a theory of history in thirty-two stages ordained by God, beginning with savagery and gradually leading up to the present stage of 'civilisation', leading, via socialism, to harmony. Harmony was the highest stage that would last 70,000 years, before descending down the stages back to savagery, at which point the world would end. There was a certain amount of flexibility, in that the hateful present stage, 'civilisation', could be shortened and the more desirable stages come sooner and last longer if the world would adopt his ideas for the ideal society quickly.

He believed that, just as Newton had penetrated the mysteries of attraction and repulsion in physical nature in his theory of gravity, showing how all the forces of attraction and repulsion could in fact create a perfect equilibrium and harmony in the universe, so he, Charles Fourier, had discovered the same principles in the human world. He would demonstrate that they could be the basis of a perfect equilibrium and harmony in society. His understanding of human nature came from a highly elaborate theory of the passions. These were God-given and as such their satisfaction must be natural and right. In fact, if only they were given free reign then a natural social harmony would, Fourier thought, inevitably result. Unfortunately, society throughout history had systematically denied and repressed 'natural passions'. This was never more so than in contemporary so-called 'civilisation', where moral conventions suffocated and repressed the passions, especially the sexual ones, creating perversion and endless misery. (To a considerable extent, Fourier anticipated Freud and some of his followers.)

In 'civilisation' according to Fourier, this oppression was compounded by the economic system. He attacked economic liberalism bitterly. Capitalism drove down wages, creating exploitation, poverty and misery. Political liberalism was a sham. Constitutionalism did nothing to check the depredations of economic liberalism and so nothing to alleviate the suffering of the people. Liberalism was a benefit for the few but a disaster for the many.

A new society needed to be built in which people could be happy. But revolution was not the answer. Fourier detested the Jacobins not merely for personal reasons, but because they represented methods of violence and terror, as well and authoritarianism and puritanism, all of which he abhorred. People should be genuinely free from the artificialities of 'civilisation', free to be themselves and be happy. Fourier had little faith in government and believed that this new world would have to be built from below, in personal relationships and small communities. He was constantly looking for patrons to take up his schemes.

The basic building block of the new society would be the small community, the *phalanstère* or phalanx. Each would have a population of around 1,700 to 1,800 (based upon a calculation of the different emotional types of human being, doubled to account for both men and women, plus a few extras). There would be communal meals and common housing and services, including child care. Apart from cases where people might be harmed, there would be complete sexual freedom and people would change partners freely. Women would be fully emancipated. The phalanx would replace the family as the primary object of loyalty and affection. Social solidarity would also be maintained by a common education for all.

After sexual freedom, Fourier's second major principle for achievement of happiness for all was pleasure in work. Everyone must be found work according to their interest and aptitude. He disliked factories and thought in terms of crafts. However, he did not believe in abolishing property. Everyone in the phalanx would be properly housed, clothed and fed, but beyond that people would have different levels of investment in their community and profits would be equitably shared among capital, labour and talent. Some would own little, yet would still be vastly better off than in any previous society.

Fourier says little about political organisation. Each phalanx would be run by a council of all members, but there is a strong suspicion that some would be more equal than others. He believed that the whole population of France, and ultimately the world, would come to live in phalanxes. Once established, they would create networks of co-operation, and eventually national networks would direct volunteer armies in great civil engineering projects. Perhaps international armies would one day undertake, for example, the reclaiming of the world's deserts for fertile use. All this would by-pass existing political systems. What would happen to these, Fourier does not say.

Robert Owen

Robert Owen (1771–1858) came from humble origins and made himself rich and successful in the cotton industry, which was leading the Industrial Revolution that was far more advanced and developing much faster in Britain than elsewhere. It was here that the working-class movement was developing and where the moral indictment of industrial capitalism was most fierce and alternatives most discussed. Owen was merely the most comprehensive and effective of the British socialist thinkers.

Owen did not begin as a socialist. He came to prominence for his creation of the community at New Lanark, which he built up after taking control of the cotton mill in 1800, providing good-quality housing, education and other facilities for the workers. Visitors came from all over Europe to see the results, which flew in the face of current wisdom that minimal pay and conditions were essential for maximum profit. However, New Lanark was nothing to do with socialism, but with that enlightened paternalism that was later associated with the model communities of Victorian industrialists like Sir Titus Salt. His ideas were set out in his best known writings: *The New View of Society* (1813) in which he laid out his ideas for factory and educational reform. His fundamental idea was that human character is infinitely malleable, and that it is perfectly possible to produce a better society by properly educating its members. This is the business of government. People's characters are determined by their environment and it is possible to manipulate that environment to produce any kind of society. He advocated a national education system and better working conditions that would lead in time to a prosperous and harmonious society for all.

In 1817 Owen was invited to join a government-appointed commission to examine the problems of poverty and unemployment following the Napoleonic Wars. He advocated the setting up by government of 'Villages of Co-operation' as a solution to poverty. People should have a right to work, and the necessities of co-operation would be educative and morally improving.

But from what was initially a solution to specific social ills, Owen developed an alternative to contemporary society. His thinking moved quickly to the left. He advocated universal non-religious education and the gradual replacement of an industry based on competition to one based on co-operative principles; principles that could then be applied to the whole of society. Despite his earlier success as an industrialist, he came to reject the growth of large-scale industry, the profit motive and private property itself. He was also hostile to established religion as a major obstacle to change. As he began to advocate the building of a new secular society, the establishment lost interest in him, although he sent his schemes to the rulers of Europe. When that failed, he went to America to found his own co-operative community of New Harmony, but it was not a success.

He returned to England in 1829 and became involved in the trade union movement and various schemes for co-operative production. He also travelled the country lecturing and published journals such the *New Moral World*, which was read all over Europe (Engels was a contributor). The country, he believed, was in a profound crisis, which could only be solved by a peaceful social transformation.

As with Fourier, Owen thought in terms of communities opting out of the new industrial system and creating industrial and agrarian villages based on principles of co-operation, common property and communal living. Working men coming together to organise themselves was his ideal. He was behind various attempts at co-operative communities both here and in America, as well as various attempts at creating producer co-operatives. Unusually, he took a fairly dim view of democracy, believing elections to be divisive. Instead, he believed that communities should be run by their older members. Eventually everyone would live in such communities and take their turn in their administration.

The creation of a radical socialist trade union movement failed, although some of Owen's followers founded the co-operative movement which still exists today. The focus of the working-class movement switched to parliamentary reform in the form of the Chartist movement, but when that collapsed after 1848 the link between working-class movements and socialism was broken for a generation.

The great Victorian economic boom effectively killed off socialism as a serious political movement in Britain until the late 1880s. There were developments in working-class organisations, in trade unions, co-operative societies, friendly societies and other forms of mutual aid, but there was little new socialist thinking. The working-class organisations were more concerned with bread-and-butter issues such as wages and cheap food.

It was the *Communist Manifesto* (1848) of Karl Marx and Frederick Engels that airily dismissed Saint-Simon, Fourier and Owen as 'utopian socialists', and the label stuck. What Marx meant by this was that their theories were not 'scientific' like his own, that they had no understanding of the dynamics of society and history and could not demonstrate that socialism was both necessary and inevitable; and for that reason their ideas were little better than useless fantasies. Marx's view is reasonable given his beliefs, but from a non-Marxist standpoint the term 'utopian', used pejoratively, was not entirely fair. Besides, when Marx wrote in 1848 they could each be seen as rival socialisms with many followers. Later, when their influence had declined, Marx and Engels were more generous.

Interestingly, there has been a revival of interest in recent years in the utopian socialists, and similar writers such as William Morris. This is partly due to the general disillusionment with centralised state socialism, and partly due to the growth of green ideas (see Chapter 11). Leading green theorists, such as Rudolf Bahro and Jonathon Porritt, have acknowledged their influence and importance.

International socialism

The year 1848 was a year of revolutions across Europe. They were liberal-inspired, although they did have the support of working-class organisations where these existed. The result was virtually universal failure, setting back the liberal cause, and the socialist cause even more so. Large numbers of socialists ended up in prison or exile, and many came to London, including Karl Marx and Frederick Engels.

Marx and the international worker's movement

There followed a long lean period in the organisation of the socialist move-ment, although it was a time when Marx and Engels were developing their system (discussed in Chapter 7) and extending their influence. Things began to move in the early 1860s. In 1864 the International Worker's Association (known as the First International) was established with headquarters in London. It was a loose gathering of representatives from a number of working men's organisations across Europe. There were socialists of various kinds, as well as followers of the French anarchist, Proudhon, together with a few radical democrats and republicans. The movement adopted a form of parlia-mentary socialism sufficiently moderate and practical for all delegations to accept.

It seemed that the British working class had lost all interest in socialism, or at least its theory, since the collapse of Chartism in 1848. Its representatives were only interested in concrete issues, such as preventing British employers bringing in cheap foreign labour. Marx became secretary of the association, and had considerable influence on its policies and workings as it helped to foster working-class organisations and recommend common policies to them. Worker's parties and trade unions grew steadily in various countries, and socialist ideas made important advances.

Marx became the leading socialist thinker in Europe, except in Britain, with only anarchists as a rival in some areas. Many European countries were indus-trialising and working-class movements were springing up and looking for their own philosophy that expressed their interests, which is just what Marxism provided. In many ways the greatest success was the German Social Democratic Party (SPD), formed in the mid-1860s by Marx's German followers, which became the largest working-class party in the world.

The French socialist movement was more fragmented, but eventually came together in 1906 as the Section Français de l'International Ouvriere (SFIO), with Marxism the dominant theoretical influence. Other parties were formed across Europe, including Russia where the Russian Social Democratic Party was illegal and its leaders had to live in exile.

These various parties and other organisations were brought together in the Second International, founded in 1889, five years after Marx's death. It met in various congresses and in 1900 created a permanent secretariat. Marxist socialism was easily the dominant form of socialism and was truly international. There was an official Marxist orthodoxy, to which most parties subscribed.

However, all this impressive show of unity did disguise deep divisions. The trouble was that things had not turned out as Marx had predicted. Society had not become more polarised or the working class more miserable and desperate. He had not foreseen growing general prosperity, the growth of democracy and the increasing recognition of workers' rights. As a consequence, Marxist parties tended to divide within themselves between those who would work for a revolution (as the orthodox line dictated) and those who wanted to extend and make use of the new democratic opportunities.

The German SPD, regarded as the Marxist flagship, became riven with internal conflict, known as the 'Revisionist Debates' (discussed in Chapter 7). They came to a head when one of its leaders, Edward Bernstein, former editor of the party's newspaper, wrote a series of articles culminating in a book, *The Preconditions of Socialism* of 1899 (also translated as *Evolutionary Socialism*) which advocated the revision of the party's official Marxist revolutionary doctrine in favour of parliamentary socialism. Bernstein's attempts to have the party's official doctrine changed failed. But although he lost the battle, there is a sense in which he won the war, for while revolutionary Marxism remained party orthodoxy, the party in fact behaved more and more like the reformist party Bernstein wanted, and with the kind of policies that he had wanted to see.

Other European socialist parties had internal conflicts, though usually less publicly. The formation of a united socialist party, the SFIO, in France disguised strong differences. One party that did actually split was the Russian Social Democratic Party. The majority view was that Russia was nowhere ready for revolution, having only a tiny and undeveloped capitalism and industrial proletariat. Lenin disagreed and formed his own Bolshevic Party to work for revolution as soon as possible.

Communism and social democracy

It was Lenin and his Bolshevics who seized power in 1917 and turned Russia into the first communist state (see Chapter 7). Lenin then condemned the Marxist social democratic parties of Europe for abandoning revolution and betraying the working class with false promises of progress through democratic means. Far from representing the interests of the working class, the social democrats were its enemies. There could be no common ground with such people, who had no intention of ending capitalism, whatever they said in theory. Social democracy did indeed become synonymous with reformist parliamentary socialism, even though such continental parties continued to pay lip service to the ultimate revolution following capitalism's inevitable collapse. Lenin insisted that only the Communists (as the Bolshevics now called themselves) could truly represent the workers.

In 1919 Lenin set up the Third International (often referred to as the Communist International or Comintern) in which only parties which adopted the Bolshevic model were allowed to join. In most Western countries there were rival communist and social democratic parties, whose rivalry was often more bitter than that with non-socialist parties. In Germany, for example, the hostility between the Communists and the Social Democrats stopped them working together to prevent the rise of Hitler and the Nazis, as a united effort might well have done. Far from being an instrument of world revolution the Third International was no more than an instrument of Soviet foreign policy. Co-operation was eventually achieved in the fight against fascism, but hostility resumed once the war was over.

The British socialist tradition

After a period of fallow lasting more than thirty years when there was little or no native socialist theory or activity, there was a revival in the mid-1880s that set British socialism on a new and distinctive path. In the last two decades of the century there were the development of anglicised versions of Marxism; the more successful development of Fabian socialism; the founding of the Independent Labour Party with its distinctive (though eclectic) ethical socialism; and all culminating the creation of the Labour Party in 1900. The numbers of people involved in these movements and affected by the theorising was very small. Only when the Labour Party really began to establish itself did this change. Most trade unions, which were the main working-class organisations, were indifferent. Insofar as trade unionists were interested in political ideas, it was the new social liberalism of the Liberal Party that was far more important.

The Social Democratic Federation

The first significant figure in the socialist revival of the 1880s was H.M. Hyndman (1841–1921). He was a rich banker, but devoted most of his adult life to propagating a heavily anglicised and idiosyncratic version of Marxism. Hyndman set out his initial views in his book, *The Text Book of Democracy: England for All* (1881). It consists of an analysis of Britain's development from a crudely Marxist point of view, to which Hyndman added some of his own distinctly non-Marxist ideas. There was a fierce nationalism, a support for British imperialism and a paternalistic concern for the lower orders combined with a distinctly elitist disdain for ordinary people's capacity to do anything without firm leadership from above, so that some socialists were inclined to dismiss Hyndman as a Tory.

Hyndman believed that capitalism was not only unjust but also disastrously inefficient. As the greatest nation in the world and the leading industrial power, it was up to Britain to lead humanity towards the far more productive and morally superior system of socialism. He wanted the ruling class to be so convinced of the inevitability of bloody revolution that they would begin to abdicate their power rather than face these inevitable horrors. The socialist transformation, together with the consequent socialist society, would need to be guided by an intellectual elite with the necessary theoretical understanding. He had little sympathy with spontaneous working-class movements such as the trade unions, which he dismissed as reactionary, and he later refused to support the Bolshevic Revolution on the grounds that it weakened the war effort and cast doubt upon his dream of Britain leading the world towards socialism.

Hyndman founded the Social Democratic Federation (SDF) in 1881 and dominated it until it broke up in 1918. It was the first Marxist party in Britain. However, its membership was never large, nor its influence great. It was one of the founding organisations of the Labour Party, but quickly left.

William Morris

Hyndman was a somewhat domineering and dogmatic figure who managed to alienate some of the early members of the SDF, including Eleanor Marx (Karl's daughter), William Morris and Belfort Bax (another unorthodox Marxist). They broke away to form the Socialist League (1884–90). This body was chiefly distinguished for the theoretical writings of William Morris (1834–96) who was an artist-craftsman, businessman, scholar, poet and novelist, but now best known as a great designer. He produced another anglicised version of Marxism; this time even more diluted (unlike Hyndman he had no interest in Marxist economics, which he claimed he did not understand and did not care to) with a more creative, consistent and attractive blending of other elements.

Morris believed in the necessity of revolution, in the sense that ordinary people would need to seize power and use it to transform society, but he cared little about how this might be done or in organising to achieve it. What did interest him was demonstrating the injustice and cruelty of the current division of society into rich and poor, and the nature of life in the kind of society that could replace it. His hatred of modern industrial capitalism was as much aesthetic as moral, although he would not have separated the two so clearly. He was influenced by the great Victorian art critic, John Ruskin, and his view that art reflects the moral quality of the society that produces it. Morris condemned the ugliness and squalor of industrialism: its destruction of craftsmanship and of the worker's pride in their work. He blamed industrialisation for an unnatural divorce of art and life, which was also reflected in contemporary notions of 'high art' that could only be appreciated by the few. The ideal society would dispense with machinery, restore craftsmanship, and with it the joy of work, and bring about a full and genuine integration of art and life.

This ideal society would not, however, be the centralised bureaucratic state envisaged by many fellow socialists (such as the Fabians, whose elitism Morris detested), but a collection of self-governing communities. In this Morris was close to the anarchists, although he insisted he was not one of them. His vision of the ideal society is set out in his novel, *News from Nowhere* (1890), which describes an idyllic way of life in which politics as we normally understand it does not exist.

Fabianism

The Fabian Society was founded in 1884 for the purpose of promoting social-ist ideas. Its most prominent early leaders included Sidney and Beatrice Webb, George Bernard Shaw, Graham Wallas and H.G. Wells. It was always a society of intellectuals and had no aspirations to become a political party. Initially it was unsympathetic to the creation of a working-class party, hoping to dissem-inate its ideas among the existing Liberal and Conservative Parties. A working-class party would be a distraction. In her account of the period (*Our Partnership*) Beatrice Webb recalled: 'The Fabian aim was, therefore, to make thinking persons "socialistic", rather than to organise unthinking persons into socialist societies' (Webb, 1975).

The Fabians did not have a fixed doctrine, but rather a general belief that socialism was what liberalism must inevitably evolve into, and that socialism was a far more rational vehicle for liberal ideals than capitalism. They believed that capitalism was chaotic, inefficient and wasteful and that steadily over time, more and more aspects of life would need to be regulated and 'rationally' planned, necessitating increasing municipal and state intervention.

They sought to back up their claims with powerful intellectual arguments and massive empirical research. The Webbs in particular were extremely diligent researchers and were the inspiration behind the creation of the London School of Economics in 1895 as a centre for social research. They rejected Marxist notions of the class war and the class nature of institutions. If the state was used to maintain capitalism, it could just as well be used to introduce socialism. The classes could and should co-operate when the reason-ableness of reform was clear to all. They believed in the 'inevitability of gradu-alness', that incremental reform would win all the fruits of revolution without its attendant dangers. (The Society had been named after the Roman general, Fabius Maximus, who defeated his opponents by avoiding head-on battles and gradually wearing them down.)

Within this broad framework there was a variety of strands. Among the most influential were the ideas of the Webbs. They were very much elitist, envisaging the state being run by a group of enlightened and benign adminis-trators who, with democratic supervision, would organise society and the economy in the most rational way that was best for everyone. The future lay in efficient central planning and efficient local administration.

The Fabian Society was one of the founding organisations of the Labour Party (although not very enthusiastically at first) and of all socialist groups has been the most influential. Sidney Webb wrote Labour's socialist constitution in 1918 and from the beginning most of the leading figures of the party have been Fabians. However, as the spectrum of belief within the Labour Party has broadened, so has the range of belief the Fabian Society has accommodated, including bitter opponents in the left–right battles of the years after 1945.

ILP socialism

The Independent Labour Party (ILP) was founded at a conference in Bradford in 1893 under the leadership of Kier Hardie, who had been elected as an independent MP the previous year. The new party was created through a coming together of various working-class socialist groups and local parties, especially in the north of England. What was important about the new party was that it was working class in both its leaders and membership, in contrast to the essentially middle-class or middle-class-led Fabians, SDF and Socialist League. The new party was committed to a form of ethical socialism: that is, to collective ownership of the economy and a simple, direct belief in the evil of capitalism and the moral superiority of a socialist alternative.

ILP socialism relied a good deal on emotional appeal against the cruelty and injustice of capitalism, rather than on any worked-out theory. G.D.H. Cole, the historian of socialism, said it was 'socialism almost without doctrines ... so undefined as to make recruits readily among persons of quite different types'. Nevertheless, there was a basic belief in the socialist implications of the 'labour theory of value', that the workers were being systematically deprived of the wealth they created and were therefore entitled to. Capitalists, because they owned the factories and machines, were able to grab the lion's share of the wealth created while the poor exploited worker received only a miserable fraction. It followed for socialists that the working classes should take control of the means of production to secure for themselves the whole value of what they produced.

However, the ILP did not reject liberalism, but rather saw socialism as the only means of making possible the fulfilment of the liberal ideals of liberty and democracy. The ILP also drew inspiration from the Bible, which, it is often said, created more socialists in Britain than Karl Marx. For Christians like Kier Hardie, the painful consequences of industrialism suggested that mutual love and brotherhood ought to replace the competitive antagonisms of the capitalist market place. This was also true of many for whom socialism was a substitute for the Christian faith they had lost. The religious element also stresses the 'international brotherhood of man', a somewhat vague internationalism which was to characterise Labour's foreign policy up to the coming of the Cold War.

British socialism

By the turn of the twentieth century, Britain had developed its own distinctive if rather weakly theoretical version of socialism, with mainly Fabian and ethical socialist strands and a strong element of 'labourism'. Labourism is a trade union outlook that merely insists that workers are not getting their fair share of the wealth they create and that it is the business of the trade unions to rectify this imbalance. It does not require the abolition of capitalism.

This loose amalgam of elements is perhaps best understood when contrasted with contemporary European socialism based on orthodox Marxism. Unlike their continental counterparts, British socialists rejected class war between workers and bourgeoisie. The enemy was rather those who did not work at all and lived off profits. They rejected Marxist economics and accepted a notion of labour being one element of wealth creation that was being denied its true share. The state was not seen as necessarily an instrument of class oppression, but potentially a benign instrument of progress if in the right democratic hands. Finally, liberalism was not seen as the enemy ideology, but rather as a set of ideals for the achievement of which capitalism was not an adequate instrument, but socialism was.

The founding of the Labour Party

Strictly speaking the Labour Party did not begin as a socialist party. As created in 1900, it was to be a federation of all organisations devoted to fostering the working-class cause, including trade unions, co-operative societies, intellectual societies and working-class parties. The intellectual societies (principally the Fabians) and the two political parties, ILP and SDF, were committed to socialism, but this did not necessarily apply to the other working-class bodies, especially the trade unions, who supplied the bulk of the membership, organisation and funds. Most trade union leaders were in fact Liberals and believed in labourism.

However, in 1918, when Labour was on the brink of displacing the Liberals as the country's second major party, it needed to be clear about what it stood for. The party wrote itself a new constitution in which socialism was firmly entrenched as the official doctrine in the famous Clause IV, which read:

> To secure for the worker by hand or by brain the full fruits of their industry and the most equitable distribution thereof that may be possible upon the basis of the common ownership of the means of production, distribution and exchange, and the best obtainable system of popular administration and control of each industry or service.

This does not actually mention socialism, but it is implicit in the phrase 'common ownership'. It is also suggested in the phrase 'the full fruits of their labour'. This implies the labour theory of value, which insists that all the value of a product comes from the amount of labour that has gone into its production. This could be interpreted in a 'labourist' way or a more socialist way. If the workers did indeed receive the full fruit of their industry, then there would be no profit, and without profit there would be no capitalism, no class system, no exploitation, and none of the ills that flow from them.

The new constitution of 1918 allowed individuals to join the party directly for the first time, instead of via some affiliated organisation. It also confirmed the basic structure of the party, which vested sovereignty and the ultimate authority to make policy, in the annual conference. Unlike the other two parties, Labour was created outside parliament. Its conference was seen as a kind of parliament of the working class, with representative of trade unions, co-operative societies, socialist societies and other organisations being represented.

However, although in principle the Parliamentary Labour Party (PLP) has always been subordinate to conference, the party has always tended to be dominated by its parliamentary leadership (elected by the MPs alone until 1981). Their policies have tended to prevail against those of the normally more left-wing constituency representatives because the leadership could usually rely on the massive block votes of the trade unions, which could outvote everyone else at conference. Later, in the 1950s and after, when the party was more radically split between left and right, the issue of who runs the party – conference or the PLP – was to become bitterly contested.

The Labour Party's socialism

The commitment to socialism in Clause IV was deliberately vague and minimal. There were elements of Fabianism, ethical socialism and a large admixture of labourism. Little was added subsequently. It is often said that the British Labour movement is averse to theory, and while there was some theorising, it had no real impact upon policy. The leader, Ramsay Macdonald, was a Fabian theorist who believed that social evolution would bring socialism in due course, but his theoretical position was no help in running the country when Labour had its first brief tastes of power in the inter-war years. He and his cabinet seemed too much concerned to show that a Labour government was 'responsible' by insisting upon economic orthodoxy, which meant massive unemployment. At the height of the crisis, Macdonald agreed to form an all-party government, but the rest of the Labour Party abandoned him. After the National Government debacle, the party developed a more realistic strategy based upon nationalisation, planning and a major role for trade unions, supplemented by Keynesian economic management, which it put into practice after 1945.

It was not until 1945 that Labour became the government on its own and backed, by a large majority in parliament, that it was in a position to put its socialist beliefs into practice. This involved the creation of the welfare state, to which all parties were committed following the Beveridge Report of 1942, but it also meant socialist planning and nationalisation as the first major steps to the creation of a socialist economy and therefore a socialist society. It was a government of extraordinary energy in the very difficult circumstances of the aftermath of war when the country was bankrupt. Among other things it created the National Health Service, the social security system, nationalised industries, the Arts Council, a comprehensive planning system, the green belt and new towns policies and the national parks.

Major steps had been taken towards socialism. Nevertheless, before the government left office in 1951 there had been a marked shift of opinion within the party. Some on the right of the party had begun to question both the necessity and the desirability of pursuing the ultimate aim of the elimination of capitalism and its replacement by a fully socialist society. Their view, widely shared across Europe, came to be called 'social democracy'.

Liberal socialism in Britain

In Britain, as in Europe following the Second World War, new varieties of socialism developed which departed from the classical socialist framework because they did not regard it as essential that capitalism be abolished. These are post-war social democracy and, more recently, the socialism of New Labour. Both tend to emphasise freedom and democracy at least as much as equality, so that 'liberal socialism' might be an appropriate label. However, they are also described as two forms of social democracy based on two different economic theories, Keynesian and 'supply-side' social democracy respectively.

For almost half a century there was only one form of social democracy, although with several variations, which established itself as the leading form of socialism in the West. It was built around Keynesian economics, the welfare state and, in Britain at least, the mixed economy. These were policies accepted by all parties, and were consequently known as the 'post-war consensus'. However, in the 1970s some of these policies failed and the consensus collapsed. The New Right dominated the scene, while Labour flirted with a renewed classical socialism, which was electorally disastrous. In the 1990s a new form of liberal socialism emerged, represented in Britain by Tony Blair's New Labour.

The social democratic analysis

The emergence of social democracy was partly a result of the Cold War. People argued that if the Stalinist Soviet empire, where the state controlled everything, showed socialism in action, then socialism was not worth having. Democratic socialists insisted that a socialist society democratically arrived at and based on democracy would be nothing like Eastern Europe, but there was nevertheless a good deal of disillusionment. The other important factor was the availability of an alternative. The consensus policies of a mixed and managed economy and the welfare state, developed by the post-war Labour government, seemed in themselves to provide a basis for a viable socialism that would combine prosperity and freedom with social justice and the possibility of a full life for everyone. They could be seen as a compromise between socialism and capitalism.

In Britain the right wing of the Labour Party adopted this programme as the basis of its ideal, while for the left (that is, the democratic socialists) these policies were regarded as merely a stepping stone to full socialism. The chief theorist of the social democratic view was Anthony Crosland, as set out in his book, *The Future of Socialism* (1956), in which he argued that the socialist ideal of owning the economy is no longer necessary. The nationalisations of the post-war Labour government plus Keynesian economic management were sufficient to ensure that a socialist government could control the economy and ensure that capitalism worked for the people. Full employment and economic growth could be assured and the surplus wealth could be taxed to provide better welfare and education and therefore equality.

As a consequence, capitalism was no longer the blindly destructive force it had been in the past and could now be the basis of a fair society. It was equality, and not common ownership, that was the great socialist value, and this could be achieved through good education for all, and through the eradication of unemployment, poverty, squalor, avoidable ill-health and other obstacles to a decent life for everyone. Common ownership for its own sake has no point if socialist ideals can be achieved more effectively by other means.

The success and failure of social democracy

These ideas led to severe internal conflict within the Labour Party in the 1950s, when the right wing adopted social democracy and the left rejected it as a betrayal of genuine socialism, which they thought must involve the replacement of capitalist society by a socialist one, as in genuine democratic socialism. The resulting conflict is sometimes referred to as the 'Revisionist Debates', a reference to a similar period of conflict within the German Social Democratic Party in the 1890s (discussed above and in Chapter 7). The issues then were different, but they too were about what the party stood for and whether it should 'revise' (in effect abandon) its traditional doctrine.

Despite the conflict, social democracy became the dominant Labour view and remained so for a generation, although after the creation of the Social Democratic Party in 1981 (by a breakaway group of Labour right-wingers) adherents within the Labour Party have an understandable reluctance to call themselves social democrats. Socialists who remained within the classical tradition, both democratic and revolutionary, have argued that social democracy was not socialism at all. Indeed, some have suggested that since the advent of social democratic ideas the Labour Party really became two distinct parties occupying the same organisation.

Crosland's vision of a good society depended a good deal on full employment with continuing economic growth, which Keynesianism seemed to promise indefinitely. During the 1950s and 1960s social democratic policies, pursued by both Labour and Conservative governments, gave Britain unprecedented prosperity shared by the whole population. It amounted to a revolution in social conditions relative to what had prevailed before the Second World War. It is true that other countries outstripped Britain in economic performance, but they did so on the basis of broadly similar social democratic policies.

However, the economic recession of the 1970s called social democratic policies into question. In particular, Keynesian economic policies could not cope with the critical economic problem of the time, the combination of inflation and growing unemployment at the same time. Keynesian remedies no longer appeared to work. Furthermore, an expanding economy was necessary to promote greater equality through social expenditure. Without such expansion the pursuit of equality is not possible without the socially divisive appropriation of the wealth of some to give to others.

The failure of social democratic policies led both parties to seek new solutions. The Conservatives chose what came to be called 'Thatcherism', while the left of the Labour Party argued that the social democratic compromise had been a mistake all along, and that the party must return to its true self, working for the end of capitalism and its replacement by a genuinely socialist society. The most forceful advocate of this view in the Labour Party was Tony Benn.

Bennite socialism and the resurgence of the left

Like Mrs Thatcher, Benn rejected the compromise of the consensus years as having brought the country into crisis, and saw a clear radicalism as the only solution to the country's problems. For him, this meant a return to the Labour Party's traditional Clause IV socialism, but also a return to the earlier roots of socialism and radical democracy in Britain going back to the English Civil War. Tony Benn's socialism was distinctive in the importance he placed on combining socialism with radical democracy. For him it was an essential principle that people should be involved in decisions that affect them. This was not only right and just, but was also conducive to greater commitment and efficiency.

Benn argued that by the 1970s the advance of democratic power had reached the point where it was dislocating capitalism. In order to fulfil legitimate popular demands for better public services, capitalism needed to be taxed to such a degree that it reduced its capacity to create wealth. The further development of capitalism could only be at the cost of reversing social progress.

It followed that a new economic system was necessary. The only alternative was to move towards a socialist economy and greater democracy, which would be able to meet the demands of the people for such progress. These ideas dominated the Labour Party in the early 1980s and led to a catastrophic defeat in 1983.

The Blair revolution

The Labour Party's abandonment of both classical socialism and post-war social democracy following 1983 was done slowly and reluctantly. But with the advent of Tony Blair in 1994, the party had a leader who embraced the change with enthusiasm. His first act was to work to have the old Clause IV of the party's constitution changed to eliminate the commitment to common ownership and in effect to classical socialism. These were replaced by commitments to the free market, to the environment, to the ending of discrimination and to equal opportunity for all.

All this was rather vague. Bennite socialism and Keynesian social democracy were lumped together and dismissed as 'old Labour', but the essential doctrine of 'New Labour' was still in an embryonic stage and took some time to emerge. Indeed, it is a process that is still incomplete. Just as Thatcherism evolved while Mrs Thatcher was in office, Tony Blair believed that his New Labour philosophy could also develop in office (although it has to be said that Thatcherism had behind it a large body of New Right theory already in place, which arguably Blairite socialism did not have). Several key terms have appeared to sum up the doctrine, like 'stakeholder society', but have faded. The most enduring has been the 'Third Way', signifying a middle path between Thatcherism and old Labour. This is still rather vague, but a distinctive outlook can be discerned. In a fact it is less a way between Thatcherism and old Labour so much as a synthesis of elements of Thatcherism with elements of social liberalism, especially in its modern form of communitarianism.

The principal Thatcherite element in New Labour is supply-side economics (although not its extreme monetarist form that Mrs Thatcher initially favoured). It is believed that only a competitive economy can be successful in the modern globalised world, and this means many of the Thatcherite policies such as low inflation, low public expenditure, low taxes and no overmighty trade unions. Keynesianism means the government controlling the national economy as a self-contained unit, which is no longer realistic; hence Blair's supply-side social democracy.

Low public expenditure and low taxation limit the amount of welfare provision that is possible, and this has caused some consternation among traditional Labour supporters. The plan has been to wean people off welfare dependency. Work is seen as the cure for poverty, not higher benefits, thus single mothers, the disabled and other welfare recipients are helped to find work. This is seen by some as Thatcherism by another name. However, it can be seen in a different light as a more responsible attitude. Along with a harsher view of crime, this is seen as a part of the need for a more responsible society advocated by communitarianism. This advocates stronger communities and more responsible attitudes towards the community on behalf of members, including a greater emphasis upon duties as well as rights. The community will provide opportunities and welfare for those genuinely unable to work, but people have a duty to seek work, not commit crime and so on.

This emphasis on duties is balanced by an emphasis on rights. One aspect is constitutional reform to bring people closer to government and give them a stronger say (for example devolution, abolition of Lords, elected mayors, and possibly electoral reform), as well as the incorporation of the European Convention of Human Rights into British law. Workers' rights are particularly emphasised, including a minimum wage and right to assistance in retraining. Policies to deal with social exclusion and discrimination against minorities are also important. The right to a decent environment brings in the green agenda.

This brings Labour close to the Liberals, and they have co-operated on some of these matters. Blair argues that the Conservatives have dominated British politics for most of the twentieth century, but only because the left of centre (which forms the majority of the electorate) was split between Labour and the Liberals, who in fact are not all that far apart. The logic of this position would suggest a proportional representation system for electing parliament, which could give a Lab-Lib coalition power for the foreseeable future. But this seems unlikely to occur because of rank-and-file hostility, especially in the Labour Party.

But there is another interpretation. It is argued that New Labour is the first postmodern party, that it has no basic principles and simply is skilled at offering what the bulk of the electorate want (through opinion polls and focus groups). This seems somewhat unfair, although there are electoral considerations here. Britain's social structure has changed to such a degree in recent decades that a party seen as representing the traditional working class (heavy industry, heavily unionised, council housed) together with the poor and disadvantaged, would be the party of a minority, and the party of those who fail. It would be extremely difficult to win any election. If the Labour Party was to succeed it had to appeal to the middle classes, and those working-class voters with middle-class lifestyles that had been the foundation of Mrs Thatcher's electoral success. In the process New Labour has stolen many of the themes of conservatism. Labour now claims to be the party of business, the party of the whole nation and so on. Much of this distresses old Labour stalwarts. Its justification is electoral success. To what extent it can properly be counted a version of socialism is a matter of debate.

But while there is an element of truth in this analysis it is perhaps unduly cynical. To understand it better we need to see Blairite socialism in a wider geographical and historical context. In the first place, it can be seen as a response to globalisation. It is perhaps significant that the leading academic theorist of the Third Way, Anthony Giddens, is also a leading analyst of the social impact of globalisation. It is also significant that Blair shared seminars on the Third Way with Bill Clinton, and drew inspiration from Clinton in the USA. Clinton was a 'New Democrat', elected in 1992 on a programme that was economically conservative, strong on law and order, avoided too close an identification with the unions, the poor and ethnic minorities, but sought to be more compassionate to those genuinely in need. In other words, a blending of left and right that was thoroughly centrist. During the 1990s and since, centre-left parties across Europe have been engaged in a similar search for new ideas and a new identity, and with similar results to New Labour's supply-side social democracy.

European socialism since 1945

Socialism has been a major force in the politics of most Western European countries since the Second World War. Unlike Britain, however, socialist parties were suppressed during the war in much of Europe, and had to begin again after 1945. For many there was a fresh start theoretically as well as organisationally. Most had Marxist origins, although they had followed the non-revolutionary route of Bernstein's revisionism.

After the Second World War, however, even this form of classical socialism was difficult to reconcile with post-war prosperity, freedom and democracy, and a general revulsion against totalitarian communism. A second major phase of revisionism became necessary. This involved an explicit acceptance of the free market about which many European socialists remained ambiguous. But Keynesian social democracy was socially and politically successful for several decades and preserved many traditional socialist values and principles. That success came to an end in the 1970s with a world recession. Since then, the impact of globalisation and the electoral success of parties influenced by New Right ideas forced a further rethink in the 1990s. As with America's Democratic Party and Britain's New Labour, this has taken the form of adopting a certain amount of the New Right analyses and policies, a process that has been labelled 'neo-revisionism'.

Germany

German Social Democrats initially believed that, since the Nazis had discredited the right, they would dominate post-war German politics. In fact, that dominance was achieved by the centre-right Christian Democrats who restored German prosperity and respectability and introduced and an extensive welfare state. After losing three elections in a row, the German Social Democrat Party (SPD) made a decisive break with the past. At a special conference in Bad Godesburg in 1959 it rejected the Marxist revolutionary principles of its official doctrine, which too many associated with the communism of East Germany and which few in the party believed in any more. Embracing the free market was seen as essential to the party's survival.

Accordingly, the Bad Godesburg Declaration set out the SPD's revised principles. There is no mention of Marxism. Instead there is a total commitment to democracy: 'Socialism can be realised only through democracy and democracy can only be fulfilled through Socialism.' There is also an endorsement of the free market and an abandonment of the objective of comprehensive public ownership: 'Free choice of consumer goods and services, free choice of working place, freedom for employers to exercise their initiative as well as free competition are essential conditions of a Social Democratic economic policy.' Furthermore: 'Private ownership of the means of production can claim protection by society as long as it does not hinder the establishment of social justice.' What this meant was Keynesian economic management, welfare and a degree of economic planning. That is, an acceptance of capitalism consistent with same kind of controls as in Britain. Beyond this there was a strong emphasis on welfare: 'The social function of the state is to provide social security for its citizens to enable everyone to be responsible for shaping his own life freely.'

It was the Bolshevic Revolution that led to 'social democracy' coming to mean, not Marxist revolutionary, but moderate parliamentary socialism. The Bad Godesburg revision was instrumental in a further shift of meaning, whereby 'social democracy' has come to mean the abandonment of the ideal of replacing capitalism with a society based on socialism (in the 'classical' sense).

The change of course of 1959 gained the SPD a place in government in 1966, from which it went on to become the dominant party in German politics from the late 1960s to the early 1980s. That dominance ceased when the Christian Democrats returned to office, where they remained, dominating the political scene under Helmut Kohl, until 1998. The SPD again had to redefine its socialism to take into account of a changed world, as well as new concerns, such as feminism and environmentalism. The latter was particularly pressing since during the 1980s and 1990s the SPD has found itself outflanked on the left by the Green Party, which gained many votes that might otherwise have gone to the Social Democrats.

In 1998 the SPD returned to power in coalition with the Greens. The party had a new leader in Gerhard Schroder, pursuing neo-revisionist centrist policies rather similar to Tony Blair's and called the 'new middle', with a closer relationship to business, commitments to lower taxes and spending, welfare reform and so on. However, more traditional socialist policies and principles were represented by Oscar Lafontaine, the former leader of the party, who seemed to pursue his own policy agenda as minister of finance. The resultant conflict was only resolved by Lafontaine's resignation in 1999.

Scandinavia and Holland

Social democratic parties have dominated the politics of Scandinavia since before the Second World War. These countries adopted the social democratic formula of Keynesian management, the mixed economy and an extensive welfare state before Britain or Germany. The result has been highly prosperous and successful economies, with high wages and full employment. But there has also been high taxation to fund, in Sweden and Norway, the most extensive welfare services and the highest level of welfare payments in the Western world. The 'Swedish model' in particular was an inspiration for social democrats in other countries. Examples included 100 per cent sickness and unemployment pay and pensions entirely funded by employers. The great emphasis is upon social equality, which includes a non-selective education system with a large proportion of students entering higher education.

However, in the 1970s Swedish prosperity faltered, as it did elsewhere, and there was growing resistance to such high levels of taxation. After being in power continuously since 1932 the Swedish Social Democrats gave way to the Swedish Conservatives in 1976–82 and again in 1991–94. The Conservatives had a neo-liberal agenda to reduce taxation and welfare spending, though modestly by non-Scandinavian standards. Swedish Social Democrats recovered power in the late 1990s, having accepted the need for restraint in spending and less control over a changed economy. However, they are in a precarious position. The Social Democratic government in power at the beginning of the twenty-first century is a minority government dependent on the Greens and the Left (former Swedish Communist Party), who regard such restraint as only temporary and want full restoration of the previous levels, as well as greater economic intervention. Social Democrats have come to accept that these are no longer realistic in a globalised world with their commitments to the EU (of which Swedes are the least enthusiastic members). The present government is sustained by prosperity, but if conditions change they are vulnerable.

Norway has a similar history of domination by a party committed to social democracy, the Norwegian Labour Party, which created a massive welfare state in the post-war years. It too had to adjust to new realities in the 1990s, but the transition was less problematic than in Sweden because the Labour Party headed a coalition, which also contains the Centre Party and the Christian Democrats. This is equally true of the Dutch social democrats who, in 1998, exchanged the leadership of a left-centre coalition for a 'purple coalition' of socialists and conservatives under the leadership of Wim Kok. Under the cover of a general coalition, and a striving for consensus (the 'polder method'), Kok has sought to move his Labour Party towards a more neo-revisionist agenda.

Italy and France

In both Italy and France, socialists have had to share the allegiance of left-voters with larger communist parties. This has helped to keep them out of power until relatively recently. In Italy the 'red taboo' kept socialist as well as communists out of any real power for most of the post-war period, when the Christian Democrats dominated. Only for a brief period in the 1980s, did the Socialists under Betino Craxi lead a coalition government, but even that included the Christian Democrats.

With the end of the Cold War the Italian Communist Party sought to redefine itself. The bulk opted to form a more mainstream democratic socialist party, the Democratic Party of the Left, while a hard-line minority founded the Communist Refoundation. But both remained far from power. However, in 1992 the whole Italian party structure collapsed in a chaos of accusations of corruption and Mafia connections. The Christian Democratic Party was the chief casualty, although others that had participated in government, including the Socialists, were also brought down. New parties and alliances emerged. In the election of 1994 the Democratic Party of the Left hoped for a long-awaited breakthrough into government, but it was defeated by a coalition of hastily constructed parties of the right and centre.

In the wake of this defeat the left regrouped into what became known as the 'Olive Tree Alliance'. Its chief architect was Romano Prodi, a centrist Catholic academic, who brought together centrists, the two former communists groups, left-wing Catholics and greens. It won power in 1996 and ruled Italy past the turn of the century.

The Communist Refoundation did, however, leave the government in protest against cuts, but was out of sympathy with its neo-revisionist policies: controlling inflation, cutting expenditure and taxes, welfare reform, law and order and so on. Italy did, however, have a particular motivation. Despite a long history of inflation, high expenditure and corruption, Italy was determined to participate fully in the European financial system and the new single currency, which it could only do by putting its financial house in order. These policies have legitimised the left sufficiently to allow the former Communist, Massimo D'Alema to succeed Prodi in 1998.

In France the long period of Gaullist dominance was finally broken in 1981 when the Socialist leader, François Mitterand, gained the presidency and worked with the Communists. However, it is widely believed that Mitterand out-manoeuvred the Communists to such an extent that the Socialists flourished while the Communists experienced a serious decline. On the other hand, despite winning two seven-year terms as president, Mitterand had to abandon many Socialist policies, including a nationalisation programme, and even for a time had to 'cohabit' with a Gaullist prime minister, Jacques Chirac, who was bent upon a programme of privatisation and other right-wing measures. Mitterand's second presidential success in 1988 led to a more moderate Socialist government which did not reverse Chirac's privatisations, although it reinstated a more Socialist social policy. However, when in 1993 another right-dominated parliament was elected and Chirac won the presidency in 1995 it seemed that the Socialists were exhausted and were set for a long period out of office.

However, under the leadership of Lionel Jospin the left won a remarkable parliamentary majority in 1997. Jospin led a coalition of all the parties and groups of the left (the first comprehensive coalition of the left for more than forty years) including Communists, Radicals, Greens, Socialists and the highly nationalistic Citizen's Movement (the MDC). This created a complex and diffi-cult policy-making process, trying to reconcile often quite different and some-times opposing agendas, which none the less proved popular. In general, Jospin embraced the business community and has been an enthusiast for privatisa-tion and welfare reform. At the turn of the century he was presiding over France's most extensive programme of privatisation, while at the same time extending workers' rights, including a thirty-five-hour week. His general approach puts him closer to Blair and Schroder than his reputation as a more traditional socialist would suggest.

Neo-revisionism and the future of socialism

During the 1990s in Britain and Western Europe (and with a parallel move-ment in the USA) the parties of the left have been undergoing a further period of revisionism, which still continues. After Bernstein and post-war social democracy this is the third phase. These revisions have often been painful, and critics have dismissed the resultant changes as a progressive abandonment of socialism, but the counter-argument has been that they have been realistic in terms of what voters are prepared to accept.

The need for fresh revision

Post-war social democratic ideas and policies were highly successful, although not confined to socialist parties. However, the recessions of the 1970s and 1980s created a good deal of disenchantment with socialist ideas of all kinds. There has since been a mood of disillusion with the omnicompetent state and a degree of resistance to the high levels of taxation needed to sustain welfare and other social democratic measures. This has been helped by the relative failure of Keynesian economics and the intellectual success of New Right criticisms of state intervention of all kinds (see Chapter 10). For Keynesian economics to work at all the economy must be a unit that can be manipulated in relative isolation from other economies, but this is no longer possible in a globalised world. Furthermore, the economy has become steadily less amenable to control because it is no longer dominated by large production units with mass workforces. The post-industrial economy is far

more fragmented and has a multitude of small businesses, in which intervention is inappropriate. Governments can only provide a general environment.

The New Right recognised this, along with the need for economic success in
globalised world, with less tax and expenditure. Furthermore, the more fragmented economy and the decline of the mass workforce meant a decline in
working-class solidarity and the rise of a more consumerist, individualist electorate, to which the New Right was also able to appeal. Consequently, the
1980s was a New Right decade, dominated by Thatcher and Reagan and the
influence of supply-side economics across the Western world. It seemed to spell
the end of socialism. Mrs Thatcher even made it her stated aim to rid Britain of
socialism altogether, a claim taken seriously.

It was to this situation that the left in Britain and Europe and America
had to respond with a new wave of revisionism, sometimes called 'neo-
revisionism'. This involved a search for a new formulation that could be
electorally popular and yet would not alienate traditional support or abandon
traditional values. Hence the array of formulations, perhaps beginning in the
early 1990s with Clinton's 'New Democrats' in America, followed by New
Labour and Third Way in Britain, Schroder's *Neue Mitte* in Germany, Jospin's
gauche plurielle in France and others elsewhere.

The success of neo-revisionism

At least in electoral terms the success of these neo-revisionist strategies has
been considerable. By the turn of the twenty-first century centre-left governments dominated much of the Western world, including America, Britain and
most of Western Europe – Scandinavia, the Low Counties, Germany, France
and Italy. What is perhaps more surprising is that between them there is a
remarkable degree of consensus in outlook and policy, indeed, perhaps more so
than at any time in the past, even though none of the Europeans would argue
that the process of 'modernising' socialism is complete.

Central to the whole process has been the absorption of principles and policies of the New Right, in order to modify and blend them with what could be
salvaged from traditional socialist values, principles and policies. This had to be
done because the New Right agenda had been much to do with surviving in a
globalised world, and since it had been seen as both popular and effective the
left needed to learn some of these lessons in order to survive electorally. A
moderate version of supply-side economics, privatisation and welfare reform
have been among the policies taken from the right and which have been
combined with policies to combat social exclusion and extend workers' rights
(such as the minimum wage) from the left. Constitutional reform and green
policies are new elements that cut across traditional left–right lines. This is also
true of attitudes to the European Union, which some see as potentially a new
means of controlling and moderating capitalism.

However, one of the means of distinguishing these supply-side socialists from their centre-right rivals is the greater emphasis upon public expenditure as opposed to tax cuts. This is true in Europe and also in America, where it emerged as a major issue of the 2000 presidential election campaign.

Is socialism dead?

Socialist parties would thus seem to be flourishing. But here we come up against the problem of what constitutes socialism. For those who feel that classical socialism is the only genuine form of socialism, then arguably it is as dead as Marxism. The abolition of capitalism and its replacement with a fully socialist economy and society is not serious politics anywhere in the world.

All viable forms of socialism are liberal and social democratic. Postwar social democracy still has its advocates but it cannot overcome basic difficulties: of isolating the national economy from the world; international financial markets punish high tax-and-spend economies; nationalisation and state planning will not be voted for by today's electorate, and so on. This leaves some room for supply-side neo-revisionist socialism, like that of New Labour. But is it socialism? For many, including significant figures in neo-revisionist parties, it is difficult to see it other than as capitalism with a human face, providing an infrastructure for a more efficient capitalist economy. The turn-of-the-century success of such parties has been against the background of general economic prosperity. When there is a downturn, it is claimed, the socialist element of the neo-revisionist synthesis will not be enough to protect ordinary people from the vagaries of capitalism. The charge of the death of socialism is therefore not surprising.

Socialism, it is suggested has been killed by global capitalism, but globalisation is not the only factor. Whether we are thought to live in a post-industrial society or more fashionably in a postmodern one, socialism seems no more suited to it than to a globalised world. Central is the decline of class and class-consciousness. When the British Labour Party was founded in 1900, the manual working class was around 80 per cent of the population; a hundred years later it is around 40 per cent and falling. Besides, the working class, conceived in terms of a mass, unionised labour force displaying class loyalty and solidarity expressed in terms of trade unionism, labour politics and a specific lifestyle, is a thing of the past. In the Western world generally, middle-class lifestyles and attitudes have expanded through much of the population. Political parties have to appeal to all sections. Being tied to the working class and its organisations, as socialist parties traditionally have been, is electoral death.

However, there is more to postmodernity than the end of class. There is also ideology. A major feature of postmodernity (see Chapter 13) is a disillusionment with grand theory, theories which purport to tell all humanity how it is going to live; accompanied by a disillusionment with all-competent government. Perhaps more than any other ideological tradition, socialism (including Marxism) falls into both of these categories. Socialism on this view is the ideology most at odds with the spirit of the age. For good or ill, the present age is one of individualism, of free choice, of resentment against what interferes with that choice.

In the light of the above it might be argued that socialism, at least beyond its most watery supply-side form, is indeed dead beyond recall. But this assumes that the present situation will go on indefinitely, which seems unlikely. In the first place, the drive towards globalisation itself generates a counter-drive towards particularity and the assertion of difference, and socialism may have a role here. Furthermore, the capitalist system is massively dynamic, and can generate massive change and evolve into something else or generate a reaction. A major economic disaster could generate a reaction against the free market and, as a consequence, today's economic orthodoxy may be rejected, as such orthodoxies have in the past.

There may be a revival of socialist ideas in the future on a regional or local or even international basis, possibly using a revised Keynesianism. After all, the New Right was the revival of ideas thought long dead and out of date. In fact, there could be said to be an ambiguity in the preferences of populations in the electorates of Europe and the USA which seems to transcend the old left–right spectrum and to lean to the right on economics and to the left on social matters. Neo-revisionism recognises this. Besides, it could be argued that politics today is much closer to public opinion, which may shift.

Though socialism may be dead, socialist values of equality and community and social justice are not, nor is the dream of an alternative society. Socialism's weakness is its lack of an alternative economics, but that could change. The prospect of a socialist revival may not be in sight, but in a fluid world it is far from impossible.

6

Anarchism

The word 'anarchy' comes from the ancient Greek and means 'without rule', and in ordinary parlance 'anarchy' means the same as 'chaos'. But there is a long-established body of political theory calling itself 'anarchism' that is based upon the idea that the state, or any other kind of political rule, is not only unnecessary but a positive evil that must be done away with. Such ideas have only occasionally inspired political movements of any size, and the tradition is mainly one of individual thinkers, but they have produced an important body of theory. The first significant anarchist thinker was William Godwin, who developed his ideas around the time of the French Revolution. However, the idea that it is possible to do without the state was not invented by the anarchists, but has a much older history in Christian theology.

There is a long tradition in European thought, going back to the great theologian and exponent of the theory of Original Sin, St Augustine of Hippo (354–430 AD), which argues that government is needed because human nature is corrupt, and that if it were not corrupt then government would not be necessary. On this view, government is essentially coercive, being there to keep the sinners in line by laying down laws and punishing those who break them. It was an idea still strong in the eighteenth century. Thus, James Madison (1751–1836), the chief architect of the American constitution, wrote:

> there is a degree of depravity in mankind that requires a certain degree of circumspection and distrust ... But what is government itself, but the greatest of all reflections on human nature? If men were angels, no government would be necessary.
>
> (*The Federalist Papers*, Nos. 51 & 55, in Hamilton *et al.*, 1961)

Neither Augustine nor Madison were anarchists, but what this line of thought did open up was the possibility that government could be done away with if the evil in the world could be eliminated.

What the anarchists did was to say that the evil in the world was not caused by Original Sin, but was in fact mainly the consequence of government. As the poet Shelley (William Godwin's son-in-law) put it:

> Kings, priests and statesmen blast the human flower
> Even in its tender bud.

(*Queen Mab*, 1812)

If government was taken away human beings would be good and all coercion and domination would be unnecessary.

Individualist anarchism

The first anarchist thinkers, in both Europe and America, saw themselves as, for the most part, continuing the Enlightenment tradition, emphasising the sovereignty of the individual and the progress of reason.

William Godwin

It was William Godwin (1756–1836), in his *Enquiry Concerning Political Justice* of 1793, who first argued the anarchist case: that the state had a corrupting influence on those subject to it, and that a much better society could therefore be built without it.

Godwin had an optimistic, Enlightenment view of human nature. Our individual natures, he thought, were the product of our environment and upbringing, although that could be improved upon by the application of reason. With the spread of science and philosophy and improved education, there was no doubt in his mind that mankind would gradually improve. The ills of war, poverty, crime and violence would disappear, since he took it for granted that the consequence of people becoming more rational is that they became more benevolent towards their fellows. He held the utilitarian view that the greatest good was the greatest happiness for the greatest number, and that any truly rational person would understand this and behave accordingly; that is, human nature as we observe it would change as the environment which nurtured it changed.

There were, however, certain obstacles on the way to progress, and chief among these was the state. The common belief that the state was necessary for social life was a myth. The state maintains itself by deception and violence, and by keeping the population in ignorance. The process artificially sets one above another, and induces competition and greed and conflict, which are the source of the ills from which mankind suffers. It is only when the domination of man over man has ceased that people can live a fully rational life. The abolition of all political institutions would put an end to class distinctions and national feeling, and the enviousness and aggression that goes with them. It would restore to men their natural equality and enable them to rebuild social life on the basis of free and equal association, governed by their reason alone.

Godwin was a radical rather than a revolutionary. Revolutions, and for that matter ordinary party politics, polarised society and aroused passions that resulted in the eclipse of reason. Social progress was entirely dependent on intellectual progress, which in turn came from reflection and discussion. The ideal could only be pursued as the entire population was gradually brought to the level of understanding presently confined to the few. It was a lengthy process, although Godwin never doubted the inevitability of its completion.

Max Stirner

The next significant work of a European anarchist was a strange book entitled *The Ego and His Own*, published under the name of Max Stirner in 1843. The author's real name was Johann Caspar Schmidt (1806–56), and he was for a time a schoolmaster before sinking into misfortune and debt. Schmidt was personally a mild and timid man, but his book is a violent expression of pure individualism, which glorified rebellion, crime and violence in the name of the uninhibited free will. The state, society, religion and morality are all denounced for suffocating the free spirit. The assertion of the self, at any cost, was the only good. The state, with all other manifestations of collectivist man, must be destroyed to make way for a world of unrestrained egoism (that is, selfishness and self-assertion); a world of unique and powerful individuals who will come together and co-operate spontaneously as and when its suits their individual interests. But what kind of a social life this would make possible Stirner does not tell us. His book shocked society when it was first published, but was then forgotten until the end of the century when it was revived and widely read by anarchists.

Both Godwin and Stirner developed versions of anarchist doctrine based on individualism, but there the resemblance ends. For while Godwin's was an Enlightenment individualism that stressed the capacity of all to participate in universal reason and be capable of rational self-direction, Stirner's was very much a Romantic individualism that stressed will and emotion and the assertion of unique individuality. Neither of them founded political movements or had much of a following, and after them the trend in European anarchist thinking was towards socialist anarchism.

Nineteenth-century American anarchism

It was in America that the individualist strand of anarchism continued to develop. Here it was perceived by its followers as a logical extension of Lockean liberalism and Jeffersonian democracy, that is, the 'natural rights' of life, liberty and property were sacrosanct, while the state's role as the appropriate vehicle for defending those rights was questioned. The American anarchists tried to show that government had 'become destructive of these ends'.

Godwin's writings were well known in America, but the first important American anarchist, Josiah Warren, was initially a follower of the English socialist, Robert Owen, and was a member of his ill-fated American colony of New Harmony. Its failure in 1827 left Warren convinced of the need to fit society to the individual and not the other way round. He was thereafter a fierce advocate of the absolute sovereignty of the individual, with which no organisation of government had any right to interfere. After the relative success of his 'time store', based on the exchange of promises of labour time, he founded a series of communities based on similar principles, without any regulation or means of enforcing decisions. The first, called the 'Village of Equity', failed because of an epidemic, but the second two, called respectively 'Utopia' and 'Modern Times' lasted for a couple of decades each and convinced their founder of the rightness of his principles.

Warren worked out a complicated economic system (set out in his main book *Equitable Commerce*, 1852) that was based on people charging for their goods exactly what, in terms of labour time, it had cost them to produce them, only modified by taking into account the 'repugnance' of the work involved. In addition there would be free credit, except where a loan involved a demonstrable loss to the lender. This is what he meant by 'equitable commerce'. A society based on honest exchange between free people, he believed, would be harmonious and prosperous, and not need government to run it. Warren seemed to have in mind an unchanging society of small farmers, craftsmen and traders, much like that envisaged by Jeffersonian democracy. Some of his followers, however, adapted his ideas to factory conditions. Workers would still be employed by bosses, but both would receive the same wages, related to hours worked, and there would be no return on capital invested. Nor would special talent or skill receive special reward, for that, according to Warren, had nothing to do with the just reward for hours worked. A system of this kind would be quite incompatible with capitalism, and was, as such, regarded as a version of socialism.

There were a number of writers and thinkers who followed Warren and developed ideas of their own, but the most distinguished contributor to the tradition in the middle of the century was Henry David Thoreau (1817–62). His attempt to live a life of absolute simplicity in the woods near Concord in Massachusetts (chronicled in his book *Walden*) was rudely interrupted by prosecution and imprisonment for his refusal to pay his poll tax. Thoreau objected to the legal confiscation of his goods for purposes from which he gained no advantage, and which immorally upheld slavery and engaged in wars with other countries. This experience prompted a passionate essay, entitled *The Duty of Civil Disobedience*, which attacks government and insists upon putting his own conscience above the law. The essay begins:

I heartily accept the motto, 'That government is best which governs least'; and I would like to see it acted up to more rapidly and systematically. Carried out, it finally amounts to this, which also I believe, 'That government is best which governs not at all'; and when men are prepared for it, that will be the kind of government which they will have.

(quoted in Woodcock, 1963, p.429)

The essay would be influential in the next century with political figures such as Ghandi, but Thoreau was ignored in his own time. Besides, he was far too much of an individualist to have a following or to try to start a movement.

Benjamin R. Tucker (1854–1939) was the leading American anarchist of the late nineteenth century. Like Warren, he also saw his ideas as socialistic, although he was much more committed to the free market, and even believed his socialistic anarchism to be consistent with classical liberalism. He argued that the reason why the free market appeared to generate exploitation and huge disparities of wealth was that it was not genuinely free. The market was rigged and distorted by monopolies, for which governments were largely responsible. If the four main monopolies of money, land, tariffs and patents were abolished, then competition in a free market would bring down prices to approximately production costs and interests rates to near zero. In these circumstances anyone could set up a business, land would belong to those who worked it, and no one need be poor or exploited.

From 1881, Tucker published the journal *Liberty*, which became a great forum for radical thought in the period. By this time, European versions of communistic anarchism and theories of violent activism, both of which Tucker detested, were arriving in America. When his printing presses were burnt down in 1907 and *Liberty* ceased publication, the native tradition of individualist anarchism was broken and did not reappear until very recently.

Although individualist, US anarchism thus far tended to see itself as leaning towards socialism in the sense of stressing an egalitarian society of free, independent individuals, seeking to appeal to the common man, and in its hostility towards the rich and privileged. On the other hand, US anarchists were not opposed to the market as such, and tended to see humans beings as intelligent pursuers of their self-interest. Unlike Godwin, they did not foresee a change in human nature, but merely the creation of a society where the pursuit of self-interest was more enlightened and mutually beneficial. Their ideas therefore relate to late-twentieth-century anarcho-capitalism. Like Godwin, they eschewed both revolutionary activity and ordinary parliamentary politics, relying on the power of reason, persuasion and education (Josiah Warren promoted his ideas through a journal entitled *The Peaceful Revolutionist*).

The immigrant strand of communist anarchism, derived from Europe, was the more dominant strand by the end of the nineteenth century. However, before turning to the socialist and revolutionary anarchists, a further strand of the individualist variety needs to be mentioned.

Personal anarchism

Since the end of the nineteenth century, there has always been number of individualist anarchists who have usually stood apart from the social revolutionaries. They have pursued freedom in their own way: either through campaigning publicly for their beliefs, or by withdrawing from society to live a life at odds with accepted social norms. What these anarchists demand is freedom from society's pressure to conform, or, as they would express it, freedom from ignorance, superstition and moral prejudice. The kinds of things they have usually had in mind have been artistic freedom, sexual freedom and freedom from religious intolerance. Society, they insist, has no right to impose these things. The individual is sovereign.

We now take for granted many of these individualist anarchist demands. This is partly because there is good deal of overlap between their demands and certain liberal ideas of the late nineteenth century, which have been extremely influential. This is the kind of liberalism particularly associated with John Stuart Mill (see Chapter 2), who argued that the state has no right to interfere in an individual's way of life, providing he or she is doing no harm to others. In this respect individualist anarchism can be seen as an extreme version of liberalism. The main difference is that all liberals accept the necessity of law and the state. What Mill advocated was maximum possible freedom within the law, whereas all anarchists reject law and the state as unnecessary.

Socialist anarchism

The main trend in anarchist thinking in Europe after Stirner was towards socialist anarchism which, while insisting on individual liberty, saw society as based on a network of communities of people working together. A number of thinkers contributed to this increasingly influential tradition.

Proudhon

The first of these was a self-educated French printer by the name of Pierre-Joseph Proudhon (1809–65). If anyone can be said to be the founder of modern anarchism as a political movement it is Proudhon, and he was the first thinker to call himself an anarchist. He developed the anarchist case against capitalism in addition to the case against the state. He is probably best remembered for his aphorism 'property is theft', although this does not accurately reflect his views. He did not object to private property as such, but only the possession of such property as gave one man power over another. Indeed, he thought it essential that every individual own his own home, together with the tools and land necessary to do his work. A minimum of property was necessary to maintain independence and liberty, and he objected to communism on the grounds that it took these away. He was fiercely individualistic, writing:

My conscience is mine, my justice is mine, and my freedom is a sovereign freedom ... To be governed is to be watched over, inspected, spied on, directed, legislated over, regulated, docketed, indoctrinated, preached at, controlled, assessed, weighed, censored, ordered about, by men who have neither right, nor knowledge, nor virtue. That is government, that is its justice, that is its morality ... Whoever puts his hand on me to govern me is a usurper and a tyrant; I declare him my enemy.

(*General Idea of the Revolution in the Nineteenth Century*, 1851,
in Proudhon, 1923, p.294)

Proudhon's ideal was a world of small independent producers – peasant farmers and craftsmen – who associated and made contracts with each other freely for their mutual benefit, and for whom a centralised coercive state was an unnecessary evil.

It is not difficult to see in Proudhon's ideas the reaction of the independent craftsman and peasant proprietor against the new age of industrialism and a longing for a world that was passing away (although he did take factory production into account, believing that this should be based on worker co-operatives), and it was among just such small producers that his ideas took hold. Yet he was more widely influential than this. His followers played an important role in the First International and in the Paris Commune of 1871. On the other hand, Proudhon disliked parties quite as much as any other kind of formal organisational structure, and he also disliked rigid structures of thought in the form of theories or programmes that everyone has to agree to. He refused to call his ideal society a 'utopia' in the sense of a system that once established could not be changed. That would be an intolerable limitation on freedom. Each generation, he believed, must be absolutely free to solve its own problems in its own way.

This points to a central difficulty in Proudhon's thought. He wanted a society based on mutualism, with free bargaining between individuals and communities. Since such free bargaining was not possible in a situation where some were more powerful than others, he was, therefore, anti-capitalist. On the other hand, he was more individualist than collectivist. He wanted a society based on a voluntary association of independent communes, but also wanted a situation where everyone was equal and could do what they wanted, and each commune could run its affairs as it chose. These are potentially in conflict (such as some becoming successful and rich through their own talents) but he was unclear how the combination could be sustained.

Bakunin

Proudhon's most famous disciple was an extraordinary Russian aristocrat named Mikhail Bakunin (1814–76). While Godwin, Stirner and Proudhon confined their rebelliousness to their writings, Bakunin was a rebel in everything he said and did. He scorned all conventions of behaviour and charged about Europe involving himself in every plot, conspiracy and insurrection he could find. He was completely devoted to revolutionary activity, with little thought of his own safety or anyone else's. Despite years of harsh imprisonment his faith was undimmed and he lived to become the father-figure of European anarchism and inspirer of generations of anarchists.

Bakunin began his revolutionary career by advocating a general uprising of the Slav peoples and the creation of a great pan-Slavonic federation under a revolutionary dictatorship that would lead mankind out of oppression towards freedom and equality. He wrote (rather ironically as things turned out):

> the star of revolution will rise high and independent above Moscow from a sea of blood and fire, and will turn into a loadstar to lead a liberated humanity.
>   (*Appeal to the Slavs*, 1848, in Bakunin, 1980, p.65)

He later abandoned ideas of revolutionary dictatorship and pan-Slavonic nationalism; but he always retained an almost mystical belief in violent revolution as a great purifying and regenerative force:

> Let us put our trust in the eternal spirit which destroys and annihilates only because it is the unsearchable and eternally creative source of all life. The urge to destroy is also a creative urge.
>   (*The Reaction in Germany*, 1842, in Bakunin, 1980, p.57)

Bakunin did not, however, believe in mass political parties as an instrument of revolution, but in small secret bodies of professional revolutionaries on the Babouvist model (which later influenced Lenin) who would inspire and lead spontaneous insurrections of peasants and workers.

Bakunin believed that mankind was oppressed by the duel power of church and state. They both relied on the myth of human selfishness, upon which was based the claim that human beings were not fit for freedom, but need the guidance of religious and political authority. Science, Bakunin believed, would put and end to religion, but it was only the people who could destroy the illegitimate power if the state.

Like Proudhon, Bakunin believed that anarchism was the logical outcome of the ideals of the French Revolution, and that revolutions were the necessary means by which humanity progressed. Bakunin believed that ultimately the whole world would be engulfed in a revolution that would destroy the class system and the nation-state. Henceforth property and inheritance would be abolished and mankind would be organised in a worldwide federation of industrial and agricultural communes based of the principle of 'from each according to his ability, to each according to his work' (not according to *need* as held by Marx and other socialists).

Bakunin's vision was more socialistic than Proudhon's. The basic unit of society is the commune rather than the individual. He argued that since all must be afforded the means to earn their living and not be economically dependent on anyone else, then property rights must belong to the community and not to individuals. Human beings must be free, yet man is by nature a social being who can only flourish in a community of equals. Bakunin marks a change in the mainstream of anarchist thought from individualism to collectivism.

But although committed to socialist ideals, Bakunin was an implacable opponent of Karl Marx, whose ideas he believed were inherently authoritarian. Although far less original and far less of a systematic thinker than Marx, his criticisms were prophetic, and were later influential among the New Left Marxists of the 1960s (see Chapter 7).

Tolstoy

After Bakunin the next two significant anarchist thinkers were, oddly enough, also Russian aristocrats. One was Count Leo Tolstoy (1828–1910), the great Russian novelist. Unlike any of the previous thinkers he was a Christian anarchist. After a life of worldly success and worldly pleasure he renounced cultivated society and his art, and tried to live a simple life close to the Russian peasantry.

Tolstoy was a savage critic of contemporary society as being based on corruption, hypocrisy and false knowledge. Science, he believed, taught us nothing of any significance, and he was scornful of the modern world's belief in progress. He rejected all state and social institutions and all organised religion. The honest simple life that was close to the soil and within the family was the source of wisdom and goodness and constituted the best life for man. Tolstoy was a pacifist, believing all forms of violence to be immoral, and consequently did not believe in revolutions. The thing to do, he said, was not to plot and plan for the good society, but to go out and start living the good life.

Kropotkin

The last of the major theorists, who built on the ideas of Proudhon and Bakunin, was Prince Peter Kropotkin (1842–1941), a distinguished Russian scientist and geographer. After a period in the Imperial army followed by scientific work in Siberia, Kropotkin visited Switzerland in 1872 where he was converted to anarchism by some of Bakunin's followers. After returning to Russia he began to promote the anarchist cause, but ended up in prison. He later escaped and spent most of the rest of his life in exile, mainly in London. He returned briefly to Russia before he died, but had little sympathy for the Soviet regime.

Kropotkin was the most thorough and systematic of anarchist thinkers and devoted several books to trying to put anarchism on a firm scientific basis. In the late nineteenth century the scientific theory that caught every imagination was Darwin's theory of evolution. Many social theorists attempted to use evolution as a basis of the own social and political ideas. They were known as 'social Darwinists'; the best known was Herbert Spencer who used evolution to justify extreme *laissez-faire* capitalism as natural and right, in the sense that free competition ensures the 'survival of the fittest', thereby promoting higher evolution and progress. But instead of glorifying competition, as did most social Darwinists, Kropotkin took precisely the opposite view by arguing that co-operation was the key to evolutionary success. Human beings were the most successful species because they had learnt to co-operate together effectively.

It is not competition, therefore, that is natural and good, but social co-operation and mutuality. The obvious conclusion to be drawn from this, Kropotkin believed, was that the ultimate stage in the evolution of human society was a social life where people freely and naturally co-operated on equal terms, and competition no longer existed. However, man's natural sociability and co-operativeness were obscured and distorted by capitalism and the coercive state. Once these have been removed, by whatever means, human society would be free to achieve its highest stage of development, which was communist anarchism. Society would then be based on a free association of communes, where goods would be produced and distributed on the basis of need (as in Marx) and not labour time (as in Bakunin).

Anarchist terrorism

In the two decades prior to 1914 the Western world was shocked by a series of anarchist outrages. Bombs were thrown into parliamentary assemblies, and into theatres and restaurants where the rich gathered; policemen, judges and other public officials were murdered; most shocking of all was a series of spectacular assassinations, including those of President Carnot of France (1894), Empress Elizabeth of Austria (1898), King Umberto of Italy (1900) and President McKinley of the USA (1901).

The press and the politicians usually portrayed these atrocities as the work of the Anarchist International (or 'Black International'), a vast international conspiracy aimed at destroying Western civilisation. In fact there was no such conspiracy and no such organisation. All these sensational acts were committed by individuals, or very small groups, working alone. Their own justification was that they were striking a blow for the oppressed. The state and the capitalist system constituted organised violence against the people, and terrorism was their only way of fighting back. An assassination was not so much an attempt to overthrow the system directly (though there was always the hope that it would spark off a popular uprising). It was, rather, a symbolic act that would reveal to the masses the true nature of the system and convince them that action to change things was possible. It was, in the anarchist phrase, 'propaganda of the deed'. Many moderate anarchists, like Kropotkin, were appalled by these outrages, but refused to condemn them on the grounds that they were the inevitable products of an unjust society.

The idea of 'propaganda of the deed' had been developed in the 1870s as a reaction against earlier reliance on propaganda and persuasion. The oppressed, it was argued, had neither the time not the inclination to read pamphlets or attend political meetings. They had to be shown by a dramatic and symbolic act against the state and capitalist property, that would highlight their oppression and demonstrate the way forward. What was originally envisaged were acts of insurrection, with anarchist bands moving from community to community, providing the spark that would lead on to a general uprising. The most serious attempts to implement this strategy were in northern Italy in the mid-1870s, which all came to nothing. Such failures led to a commitment to terrorism, and the expression 'propaganda of the deed' acquiring more sinister connotations.

It might be argued that 'propaganda of the deed' grew out of two other kinds of failure. One was a failure of insight. Anarchists were given to believe (as Marxists often were) that the oppressed masses were ready for revolution, and that all that was needed was the spark that would set alight a revolutionary conflagration across Europe. The resort to terrorism was a desperate attempt to find the right kind of spark, and was more successful than previous strategies. But also, anarchists seemed to be neither inclined nor capable of creating the kind of disciplined organisation their aspirations called for. Organisation based on entirely voluntary co-operation and acceptance of decisions could not be effective. The systematic application of anarchist principles to anarchist organisations appeared to condemn anarchism to impotence, even when events seemed propitious. For example, they failed to take advantage of their substantial following in Russia to resist the Bolshevics in the revolutionary period.

Anarcho-syndicalism

Most anarchists believed that the existing order needed to be overthrown by a spontaneous popular insurrection, whether or not it was sparked off by terrorism. There was, however, one strand of anarchism in this period which put its faith in economic action rather than political. This was anarcho-syndicalism (from the French *syndicats* = trade unions), which has been the nearest the anarchists have come to creating a serious political mass movement capable of challenging for power in a modern society.

Syndicalist theory developed in France, and is essentially revolutionary trade unionism. Syndicalism was about class war, using whatever was necessary by way of direct action – strikes, boycotts, sabotage and, where necessary, personal violence – to fight for better conditions and prepare the workers for the revolutionary general strike that would finally cripple and destroy the capitalist system. The syndicalists were deeply suspicious of party politics, and saw the emancipation of the working class as something to be achieved by the working class themselves, and by means of their own institutions.

Syndicates were local trade unions, normally based on an industry, although sometimes a craft or profession. They were under the democratic control of their members and entirely autonomous, and in syndicalist theory must remain so. There must be strong links with other local syndicates, and with a national organisation for each industry. But these wider organisations were only for purposes of co-ordination. Each local syndicate was sovereign, and joined these wider organisations and took part in common action on a purely voluntary basis.

Not all syndicalist leaders were thoroughgoing anarchists. For some the main object was destroying capitalism, and the abolition of the state was a minor matter to be settled when that object was achieved. But most were anarcho-syndicalists who did see the stateless society as central to the ideal. The state was not only undesirable but unnecessary, since the federation of syndicates, freely co-operating in the interests of all, would not only create the revolution but were perfectly adequate for running the post-revolutionary world without the need for the state apparatus of oppression. (However, it must be said that revolutionary fervour was confined to a minority.)

Although it never made much impact in Britain, anarcho-syndicalism became a major political movement in France, Italy and Spain. In the years before the First World War it was a serious rival to socialism and Marxism. In France, half the workforce belonged to anarcho-syndicalist-dominated unions, and even in America the anarcho-syndicalist union, the International Workers of the World (the 'Wobblies'), had over 200,000 members.

After the war the influence of anarcho-syndicalism waned in most countries. The exception was Spain, where it went on growing as a mass movement and played an important role in the Spanish Civil War. The anarchist trade union, the Confederacion Nacional de Trabajo, in the mid-1930s achieved a membership of over one million, and fleetingly controlled large parts of Spain. But with Franco's victory the anarchist tradition more or less died out.

Since then, however, it has not been a significant political movement anywhere in the world in terms of mass politics, although anarchist theorising has continued along several paths. There was something of a revival of anarchist ideas among the student left of the 1960s, although mainly on the fringes of the New Left which was dominated by neo-Marxism. More recently there has been the development of 'green anarchism' and 'anarcho-capitalism'.

Anarchism and Marxism

Curiously, Marx knew well all the leading anarchist thinkers in Europe in his lifetime. Stirner was, for a time, a fellow Young Hegelian in Berlin. When Marx first went into exile in Paris he was on friendly terms with Proudhon, although this subsequently turned to hostility. Finally, it was Bakunin who led the anarchist faction in the First International and was Marx's chief opponent. In the second half of the nineteenth century, and up to the First World War, support for the revolutionary left was divided between Marxists and anarchists.

Differences and similarities

Proudhon and Bakunin objected to Marx's authoritarianism, both organisational and intellectual. Marx wanted the workers to form centralised and disciplined mass parties co-ordinated by an international body led by Marx himself. But Bakunin and other anarchists would have none of this. They were against disciplined parties and intellectual elites possessed of the 'truth'. They thought Marx's theory of the dictatorship of the proletariat implied a post-revolutionary tyranny not much better than what it replaced.

Anarchists objected to the whole notion of 'scientific socialism', with its economic determinism and its necessary stages of history, which seemed to suggest that it would all happen automatically anyway. This must, they argued, undermine the revolutionary fervour necessary to overthrow the system. Revolutions were about will and leadership and courage, not about having the correct analysis. Besides, if it was all scientific, that implied a class of experts to run not only the revolutionary party but the post-revolutionary world: only they would know the right moment to act and the right thing to do; they would constitute a new and permanent priesthood.

Another objection was to the role of the proletariat. Marx saw the revolution being undertaken by an army of disciplined urban factory workers. But the anarchists did not believe the working class was the solidly united force Marxists believed. The top strata were reasonably prosperous and unlikely to participate in revolutionary activity, let alone lead it. Much more likely material, anarchists believed, was the lower strata, the most exploited, the unemployed, the poor, as well as landless peasants and other groups. Furthermore, apart from regarding the whole notion of a post-revolutionary dictatorship as inherently wrong, it was completely unacceptable that it should be in the hands of one narrowly defined social group and not all the oppressed. At best it would rule in the interests of that narrow class and suppress the spontaneity and creativity of the whole society released by the revolution.

Finally, the notion of the 'dictatorship of the proletariat' was anathema. The means must be consistent with the end. Revolutions must be accomplished in accordance with the same values they are intended realise. To create a tyranny in order to end all tyranny was absurd.

Marxists tended to reply that the anarchists were so disorganised, they would never achieve anything. Nevertheless, despite the rivalry Marxism and anarchism had much in common. They were both equally hostile to capitalism and the bourgeois state. Marx believed that the state was an instrument of class oppression, and that in the future classless society the state would necessarily cease to exist. Thus, Marx's ultimate future (to the very limited extent that he outlined it) was an anarchist one.

Until the First World War, the anarchists were the only serious revolutionary rivals to the Marxists, although only in a few places of equal importance. But, Spain apart, the anarchist movement collapsed after the war. There were several reasons for this, but one was the success of the Bolshevic Revolution, which seemed to show the true and effective way of accomplishing a revolution. In fact the anarchists, both within Russia and elsewhere, were the Bolshevic's severest critics on the left. Indeed, as time went on anarchists were increasingly clear that all their criticisms and suspicions of Marxism had been well founded, and that the 'dictatorship of the proletariat' had turned into the monstrous tyranny they had predicted. Their prescience did not, however, prevent the demise of anarchism as a mass movement.

Anarchism and the New Left

The New Left (discussed in Chapter 7) was a remarkably disorganised and inchoate movement, with no overall organisation and no clear goals. Its theory was fluid and eclectic. Marx and Marxists were the most important figures, but psychoanalysts, psychiatrists, phenomenologists and various cultural critics also contributed. Anarchism was a strand, but also a central part of the general New Left outlook, as is apparent in the writings of such leaders as Danny Cohn-Benditt, the French student leader, and in the thinking of student groups like the French 'Situationists' and the Dutch 'Provos' and 'Kabouters' and the whole American 'counter-culture' movement. The New Left as a whole was profoundly anti-authoritarian, such that it could fairly be described as 'anarcho-Marxist'. It is Marxist with all the old anarchist criticisms taken to heart. This can be seen in number of ways.

First of all, the New Left's rejection of orthodox communism as a corrupt and bureaucratic tyranny reflected the old anarchist fears of the idea of a 'dictatorship of the proletariat', that were borne out in the experience of modern communism. The modern bureaucratic state was almost as much an object of hatred as the ruling class. There was no national or international leadership and no attempt was made at creating a disciplined party; reliance was placed upon a network of independent democratic groups.

Second, the New Left rejected Marx's economic determinism and the whole emphasis on the working out of historical necessity. Third, the idea of the proletariat as the instrument of revolution was abandoned in favour of, as Bakunin wanted, the oppressed and disillusioned, the more prosperous working class having, to a considerable extent, been bought off (more so in the age of consumerism). Finally, the New Left emphasis was on revolt now, leading to liberation now, and a new society now, all based on a transformation of consciousness, and not the juggernaught of historical inevitability being played out in the fullness of time, independent of anyone's will.

Part of the whole student-New Left ethos of the 1960s was the rejection, not just of the power-structure of class and state but the whole consumer culture and bourgeois values of mainstream America. Part of the New Left revolt was a rebellion among the young who sought to revolutionise everyday life, to create alternative ways of living. This led to what is called the 'counter-culture', manifested in 'hippies', 'flower power', 'drug culture' 'sexual liberation' and the fashion for 'communes', all of which were expressions of a distinctly anarchist outlook.

Recent developments in anarchist theory

In the New Left there was a kind of merging of the Marxist and anarchist traditions. However, there were several distinctively anarchist outcomes remaining after the youthful rebellion had died down. These included deschooling theory, feminist anarchism and green anarchism. The same period has also seen an entirely new strand of anarchism developed, anarcho-capitalism, which has far more to do with the New Right than the New Left. Both of these have affinities with more recent postmodern developments.

Deschooling society

One of the most odd, yet most influential, movements that grew out of the New Left was the 'deschooling' movement, associated with Paul Goodman, Paul Reimer and, most famously, Ivan Illich (*Deschooling Society*, 1970). It was essentially an educational theory, and followed a distinguished tradition of educational theorising by anarchists, starting with William Godwin. Education must be central to the anarchist vision. It is the only viable alternative to revolution as a means of creating the anarchist society, and, even where revolution is the means, it would still be essential to the maintenance of society the revolution had created. However, deschooling theory became a fashionable educational theory for a while, far beyond the confines of radical intellectual circles.

Essentially, deschooling theory argues that schooling as we know it does not in fact educate. All it does is to process and certificate people for modern industrial society; and it is essentially the same process in liberal democratic states as in communist ones. Many spend years being 'schooled' and learn virtually nothing. The formal education system all needs to be replaced by a voluntary network in which people take charge of their own education, just as in the wider world they need to take charge of their own adult lives. The key to transforming society is the abolition of the schooling system.

Illich in particular emphasises the sheer inability of the compulsory state schooling system to perform the very task it is set up to do, and links this with the inability of massive state bureaucracies to do any of their appointed tasks.

Thus we have a defence system that fails to provide security; a social security system that perpetuates poverty; a health service that does not make people healthier; and so on. (This argument is one of the very few links between New Left anarchism and New Right anarchism, although the explanations and remedies are different.) The general reason for this failure, Illich believes, is that people are not, as they ought to be, in charge of their own lives.

Feminist and green anarchism

Another outcome of New Left anarchism is anarchist feminism (sometimes called 'anarcha-feminism'), in which the state is seen as an expression of male dominance, a dimension of patriarchy that must be abolished if women's emancipation is to be accomplished. As with the New Left movement itself, there is among radical feminists generally a specific and self-conscious strand of anarchism, but also anarchist ideas and attitudes have a pervasive influence over the whole movement. There is the traditional anarchist rejection of conventional politics: there has not been (nor is there any prospect of) a Women's Party. The emphasis is on decentralisation and co-operative small-group democracy, with no national leaders. The same could be said of probably the most important area of anarchist influence today, the green movement (see Chapters 11 and 12 for fuller accounts of feminist and green thinking).

Murray Bookchin, one of the leading figures of the American green movement, sees what he takes to be the authentic green movement, or 'social ecology' as he calls it, as the culmination of the various radical movements of the 1960s, and as fully in the anarchist tradition:

> Social Ecology draws its inspiration from outstanding radical de-centralist thinkers like Peter Kropotkin, William Morris, Paul Goodman, to mention a few, amongst others, who have advanced a serious challenge to the present society with its vast, hierarchical sexist, class-ruled status, apparatus and militaristic history.
>
> (quoted in Porritt and Winner, 1988, p.236)

He insists that it is not individuals that are responsible for the world's appalling condition, but the racist, sexist capitalist system. He sees the impulse to dominate other human beings (in the first instance, of women by men), and the impulse to dominate nature, as a continuum, and all to be resisted.

Bookchin is a self-conscious anarchist, but the movement has strong anarchist characteristics quite independently of this, and what are clearly anarchist ideals are held by a great many who are entirely innocent of the anarchist tradition of political thought. For many greens the future sustainable society needs to be stateless and composed of a network of self-sufficient communes, based on equality, participation and direct democracy.

Anarcho-capitalism

At the same time, a quite different form of anarchist theory was developing at what would, at first thought, seem to be hostile territory at the opposite end of the ideological forest, amongst the writers and thinkers of the New Right (see Chapter 9).

The New Right sought a reduction of the state in favour of the free market. Some New Right theorists, such Robert Nozick in his book *Anarchy, State and Utopia* (1974), take the view that the only thing the state should do is provide law and order. Indeed, Nozick insists that for the state to take citizens' property, as taxation, for any other purpose is positively immoral (see Chapter 2). It is only a very short step beyond this 'minimal statism' to downright anarchism. Among those who have taken this step the most important are David Friedman (son of the leading New Right economist Milton Friedman) and Murray Rothbart. In books such as Friedman's *The Machinery of Freedom* (1973) and Rothbart's *For a New Liberty: The Libertarian Manifesto* (1973) they argue against there being any form of state at all, leaving everything to free-market capitalism. Hence the name, 'anarcho-capitalism'.

There are many anarchists of the more traditional variety who would not recognise such ideas as authentic anarchism, and for whom rampant unregulated capitalism would be an evil of horrifying proportions. It would reproduce all the horrors of the industrial revolution and worse; poverty, exploitation and squalor would again be the lot of the workers. Needless to say, the anarcho-capitalists do not see their ideas in this light. They see their primary concern as human freedom and, like all anarchists, they see the state as its chief enemy, a 'protection racket' as Rothbart calls it. They see capitalism as benign, and any faults it is thought to have as the result of state intervention. State regulation creates monopolies, or reduces the number of producers, in a multitude of ways, and it is in such situations that exploitation takes place. In a stateless situation that is genuinely free, there will be prosperity and opportunity for all, and the only differences of wealth will arise from differences of talent and application. Society will be characterised by a spontaneous harmony.

Much of the literature of anarcho-capitalism is devoted to demonstrating how government attempts to help people through collective action end up doing more harm than good, and how the free market could provide whatever was necessary more cheaply and efficiently and to the greater satisfaction of all. This even applies to law and order, the key difference with the minimal statists.

Anarcho-capitalism began as the outlook of a relative handful of intellectuals, but its ideas have spread and found resonance on the right of the American political spectrum. Murray Rothbart in particular has made common cause with minimum statists in the Libertarian Party, now a significant small party devoted to a drastic reduction of American government to defence and law and order. There are links here with the right wing of the Republican Party, which also seeks to reduce government, as seen in the

'Contract with America' of Newt Gingrich and the Republican majority in Congress in the early 1990s.

There is, however, a more sinister link with the American far right. In 1995 the federal building in Oklahoma City was blown up, killing 169 people and injuring 500. It was the act of a few people acting alone, but they had links with the state militia movement which believes that the federal government is part of an international conspiracy to deprive ordinary Americans of their rights. These people arm themselves against the day when there is a confrontation with the federal government (see Chapter 8). Hatred of government is strongly felt in certain sections of American society, and has increased with the end of the Cold War, so that the government's role of defending against the evil of communism is redundant.

Finally, it is not in fact the case (as is sometimes thought) that anarcho-capitalism came out of the blue, without past or pedigree. It has a good deal in common with the earlier American tradition of individualist anarchism, particularly that of Benjamin Tucker. There is also a link with the extreme version of classical liberalism represented by Herbert Spencer and his followers, who saw the role of the state progressively diminishing as free-market capitalism, and therefore social progress, advanced. However, whatever the independent history and standing of anarcho-capitalism might be, its fortunes seemed bound up with those of the New Right generally, and will advance or decline as they do.

Anarchism and postmodernity

One of the features most associated with the claim that we now live in a postmodern world is the rejection of authority. Postmodern thinking tends to be libertarian and anti-authoritarian, celebrating freedom and choice and variety in all things, and questioning the right of those, including the majority, to impose their views on those who are different or think differently. Anarchism might be said to fit well with the spirit of the age.

With the decline of Marxism since 1989, anarchism has flourished among groups who reject modern society, protest against its manifestations and seek alternative lifestyles. These include New Age travellers, eco-warriors and others. In the summer of 1999, anarchists organised a seemingly peaceful protest against capitalism in the City of London which in fact turned into a riot. It subsequently appeared that the event had been organised through the internet and that a considerable network of such groups existed across Europe and America. Subsequent meetings of international financial bodies in Seattle, Washington, Prague and elsewhere were accompanied by more rioting. The organisation of these protests has been without overall leadership, through multiple voluntary networks in true anarchist fashion. They have drawn together a host of protesters, concerned with green issues, Third World debt and other matters. More recently, meetings of the EU have become a target.

One of the features of contemporary anarchist thought is its diversity and willingness to explore possibilities of culture and technology as arenas for protest and subversion of power and authority, through hacking into capitalist information systems, encouraging free access to commercial music, resisting attempts to control or regulate the internet, popular participation in urban renewal and many other issues.

There seems little chance of anarchism becoming a serious political movement as it once was, but equally there seems little doubt that it will continue as an expression of freedom to differ for a long time to come. However, as a serious political theory it does have considerable difficulties.

Fundamentals and criticisms

Anarchism covers such a wide range of beliefs, from extreme individualism to extreme collectivism and from extreme capitalism to extreme communism, that it could be argued that there cannot be much, if anything, that unites all the strands. The question of whether there are such common principles turns on the question of whether there is a specifically anarchist conception of human nature and its relationship to society. Upon this answer turns the further question of the viability of anarchism as a political doctrine.

Anarchism and human nature

Anarchism can be said to rest upon certain basic assumptions about human nature and its relation to society:

a Society is based on free association between people and is natural.
b The state is based on the domination of some by others, is maintained by coercion, and is not natural.
c Humanity is essentially good, but is corrupted by government.
d Government cannot be reformed, but must be destroyed altogether.

Anarchists of all kinds agree that human nature is such that it will not flourish in conditions of coercion and domination, especially those represented by the state. Human beings will live more fully and happily once the state has been removed. Only then will humanity's natural sociability assert itself and create a spontaneous natural order superior to any that could be imposed from above.

This, however, is only a partial and initial account of human nature. To complete it we have to see the kind of spontaneous order and harmony that anarchists believe the ending of the state will call forth. It is at this point that different anarchist strands disagree.

Thus, Godwin emphasised human rationality and believed in a natural order arising spontaneously if human beings were free to exercise their reason.

Kropotkin believed humanity's naturally evolved instinct for co-operation and community would assert itself. Green anarchists put their faith in man re-establishing a natural harmony with nature, following which everything else will fall into place. Finally, the market anarchists believe that giving free reign to man's natural instinct to pursue his own self-interest will result in the natural order of the market.

Anarchism is open to a variety of criticisms. Some of these apply to anarchism in general while others apply to individual strands within the broader tradition.

Rules and authority

The most fundamental criticism of anarchism is that if we take it to its logical conclusion it simply does not make sense. That is, if we take seriously the idea that 'anarchy' implies without rule or authority. We might imagine extreme anarchists who, on principle, refused to follow any rule they did not make up themselves. Such a policy could not be pursued consistently, and would be self-defeating. Take, for example, the case of language. If this individual refused to follow the rules of sentence construction, and put words in their own peculiar order, then they would not be able to communicate with the rest of us. A more general point can be made about rules of behaviour. To be part of any community involves shared beliefs and values, as well as shared ways of doing things and ways of behaving. If the individual refuses to share any of this it is difficult to see in what sense they would be a member of the community. Certainly it would not make sense to talk of a community composed of such individuals.

Anarchists are inclined to say that they only reject coercive authority and since nobody is formally punished for using language incorrectly, following generally accepted authoritative rules is unobjectionable. The question then becomes where one draws the line. At this point anarchists divide between individualists and communists. Individualists who are 'doing their own thing' may not be able to work together to form a community, to do the necessary tasks, to get things done. Communist anarchists require a high degree of co-operation and authoritative decisions (usually by means of direct democracy), which cannot accommodate the dissenting individual who may not accept the authority of the majority.

This argument becomes a practical one of what will and will not work. All forms of anarchism involve a reliance on natural harmony, such as the unhindered market or unhindered reason or unhindered sociability, that will assert itself once the hindrance of the state has been removed. Anarchists are sustained by a faith in one or other of these harmonies, while the rest of us tend to be sceptical. The seventeenth-century philosopher, Thomas Hobbes, argued that with the removal of the coercive authority of the state, society would degenerate into a war of all against all in which the life of man would be 'solitary, poor, nasty, brutish and short'. Most people are inclined to believe that the taking away of all forms of coercive authority would lead to conflict. To believe otherwise requires a considerable degree of faith.

Problems with socialist anarchism

Socialist anarchism is based on common ownership and distribution on the basis of need. It would appear to presume a considerable degree of discipline and commitment among the members of the community and a good deal of agreement. What happens to people who do not pull their weight; or to those who do not accept the authority or discipline of the community; or who do not agree with the distribution; or who want to go off and do their own thing, start a business or whatever? It is all very well to assume that all will share the same values, but if they do not then there will be divisions. There are, therefore, doubts about the practicality of anarchist communities.

The evidence is in fact ambiguous. It is true that there have been anarchist communities that have shared and lived together. These have been of several kinds, and had with different outcomes. The communities of the kind inspired by individualists, such as Josiah Warren, discussed earlier, were fairly successful. But they were not communistic; everyone minded their own business and did their own thing, and they gradually evolved into ordinary communities. Communities based on sharing tended not to last, unless there was some religious inspiration. As with the hippie communes of the 1960s there were difficulties in making sure people did their share of production, and even of chores; people joined and drifted away as the spirit moved them.

Anarchism has seemed to work best with established communities living a traditional way of life (as in parts of Spain during the Civil War). This tends to reinforce the idea that the appeal of socialist anarchism is to a lost past of social solidarity that is quite incompatible with our contemporary devotion to individualism and personal freedom. The present-day version of social anarchism that has the greatest following, green anarchism, seems to rely on a similar appeal. The social cohesion to make this possible is just not there any more. On the other hand, it is argued that we must recreate it if we are to survive.

Be that as it may, it is the case that where anarchism seems to work, if only for a time, is in small, simple, self-sufficient communities. It is not at all clear that it is remotely compatible with modern society, with its high degree of integration and complex mutual interdependence.

Problems with anarcho-capitalism

Modern individualist anarchism, now most forcefully represented by anarcho-capitalism, has its own problems. There are basically three of these, failure to solve any of which could be fatal to the enterprise. The first is the problem of law and order. Anarcho-capitalists insist that this can be dealt with through private protection and arbitration agencies, but only the most fervent believers find this convincing.

Second, there is the problem of public goods. These are goods, like public parks, street lighting, roads, clean air, defence and so forth, which cannot be supplied individually to people who pay for them. We presently pay for them through government taxation. But if there is no government and all things are provided by the free market, how could private firms ensure that everyone pays who uses these things? If they were provided anyway, it would be in an individual's interest to enjoy the good but not pay, to be, as the Americans say, a 'free-loader'. Because of free-loading, many would then not pay for others to take advantage, and then the firm providing the good would give up the business and nobody would have it. Again, while anarcho-capitalists offer ways around this, few find them plausible.

Finally, there is the argument that letting capitalism do whatever it wants will lead to mass exploitation and all the horrors that go with it. The anarcho-capitalists deny this would happen, while others are sceptical. In the end, as with all these criticisms, it all boils down to faith. This is true of every ideology, but anarchism appears to require a bigger dose of it than most.

7

Marxism

Marxism is a form of socialism, but one that deserves separate treatment, for it is a theoretical world of its own, often at odds with the rest of the socialist tradition. It is the most densely theoretical of all ideologies and it has been one of the most influential of the modern world. It takes its name from its founder, Karl Marx, and it helps to understand Marxism if we know a little about his life and how his thought developed.

Hegel, Marx and Engels

Marx was born in 1918 in Trier, Germany, the son of a Christianised Jewish family. It was intended that he should follow his father's profession as a lawyer, but at university he instead became absorbed in philosophy and politics. At that time, German philosophy was entirely dominated by the ideas of G.F.W. Hegel, who had died a few years earlier. Hegel was an extraordinary thinker whose ideas many people (including some distinguish philosophers) find baffling, but who has influenced other important thinkers, including Marx.

Hegel's philosophy

Hegel was an idealist, which means he believed that mind or spirit is the ultimate reality and the physical world could not exist without it. His theory was that 'Mind' (that is, Mind as such, of which each individual human mind is a manifestation) must strive to understand itself, and that the whole of reality and the whole of history has existed so that this can be achieved. To begin with, Mind is unconsciously embodied in physical nature, and only attains consciousness with the advent of human beings. History is the process through which Mind, and therefore humanity, explores its own potentiality, and thereby achieves self-consciousness and freedom. History, therefore, is a single process. Each succeeding civilisation is a stage in this process, and each civilisation is a totality: ideas, morality, art, religion, laws, institutions, literature, and above all philosophy, are all linked expressions of Mind at a particular stage of its development.

These civilisations each represent stages in a necessary process which is dialectical. The idea of the dialectic comes from argument, where one person puts forward a point of view (the thesis), another person puts forward a contrary view (the antithesis), and in the course of the discussion a third view emerges which combines the best points of the other two (the synthesis). Hegel believed that the human mind naturally developed in a dialectical way, and so does human history. As a civilisation develops, he argued, contradictions begin to appear which prevent its further development, and as a result of which an opposite kind of civilisation develops which, in course of time, gives way to a third which embodies the best of the first two. This third civilisation then becomes the basis of a fresh cycle, and so the process goes on.

Hegel believed that human history was exactly like the development of the individual, through babyhood, childhood, adolescence, early adulthood to full maturity; at each stage gaining in capacity, fulfilling potential and growing in self-understanding. Hegel considered that his own world was the final and ultimate stage of history, which had overcome all contradictions, and where the Prussian state, the Protestant religion and Romantic art were the highest possible development of these forms. Crowning all was his own philosophy which comprehends all reality and through which Mind finally achieves full self-knowledge, maturity and freedom.

However, Hegel had a peculiar idea of freedom. For him people were only free when they willingly obeyed the law and behaved morally. He certainly did not see freedom in terms of democracy. His ideal was an authoritarian state which every citizen accepted as right and proper.

Young Hegelians

Hegel's extraordinary conclusion, that his own philosophy was the final culmi- nation of all reality, was accepted by most of his followers, who believed that all that was necessary was to elaborate his ideas in more detail. But a group of his followers, known as the 'Left' or 'Young Hegelians', had more radical views. They thought Hegel was wrong in believing that his dynamic of history was complete. There was one final and highest stage of history still to come, one that would see the end of all oppression, the dawn of true enlightenment and the final emancipation of all mankind.

Karl Marx became one of these Young Hegelians, believing that a popular revolution in Germany would lead the way for the rest of mankind and begin that final stage of human history. He took up radical journalism and wrote in support of oppressed groups and of radical political action. This brought him into trouble with the authorities and he was forced to leave for France in 1843.

Collaboration with Engels

By this time Marx's views were being influenced by those of another young radical writer, Frederick Engels, who was to become Marx's lifelong friend and collaborator. Engels came from the Rhineland and was the son of a rich family of manufacturers who owned factories in Manchester. He had spent some time in Manchester learning the family business and observing the Industrial Revolution at its most advanced. His observations of its impact on the lives of ordinary people was the basis of his first book, *The Condition of the Working Class in England* (1844).

Engels convinced Marx that the future lay not in raising the consciousness of oppressed classes in backward Germany, but had to do with what was happening in England, and that the key to understanding this was economics. Marx made a detailed study of economics and social history and went on to develop his own theories of economic development and its social impact. He settled permanently in London in 1848, by which time the basic framework of his ideas was complete.

Although they had collaborated on a number of books prior to 1848, it was in that year that Marx and Engels produced the first short, clear but comprehensive account of Marxism with their *Communist Manifesto*. After this Marx spent the rest of his life in London, working mainly in the library of the British Museum developing his theories in a series of books and articles and trying to organise the international working men's movement. He lived mainly through occasional journalism and gifts from Engels. He died in 1883 and is buried in Highgate Cemetery. Engels lived mostly in Manchester, managing the English end of the family business. He was able to combine the activity of a successful and prosperous businessman with that of a revolutionary communist for the rest of his life. After 1883 he edited Marx's papers and wrote his own theoretical works. He died in London in 1895.

The Marxian synthesis

Although Marxism was a highly original system of thought, it was shaped by three major theoretical influences: Hegelian philosophy, British economic theory and French Revolutionary ideas.

Marx took from Hegel the conception of history as a single dialectical process proceeding through a series of necessary stages to a predetermined end, culminating in a final stage when all contradictions and antagonisms will be resolved and mankind will be fully developed and fully free. On the other hand, he rejected the Hegelian conception of history as the progress of Mind towards self-understanding as so much mystical nonsense.

What Marx believed did unite all the elements of human existence was not the 'spirit of the age' but the material conditions of people's lives. It was the economy, and the social structure that went with it, that determined the character of any age; and it was changes in these basic factors that were the driving force of history and responsible for the revolutions that marked the transitions from one stage of development to the next. Marx, therefore, had a 'materialist' conception of history and his basic theory is sometimes called 'dialectical materialism'. His system of ideas is also sometimes referred to as 'scientific socialism', since Marx believed that all his theories were fully scientific, based on the sciences of sociology and economics, and that they 'proved' that the final predestined end of history was the most complete form of socialist society, communism.

To examine Marx's ideas more closely we need to begin with his account of how the various aspects of society are related together and how they generate social change.

The analysis of society and social change

Marx believed that the most basic fact about any society is the nature of its economic organisation, its 'mode of production'. This involves two things: the methods of production (the type of agriculture or industry, and so on), and, second, the way in which production is socially organised in terms of who owns what and who does which job. The distribution of wealth and work is the basis of the class structure. Although this structure might be quite complicated, Marx insisted that in any society with a class system there is always a fundamental division between those who own the means of production, and who thereby constitute the ruling class, and those who do the work.

Base and superstructure

For Marx, the socio-economic organisation of society is fundamental because not only does it make all the other aspects of society possible, it also determines the nature of all those aspects. Consequently, in any society the kinds of laws, government, education, religion, art, beliefs and values it has are a direct result of the kind of social and economic organisation it has. Marx called the socio-economic organisation of a society its 'substructure' or 'base', while everything else belonged to the 'superstructure', and it is a basic principle of Marxist theory that base determines superstructure.

The crucial link between the base and the other elements of society lies in the need of the ruling class to maintain its power. Thus the state – with its instruments of law, police and armed forces – exists to protect the property of the ruling class, and therefore its control of the economy. But the ruling class cannot maintain its control by force alone; it needs the active co-operation of most of the population. This is where, according to Marx, religion, education, the arts and prevailing ideas play their role. They help to maintain the position of the ruling class by teaching people to believe that the way society is organised is natural and right and should not be questioned.

The base, therefore, does not just determine the various institutions of society, but also determines the way people think: 'It is not the consciousness of men that determines their existence, but, on the contrary, their social existence that determines their consciousness' (*A Critique of Political Economy*, Preface, in McLellan, 1977, p.388).

Marx used the term 'ideology' to refer to ideas, beliefs and values that reflect the interests of a particular class. In any society, he argued, the dominant beliefs and values are always the beliefs and values of the ruling class, while those of the rest of society who accept them (that is, most people most of the time) are in a state of 'false consciousness'. Thus, ideology is also an instrument of class domination, along with all the other elements of the superstructure.

Feudalism and capitalism

We can illustrate these points with the two examples Marx was most concerned to analyse. The feudal society of the Middle Ages was based upon subsistence agriculture. The peasant class did all the work, while the nobility owned all the land. The power of the nobility was sustained by law and custom, and upheld by the king's courts and by force if necessary.

The mediaeval church was closely bound up with the feudal system and its teachings were designed to maintain the existing order. It taught that the universe was a vast cosmic order, created and ruled by God, in which everything had its appointed place. Human society was part of this order, so that everyone's place in it, from the king to the humblest peasant, had been ordained by God. To try to change the order, or even one's own place in it, was to defy the will of God and was therefore sinful. Mediaeval art and literature was either religious, and therefore reinforced these teachings, or else was a celebration of the chivalrous exploits of the aristocracy, thereby displaying its fitness to rule.

In contrast, those who constitute the ruling class in capitalist society are not the possessors of land but the owners of capital. This is the bourgeoisie, who control the finance, the factories and the machines upon which modern industrial production is based. Because of this control over the means of production, the bourgeoisie can exploit the industrial workers, the proletariat, just as the feudal aristocracy exploited the peasants. Here again, the state and its instruments supports the property and interests of the ruling class, and again the beliefs and values that prevail in capitalist society help to portray the existing state of affairs as natural and right.

The dominant ideology of bourgeois society is liberalism, by which Marx meant the classical *laissez-faire* liberalism of the early nineteenth century, with its principles of free markets, individual liberty, equality of opportunity and limited parliamentary democracy. A society founded upon such principles is portrayed as the good society which works for the benefit of all. In practice, what these beliefs and values do, according to Marx, is to justify the wealth and power of the bourgeoisie who are seen as having legitimately earned them in the competition of life in which we all have an equal chance. But freedom, equality and democracy are all seen as a sham so long as the ruling class owns the means by which the masses earn their living. While the exceptional few might be able to climb the social ladder, the great majority are exploited and oppressed, and the bourgeoisie is able to maintain its economic power over time by means of inheritance.

Religion, although not as important as in the feudal world, also makes its contribution to the bourgeois world view. Protestantism emphasises individuality, and (in some sects at least) views worldly success as a sign of God's grace; while at the same time, as with mediaeval religion, it reconciles the exploited to their sufferings by telling them that it is God's will and that their reward will be in Heaven. Art and religion also play their part by reinforcing such bourgeois virtues as individuality, freedom and the accumulation of property. Thus, all the elements of the superstructure operate in the interests of the ruling class and consequently are a direct reflection of the socio-economic organisation of society.

The dynamics of social change

These brief and simplified sketches of feudal and capitalist societies pose an obvious question as to how, if the ruling class is so solidly entrenched, one type of society can ever change into another. It is clear from the principle that base determines superstructure that, for Marx, it is social and economic forces that bring about historical change. Great events, such as the Reformation or the French Revolution, do not come about because of changes in people's ideas or because of the actions of great individuals. These are merely the surface manifestations of much deeper substructural changes.

Marx's theory of the basic dynamics of historical change is built around four interconnected ideas: economic development, class conflict, the dialectic and revolution. Each mode of production, Marx believed, had its own inner logic of development. Economies change and develop over time through technological innovation, new financial techniques or growing trade and prosperity. Such developments give rise to strains and contradictions within the system; a new kind of production evolves along with a new class to exploit it. Eventually, the old structure of society can no longer contain these new developments, and the new class challenges the old ruling class for supremacy. All the contradictions and conflicts can only be resolved by a revolution, since the old ruling class will cling on to its power by any means. But once the revolution is complete, the new ruling class will transform society in accordance with its own mode of production and its own ideology.

This intricate mechanism of change was supposed to explain how the various stages of human development evolved into each other, although Marx only applied it consistently to the latter part of the sequence. Before there was any settled civilisation, societies were characterised, Marx believed, by a primitive communism, where all property was the property of the tribe. When people settled down and created the first civilisation proper, something of this early communal ownership was retained in village life, although the surplus was paid as tribute to a despotic state which organised great public works to irrigate or defend the land. Marx called this the 'Asiatic' mode of production, since it had persisted in Asia while other parts of the world had moved on to later stages of development. The Asiatic mode is succeeded by the 'Classical' mode, which is an economic system based on slavery. This in turn gives way to the feudal mode, which is eventually succeeded by the capitalist or bourgeois mode.

Marx paid particular attention to the transition from feudalism to capitalism. The development of the feudal economy led to a growth in trade, and with trade came towns and, eventually, a new class of merchants, the bourgeoisie. Urban life and the new middle class did not fit well into the feudal social structure. This became increasingly true as the bourgeoisie grew ever more rich on domestic trade, foreign ventures and eventually capitalist finance of industry (for example the 'domestic system' of wool manufacture). The feudal system became more and more of a restriction of the development of the capitalist economy, and this contradiction could only be resolved in a new kind of society. The bourgeoisie, whose wealth had come to outstrip that of the feudal aristocracy, eventually came to challenge the power of the old ruling class.

How the bourgeoisie came to take over as the new ruling class varied from country to country. In England it was through the Civil Wars of the seventeenth century, while in France it was through the most spectacular of all social upheavals, the French Revolution. In each case, revolution was followed by a transformation of society: feudal restrictions and feudal relationships were swept aside; new science and new technologies were inspired by industry and commerce; feudal agriculture was replaced by commercial farming. The old mediaeval view of the world was replaced by new ideas that were scientific and secular; new art and literature began to flourish; new ideas of liberty and constitutional government began to be advocated.

The capitalist world is not the end of the historical process. By following the dynamic of historical development to its logical conclusion, Marx believed that the transformation of the capitalist stage into one further and final stage, communism, could be predicted. It would necessarily be the final stage since it would resolve all conflicts and contradictions yet synthesise the best in all previous societies. To understand why Marx thought that this ultimate outcome was inevitable it is necessary to look more closely at his analysis of capitalism.

Capitalism, revolution and human nature

The capitalist system developed through a number of phases and over a number of centuries before reaching modern industrial capitalism. It was only as this phase was beginning that the theory of how capitalism worked emerged, through the classical economics of Adam Smith and his followers. They were writing at a time when capitalist enterprise was creating the Industrial Revolution, which transformed Britain and would eventually change the entire world.

Marxist economics

Marx admired the classical economists, but believed that their economic laws only applied to a temporary phase of human development, and that as time went on the free market would bring only increasing misery to the majority. He adopted some of their ideas and used them to develop an entirely different theory of his own. The main idea Marx borrowed was the 'labour theory of value', which is an answer to the problem of what determines the value of any object. The theory argues that it is the amount of labour that has gone into producing the object that determines how valuable it is; the more labour has been expended on making or extracting the object the more valuable it will be. This value is a fixed quantity and is different from the price at which it can be bought, which can fluctuate according to the market. (When we think an object in a shop is 'overpriced' or 'underpriced' we are making an unconscious distinction between its price and its value. However, modern economics assumes that the price and value are the same thing.)

In the capitalist economy the workers produce all the wealth and yet remain poor, while the capitalist's wealth grows. Marx used the labour theory of value to explain how this comes about. The workers generate value by turning raw materials into finished products, but only receive a fraction of this value back in the form of wages; the rest, what Marx called 'surplus value', goes to the capitalist as profit. Because he controls the means of production, the capitalist can buy labour cheaply with just enough wages to live on, while keeping most of what that labour has earned for himself. The capitalist, therefore, exploits the workers, and the more he can exploit them the more successful he will be. According to Marx, the capitalist himself adds nothing to the process of value-creation, and so the capitalist class as such is entirely parasitic.

The capitalist, however, has his own problems. Unlike the feudal lord, he must compete. The capitalist economy is based on competition. The capitalist must constantly strive to better his rivals by producing more goods at lower cost. This can be done in two ways: first, by new and better machinery which increases the value-creating power of the worker; and second, by reducing the worker's wages. There is constant pressure on the capitalist to exploit his workers more and more, to extract ever greater quantities of surplus value.

This fierce competition inevitably produces winners and losers: the stronger capitalists flourish while the weaker ones go out of business. Thus, the capitalist class grows smaller and richer, while the proletariat grows larger and more wretched.

This is the natural tendency of capitalism, although the process is not smooth or continuous. By the time Marx was writing, the 'trade cycle' had become a recognised feature of economic life. This was the regular progression of boom and slump, of rapid growth and sudden collapse of industrial production. Marx explained the trade cycle in terms of what he believed was the most fundamental contradiction of capitalism.

On the one hand, he argued, there was ever greater production of goods based on ever greater exploitation of the worker, while on the other hand, that same exploitation reduced the worker's ability to buy the goods produced. Consequently, there is always a tendency in capitalism to overproduce, for production to outstrip demand. When this happens, goods go unsold and so workers are laid off and factories close, which reduces demand still further and so more factories close, and so on until the whole economy collapses. There is widespread unemployment and distress, and wages are forced lower and lower. Eventually, wages will be so low that some capitalists will find it profitable to start production again, demand will increase and the economy will begin to recover. But the slump will have driven some capitalists out of business, and only the stronger ones will be left to take advantage of the recovery. With each slump the capitalist class grows smaller as the working class grows larger and suffers more.

The inevitable collapse of capitalism

Marx believed that each successive boom would develop faster and higher, and each successive slump would be deeper and more catastrophic than the last. Eventually the slump would be so great that the impoverished working class would be forced by sheer necessity to overthrow capitalism and establish a worker's state. Thus, the capitalist system is driven to destruction by its own nature, by the working out of its own inner logic.

It is a peculiarity of the capitalist system, Marx thought, that it must train its future destroyer. Unlike other modes of production, industrial capitalism must concentrate its workforce (in factories and workshops) and teach it discipline and mutual dependence. In these circumstances the proletariat has the opportunity to organise and achieve a common understanding of its own experience and what needs to be done; in other words to achieve what Marx called 'class consciousness'.

The progressive enmiseration of the proletariat forces it to see its own situation clearly, undistorted by bourgeois ideology. It will see that capitalist society cannot survive, that the proletariat can and must itself take over the means of production, and dispense with the capitalists whose role in production is unnecessary and parasitic. In short, the working class will come to realise (assisted by intellectuals like Marx and Engels who defect to the proletarian cause) that communism is the true outlook of the working class, and the only hope for the future of humanity. Thus, when the revolution does come the workers will understand what their historical task will be, which is not only to seize control of the means of production and the instruments of the state, but to go on to build a communist society.

Marx believed that the communist revolution was inevitable. Capitalism could not be reformed, nor the lot of the worker permanently improved. Capitalists cannot change their ways, but must go on increasing exploitation or cease to be capitalists; in this sense they are as much victims of the system as anyone else. The dynamic of capitalist development was so powerful, and its internal contradictions so fundamental, that it must eventually drive itself to destruction. Marx insisted that only through a violent revolution and creation of a communist society could all these contradictions be finally resolved.

Revolution and the dictatorship of the proletariat

Marx believed that the communist revolution would only come when capitalism had reached the full peak of its development. Consequently, he looked to see the revolution begin in the industrially advanced West, above all in Britain (although he was less certain of this towards the end of his life). But wherever it began it would be a worldwide revolution, because one of the unique features of capitalism was its capacity – through trade and the exploitation of colonies – to bring the whole world within its network. Marx thought that nationalism was an aspect of bourgeois ideology, whereas proletarian class consciousness was truly international: that is, workers had more in common with fellow workers in other countries than with their own bourgeoisie. When the communist revolution began in one country, therefore, it would quickly spread to others and eventually the whole world, so that the whole of humanity would be emancipated together.

However, Marx did not believe that the communist revolution would be immediately followed by the establishment of the communist society. There would have to be a transitional period, which Marx called the 'dictatorship of the proletariat', in which the workers would be in control. The state and its instruments would still be the means by which the ruling class overtly maintains its domination, only now the ruling class would be the workers, the majority. The dictatorship of the proletariat has two tasks. The first is to preserve and extend the revolution. The second is to prepare the way for the ultimate stage of human history, the establishment of the classless, stateless communist society, the kind of society appropriate for human nature.

Human nature and alienation

Marx was very suspicious of theories about essential human nature, especially where they appeared to set limits to what was socially and politically possible (for example by depicting human beings as essentially selfish, aggressive and competitive). He believed that human nature expressed itself in different ways in different epochs. In particular, he saw the creation of communist society as involving a transformation of human nature. However, despite his disclaimers, Marx did have a theory of human nature that underlay its transformations.

For Marx the most crucial feature of humanity, that which distinguished the human being from all other animals, was the capacity to produce. Through social labour, both physical and mental, human beings can make the things they need and build their own world, a world of artefacts and organisations and of ideas. Human needs and the ability to fulfil them develop over the centuries, and they develop socially. Human sociability, the need for the shared life of the community, is another crucial feature of essential human nature, though not unique to the species.

The development of human needs, capacities and social organisation through history has been achieved only at huge cost to the majority of individuals. The price mankind has paid for progress has involved immense exploitation and suffering, the denial of natural human sociability through class differences and conflicts, and the warping of the natural creative labour of individuals into the narrow channel of producing goods mainly for the profit of others. As a consequence, instead of humanity enjoying the world it has created, it is oppressed by it.

In an early unpublished work, known as the *Paris Manuscripts* of 1844 (which only came to light in Russia in the 1920s), Marx described mankind in this oppressed condition as being in a state of 'alienation'. This is a rather strange metaphysical concept which Marx adapted from Hegel. It roughly means that a person's inner self is divided so that they are alienated or estranged from the world, from their fellow human beings and from themselves. This fragmentation and distortion of human personality was, Marx believed, a condition of all societies based on property and class division, but it was at its most severe under capitalism, where human beings are most exploited and where labour is reduced to mindless drudgery. Only in a communist society will alienation cease, will human beings recognise and be at home in their own creation, and will mankind's fragmented self be restored to wholeness.

Communist society

What, then, will communist society be like? Marx was decidedly vague about this and deliberately so, insisting that communist society was not some utopian blueprint that people must aspire to but the actual society that they would build as they thought best. However, some general features can be given. It will be a world without class divisions and without private property; there will be no more poverty or wealth. It will be a world without the state, at least as we have known it, since Marx sees the state as an instrument of class oppression, so that in a classless society the state will, in Engels' phrase, 'wither away'. For the same reason there will be no more ideology, no more distorted perception, and people will see the world as it really is.

It will also be a world of abundance. Capitalism has taught mankind the secrets of production, and once production is designed to meet human needs and not the need for profit there will be more than enough for all. Consequently, society can be organised on the principle of 'from each according to his ability, to each according to his need'. In other words, everyone will contribute to society according to their talents and capacities, and all will take whatever they need from the common stock.

In this society every individual will be able to develop all their talents – physical, intellectual and creative – to the full. In a famous passage Marx wrote:

> In communist society, where nobody has one exclusive sphere of activity but each can become accomplished in any branch he wishes, society regulates the general production and thus makes it possible for me to do one thing today and another tomorrow, to hunt in the morning, fish in the afternoon, rear cattle in the evening, criticise after dinner, just as I have a mind, without ever becoming hunter, fisherman, shepherd or critic.
>
> (*The German Ideology*, 1845–46, in McLellan, 1977, p.169)

This is perhaps a little fanciful, but it does emphasise Marx's insistence on the all-round development of every individual instead of people being restricted to one job. He foresaw a society in which 'the free development of each is the condition for the free development of all' (in McLellan, 1977, p.169).

Marx believed that many of the divisions in life that we take for granted will have no significance in a future society: the division between the individual and society, between intellectual work and physical work, between town life and country life, and so on. Finally, Marx did not believe that history would come to an end in a kind of static perfection, but merely that all that oppresses and distorts human nature would be thrown off. Indeed, with humanity at last becoming master of its own destiny, genuine human history could really begin.

It should be clear that Marx's ideal was a fully free and creative humanity, which is very far from the totalitarian communism of the twentieth century. But before considering the later development of Marxism, it will be useful to pause and examine some of the objections to Marxism in its original form.

Objections to Marx's theories

A great many objections to some or all of Marx's ideas have been put forward, some of which are telling and perhaps fatal.

False predictions

The first and obvious point is that Marx's predictions concerning the future development of capitalism have proved false, at least in the short run. In fact, exactly the opposite has happened. Instead of shrinking, the middle classes have expanded and diversified with ever greater ownership of capital. At the same time, the working class has become progressively more prosperous, has gained considerable political power, and in the second half of the twentieth century has steadily diminished in size. Furthermore, capitalist society has reformed itself in a manner Marx could not have conceived, with the welfare state and intervention in the economy. Finally, Marxist-inspired revolutions have only occurred in undeveloped countries, while the most developed states seem the least likely to follow a revolutionary road.

Although Marxists still believe that capitalism will, eventually, collapse under the weight of its own contradictions, they do have to keep adapting their theory to explain away the world's persistent refusal to conform to Marx's projections. This undermines the plausibility of the original theory and calls into question the scientific status it claims to have. Indeed, it has been pointed out (most notably by Karl Popper) that the way Marxist theory is freely adapted to explain any circumstance whatever, means that it cannot be tested against experience. We cannot say what would have to happen to prove it wrong (as finding a metal that shrinks when heated would disprove the law that all metals expand when heated) because it can always explain whatever happens.

Determinism and free will

Another problem is that of determinism. Marx and Engels insisted that their work was thoroughly scientific, and their conception of science was entirely positivist. This means that the social sciences must be like the physical sciences, such as physics, and so based on the assumption that everything that happens, including all human behaviour, is causally determined according to laws of nature. This is a view that has been widely held by social scientists, especially in the nineteenth and early twentieth centuries. However, it has come in for strong criticism. This is mainly because the consequence of this view is that we have no responsibility for our actions, that our belief in our own free will is an illusion, and that human being are little better than sophisticated robots.

Positivism means that everything we do and everything that has ever happened in history had to happen the way it did by necessity and could not have happened in any other way. In fact Marx, unlike Engels, is rather ambiguous about this and does sometimes talk as though human beings do have genuine freedom to choose their actions. Marx may have thought that individual freedom was compatible with historical necessity and natural laws governing the way society behaves (a view known as 'compatibilism'). Nevertheless, the whole thrust of his theory is thoroughly deterministic: necessary stages of history, base determining superstructure, the inevitable collapse of capitalism, and so on. Now if people also have free will then they must be capable of behaving in ways that prevent anything being inevitable. If, on the other hand, there is strict determinism in human affairs then there is something peculiar about the idea that after the revolution we will be free, and that at last mankind will control its own destiny. There is also something odd about writing books to persuade people to work for the revolutionary cause if it all has to happen anyway.

Positivist social science has come in for a great deal of general criticism in recent decades. Reasons for this include the fact that no social scientist has ever come up with an empirical law of social behaviour that can be tested; and second, human actions involve the actor having an understanding of what they are doing, an understanding that cannot be analysed in terms of cause and effect. Human beings simply cannot be predicted in the way that physical objects can, and therefore the future course of human history cannot be predicted either.

A further aspect of determinism that is particularly important is Marx's insistence that social conditions determine consciousness and not the other way round. In other words, our ideas and beliefs are determined (and not merely influenced) by our social background. But it is a commonplace that people of the same social background, and even the same family, often have different ideas and beliefs. And it could hardly be said that the ideas of Marx and Engels were a product of their social backgrounds. Furthermore, if social conditions do determine ideas and beliefs then it is difficult to make sense of Marx's theory of false consciousness, which requires that the exploited class have their ideas and beliefs dictated to them by the ruling class.

Dialectics and history

The scientific status of the dialectic is also dubious. Very few non-Marxists take the dialectic seriously, either as a system of logic or as an explanation of historical development, and least of all as a means of analysing the physical world. It adds nothing to our understanding of historical conflicts to say that they are the result of 'contradictions', or that a resolution of a conflict is a synthesis. The application of such terms is entirely arbitrary. Engels attempted to systematise the dialectic and apply it to the physical world in his book *The Dialectics of Nature*, but produced nothing that would help any scientist to better understand any aspect of nature. To regard ice as the thesis, water as the antithesis and steam as the synthesis tells us nothing whatsoever.

The dialectic is principally an aspect of Marx's theory of historical change. Engels once said that just as Darwin had discovered the law of evolution in organic nature, Marx had discovered the law of evolution in human history. In fact Marx never applied his theory consistently, and there are many instances where it is difficult to see how he could. To take just one example, the end of the classical world was nothing to do with the operation of the dialectic, or with economic development, or with a new class leading a revolution against the old. The classical world collapsed under the impact of the Barbarian invasions, which are impossible to fit into Marx's scheme. Indeed, it takes an immense amount of ingenuity to explain all significant historical change in terms of socio-economic developments. Looking at the sheer variety of human existence, the idea that social development can be summed up in four stages between a doubtful primitive communism and a shadowy future communism is not really very plausible.

These are just some of the objections to Marxism that have been put forward at various times. Needless to say, Marxists have developed a large and elaborate set of counter-arguments, some of which will be discussed in the next section.

Revision and revolution

Marx did not confine himself to thinking and writing, but was actively engaged in fostering working-class movements. In 1864 he was closely involved in setting up the International Working Men's Association (known as the First International) and although this was by no means a Marxist organisation, Marx personally dominated it until its collapse in 1872 (see Chapter 5). Meanwhile, Marxist groups and parties were being set up in various countries, and although Marx's ideas made little impact in Britain they were widely influential in continental Europe, especially in Germany. The major German workers' party was the German Social Democratic Party (SPD) which was fully committed to Marxism. It looked to Marx for advice and guidance, a role taken over by Engels after Marx died.

Bernstein and revisionism

However, after Engels died in 1895 there was no longer an authoritative voice to whom all could defer for the correct interpretation of Marx's ideas and strategy. As a result the Marxist movement began to fragment. The first major division was in the SPD over what is known as the 'revisionist controversy'.

This arose from the writings of one of the party's leading figures, Edward Bernstein (1850–1932). He was a pillar of orthodoxy and close to Engels, but after the SPD was banned in 1878, Bernstein spent more than twenty years in exile, mostly in Britain. He initially took the Engels line that the party should pursue parliamentary tactics and legislation as a means of keeping it together against the day when conditions were ready for revolution, but that whatever gains were made could not be permanent or ultimately important. Bernstein came to reject this and argued that gains for the working class were real and that so long as the working class was properly represented (the ban on the party was effectively lifted in 1890) then a revolution was unnecessary. He set out his ideas in his main book, *The Preconditions of Socialism* of 1899 (also translated as *Evolutionary Socialism*).

Bernstein argued that Marx was essentially a social scientist who had discovered an important way of analysing society, and who had, on the basis of his analysis, identified certain trends, made certain predictions and devised a certain programme of action. But the world had not worked out the way Marx had expected: the bourgeoisie was growing instead of shrinking, while the working class was becoming more prosperous and more politically powerful. The good Marxist social scientist should, therefore, reassess the situation in the light of this new evidence and modify his predictions and his programme of action accordingly. Thus, Bernstein believed that the SPD should abandon its doctrine of the inevitability of communist revolution and its programme of working towards it. Instead it should adopt a doctrine of 'evolutionary social-ism' and a programme of working towards socialism through parliamentary means.

Democracy and freedom and civil rights were not, Bernstein insisted, to be dismissed as 'bourgeois values' of no significance to the working class, but were genuine gains and necessary features of a civilised society. Given democratic procedures, steady progress could be made in creating a better society for all. It was absurd to put faith in a single giant leap into a perfect world. In democratic circumstances it would be immoral and terroristic to violently overthrow the government and expropriate everyone's property. Socialism could and should be achieved by evolutionary and democratic means.

Orthodox Marxists were horrified by Bernstein's attempt to 'revise' Marx (hence the term 'revisionism', which became a term of abuse in the Marxist vocabulary roughly equivalent to 'heresy' in religion). The 'revisionist debates' were fierce and bitter, but the final outcome was in fact a compromise. The doctrine and the official programme of the party was not changed, while the actual policies on which it fought elections were more in line with Bernstein's views than with orthodox Marxism.

Bernstein became more and more critical of Marx. His ideas would eventu-ally triumph in 1959 when the party finally abandoned its commitment to Marxism at its conference at Bad Godesberg. However, in 1914 the controversy was still smouldering when the First World War broke out. Both Bernstein and the orthodox leaders argued that this was a capitalist war which the workers should refuse to fight. But a wave of nationalist feeling gripped the working class and the movement's leaders were ignored. By the time the war was over, the attention of world Marxism had shifted to Moscow.

Lenin and the vanguard party

Towards the end of the nineteenth century a Marxist party, the Russian Social Democratic Party (RSDP), was established in Russia and began to recruit among the comparatively small industrial workforce. But unlike the German SPD it was not legal, and so was hounded by the Tzarist police, its leaders lived in exile, and its effectiveness in organising and supporting the working class was small. This was the party that Lenin (real name Vladimir Illyich Ulyanov) joined as a student in St Petersburg. There was already a strong revolutionary tradition in Russia before Marxism arrived, and Lenin was already a revolutionary before he became a Marxist (his elder brother had been executed for involvement in a plot to assassinate the Tzar).

Lenin's zeal and organising ability soon made him a leading figure in the party and led to his exile. As time went on Lenin became increasingly disillusioned with the RSDP and became convinced that its whole programme and strategy were wrong. The leadership was fatalistic about the possibilities of revolution, believing that Russia must first pass through a long capitalist phase before it was ripe for revolution, which would in any case first begin elsewhere. Lenin disagreed and insisted that the party should work for revolution in Russia as soon as possible, irrespective of what was happening in other countries.

He also disagreed with the strategy of building a mass party on the model of the German SPD. The conditions in Russia were just not the same, the party being illegal, wide open to police penetration and largely restricted to backing worker's demands for better pay and conditions. Lenin's alternative was set out in his most important work, *What is to Be Done?* (1902). In this he argued that left to its own devices the working class would only develop what he called 'trade union consciousness' and not the necessary 'revolutionary consciousness'. What the workers needed was leadership from a new type of party which did possess the necessary revolutionary consciousness, plus the theory and tactics to go with it.

Lenin proposed, therefore, the creation of a small party of dedicated professional revolutionaries, trained in revolutionary activity and thoroughly grounded in Marxist theory. The organisation of the party would be based on the principle of 'democratic centralism'. That is, open discussion and opinion passing up through the hierarchy, but once a decision has been made at the top it must be rigidly enforced throughout the party. This new party would be the 'vanguard of the proletariat', meaning that it is not separate from the working class, but is its elite, the most class-conscious part of it. Lenin also insisted that whatever was done to further the revolutionary cause was justified, no matter how immoral it might seem. In other words, the end justifies the means.

Lenin's ideas split the leadership of the RSDP, and his faction broke away to form their own party that came to be called the 'Bolshevics'. The party he left came to be known as the 'Menshevics'. Some sympathised with Lenin's belief in working for an immediate revolution but could not stomach his dictatorial leadership, most notably Leon Trotsky, who had an independent reputation as a writer and revolutionary, although he returned to the Bolshevics after the Revolution broke out.

The theory of capitalist imperialism

Lenin's second major contribution to Marxist theory dealt with the problem of Marx's predictions. His solution is suggested in his main work on the subject: *Imperialism, the Highest Stage of Capitalism* (1916). The late nineteenth century was the period when the major powers competed to carve up Africa and other uncolonised parts of the world. Lenin argued that this process constituted a higher stage of capitalism which Marx could not have foreseen. Capitalism increasingly exploits the undeveloped part of the world and uses part of the profits to 'buy off' the domestic working class with a higher standard of living and state welfare. The exploited masses of the colonial world were thus the new proletariat. The First World War was essentially a war for colonial possessions, so that the capitalists of the winning country could extend their exploitation and profits. Consequently, the communist revolution would not necessarily take place in the advanced West.

The country that was in fact particularly ripe for revolution, Lenin argued, was Russia. It was not economically advanced, but then the workers had not been bought off, and its industry, largely financed by foreign capital, was the 'weakest link' in the chain of capitalist imperialism. A revolution in Russia would begin the process which would spread to the rest of the world and bring the whole system crashing down.

In February 1917 the Tzarist regime collapsed under the strain of the First World War, and shortly afterwards Lenin's Bolshevics, joined by Trotsky, seized power in November (October according to the old Russian calendar that was then still in use, hence the 'October Revolution'). Once in power Lenin suppressed all opposition parties and encouraged the peasants and workers to seize the land and the factories. Despite civil war and foreign intervention the Soviet Union had been established by the time Lenin died in 1924.

Marxism-Leninism

It was Lenin's particular interpretation and extensions of Marx's theory, known as Marxism-Leninism, that became the official doctrine of the Soviet Union and of all subsequent communist regimes (although sometimes with native additions, as in China). It is the version of Marxism that we know as 'communism' and became the only orthodox version until the 1960s. Its reputation as the only authentic Marxism was simply a result of Lenin's success. It was also reinforced by Lenin's creation of the Communist International (known as the 'Comintern') in 1920, which he dominated, insisting that all member parties adopt his doctrines and his system of party organisation, as well as recognising Soviet leadership.

Marxism-Leninism is in fact a rather crude version of Marxism, relying on Marx's later works and especially Engels' popular expositions. For one thing, it is very mechanical, putting great stress on economic determinism. Democratic centralism is extended from a principle of party organisation, where it amounts to rigid control from the top, to a principle of social organisation with party control of every significant social organisation and any kind of opposition is suppressed. Thus, Article 6 of the Soviet Constitution read:

> The leading and guiding force of Soviet society and the nucleus of its political system, of all state organisations and public organisations, is the Communist Party of the Soviet Union. The CPSU exists for the people and serves the people.
>
> The Communist Party, armed with Marxism-Leninism, determines the general perspectives of the development of society and the course of the home and foreign policy of the USSR, directs the great constructive work of the Soviet people, and imparts a planned, systematic and theoretically substantiated character to their struggle for the victory of communism.

All other communist regimes had similar clauses in their constitutions, producing totalitarian one-party states.

The justification of this in Marxist terms is based on Marx's theory of the 'dictatorship of the proletariat', which was seen as the temporary phase of working-class rule prior to full communism. Since, in Lenin's theory, the party *is* the proletariat, its vanguard, the party has the right to rule on behalf of the rest of the workers. Various justifications were also offered on democratic grounds. It was said that multi-party systems reflected class divisions, which did not exist in communist countries, and that the Communist Party could alone represent the interests of the people. It was because of arguments like this that communist regimes styled themselves 'people's democracies', as distinct from liberal democracies which were dismissed as a sham because the people had no real power.

On the other hand, while communist regimes claimed to be 'worker's states', they saw themselves as being a long way from achieving a communist society. When Lenin seized power in 1917 he was convinced that his revolution could not succeed unless the workers of other countries followed the Russian lead. This, of course, did not happen. In Marxist terms all communist states are stuck in the transitional phase of the dictatorship of the proletariat (which Marxists, rather confusingly, sometimes refer to as 'socialism' as distinct from the final phase of 'communism') and must maintain a powerful state so long as they are surrounded by hostile capitalist states. Only when the rest of the world has its revolution and catches up can mankind progress together towards a truly communist society.

Lenin's theory of the vanguard party still dominates wherever communist regimes remain. But at least since the 1960s it has been criticised as a distortion of Marxism by many Marxists in the West. The theory of imperialism, however, retains its appeal for all Marxists since it overcomes objections based on Marx's failed predictions. It is still widely adhered to despite the ending of Western colonialism after the Second World War. The argument is that although overt political control may have gone, the Third World is still dominated and exploited by the capitalist West, only now through more subtle economic means.

The communist world after Lenin

Following the death of Lenin early in 1924 there was a struggle for power in the CPSU. Trotsky was the obvious successor, but he was outmanoeuvred by the party secretary, Joseph Stalin, and in 1929 was forced into permanent exile. Thereafter, Stalin rapidly established himself as the supreme ruler of Soviet Russia.

Stalinism

Through a series of 'show trials' and executions, Stalin virtually wiped out the old Bolshevic party and created a new party in his own image. He ruled through terror, as a result of which millions of people died in labour camps or were executed. Whole nationalities were liquidated. The leading people in every walk of life were frequently 'purged' to eliminate anyone even suspected of dissent, with those that were left reduced to grovelling subservience. The history of the October Revolution was rewritten to give Stalin a more prominent place, and he was presented as the benevolent father of the nation. The Soviet people were taught to revere him almost as a god, and his portrait was everywhere (a process that became known as the 'cult of personality').

Stalin's policies were summed up in the slogan 'socialism in one country'. This meant concentrating on building up the Soviet Union as a great fortress against a hostile capitalist world, rather than the promotion of world revolution. Stalin was very much a nationalist leader who encouraged patriotism and sought to make the USSR a great power. He was happy to encourage subversion in other countries, but only as a means of promoting Soviet interests; he was quite prepared to abandon fellow communists if it suited him.

At home his first priority was industrialisation, undertaken through a series of 'five-year plans' beginning in 1928, and which eliminated what was left of free enterprise overnight. This was soon followed by the 'collectivisation' of agriculture, enforced with great brutality. A whole class of well-off peasants, the 'kulaks', were declared to be enemies of the state and were wiped out; millions were allowed to starve to death while grain was exported to pay for industrialisation. To ensure that his policies were carried out, Stalin created a gigantic bureaucracy which, along with the secret police, came to control Soviet society in minute detail. By these means, the Soviet union was turned from essentially a peasant nation to a major industrial power; and by the time of Stalin's death in 1953, one of the world's two 'superpowers'.

Trotskyism

The outstanding communist critic of Stalin was Leon Trotsky (1879–1940). After his expulsion from the Soviet Union in 1929 he devoted himself to writing historical works on the Russian Revolution, commenting on world affairs and analysing Stalinism. He lived in several countries before settling in Mexico, where he was murdered in 1940 by one of Stalin's agents.

Trotsky's main contribution to Marxist ideas was his theory of 'permanent revolution', which he began to elaborate as early as 1904. He argued that the Russian bourgeoisie was so small and weak and dependent on foreign capital that it could not carry through and sustain a bourgeois revolution on its own, as had happened in the French Revolution. What would have to happen, therefore, was that the bourgeoisie would need the assistance of the proletariat; but once the revolution was under way the working class would have to keep going until it had created a dictatorship of the proletariat. In other words, the bourgeois and communist revolutions would be telescoped into one, and this would stimulate proletarian revolutions in the rest of the world. Though at first rejecting it, Lenin came to adopt this theory by 1917, and the events of that year were seen as a vindication of it.

Later in exile, Trotsky developed the theory further. He believed that in the underdeveloped world, small and heavily exploited proletariats would be the force behind nationalist revolutions to rid their countries of capitalist imperialism. But, as in Russia, they would not be content with bourgeois democracy but would establish worker's dictatorships. Their success would throw the advanced world into crisis and create conditions for communist revolution there. The process would not cease until the whole world was under proletarian control, and the movement towards true communism could begin.

Trotsky consistently argued that the primary task of the Soviet Union was to stimulate and aid this process. But Stalin had betrayed the revolution, creating a 'degenerate worker's state' (or 'state capitalism' as Trotsky's followers called it) in which the Party and a vast new bureaucracy had become the ruling class that also needed to be overthrown.

By the 1950s, many revolutionary socialists shared the general revulsion against Stalin and the system he bequeathed, but there was still Trotsky's ideas to keep alive the idealism of the early Bolshevics. Trotskyite groups provided an alternative to the traditional pro-Soviet Communist Parties (CPs) in many Western countries, although they have been prone to faction and split over differences of the 'correct' analysis and tactics.

Trotsky's most famous tactical suggestion for his followers in the West was 'entryism'. That is, not attempting to change CPs, but secretly penetrating mass social democratic parties to win recruits and eventually control. In Britain only the Militant Tendency systematically pursued this tactic until driven from the Labour Party in the late 1980s. But whatever their tactics, all such groups follow Trotsky in refusing to contemplate any suggestion that Stalinism was inherent in the ideas of Lenin. Trotsky had, perhaps, a rather romantic idea of the revolutionary potential of the working class and its expression in the pure bolshevism of 1917. He believed absolutely in the Bolshevic's rather crude Marxism and in the concept of the 'vanguard party'. He saw himself as the true heir of Marxism-Leninism. However, despite his standing, none of the extensions of the communist world since 1945 have been inspired by Trotskyism.

The spread of communism

The Second World War left the Soviet Union with a huge empire in Eastern Europe which had been liberated from Nazi rule by the Red Army. Two other communist states existed by this time in Yugoslavia and Albania. These had achieved their own liberation under partisan leaders, Tito and Enver Hoxa respectively. They were therefore less inclined to take orders from Moscow and soon fell out with Stalin. Albania was, however, to remain true to Stalin's legacy and become the most oppressive regime in Europe, accusing Stalin's Soviet successors of 'revisionism'.

Meanwhile in 1949 another major extension of communism occurred when the Chinese communists, led by Mao Tse Tung, took over the country following a civil war. The Soviet Union was initially friendly and helpful, but this soon turned to hostility and remained so thereafter. By the time of Stalin's death in 1953, the communist world had grown considerably, but it was not the monolithic Moscow-dominated bloc he had wished for. In particular, China had become a rival centre of communist orthodoxy.

Over the next twenty-five years communists came to power in several new parts of the world, including parts of Africa, Arabia, Indo-China, South America and the Caribbean. None of these were dominated in the way Eastern Europe was dominated by the Soviet Union, and many regimes were as nationalist as much as they were communist. The result was a communist world that was complex and various, with China and the Soviet Union competing for the allegiance of new communist regimes.

Mao Tse Tung

Mao Tse Tung was a Marxist-Leninist, but with significant variations of his own. Soviet communism is built on the proletariat in orthodox Marxist manner; but in China the proletariat played no part in the revolution and Chinese communism was built upon the peasantry. Instead of the Soviet policy of industrialisation at all costs, Mao put much more emphasis on agriculture, upon the revolutionising of consciousness (that is 'cultural revolution'), and upon the community. Although Mao did attempt a sudden dash for industrialisation in the 1950s, known as the 'Great Leap Forward', it was with disastrous economic consequences.

In his writings, Mao was hostile to the Soviet belief that the party had to be omniscient and infallible, and that the 'correct course' had to be imposed on the masses from above. He wrote of his great faith in the wisdom of the masses, and argued that the party is prone to error and must learn from the masses (although how far this did or could happen in practice must be doubted). Mao's China was in fact as totalitarian as the USSR. Nevertheless, it had more appeal to Western youth in the period of the New Left than its Soviet counterpart.

The New Left and after

Following the success of the Bolshevic revolution it was inevitable that Marxists all over the world should look to Moscow for leadership, both political and theoretical. There were some Marxist thinkers in the West who took an independent line, but for most people Soviet communism *was* Marxism. However, the horrors of Stalinism eventually led to a reaction, and the work of some of these independent thinkers became important. In the 1950s and 1960s a variety of new Marxisms flourished in the West. The Soviet version seemed moribund and discredited, having been used for too long to justify a monstrous regime.

Neo-Marxism

Inspiration for much of the new thinking came from Marx's earlier writings, which had not been published and which had only recently became available (particularly the *Paris Manuscripts* of 1844, only discovered in the twentieth century and not widely available until the 1950s). These revealed a 'new', more humanistic Marx, preoccupied with human alienation, the fragmentation of human existence and the need for liberation. They provided the basis of a fresh interpretation of Marxism that is sometimes referred to as 'neo-Marxism'.

The significance of these early ideas had been suggested by a group of German thinkers, including Max Horkheimer, Theodore Adorno and Herbert Marcuse, and known as the Frankfurt School. They had been attempting to take a fresh approach to Marx since the 1930s. They began with the conviction that Marx's thought had been distorted by Engels and the Marxist-Leninists, who put too much emphasis on economic determinism, and that Marx himself had been too influenced by positivism in his later years.

More important, they thought, was Marx's analysis of consciousness, and his discussion of human nature and the distorting effects of modern society upon it. They were particularly interested in the relationship between the concept of alienation and modern psychological theories, such as psycho-analysis. Their style of thought is known as 'critical theory', reflecting their aspiration to create a form of Marxist analysis that would reveal the true oppressive nature of modern society, but not based on political economy or class analysis.

When these ideas began to circulate more widely from the mid-1950s onwards they struck a chord, especially among the young. They came at a time when there was not only disillusionment with orthodox communism, but also a certain disillusionment with the prosperous materialist West. This sparked off a wave of new theorising which linked Marxism with the ideas of Freud and Wilhelm Reich, with existentialism, phenomenology, black nationalism, 'anti-psychiatry', and with other bodies of thought and social movements.

The critique of society

These ideas, together with the movements they inspired (above all, the student protest movement of the 1960s) came to be known collectively as the New Left. This was an international movement, though there was little national or international organisation and no fixed body of doctrine common to all. It was all highly anti-authoritarian and displayed a strong anarchist strain (see Chapter 6).

One major theme was that modern society, both East and West, was bureau-cratic, oppressive and alienating. There was no thought of waiting for capital-ism to collapse under the weight of its own contradictions; mankind must be liberated immediately through a transformation of consciousness. Thus, in New Left theory economics was largely ignored in favour of the psychology of oppression and liberation, and the critique and analysis of culture.

A major aspect of social oppression was deemed to be sexual oppression, hence the influence of Sigmund Freud's works, together with those of his more radical follower Wilhelm Reich. Traditional morality and beliefs were seen as restricting sexuality to joyless conformity, as part of a wider conspiracy to maintain those in authority and keep the rest of us working for the capitalist system. Reich went beyond Freud's theories of sexual repression, and argued that society's systematic repression of sexuality (from the forbidding of masturbation to the monogamous marriage) generated unhappy, neurotic personalities and was responsible for aggression and sadism and the desire for power over others. Society's instrument was the patriarchal family, that was based on authoritarianism, was fearful of youthful instinct for freedom and sexual expression, and was productive of the authoritarian personality and ultimately of such life-negating ideologies as fascism. Reich put his faith in rebellious youth to liberate mankind from sexual, and therefore political, oppression.

In the 1960s especially, there was a strong sense that all things were possible, even the final emancipation of humanity, if only people had the right understanding. This involved a rejection of conventional lives and conventional morality. The fashion was to 'opt out', into communes, drugs, Eastern religion, and indeed virtually any belief or practice that was deemed to be in conflict with the prevailing order of society.

Heroes of the New Left included Trotsky, Che Guevara and Ho Chi Minh, all rather romantic figures fighting against overwhelming odds. Guevara was a particular favourite, since having played a leading role in the Cuban revolution he refused to be tied down by government and went back to South America to continue the revolution, where he died fighting in Bolivia. Ho Chi Minh was the communist leader of North Vietnam, who had fought the Japanese and then the French and was, in the late 1960s, fighting the Americans for the control of South Vietnam. It seemed a hopeless struggle of a very small and very poor country against an economic and military giant. Intellectual heroes included Jean-Paul Sartre (the existentialist philosopher and Marxist), Frantz Fanon (theorist of anti-colonialism) and R.D. Laing (the psychiatrist who thought that it was irrational society that was the cause of mental illness). But perhaps the most characteristic and influential thinker of the New Left was Herbert Marcuse (1898–1979).

Herbert Marcuse

Marcuse had been one of the founder members of the Frankfurt School in the 1930s and had moved with it to the USA after Hitler came to power, later becoming a professor of philosophy at the University of California. He was especially concerned to analyse the way in which human freedom, spontaneity and creativity were systematically crushed out of people by modern society. To flesh out his new interpretation of Marx, Marcuse made use of the ideas of Max Weber and Freud.

The attraction of Weber was his analysis of bureaucracy (in *Economy and Society*, 1921–22 and other writings; see Weber, 1964) which pictured the modern world as increasingly subject to domination and control by bureaucratic structures, so much so that Weber talked of the 'iron cage of modernity'. We all become mere cogs in an ever more elaborate machine, controlled and regulated in ever greater detail of our lives in the name of greater production, efficiency and 'scientific' organisation. Weber wanted to show that both capitalism and bureaucracy were expressions of a particular kind of rationality that was distinctly Western and distinctly modern. This was scientific rationality that assumed everything in reality was subject to rational understanding and control through science, that everything was subject to cause and effect and could therefore be calculated and controlled and that this could be applied to human existence, making ever more complex organisation possible. Weber saw no end to the increasing prevalence of this kind of thinking and its social consequences of ever greater control of social life. He had, therefore, a somewhat bleak view of the modern world and its prospects for the future.

Marcuse shared this view and added his own Marxist twist. The increasing subjection of the world to technical rational control was merely the latest stage in capitalist development. He interpreted science in general, not as a form of objective knowledge and a means of acquiring it, but as a means of domination and control over nature. It was not truth that was the essence of science, but technology. This is used in the capitalist system of the modern world in the form of 'scientific' management and administration, to dominate and control human society. At the same time, in the communist world people were equally oppressed by a bureaucratic monster, spuriously justified by a version of Marxist theory systematically distorted by positivism.

He went on to argue that the alienation of modern man is linked with sexual repression (as analysed by Freud and Reich) and that humanity is in need of sexual as well as economic and political liberation. He further argued that in the modern prosperous West, capitalism had been clever enough to keep the working classes in their exploited condition, not by overtly oppressive means, but by using advertising to manipulate their desires towards trivial material possessions and satisfactions (such as consumer goods and cheap entertainment) which can easily be satisfied by the industrial system. Through welfare and the consumer society, an artificially induced sense of well being, and a spurious freedom and tolerance, diverts them away from demands for economic and political power. This system was so efficient that the capitalist system's grip was becoming unbreakable. It was a comfortable prison reinforced by sexual repression that kept us all in awe.

This rather gloomy picture was the burden of Marcuse's best-known book, *One Dimensional Man* (1964). However, the New Left student protest movement gave him optimism. The traditional working class had ceased to become a vehicle for revolution. Instead, Marcuse put his faith in those who had not yet been brainwashed and neutered by the system, together with those who missed out on the benefits of the consumer society: that is, the students, blacks, gays, very poor, and all the misfits and the discontented. These together could be a force for revolution and liberation from the tyranny and alienation of the modern world.

Climax and anti-climax

The 1960s was the great age of student protest. Some protest movements were directed against what were deemed to be oppressive governments, as in France. Others supported oppressed minorities, such as the civil rights movement in the USA. But the most famous cause, and the one that had most international support, was the protest against the war in Vietnam. It seemed to symbolise America's role as the leader of the racist, capitalist, imperialist system, using its massive military might to crush a poor Third World country that dared to seek its liberty.

However, much of the student protest seemed to be just against society itself and any kind of social order, and usually (and infuriatingly) without much conception of what they would put in its place. On the other hand, they could argue, as Marx had done, that the revolution itself would transform human nature in ways that could not be predicted, and only after this transformation could a new society be built to suit it.

Student protest reached a climax in 1968. In May of that year riots in Paris brought down President de Gaulle. Later the Vietnam War protest ended the presidency of Lyndon Johnson. It climaxed in a summer of considerable violence in the USA, with major riots in several American cities, and which saw the assassination of, among others, Martin Luther King. But there was no social revolution anywhere, and after 1968 the protest movement all over the Western world began to subside.

The student protest movement died out in the 1970s. The Left took up new causes, such as the cause of women, gays, ecology and the peace movement, but the term 'New Left' no longer seemed appropriate and fell out of fashion. The dream of revolution faded, only remaining strong for those who had become disillusioned with the politics of protest and who had turned to urban terrorism, such as members of the Baader-Meinhof Gang in West Germany, the Red Brigades in Italy and the similar groups in Japan and elsewhere. These petered out in the 1980s.

The collapse of communism

During the 1960s the Soviet Union was a global superpower and Communism was spreading. It seemed that the Cold War would go on indefinitely.

Soviet decline

In the 1970s, communism continued to spread to Asia, Africa and Latin America. Massive resources continued to be poured into Soviet military expenditure, especially into nuclear missiles and the creation of a global fleet. When national security was deemed to be at stake there was no hesitation in taking vigorous military action. Thus, Afghanistan was invaded in 1979 to prevent a communist regime being toppled.

At the same time, the Soviet Union was growing weaker economically. The vast central planning system, GOSPLAN, which controlled the entire Soviet economy and decided exactly who produced how much of what, every price and every wage, was working less and less well. There was immense corruption, virtually everybody lied about what they were producing and there were endless dislocations. The economy was grinding to a halt.

Eastern Europe was still under firm control with all dissent suppressed, but Western communist parties increasingly distanced themselves from Moscow, a process known as 'Eurocommunism'. Soviet policies were criticised, parties became less authoritarian, and they increasingly accepted the liberal democratic systems they operated in.

Soviet weakness was cruelly exposed in the early 1980s when America embarked on a new phase of the arms race, known as 'star wars', which was based on the latest technology which the USSR could only cripple itself trying to match.

Gorbachev and the fall of Soviet Communism

Under a new leader from 1985, Mikhail Gorbachev, the USSR began to change its policies. Gorbachev believed that the economy had to be restructured ('*perestroika*') with far more freedom and market forces, and that political reform was also needed, with more openness ('*glasnost*') and freedom, and less repression. In this way, Gorbachev hoped to restore the Soviet Union and preserve the Communist Party's power as a modern democratic party instead of an oppressive totalitarian one. These aims were not achieved, partly because the Soviet economy refused to respond to reform, and partly because of events in Eastern Europe.

In 1989 the East German regime collapsed and the Berlin Wall was breached amid great jubilation. Other communist regimes collapsed in rapid succession in Czechoslovakia, Hungary, Bulgaria and Romania. The Yugoslav Federation began to break up in ethnic conflict and even Albanian communism began to collapse. In the Soviet Union President Gorbachev was prepared to accept the ending of Soviet power in Eastern Europe but strove to keep the Soviet Union together. A failed communist coup to oust Gorbachev resulted in disaster for the communists, who were completely discredited. Gorbachev's successor, Boris Yeltsin, banned the Communist Party and appropriated its assets. The Soviet Union itself promptly collapsed with all of the republics claiming independence from Moscow. They subsequently formed a very loose alliance, called the Commonwealth of Independent States (CIS) but with no central authority at all. Other communist states have fallen apart under nationalist pressure (see Chapter 4).

China and the wider world

The collapse of the Soviet Union was accompanied by fall of communist regimes in other parts of the world, including Ethiopia, Angola and Afghanistan. Only a handful of regimes remained, the most important of which was China.

The death of Mao Tse Tung in 1976 was followed by a change of direction. His eventual successor Deng Xiou Ping was more moderate and pragmatic and began to move towards economic reform. Mao's collectivisation of agriculture had been a disaster and was gradually abandoned in favour of a free market in agricultural goods, resulting in a big increase in production. The more complex problem of industry was being approached more gradually, when an upsurge of demand for democracy, spearheaded by students occupying Tienamen Square in central Beijing, was put down with great bloodshed and repression in 1989. China became isolated from the world and reform stopped dead. It was several years before changes began again, but since the mid-1990s it has moved steadily towards a market economy. The government, however, remains determined that this will not be accompanied by democratic reform. The Communist Party still retains power and still justifies its actions in terms of Marxist ideology, although with ever decreasing credibility.

Of the remaining communist states, Vietnam is a poor country in need of foreign aid and investment, and is losing the rigour of its orthodoxy. North Korea after the Second World War became, under Kim Il Sung, a monstrous tyranny where the adulation of the leader, virtually as a god, was sedulously cultivated. His son managed to retain the power and the North Korean economy is in a state of collapse, but it still poses a military threat to its neighbours. Finally, there is Cuba. Fidel Castro has ruled there since he led the revolution in 1959, and has set his face against all change. However, the ending of Soviet aid has, many believe, doomed Cuba to economic collapse sooner or later.

The end of Marxism?

Orthodox communism is clearly dying in its few remaining areas. Nevertheless, throughout the period of communism's decline and collapse, Marxism as an intellectual movement continued, although it has now lost some of its credibility and Marxist theorists have struggled to come to terms with many aspects of the postmodern world.

Structuralist Marxism

The decline of the New Left in the 1970s was partly to do with a change in economic climate. In the 1960s people believed that mankind's economic problems had fundamentally been solved and that steadily growing economic prosperity would continue indefinitely; but the coming of worldwide economic recession in the mid-1970s put an end to that. Western Marxism changed its emphasis away from a preoccupation with consciousness, alienation and cultural criticism. Once more human beings seemed the victims of great social and economic forces they could neither understand nor control, and so more traditional Marxist concerns with economics and class division appeared to be relevant again.

Orthodox Marxism-Leninism was no longer acceptable, but there was a new version of it linking Marxism with fashionable theories of structuralism. This new version was principally the work of the of the French communist theorist Louis Althusser (1918–90). He had in fact developed his main ideas in the 1960s as an antidote to current neo-Marxism, but it was in the 1970s that his ideas came to prominence.

Structuralism was an intellectual movement that developed in France in the 1960s and which argued that in many aspects of life, our thinking and acting are in fact governed by deep structures, largely embodied in language, of which we are usually entirely unconscious. What Althusser did was to interpret Marx in the light of these ideas. Althusser dismissed all the recent, humanistic interpretation of Marx, by arguing that the early writings, such as the *Paris Manuscripts*, were so much juvenilia which Marx never published because he had in fact abandoned the ideas they contained.

Althusser insisted that what Marx had created in his later work, especially *Capital*, was a new science, on a par with the work of Newton or Darwin. He had penetrated the surface of social life and demonstrated how society worked and changed through the interaction of deep structures. Althusser himself developed these ideas with his theory of 'overdetermination', which says that the determination of the superstructure by the base (in other words, economic determinism) was not a simple determination but much more complex, since different elements of both interacted with each other, so that any given outcome was the result of multiple causes. He also developed ideas about what he called the 'ideological state apparatuses', whereby the state's effective control over the educational system, media and church reproduce the conditions for the continuation of capitalism. All of this gave the crude economic determinism of Marxism-Leninism greater sophistication and plausibility.

Structuralist Marxism did, however, become less fashionable in the 1980s as post-structuralist theory came increasingly into vogue (see Chapter 13), although Althusser's own private life – his imprisonment for the murder of his wife – did not help his cause.

Jurgen Habermas

Despite the advent of structuralism and post-structuralism, theorising in the neo-Marxist mode did not cease. In the 1970s, the mantle of the Frankfurt School fell upon Jurgen Habermas (born 1929). Habermas has been an extremely prolific writer, although his work is highly abstract, dense and difficult. He has concentrated particularly on the nature and scope of human rationality and its social consequences.

Like Marcuse, Habermas sees positivist social science and 'scientific' management as the modern means by which the capitalist system controls the population. People are treated as objects of science and in the process are baffled and manipulated. Thus, problems such as poverty and disadvantage are treated as technical problems of administration, instead of moral issues over which a public discussion would call into question the justice of the capitalist system. However, because the system cannot solve these problems its credibility is undermined and modern governments consequently face a 'crisis of legitimacy'.

This misuse of science, Habermas believes, is part of a wider distortion of all knowledge and reasoning. His theory is roughly as follows. We have a notion of the ideal human society that is built into the way we communicate as human beings. The simple matter of entering into a discussion with someone implies the acceptance of shared values of mutual trust, respect for truth, the need for assertions to have a foundation in fact, and the recognition that the best argument should prevail. This, however, is an ideal state of affairs that requires all the participants be equal with each other. Since equality does not prevail in society generally our discussion of human affairs, of how society should be organised and how society's problems dealt with, is systematically distorted by the power relations that exists. Public discussion becomes clouded by ideology that masks and justifies the power differences and the exploitation and oppression that are their consequence.

What is needed, Habermas believes, is a 'critical theory' based on dialectical reasoning, that is capable of revealing the distortions of the system and pointing the way to a better society. His aim is a more egalitarian society in which all can have their say. He has abandoned class war and revolution and puts his faith in 'new social movements' – feminism, the green movement and other groups – to help society move towards a much fuller democracy.

In developing these ideas, Habermas has moved further and further away from Marx, to the extent that some would argue that he cannot be properly called a Marxist. However that may be, he does share with many Marxists a hostility to postmodernist thinking, believing that the Enlightenment 'project' of creating a world based on universal reason, which postmodernists firmly reject, is still a viable ideal and one we should still strive to realise.

Postmodernism, postmodernity and Marxism

Not all latter-day Marxists are hostile to postmodernism and attempts have been made to unite Marxism with some aspects of postmodern thought. One such is 'post-Marxism', a term used to cover a number of thinkers, the most important of which are Ernesto Laclau and Chantelle Mouffe. In *Hegemony and Socialist Strategy* (1985) and other works, they try to reconstruct Marx for the present time and thereby 'rejuvenate' it. They abandon the politics of class as the only meaningful politics. Many political conflicts today arise from the unsuccessful attempt to express identity. For classical Marxists, class identity is really all that matters, which is potentially totalitarian. Laclau and Mouffe put their hopes in new social movements (such as feminists and greens) working together to create a more democratic society. Their aim of radical democracy seems insufficient to traditional Marxists who see post-Marxism as little more than an attempt to adopt ideas that are currently, but temporarily, in vogue.

Marxism and postmodernism do not fit together very well because postmodernism's whole aim is to challenge and undermine any system of universal truth, whether Marxist or any other kind (although it is arguably itself a universal theory or ideology: see Chapter 13). Most of the leading postmodern theorists, like Foucault, Lyotard and Baudrillard, are ex-Marxists who could not synthesise such antithetical sets of ideas. Furthermore, it is not just on a theoretical level that Marxism does not fit in with postmodernity. Postmodern politics is about small-scale social movements, the politics of identity and multiculturalism, rather than the issues that are central to Marxists.

Nevertheless, despite the collapse of communism and the unfavourable intellectual climate, fairly orthodox Marxist thinking still goes on. Marxists argue that the fall of communism in no way invalidates the theory, which is strictly true, although it will inevitably undermine its plausibility to some degree. Various explanations are suggested for the failure. There are, for example, those who argue that Lenin got it wrong and that his contemporary Marxist critics (including the Menshevics) were right to say that the leap from an essentially feudal economy to a socialist one was illegitimate. Capitalism has still a long way to run and we have to learn democracy thoroughly first. There are many variations of this line (see Cullenberg and Magnus, 1995). However, there seems little likelihood of a matching political movement with such ideas in the foreseeable future.

8

Racism and fascism

Racial prejudice is an ancient prejudice, but racism as a formulated doctrine is a product of the nineteenth century. Fascism, on the other hand, is a twentieth-century doctrine. There is no necessary link between racism and fascism. Italian fascism, for example, had no interest in racial matters. Nevertheless, there are strong historical links. Both are characteristic of extreme right; but more important is the fact that in Nazi ideology the most complete fascism and the most complete racism are fused. Initially, however, we need to examine their separate developments.

Nineteenth-century racism

Racial attitudes, prejudices and beliefs are very old indeed. The Ancient Greeks thought of themselves as obviously superior to non-Greeks because they considered their civilisation so much superior. The Chinese regarded Westerners in the same light, while Europeans considered the native peoples of areas they conquered as inferior. Such assumptions were perhaps natural enough in their day; just as in ordinary life, those possessed of power or position are inclined to regard themselves as superior to those who do not have these things. Christian assumptions about all being equal in the sight of God did nothing to prevent Europeans inflicting atrocities on indigenous peoples of Africa, the Americas and elsewhere, nor their persecution of Jews as the people who had 'murdered Christ'.

Early racist theory

However, racist thinking is not confined to relations between continents. Developed racist theory enters European politics at the time of the French Revolution with claims that the French aristocracy had a right to rule because it was descended from the Frankish conquerors at the end of the Roman

Empire. It was countered by the argument that the ordinary people of France were reasserting their rights after centuries of unjust and illegal rule by usurpers. Arguments of this kind were in fact a common feature of French politics in the nineteenth century and into the twentieth. A similar point made by Tom Paine in his *Rights of Man* (1791) where he said that the English aristocracy was descended from 'the French Bastard and his armed banditti'.

Such arguments were based on history, but during the nineteenth century there were new sources of racial ideas developed that were based on a variety of what were taken to be 'human sciences', growing out of the Enlightenment belief in the efficacy of applying the methods of the physical sciences to the human condition. Anthropology was among the first of the human sciences to classify different human types according to colour and other characteristics. Later this descriptive anthropology became more 'scientific' when an army of fieldworkers, equipped with much ingenious gadgetry, went around measuring all parts of the human body, and relating their data to the variety of specially devised indexes. The most popular of these was the 'cephalic index' for relating head measurements. For much of the nineteenth century academic debate raged over the alleged superiority of dilochocephalic (long-headed) over brachycephalic (round-headed) types.

Racist ideology developed when such classification and analysis was related to wider frameworks that purported to explain the social significance of the scientific conclusions. Many anthropologists drew explicit political conclusions from their work, directly justifying slavery, or imperialism, or nationalistic assertion, or warning of racial degeneracy through racial mixing. Crucially, the distinguished French anthropologist, Georges Cuvier, claimed in 1830 to have demonstrated a consistent and necessary correlation between physical and mental characteristics. The significance of this alleged discovery (later shown to have been mistaken) was that it appeared to prove that it was racial characteristics that determined the culture and achievements of a people. Since the superiority of the culture of European peoples was taken for granted (the development of science and technology, arts and philosophy, were all presumed to be superior compared with other races) then it was equally taken for granted that superior racial characteristics were the reason.

Although the jump from anthropology to politics was frequently made , it was not a necessary jump. There were some who did not believe in inherent racial superiority, while others who did make that assumption refused to draw the usual political consequences. For example, Charles White, an eighteenth-century amateur anthropologist, littered his writings with references to the greater intelligence and beauty of the white race, yet he none the less insisted that his writings were no justification for slavery. Indeed, he pointed out that many negroes were of equal intelligence and ability to many Europeans and that they were entitled to the same liberty and equality as anyone else. Robert Knox (1798–1862), the famous Edinburgh anatomist and surgeon who had been a student of Cuvier, in his book *Races of Man* (1850), developed a theory that he called 'transcendental anatomy' which, while insisting on the inequality of the races and the vital importance of race for civilisation, equally insisted that each race had its natural homeland and should stay there; imperialism, therefore, being mistaken and wrong.

The Aryan myth

The supposed necessary link between physical and mental characteristics also seemed to confirm and justify similar assumptions made in cultural studies. It was quite common in the nineteenth century to explain differences of art and literature between different countries in racial terms.

Linguistic palaeontology, the study of the origins of languages, took a prominent part in the fashionable passion of the time for the discovery of national origins and identity. It was this field that also gave rise to one of the most potent of racist myths. It was claimed that almost all European languages had a common root in Sanskrit (a language of ancient India). And it was in Sanskrit texts that were found the legend of a noble race of Aryan conquerors. Thereafter the Aryan myth of a splendid race of warriors, who were also the originators of all civilisation and all noble values, developed steadily. Count Gobineau, Houston Stewart Chamberlain and Hitler were the best-known exponents of it, although it was widely used to justify political beliefs of various kinds from the 1850s to the 1940s, with various people claiming their particular nation or aristocracy or other group to be the true Aryans' descent.

The most fully developed racist theory of the nineteenth century was that of the French aristocrat, Count Joseph-Arthur de Gobineau (1816–82). He combined various theories from history, anthropology, linguistics and other sources to produce a most comprehensive and complex racist ideology in his book *Essay on the Inequality of the Races of Man* (1853–55, in Biddiss, 1970). He believed that the rise and fall of great empires can be accounted for in terms of race. A people had the vigour and will to create an empire when it was racially pure. But in success were the seeds of defeat, for the inevitable mixing with conquered peoples necessarily produced a dilution of the racial stock, followed by decadence and decline. Miscegenation (racial mixing) debilitated the race and weakened its will and ability to fight.

There was, Gobineau insisted, a definite hierarchy among races. Broadly, the whites came top, followed by the yellows and then the blacks. The whites were noble, spiritual and creative, the yellows were materialistic and only concerned with making money, while the blacks were physical, feckless and unintelligent. He related this in turn to French society, identifying the aristocracy as white, having been descended from the Germanic Frankish conquerors, the bourgeoisie and working class with the yellows, and blacks as the indigenous Gauls. French greatness had declined because of the racial mixing of these groups, and its restoration depended on restoring and maintaining as far as possible these racial hierarchies. Above all, of course, the aristocracy must preserve its racial purity.

Social Darwinism

In the second half of the nineteenth century the scientific debate over race shifted from anthropology to biology, finally centring around the work of Charles Darwin. Despite the fact that Darwin's theory of evolution has no necessary social or political implications whatsoever, it was nevertheless used by ideologists of all kinds to justify quite opposite views (see Chapter 3).

Darwin said nothing about race, but ideologists drew various racial implications according to their prior beliefs. For some, the demonstration of evolution clearly showed that all humanity derived from a common stock and hence were all 'brothers'. But most took a different view and saw in evolution the equally clear demonstration that inequality was 'natural' since some races were thought to be obviously at a higher stage of evolution that others. Various theories of 'social evolution' were developed in which the principle of 'the survival of the fittest' was taken to apply to internal politics, international politics and imperial politics, justifying elite classes, elite nations and elite races.

Success in war, or in other struggles, was deemed a particular mark of racial purity. Such thinking became a standard feature of much political, and especially right-wing, theorising in the late nineteenth and early twentieth centuries. Indeed, various ideologies created racist variations. Even liberalism and socialism, ideologies most committed to notions of universal equality, developed one or two hybrids, though no influential ones. It was conservatism and nationalism that were the traditions most open to racist thinking.

Anti-Semitism

The age-old prejudice of anti-Semitism was given new force and respectability through this kind of racist theorising, particularly in Germany and Central Europe. Wilhelm Marr argued in a widely read pamphlet of 1873 that all Germany's problems could be traced to the influence of Jews and that such influence had to be eliminated from German life. It was a view given support by Heinrich von Treitschke, the most distinguished German historian of the time. The great composer Richard Wagner vigorously promoted his views that the Jews were an inferior race incapable of contributing to European culture. Wagner's Germanised English son-in-law, Houston Stuart Chamberlain (1855–1927), produced a similar theory to Gobineau's, although more ferociously anti-Semitic and based on social Darwinism, in his *Foundations of the Nineteenth Century* (1899), which argued for a hierarchy of superior and inferior races with Jews at the bottom and the Germanic Aryans at the very top. He wrote of a great race war that existed between Aryan and Jew that was coming to a climax, but the Aryans would eventually conquer all because of their 'superior genetic gifts'. Since Christianity had plainly contributed much to Western civilisation he could not accept that Jesus had been a Jew, but must have been an Aryan. His book was widely read in Germany in the early years of the twentieth century.

All these writers and theorists produced an intellectual climate of anti-Semitism that had an influence on social opinion but also influenced politics. The Jews had provided a convenient scapegoat since the Middle Ages, and were blamed for famines, plagues and other disasters. In the latter part of the nineteenth century, a series of crises in capitalism across Europe caused unprecedented distress and unemployment in areas where capitalism was new, and these were blamed on Jewish finance because people did not know who else to blame.

The growth of national consciousness, especially the aggressive and xeno-phobic nationalism developed by the conservative right in the late nineteenth century, also contributed to anti-Semitism, which was in turn a major factor in the development of nationalism in Eastern Europe. In the 1890s anti-Semitic groups and parties were common in Germany, Austria and the rest of Central Europe, while conservative parties, and sometimes governments, adopted policies of discrimination against Jews. Anti-Semitism also became distinctive of the far right in a number of Western Europe countries, especially France.

The worst case was in Russia, where anti-Jewish rioting was encouraged by the government in the huge pogroms of the 1880s, 1890s and early years of the twentieth century in which many Jews died and many more left with homes and livelihoods destroyed. The result was massive Jewish emigration to North America and to Western Europe which increased anti-Jewish sentiment. After the First World War, Russian émigrés fleeing from the Revolution put about notions of a mythical world Jewish government, the 'Elders of Zion' who were plotting to take over the world, by creating chaos through their control of international finance, and instituting revolutions, beginning with Russia. Austria and Germany, having suffered a humiliating and (in their view unwarranted) defeat in the war, followed by economic disaster, were fertile ground for the propagation of such a myth, as well as other manifestations of anti-Semitism.

Racial thinking was a commonplace of Western thought throughout the nineteenth century and into the twentieth. It was the shock of the Nazi experience that brought all racist thinking into disrepute and stimulated a re-examination of the scientific evidence on race which revealed that no link whatsoever can be established between race and culture or achievement, or even of any clear demarcation between races.

Racism still exists today, but is almost universally condemned by states, by international organisations and by educated people everywhere. Where it exists it is usually associated with fascist thinking, although in its original form fascism was not racist.

Italian fascism

Today, 'fascist' is often used as little more than a term of vulgar political abuse, meaning 'authoritarian' or 'dictatorial'. In a similar way it is sometimes used to mean 'totalitarian' (where there is one political party which controls everything in society and everyone is told to think the way of the party); hence the seemingly contradictory phrase 'the fascist left'. But properly used 'fascism' refers to a group of political doctrines that flourished mainly in Europe from the 1920s to the 1940s, when the prime examples were Mussolini's fascism and Hitler's national socialism (or 'Nazism'). Some have argued that they are two separate doctrines; but it seems more sensible to regard them as two variations of the same thing. Hitler adopted Mussolini's basic fascist ideas and added a large racist dimension.

Mussolini's career

Fascism was invented by Benito Mussolini (1883–1945) in the early 1920s. He had originally been a Marxist journalist, although significantly one who believed in the importance of will rather than economics. But he was disillusioned by the in-fighting among various socialists and communists at a time when Italy was in chaos and plainly in need of strong leadership. The First World War taught him that national feeling was a far more powerful political force than social class. Using a variety of current ideas, he put together a potent concoction of nationalism, authoritarianism and collectivism that played on people's fears and prejudices, and which, with skilful propaganda, could excite an unthinking mass following. He built a fascist paramilitary organisation, the Blackshirts, and his followers fought elections using violence and intimidation. Finally, Mussolini himself seized power after an audacious march on Rome in 1922 (which could easily have been frustrated had his enemies worked together). Opposition was then ruthlessly suppressed and Mussolini ruled Italy for the next twenty-one years.

Mussolini's ambition was to build Italy into a major world power. This meant the creation of a powerful economy as the basis for imperial expansion and European war. An alliance with Hitler, setting up the 'Rome–Berlin Axis' in 1936, seemed initially successful but led to the Allied invasion of Italy and the German army being sent in to prop up his rule. As the Allies advanced Mussolini was seized by anti-fascist partisans and murdered in 1945.

The fascist state

Like Hitler after him, Mussolini tended to make up theory as he went along, according to need. Nevertheless, there was a fairly consistent body of belief, the core of which centred around the state. The term 'fascism' comes from the Italian *fascio* meaning 'bundle' or 'bound together', which had implications in

Italian politics of an insurrectionary brotherhood. It also comes from the same Latin root as the *fasces* which was the bundle of rods with axe-head carried before the Consuls in Ancient Rome as a symbol of state authority: the bundle represented the unity of the people under the state represented by the axe. Mussolini coined the term 'fascism' and used the fasces as a symbol of his regime. Such Roman symbolism was important to Mussolini, the implication being that he was recreating the greatness of Ancient Rome.

Fascists glorify the state as representing the unified people, and absolute unity is the ideal. All division and diversity is anathema. Hence fascism is totally opposed to liberal democracy with its divisions of opinion, right of dissent, tolerance, pluralism and party conflict; and above all it rejects liberalism's emphasis on individualism. At the same time, the fascist system is claimed to be superior to liberal democracy and capitalism in that it caters for all groups in society and not just those to whom the system gives an advantage. Equally, fascism rejects socialism's egalitarianism and its insistence on the reality of class division and the necessity of class conflict.

Instead, fascism aspires to total unity with discipline imposed and inspired from above. The individual must be subordinated to, and if necessary sacrificed for the sake of the state. People are therefore expendable, for value lies not in the individual but only in the unified whole. Society is an organism and the destiny of the individual is bound up with the destiny of the whole. It is the organism that is important and not the individual. This is fully understood by the great leader, to whose will the masses must be moulded.

Fascism is consciously and explicitly totalitarian, with no organisation capable of resisting the state allowed to exist. The state has complete control of the media and education, and imposes ideological uniformity. The term 'totalitarian' was coined in Italy to describe Mussolini's regime, and he adopted it and used it with pride. (Hitler ignored the word, while communists always indignantly deny that it applies to them.) In 1932 Mussolini wrote:

> The keystone of Fascist doctrine is the conception of the state, of its essence, of its tasks, of its ends. For Fascism the state is an absolute before which individuals and groups are relative. Individuals and groups are 'thinkable' insofar as they are within the state ... When one says Fascism one says the state. The Fascist conception of the state is all-embracing; outside it no human or spiritual values can exist, much less have value. Thus understood, Fascism is totalitarian, and the Fascist state – a synthesis and a unit inclusive of all values – interprets, develops and potentiates the whole life of a people ... This is a century of authority, a century tending to the 'right', a Fascist century.
>
> ('Fascism: doctrines and institutions', in *Encyclopedia Italiano*, XIV, 1932, quoted in Lyttleton, 1973, p.53)

(It is worth noting that Mussolini did not succeed, as Hitler did, in subordinating or intimidating all organisations; for one thing he could not control the Catholic church.)

Both Hitler and Mussolini conceived of the state as an organism and its organisation as ideally corporatist. Mussolini wrote: 'Every interest working with the precision and harmony of the human body. Every interest and every individual working is subordinated to the overriding purposes of the nation' (Lyttleton, 1973, p.56). In Italy this meant the different aspects of the economy were represented by corporations of workers and employers (in fact dominated by fascists) who planned everything in co-operation with the state. The system is known as 'corporatism'. Mussolini borrowed the idea from the syndicalists (see Chapter 6), but instead of just workers there would be capitalists as well. In practice the workers were disciplined while the capitalists could exploit them as they wished so long as they did what the national plan required. The aim was to build up the Italian economy and make it strong and independent, although in fact it ended up corrupt and inefficient. Economic self-sufficiency was one of the preoccupations of the aggressive nationalism of the late nineteenth and early twentieth century (as distinct from the liberal belief in free trade). Hitler had similar corporatist aims for much the same reasons, but was rather more effective at achieving them than Mussolini.

Leadership and struggle

As well as the state, fascists also glorify leadership. Mussolini called himself '*il Duce*' and Hitler '*der Fürer*', both meaning 'the Leader'. The Leader is the symbol of his people and their struggle. Both Mussolini's *Autobiography* and Hitler's *Mein Kampf* (meaning 'My Struggle') were romanticised and mythologised versions of their authors' lives with which the people were supposed to identify and gain inspiration. It is the great leader alone who can understand and articulate the 'true' will of the people. The great leader has the right to hold absolute authority over his people and demand their absolute obedience; it is what Hitler called the 'leadership principle' or *Führerprinzip*. This was absolute dictatorship, but because the leader was supposed to fully express the people's will, the fascists also claimed it to be the purest democracy.

The leader is the best of his people and has proved this by having struggled to the top. This idea comes from the social Darwinism that both Mussolini and Hitler embraced. It is the idea that life is a struggle in which only the fittest survive. It was claimed to apply both to the struggle between nations (and between races in Hitler's case) and within nations. Those who rise to the top are *ipso facto* the elite, and he who rises to the very top is the best. Hitler called this the 'natural order', the 'aristocratic principle of Nature'. Mussolini's fascists and Hitler's Nazis were thus the elites, the natural aristocracies of their respective peoples. The fact that they achieved their positions by violence merely confirmed their superiority.

Action, struggle and violence are natural and good. Hence the fascist glorification of war. Mussolini wrote:

Fascists above all do not believe in the possibility or utility of universal peace. It therefore rejects the pacifism that masks surrender and cowardice. War alone brings all human energies to their highest tension and sets a seal of nobility on the people who have the virtue to face it ... For Fascism the tendency to empire, that is to say the expansion of nations, is a manifestation of vitality, its contrary is a sign of decadence. Peoples who rise, or suddenly flourish again are imperialistic; peoples who die are peoples who abdicate.

> ('Fascism: doctrines and institutions', in *Encyclopedia Italiano*, V, 1932, quoted in Lyttleton, 1973, p.56)

Fascist values reach their highest expression in war. It is in war that the nation is most united, disciplined and possessed of a sense of purpose and national pride. War is thought to 'purify' and strengthen the people; the individual is submerged in the mass, while being the opportunity for individual courage and self-sacrifice for the good of the whole. In war the state is supreme and leadership responds to its greatest challenge. The people forget their difficulties and conflicts and respond to leadership with a heightened sense of national emotion and participation. Not surprisingly, fascist regimes tended to be highly militaristic.

Fascist ideas and methods tended to be intellectually crude; indeed, fascists despised intellectuals and sophisticated theory. Instead, they stressed instinct, emotion, will and above all action. There was, therefore, a strong irrationalist element in fascism: emotion and will are the basis for action, rather than reason (Mussolini exhorted his followers to 'think with your blood'). In consequence, fascism is widely understood as a relapse into barbarism, a return to the primitive, and a denial of the basic values of civilisation.

Popular dictatorship and socialism

Fascist dictators have not been remote autocrats, but demagogues appealing directly to the people. They have sought to arouse mass passion and maintain a heightened emotion of mass solidarity against those identified as enemies within and without. Some writers have argued that this constant state of emotion and tension is essential for fascism; that it inevitably results in constant war, which must eventually end in defeat; and that therefore fascism is inherently and necessarily self-destructive. Certainly fascist regimes have been characterised by constant mass manipulation through propaganda. Control and use of the mass media (especially radio and film, but also newspapers) is a crucial element in fascism, and helps to make it a peculiarly twentieth-century phenomenon. Emotional rhetoric, especially the rhetoric of hate, played a central part; and Mussolini, Hitler and Goebbels were all masters of swaying mass audiences.

Great emphasis was put on symbolism and ritual, with flags, uniforms, insignia, rallies and parades to excite and unify the people with a common emotion. Mass adulation of the leader was generated and sustained, in a way quite different from mere fear of a ruthless dictator. It is an uncomfortable thought that both Mussolini and Hitler were immensely popular when at the height of their power.

One of the curiosities of Italian and German fascism was their relationship with socialism. Socialism proper was despised and rejected for its emphasis on class conflict and its ideals of equality and universalism. Yet Hitler called his system of ideas 'national socialism' and Mussolini claimed that his ideas had a socialistic element. Part of the reason for this is that both of them wished to appeal to the working masses and wished to harness the loyalty that socialism commanded. But also, fascism does share with socialism a collectivist approach and an aspiration to solidarity, as against liberal individualism. Capitalism is suspect because it encourages the pursuit of individual self-interest, which conflicts with fascist demands for total devotion to the collective will. On the other hand, neither Hitler nor Mussolini had any thought of abolishing capitalism and still less of promoting equality. It is in respect of such values that the real differences lie, and from which it is clear that fascism and socialism proper are diametrically opposed and should not be confused. In fact both Hitler and Mussolini often talked of their systems as a 'middle way' between liberalism and socialism, while transcending both.

Hitler's national socialism

The common elements of fascism, such as extreme nationalism, social Darwinism, the leadership principle, elitism, anti-liberalism, anti-egalitarianism, anti-democracy, intolerance, glorification of war, the supremacy of the state and anti-intellectualism, together form a rather loose doctrine. Fascism emphasises action rather than theory, and the theoretical writings are always weak. Hitler's Nazism had rather more theory, though its intellectual quality is appalling. This greater theoretical content is mostly concerned with race, and it is Hitler's racial theories that distinguish nazism from Italian fascism.

Hitler's career

Hitler was not in fact a German citizen by birth. He was born in Austria in 1889 and studied art in Vienna where Pan-German ideas and anti-Semitism were common. He was unsuccessful as an artist but joined the German army in 1914 and won medals for bravery. Like many Germans he thought the German surrender in 1918 was entirely unnecessary and the result of political betrayal, and was bitter and angry at Germany's subsequent humiliation. Against a background of mass unemployment and hyper-inflation, he built up his National Socialist German Workers Party ('Nazis' for short) into a major

electoral force. Its programme and ideology was set out in Hitler's autobiography, *Mein Kampf*. When the Nazis became one of the leading parties in
parliament, Hitler was invited to become chancellor (prime minister), and he
immediately began destroying all opposition and giving himself dictatorial
powers.

He then began implementing his programme of uniting all Germans in a
single state and creating a German empire in the east, policies which precipitated the Second World War. As to the racial programme, the Jews were systematically persecuted from the moment the Nazis came to power. They lost jobs,
had their businesses destroyed, were subjected to endless humiliations and
then herded into concentration camps. The next step was Hitler's 'Final
Solution', the decision to systematically slaughter all the Jews that could be
found. Around six million died, mostly in the gas chambers of Hitler's concentration camps; almost two-thirds of all Jews in Europe. Known as the
Holocaust, it was one of the worst and most obscene crimes in human history.
The full horror was only discovered by Allied troops towards the end of the war.
Hitler shot himself in his Berlin bunker blaming the German people for letting
him down, still convinced of the truth and rightness of his beliefs.

Nature and race

Like Mussolini, Adolf Hitler had constructed his own ideology in the 1920s
using materials around at the time; but he made greater use of social
Darwinism and racial theories that emphasised the superiority of the Aryan
race. He produced his own synthesis based on Germany's current condition
and his own particularly virulent brand of anti-Semitism. He often referred to
it as the *Volkish* philosophy (*volk* means 'folk' or 'people').

In Nazi ideology there is much emphasis on nature and man's part in it. It is
not the ordered and rational nature of earlier centuries, but post-Darwinian
nature, competitive and brutal. Like every other species, man must struggle
with his kind and with the rest of nature for survival on a crowded planet. This
involves struggle within society, but more important is the competition to
survive and flourish among the different races or peoples (Hitler used the terms
interchangeably). Peoples are in permanent competition: all seek to grow and
expand, and need territory as living space to do so.

Upon this naturalistic picture Hitler superimposed a system of values which
he called 'race-values'. To win and to dominate is good and glorious and a mark
of superiority. Hitler wrote in *Mein Kampf*:

> And so the Volkish philosophy of life corresponds to the innermost will of Nature,
> since it restores that free play of forces which must lead to a continuous mutual
> higher breeding until at last the best of humanity, having achieved possession of
> this earth, will have a free play for activity ...
>
> (quoted in Jäckel, 1972, p.97)

Those races that are superior by nature not only dominate but also produce culture. Some races are culture-creating (above all the Aryans), others are culture-carrying (most of the rest), but some are inherently culture-destroying. In the last category the Jews are pre-eminent. They are a people who must struggle to survive and dominate like any other, and are just as intent on preserving their race purity. The Jews, however, are special. On grounds that are not very clear, Hitler insisted that there was some kind of natural relationship between the possession and acquisition of territory and the development of culture. What made the Jews different was that they had no territory, no state, and were incapable of creating or defending one.

The Jews are an unproductive people, lacking any race-value, who must live off the races who are productive. They are, in some sense, an unnatural people, and their methods are correspondingly unnatural. Not the honest nobility of war, but a more insidious and evil undermining of the strength of the people they live among, destroying their race-purity and polluting their race-culture with alien and socially debilitating ideas such as internationalism, pacifism, equality and democracy, while maintaining their own belief and racial purity. The overall purpose of such methods is to dominate the host states (as in Russia and elsewhere) and eventually the world. They would denationalise the world and thereby destroy the meaning of history. Thus, when Hitler spoke of the Jews as 'parasites' it was not only crude abuse but part of his theory.

To make such assertions involved considerable distortions of history. The notion that the Jews could not maintain a state ignores the Biblical state of Israel's thousand years of existence. More difficult to ignore was Christianity, an offshoot of Judaism, which undoubtedly made a very great contribution to Western civilisation. The Nazis followed Chamberlain in insisting that Jesus must have been an Aryan. Those aspects of Christianity they despised, like universal brotherhood, were attributed to his Jewish followers. Nor were they thrown by the fact that some of the most influential intellectual figures of recent Western history – Marx, Freud and Einstein – were German Jews. Marx was regarded as part of the Jewish plot to conquer the world; Freud's ideas were dismissed as degenerate, while Einstein was simply ignored.

Struggle and history

While the race (or people or 'folk') was the most important entity, Hitler also dealt with the world of individuals within a people. This too is a competitive struggle, within which the equivalent of race-value is 'personality-value'; that is, some are naturally superior to others. In a properly ordered society, a 'just' society, the superior will dominate the inferior, the ability to dominate being a mark of superiority. He called this the 'aristocratic principle of Nature'. Politics was a natural struggle for power according to the laws of the jungle. Succeeding in the struggle and dominating all will be the Leader, whose task it is to ensure that every aspect of social life is controlled that it may subserve race-purity and national greatness. The unjust and unnatural equalising of people in democracy is a Jewish idea designed, like internationalism and pacifism, to destroy the natural vigour of the people.

History is the natural struggle of individuals and peoples to survive and prosper. But it is not a blind and formless struggle (as the Darwinian picture of natural selection would actually imply); for over and above all particular struggles, setting them all in perspective, is the world-historical struggle of Aryan and Jew. Contemporary Germany was the centre of the drama, the home of the Aryan, and the setting for the final act. For this reason the Jews were determined to destroy Germany by means of a world plot embracing both international finance and communism (a somewhat unlikely combination). It was the Germans, or more generally Nordics, who were the true descendants of the Aryans, the purest and finest remnant. They were the 'master race' whose natural destiny was to rule the other 'inferior' races, enabling them to cleanse culture of degenerate influences and reach new and more glorious heights of culture and civilisation. But to do this the Aryans must be hard and ruthless, suppress compassion and learn to treat lesser people as subhuman to be enslaved or destroyed like vermin.

Jews had betrayed Germany in the First World War, and engineered her humiliation and territorial emasculation. But inspired by a great leader, the German people would rise from defeat, expand territorially to create *lebensraum* (living-space) at the expense of the inferior Slavs, create a network of alliances with comparable great powers (Italy dominating the Mediterranean and Britain the High Seas), and eliminate European Jewry. Thus, a just and rational world order would arise with the Aryan dominant and the Jew destroyed, all for the good of mankind and in accordance with nature.

This was Hitler's ideological vision that he developed in the 1920s. After Hitler's death it was common to suggest that he had no doctrine, that he was an opportunist who simply made theory up without believing it. Others have said that, in particular, his racial ideas were simply an excuse to whip up emotion against an internal enemy and were not based on any sincere belief. But this seems unlikely. When, for example, the war was being lost, Hitler would not release troops from the extermination camps to defend Germany.

Admirers and followers

Mussolini and Hitler both had their admirers throughout Europe and beyond. They each insisted that theirs was a universal doctrine destined to displace decadent liberalism and its form of government with the state of the future. By the mid-1930s every European country had its fascist party. Fascist governments came to power in Hungary and Romania in alliance with right-wing conservatives. Most, however, came to power in the wake of conquest by the German armies, as was the case in Norway and Holland.

British fascism

The fascist party in Britain was founded in 1932 by Oswald Mosley under the title of the British Union of Fascists. Mosley had been a Conservative, an Independent and a Labour MP (he was expelled from the Labour Party in 1931). He finally came to believe that fascism was the answer to the persistent economic distress and crises of the 1920s and early 1930s. Initially he had been an admirer of Mussolini, but increasingly came to see Hitler as his model, and his ideas becoming more racist as a result. Britain's problems could only be solved by a charismatic leader (himself) substituting authority, discipline and a sense of national purpose for the party bickering and class conflict common to the age.

Free-market capitalism had failed. The world was moving towards protectionism and state intervention, and Britain should do the same. The state should supervise the economy to make sure all parts worked together in harmony like an organism, with workers and employers reconciled, and all in the interests of the nation. Strikes and lockouts would be banned. Corporatism combined with Imperial self-sufficiency was the answer to Britain's economic ills. This meant centralised direction and planning of a capitalist economy. It would be forbidden to import goods that could be made in Britain and the empire would provide everything else. In this way the British Empire would be economically self-sufficient.

Mosley believed that the traditional parties ('the old gangs' as he referred to them) and the parliamentary system were useless and out of date. In keeping with his corporatism, he believed that the House of Commons should be elected on the basis of occupational groups. The first parliament with a fascist majority would grant the government extraordinary powers to introduce the corporate state. Thereafter, parliament would have only an advisory role, while the Lords would be replaced with a new chamber made up of technical and managerial experts of various kinds that can assist government. The government would then make periodic appeals to the people in the form of plebiscites to confirm its power. The party system could then be dispensed with. Mosley wrote:

> In such a system there is no place for parties and for politicians. We shall ask the people for a mandate to bring to an end the Party system and the Parties. We invite them to enter a new civilisation. Parties and the party game belong to the old civilisation which has failed.
>
> ('The philosophy of fascism', *Fascist Quarterly*, 1935)

It would then be possible to end all divisions, merge everyone into the greater whole and ensure that everything is subordinated to the national purpose.

The nature of British politics, which was very different from Italy or Germany, required Mosley to be more circumspect in what he said. His anti-Semitism was usually expressed in coded phrases ('alien influence', 'international finance') but everyone understood his meaning. He in fact envisaged depriving Jews of British citizenship and deporting any whose activities he did not approve of. Ultimately, he wanted a place set aside for Jews in some barren area of the world to which they could all be sent. Similarly, while he said he would govern with the help of parliament, and gain it with the consent of the British people, nobody doubted that, given the chance, he would establish a dictatorship, or that he would seize power in a coup. Certainly his methods – black-shirted paramilitary displays, great rallies, beating up opponents, and so on – were modelled on his heroes. He never had the popular support or the support of other groups in society, such as big business, that continental fascists enjoyed, he made no intellectual impact and since Britain's politics were highly stable (compared with Italy and Germany) he made no political impact either. When war broke out in 1939 Mosley was locked up for the duration.

Spain and Argentina

The utter defeat of Italy and Germany and the revealed horrors of the Nazi concentration camps completely discredited fascism as a doctrine. In only two places did any kind of fascist regimes survive, and this was more to do with the abilities of the leaders than any doctrine they espoused. These were the parties of the Spanish and Argentinian dictators, with that of Spain being the most successful. This was the Falange party, led by General Franco, which came to power in 1936 as a result of the Spanish Civil War in which it had German and Italian backing. Falange had many of the methods and trappings of Italian fascism in particular, though it was not as thoroughgoingly totalitarian. Besides, the party was, at least for Franco, less important than the army.

Once in power, Franco became less interested in making all Spaniards think the way of the party ideology, and concentrated on consolidating his personal power. It could be said that Spain evolved away from fascism, and Franco remained as a fairly conventional dictator for the next thirty years. His rule was entirely personal, and after his death in 1976 the country returned to constitutional monarchy and liberal democracy.

Juan Perón of Argentina modelled himself on his hero, Mussolini. He created his own party, the Partido Laborista, and was elected president in 1946. He was a charismatic figure who courted the working class with better wages, conditions and welfare. Together with his first wife, the equally charismatic Eva (known as 'Evita'), he dominated post-war Argentinian politics. He used his power ruthlessly to promote his followers and generated mass adulation through his command of propaganda, but he did not create a one-party state or try to impose an ideology on the whole population. After the death of Evita in 1952 his regime became progressively more corrupt and he was forced into exile in Spain by a military coup in 1955. Power alternated between Perónist supporters and the military right up to the Falklands War of

1982, although Perón himself only returned briefly to power shortly before his death in 1973.

True to fascist principles, Perón was an aggressive nationalist, and made claims to adjacent territories on the borders of Chile and Paraguay, but particularly to the Falkland Islands, which previous Argentine governments had ignored. Perón had all Argentine children learn in schools that the 'Malvinas' belong to Argentina, which has remained so since, and part of the reason why Argentinians are so passionate about the subject. It led to an unsuccessful war against Britain in 1982.

However, his main legacy was 'Perónism' which amounted to policies that were a mixture of left and right. Such was the power of his name that virtually all main parties of the post-war period, both left and right, called themselves 'Perónist', even though their politics were diametrically opposed. It was not until the defeat of the Falklands and the discrediting of the military that a non-Perónist party was elected to power for the first time, giving hope that Argentina had at last laid the ghost of Perón and would settle down into being a normal liberal democratic country.

The experiment ended in economic chaos and another Perónist, Carlos Menem, was elected in 1988. He promised strong government and measures to help the masses in true Perónist fashion, but has in fact pursued orthodox right-wing policies of monetarism and privatisation and cutting public expenditure. Some say that Menem in fact represents the death of Perónism.

Neither the Spanish or Argentine versions of fascism were racist. The horrors of the Nazi regime discredited racist ideas more completely than anything else. Nevertheless, there are a number of instances where race has been important in post-war politics and since.

Race and ideology outside Europe

Beyond Europe a racial element appears in several parts of the ideological spectrum the immediate past and today.

Zionism

In the aftermath of war, the world was horrified at Nazi atrocities against the Jews. This gave an impetus to the Jewish dream of a homeland of their own, which they had not had since Biblical times. This aspiration is embodied in a political movement called 'Zionism' and is of relatively recent origin. Jews had hoped for assimilation into European society (as opposed to being confined to the ghetto) as a result of the development of liberal ideas that suggested that all human beings were entitled to civil rights and toleration. Certainly there was progress along these lines during most of the nineteenth century. But the growth of anti-Semitism and the persecutions and pogroms towards the end of the century convinced some that emancipation was an unrealistic dream. They argued that Jews would only be regarded as equals in the modern world if they had their own state.

Zionism developed as a movement in the early years of the twentieth century and triumphed in 1948, when the state of Israel was founded in the area of Palestine, with United Nations backing. However, this provoked the hostility of the Arab world over the fate of the displaced Palestinians. It has created massive problems and made the Middle East the most difficult of trouble spots.

Zionism might be said to be a nationalist doctrine with a racial content. It has no necessary racial theory of history or notions of racial superiority or inferiority. It does, however, come in a variety of forms: including socialist, conservative and liberal. In the 1930s and 1940s among settlers in Palestine itself it was the socialist version which became dominant. This represented a revolt against much of Jewish social and religious orthodoxy. It saw a regeneration of the Jewish nation through a return to nature and the soil, which the dispersion of the Jews had made impossible. The result would be a new society of producers and farmers, instead of the nation of shopkeepers, traders and capitalists the Jews had become. National regeneration involved social regeneration, with a new society based on pioneering ideals and collectivist values, as expressed above all in the *kibbutzim*, the farming communities run on collectivist lines.

At the other end of the spectrum there were 'revisionist' Zionists who supported the capitalist and business tradition and also advocated a tougher and more militaristic approach, with the creation of a Jewish army among settlers and the eventual imposition of Jewish sovereignty over the whole of Palestine. This right-wing version came to be represented by the Likud Party.

The Second World War and the Western sense of guilt over the Holocaust gave impetus to the creation of the Jewish state. For its first quarter century, and through three defensive wars, Israel was governed by the socialist strand of Zionism, represented by the Israeli Labour Party. But from 1977 to 1992 it was the right, led by the Likud Party, that was in power. Initially the right had not been a religious party, but since the 1967 war when Israel conquered substantial Arab lands, there has been a growth of Jewish fundamentalism, which insists that these lands be permanently incorporated into Israel, because they are part of the Biblical land of Israel given to the Jews by God. It is therefore a religious duty of the Jews to settle those lands and permanently incorporate them into the Israeli state (see Chapter 12). Successive Likud governments allowed settlements despite international opposition based on the belief that only the return of the conquered lands, and the creation of a Palestinian state in the West Bank and Gaza Strip, could be the basis of a lasting settlement.

Israel has become the military superpower of the Middle East, and enjoys massive military and financial backing from the United States (where there is a large and powerful Jewish lobby in the American Congress). However, Israel lost much sympathy after the invasion of Lebanon in 1982, an aggressive, rather than a defensive war, by a regional superpower against a more or less defenceless state. In turn international sympathy for the Palestinian cause was diminished by their support for Saddam Hussein of Iraq in the 1991 Gulf War. This led to the 'peace process' to establish a Palestinian state of some sort in the West Bank and Gaza, but despite progress, the process collapsed in 2000. Israeli treatment of the Palestinians have led some to say it is the Israelis who are the modern racists.

Apartheid

The doctrine of racial superiority only survived after 1945, as anything more than fringe political ideas, in the beliefs of the white elite in colonial or ex-colonial areas, especially Africa. As most of Africa was given independence with power for the indigenous black or Arab majority, it became the state of South Africa which almost alone in the world possessed a regime inspired by notions of white supremacy. In 1948 the Afrikaaners (that is, descendants of Dutch and German settlers) elected their own Afrikaaner Nationalist Party that ruled South Africa thereafter. It was this party that created the racist doctrine and policies of apartheid.

What the Afrikaans word 'apartheid' literally means is 'apartness' or 'separateness'. The theory was that racial differences are a fundamental and fixed part of human existence. Each race has its own characteristics, and therefore it's own 'natural' development. Racial mixing interferes with such natural development and, in consequence, can only be bad. The different races of South Africa must therefore each have their own territory, education and institutions so that they may develop separately. However, the whites must remain dominant, since they are the superior race and have a responsibility to maintain the system as a whole. Many Afrikaans regarded this as a religious duty, a view that was promoted by the main Afrikaans church, the Dutch Reformed church. The Afrikaans, it was argued, are a special people, chosen by God to perform a purpose in southern Africa and given the land of South Africa as a divine gift. To fulfil their destiny, the Afrikaans must maintain the distinctive culture and position, and so must remain a race apart.

The policies inspired and justified by these beliefs involved a racial class-ification and segregation for all South Africans. Four racial categories were introduced: Whites, Asians, Coloureds (that is, those of mixed race) and Africans. The latter constituted over 70 per cent of the population yet were denied all political rights in South Africa whatsoever. Moreover, they were arbitrarily assigned to one of ten tribal 'homelands', such as Transkei, which were pockets of barren lands on the fringe of South Africa. On this basis black people could be assigned a homeland thousands of miles away from where they had always lived. Black people living in the 'white' areas (most of the country), such as in the black townships on the outskirts of the great cities, were effectively foreign residents; they were only there by special permission of the authorities, and the system was enforced by the notorious 'pass laws'. Further laws forbade mixed marriages and sexual relations between different races. There was rigid separation of whites and others in all public places: parks, cinemas, buses, beaches and so on. As a result of these policies, South Africa became a pariah state, shunned by the world.

However, by the late 1980s international pressure was so great that it began to be clear to many whites, including many businesspeople, that the situation could not go on indefinitely. Tentative moves began to move towards negotiations with the banned African National Congress. Its leader, Nelson Mandela was released after twenty-seven years in gaol. There was fierce opposition from the right. A new Conservative Party was created from the right wing of the Nationalist Party to resist change, while further to the right arose an overtly neo-Nazi, racist party, led by Eugene Terrablanche, preaching race war. But despite many difficulties a new constitution was negotiated creating a multiracial government. The first multiracial elections were held in 1994, and a few years later there was a peaceful transition to majority rule.

Black consciousness

Although South African apartheid was the only overtly racist regime in the world, and although racist doctrines have been anathematised by the world community since the Nazi experience, this is not to say that racial prejudice ceased to exist in 1945. It remained strong and to some extent still does. Next to the Jews, the ethnic group which has suffered most from racist attitudes over the centuries has been the black Africans. They have suffered not only colonial rule in their own continent, but alone have suffered mass slavery, so that in the Americas and to a lesser extent in Europe there is the legacy of a transplanted and deracinated (rootless) people whose history has been one of humiliation, degradation and deprivation; who have little of the cultural traditions of their African forbears; and have been obliged to grow up in an alien society that very largely regarded them with contempt. Consequently, the ending of slavery left appalling problems of racism, especially in the USA. The American Civil War emancipated the slaves, but the price of reconciling the rebellious South to the Union was a studied Federal indifference to the 'negro problem'. Negroes remained second-class citizens, a despised and often persecuted underclass.

Real change began in the 1960s, when the civil rights movement, led by Martin Luther King Jnr, became active and forceful. It made significant progress in the recognition of legal rights and the outlawing of discrimination. King had been greatly influenced by Mahatma Ghandi (see Chapter 4) and insisted on a strategy of non-violent protest.

But the 1960s was also an age of rebellious youth and the New Left revolt against the materialism of American consumer society (see Chapter 7).

The black cause became part of the general New Left movement, which it also influenced. The New Left was Marxist inspired, although not the kind of Marxism of communist regimes, being one more concerned with liberation and consciousness and the overcoming of alienation. For many, the mere acquisition of formal legal rights on the same basis as whites was simply not enough; black liberation had to mean something more. It had to mean the overcoming of alienation and a transforming of consciousness; it had to restore to black people a sense of identity of which they could be proud.

Part of the inspiration came from ideas about African independence. In the 1930s a number of black writers in French Africa (Leopold Senghor and Aimé Césaire were the main ones) developed the idea of *negritude* (French = 'blackness'). The idea was that black people should rejoice in their African heritage and take pride in the music, art and literature of Africa, which was in no way inferior to white culture. Their main concern was the policy of French colonial governments to impose French culture on the native population

These ideas were developed among American blacks in the 1960s and 1970s and included attempts to recover black history, whether African history or of the slave past; also pride in black cultural achievement, in music (jazz, blues, rock and roll, negro spirituals) as well as poetry and other literature. There is also a concern with language, with finding slogans and alternative terms to those imposed by whites. 'Black is beautiful' is one example, as is the insistence on the terms 'black' or 'Afro-American' instead of 'negro'. Other sources of cultural pride and identity included the wearing of African dress and 'Afro' hair-style.

The purpose of such symbols is to assert black dignity and sense of self-respect, an antidote to feelings of inferiority and alienation. That alienation manifests itself, so the theory goes, in blacks' acceptance of their own inferiority; and in the more psychologically destructive form of self-hatred (that is hatred of white oppression repressed and internally transmuted into self-loathing, a feature of black psychology widely observed by black writers). American psychoanalysts have suggested the concept of 'black rage'; that is, rage against white oppressors turned on themselves and each other. This concept, combined with poverty and social deprivation, is used to explain high rates of murder, crime and drug addiction among the black population in the US. The phenomenon was also analysed by Frantz Fanon in his *Black Skin, White Masks* (1952), in which he argued that black people must only purge their imposed sense of inferiority and assert their own dignity through violence against the oppressor. Fanon was an important figure in the liberation movement in French North Africa, whose writings were an important influence on the New Left generally. His violent message was particularly taken up in America by the Black Panthers, founded in 1965, who preached race war and a separate Marxist black state.

One way for black people to differentiate themselves from their white oppressors and generate a sense of pride has been to turn to Islam. This has happened among American blacks. The most important Muslim group has been the Nation of Islam, founded in the 1930s. Its somewhat unorthodox theology teaches that white men are a race of devils that by various means, including Christianity, had enslaved the culturally and morally superior black race. Followers must prepare for when the white people are defeated and blacks come into their inheritance. The movement was very small until it rose to prominence in the 1960s, inspired by the militant preacher, Malcolm X. He was assassinated when he tried to form a more orthodox breakaway movement. After several splits and changes of identity, something of the original vision and fervour was restored in the early 1980s by Louis Farrakhan.

Farrakhan has consistently courted publicity and controversy with his open hostility to whites and Jews, and insistence on black supremacy. America is portrayed as a civilisation in terminal decline with immorality and crime endemic. Armageddon is immanent. But in the meanwhile black should be given their own separate state in a rich part of America as compensation for past treatment at the hands of whites.

Neo-fascism

Despite the discrediting of fascism and racism after the Second World War, and the success of welfare capitalism, there has been a continuing presence of fascism on the fringes of mainstream politics, which is not always easy to explain. One of the most striking features of this neo-fascist revival has been an almost total absence of those social and economic conditions of the 1920s and 1930s in which fascism first thrived, including conditions of political instability, severe economic distress, fear of communism and a widespread sense of national humiliation and thwarted aspirations. The one present factor upon which today's fascists thrive is immigration, especially where it is exacerbated by economic recession (although, of course, nothing like the economic distress of the inter-war years).

In a number of West European countries there has been the problem of immigration, which becomes a political issue in times of economic difficulty. In these circumstances, which became increasingly common in the 1970s, 80s and 90s, people's economic anxieties and racial prejudices can easily be manipulated by parties with affinities with fascism and Nazism. Except for one or two cases (such as Italy and Argentina), neo-fascism seems to be little more than politically organised racial hatred. This certainly seems to be the case in France, Germany, USA and Britain.

Neo-fascism in Germany, Austria and France

In post-war Germany there were a substantial numbers of Nazi sympathisers, which is perhaps not too surprising after the defeat of a movement that demanded and received fanatical loyalty from its followers. The West German government, fearful of a revival of extremism, banned anti-constitutional parties and barred their members from government employment. Despite this, there were many small Nazi groupings, but of no political significance and with a progressively ageing membership. In the 1960s, however, a number of these groups coalesced to form the National Democratic Party (NPD) that was able to attract a new generation of activists. Lip service was paid to the constitution but the party pursued a far-right agenda of aggressive nationalism, while its younger adherents developed a reputation for violence. But after some modest electoral success it declined into essentially a propaganda organisation. The NPD's mantle was taken up in 1984 by the newly formed Republican Party (REP) which has since been the 'respectable' face of the far right in Germany, staying within the constitution but advocating far-right policies.

The REP stood not only for reunification of Germany but for the restoration of pre-war boundaries. It is hostile to the European Union and wishes to assert German identity and greatness. It is hostile towards immigrants and 'guest workers' who it believes should be sent home. The REP does not publicly defend the Nazi past, but rather suggests obliquely that Hitler was not entirely responsible for the Second World War and that his crimes have been exaggerated (a hint at 'Holocaust denial', the claim of the extreme right that the evidence of the death camps was put there by the Allies in 1945 to discredit Germany). Like its predecessor, the NPD, it strives for respectability but is hampered by the violence of its younger followers. The collapse of the East German communist regime and the rapid reunification of Germany in 1990 were followed by economic recession for most of the 1990s. Violence against foreign workers rose to a climax in 1992 and some neo-Nazi groups were banned. The violence frightened off support for the REP which began thereafter to decline.

Much more successful has been the Austrian far right party, the Freedom Party (FPO). This is a party led by a young and charismatic leader, Jörg Haider, who has expressed approval for some of Hitler's policies and has demanded a stop to immigration and foreign workers. He is also hostile to the EU, which insists on the free movement of labour among member countries. This has struck a chord with the electorate, in spite of Austria being one of the most prosperous countries in Europe. In the national elections of October 1999, the FPO's share of the popular vote leapt to 28 per cent making the party the second largest in the national parliament, behind the Social Democrats with 33 per cent of the vote. It formed a coalition government with the centre-right People's Party that caused outrage across Europe and elsewhere and provoked diplomatic sanctions. Shrewdly, Haider himself declined to become a minister and even relinquished the leadership of his party (although he retains a dominating influence). The furore gradually died down, leaving the party an ominous presence in government.

Experience of immigration and concern of future prospects also fuels neo-fascist activity in France. In the French case, as with Britain, much immigration is related to the legacy of empire. There is a very large number of North African immigrants and 'guest workers', and with the prospect of many more (as a result of famine and civil war in many parts of northern Africa) there is growing anti-immigrant feeling. This has been exploited by the National Front Party (FN) of Jean-Marie Le Pen.

The FN was founded in 1972, from the coming together, as the name implies, of a number of groups on the far right, including monarchists, neo-Nazis, Catholic fundamentalists and extreme nationalists of all kinds. It struggled in the 1970s but it rose to prominence with the coming of recession and high unemployment in the early 1980s. It was also helped by political changes. In 1981 the French elected their first socialist government for a generation, led by François Mitterand as president, who included communist ministers in his first cabinet. A change in the electoral system to proportional representation also helped the FN win seats in the National Assembly, although the change was soon reversed.

When unemployment reached three million, Le Pen argued that deporting three million immigrants would solve the problem 'at a stroke'. He spoke of the increasing 'Islamicisation' of parts of France and the consequent threat to French identity and culture. But apart from the overriding issue of race, the National Front has other right-wing policies, including the restoration of capital punishment, the abolition of taxes on wealth and income, steps to dismantle the welfare state, and, more recently, the compulsory isolation of AIDS victims. However, Le Pen is unusual among neo-fascists in having more free-market views and in supporting democracy (although with a strengthened presidency). He is also prone to blunders, as when he referred to the Holocaust in 1989 as an 'historical detail'. Despite this, Le Pen had considerable popular appeal, polling 15 per cent in the 1995 presidential election. But in the late 1990s Le Pen became too old to dominate his party as he once did and it split and began to disintegrate. The anti-immigrant case began to be taken up by some mainstream parties, while at the same time there was increasing acceptance that France had became a multiethnic society. This was symbolised in the country's multiethnic football team becoming world and European champions in 1998 and 2000.

Italian neo-fascism

Italy is the one European state where neo-fascism has been of permanent significance in national politics. It has a small but stable following, so that since 1951 it has never gained less than 4.5 per cent of the vote at national elections. It has maintained a block of seats in the Italian parliament since 1949. At its height, in 1972, the Movimento Sociale Italiano (MSI) gained 9 per cent of the popular vote (compared with, say, the National Front in Britain, which has never gained as much as 1 per cent of the national vote at an election). This is because the fascism of Mussolini still has a hold on some sections of Italian society, especially in the more traditional south, among whom the failure of Italian fascism was due to the unfortunate association of Mussolini with the doomed Nazism of Germany. As in the time of Hitler and Mussolini, Italian fascism is far less racist than its German counterpart. It is not other races that are seen as the principal enemy, but communism. Fascism played a role in Italian politics as the opposite of the powerful Italian Communist Party, whose very existence provoked the extreme right, who argued that the communist threat could only be dealt with by non-democratic methods.

The MSI was founded in 1946 from former members of Mussolini's Fascist Party. It argued for a 'third way' between capitalist democracy, with its instability, materialist values and individualism, and communism, with its atheism and state control of everything. Fascism offered national unity and stability, the end of class conflict and support for Catholicism as the state religion. Ironically, at least some of the political instability which the MSI continuously emphasises arises from the proportional electoral system, without which it could not survive as a national party. It established some degree of legitimacy after the Second World War because in an era of Cold War and in a country with a large and powerful Communist Party, it could present itself as the defender of 'Christian civilisation' against Bolshevism, against which liberal democracy was useless.

Initially, the MSI sought respectability and from time to time supported the Christian Democrats in government and forged links with other right-wing parties. However, greater political polarisation in the 1960s led to greater efforts to undermine and discredit Italian democracy, and there was involvement in the planning of at least one coup to overthrow the Italian government. Some of the more radical were members of underground fascist groups that were resorting to terrorism in response to the growth of the New Left and its movement to violence. But during the 1980s the MSI returned to its earlier search for respectability and left anti-democratic subversion to other clandestine groups.

Perhaps because of the demise of European communism, the MSI was in serious decline in the early 1990s. But then in 1992–93 the Italian Christian Democratic Party, which had dominated Italian politics since the Second World War, became involved in a waive of corruption scandals and collapsed. The resultant vacuum on the right of Italian politics was filled by several parties, including Forza Italia, an entirely new party created in 1994 by the media tycoon Silvio Berlusconi, and the populist Northern League led by Umberto Bossi. In 1994 these two parties formed a right of centre coalition government along with the MSI, the first time fascists had been in government since the Second World War. This government, led by Berlusconi, collapsed within a year, but it gave the fascists the respectability they had long craved. Under its charismatic young leader, Gianfranco Fini, the party has changed its name to the National Alliance Party and committed itself to democracy and against totalitarianism and racism. On this basis it seems to have bright future, although economic difficulties bring out the authoritarian and anti-immigrant strands among its more radical members.

British neo-fascism

After the Second World War there were attempts by Oswald Mosley and his admirers to revive fascism as a national movement in Britain, but without success. Eventually, however, a party was created that managed to attract national support, and which became Britain's principle fascist grouping. This was the National Front (NF), founded in 1967.

At the levels of both policy and theory, race is central to NF thinking, although there are important differences between the two levels. At the policy level the central theme is black immigration. Black Britons are blamed for every kind of social ill: poverty, crime, drugs, vandalism, bad housing, disease, unemployment and more. Worst of all, it is claimed, blacks are the greatest threat to the British people through the mixing of blood. Thus, a member of the NF leadership wrote:

> The greatest danger this country has ever faced is that it has imported millions of aliens who are members of backward, primitive races, and whose large-scale racial intermixture with the indigenous Anglo-Saxons would not only put and end to the British as a distinct and unique ethnic entity, but would produce an inferior mongrel breed and a regressive and degenerate culture of tropical squalor.
>
> (*Spearhead*, October, 1976)

The answer is the compulsory repatriation of black Britons. Other NF supporters have advocated racial laws against marriage between 'Aryans' and 'non-Aryans' in order to preserve racial purity. Beyond this, there are conventional fascist concerns with national assertion and self-sufficiency, such as withdrawal from the European Union.

At the level of theory, however, the principal theme was not anti-black but anti-Semitic. It was a slightly modernised version of the old Nazi theory of an international Jewish conspiracy. Thus, both 'international finance' and communism are instruments of a Jewish plot to destroy Western economies and society with recession and communist revolution and to destroy racial purity through internationalism, immigration and other forms of racial mixing. All this is in order to subjugate everyone to a world government based in Israel.

To the great majority of the population, such ideas are puerile and disgusting. Their main appeal in terms of membership has been to those blinded by hatred or to ignorant young men with a taste for violence, such as football hooligans. For electoral purposes, much of the uglier side of NF thinking was not made public, and there was a more subtle appeal to fears and prejudices and to 'Britain first', which in times of economic difficulty such as the 1970s has given them up to 16 per cent of the vote in certain constituencies.

The National Front was created in 1967 through the amalgamation of a number of extreme right groups. Their collective membership amounted to around 4,000, but rapidly increased to its peak of around 17,500 in 1974. Elections in that year also gave the NF its highest ever popular vote of 113,000, although this was merely 0.4 per cent of the national vote and it came nowhere near winning any single seat. However, support for the NF began to wilt with the advent of Mrs Thatcher as a Conservative leader committed to stricter controls on immigration and firmer policies on law and order. The 1979 general election was a disaster for the NF. Within a couple of years its number was as large as in 1967. The party split, producing an array of groups of various degrees of political nastiness. The most important of these was the British National Party which, under John Tyndall's leadership, took up where the old NF left off, with similar outlook and policies. But this has become a tiny fringe party, partly because of the return of prosperity in the late 1990s, but also because of a wider acceptance that we live in a multicultural society. Besides, most black Britons are no longer immigrants, but born and brought up in Britain. The policy of repatriation, therefore, no longer makes sense.

The extreme right in America

There is a different attitude in American culture in general towards immigrants. The USA is a land of immigrants and traditionally there is usually a benign sympathy to those who come to work hard and become Americans. Furthermore, because of slavery the black population has been established for 300 years or more and are not immigrants in the way they are in Europe. There are a few neo-Nazi groups, but in addition America has its home-grown equivalents as unpleasant as any in Europe. However, apart from racists, authoritarians and aggressive anti-communists, the extreme or violent right in America has another strand that is absent in Europe and which is growing in importance; that is, anti-government extremism. We will look at the various strands in turn.

The Klu Klux Klan and Christian Identity

The institution of slavery in America was based upon the assumption of white superiority, and its abolition after the Civil War of the 1860s did not abolish that assumption. The defeated Southern states defied the spirit of the Northern victory and sought to deny former slaves and their descendants the full citizenship to which they were legally entitled. This was done through discriminatory 'Jim Crow' laws, segregationist practices, and through the activities of terrorist vigilante groups of which the Klu Klux Klan was the most famous and successful. The Klan declined toward the end of the nineteenth century because the black population had been successfully cowed and the federal government accepted this situation as the price of the South's acceptance of the Union from which it had tried to secede.

The Klu Klux Klan was refounded in 1915 on a different basis, in response to the waves of immigration in the previous two decades, especially from eastern and southern Europe. As well as blacks, the Klan now targeted Jews, Catholics and promoters of 'anti-American ideas' such as socialism (meaning in effect anything that was not aggressively right wing). In the national mood of xenophobia following the First World War, the Klan flourished as never before. By 1925 it had between four and five million members and considerable political influence. However, from this peak, numbers dropped steeply so that by the 1950s there were probably less than 10,000 Klansmen. Part of the reason for the decline was that white supremacy was not in fact challenged. When this began to change with the growth of the civil rights movement in the 1950s and 1960s, Klan membership and activity began to revive (up to 55,000 at its height in 1967). A particular target was civil rights activists and many were murdered, but the white supremacist backlash ultimately failed and membership again declined, with only occasional upturns, through the 1970s and 1980s, along with a general breaking up into rival factions.

In the meanwhile other racist organisations have emerged, including neo-nazi groups such as the National Socialist White People's Party, and some little more than propaganda organisations, specialising in anti-Jewish literature, such as Holocaust denial. But perhaps the most successful and disturbing has been the church of Christian Identity centred in Idaho. This takes its inspiration from a nineteenth-century British sect called the British Israelites who believed the Anglo-Saxons were the 'lost tribe of Israel' and God's true chosen people. The Christian Identity church classes non-Aryan races as 'mud-people' devoid of souls and spirituality. It argues that Christ's Second Coming cannot come about until the world is cleansed of 'Satanic influences' such as Jews, homosexuals, abortionists and others. The church has a substantial following, an extensive propaganda recruitment machine using new technologies like the internet, and has links with many other extremist groups such as the citizen's militias. It has also been accused of infiltrating unsuspecting New Age sects in Britain and elsewhere. It was one of the groups closely watched by the federal authorities over the Millennium period, in case some violent conflict or incident was taken as the beginning of Armageddon and therefore an excuse to start killing 'God's enemies'.

Birchers and survivalists

The Cold War generated its array of extremists, the best-known group being the John Birch Society founded in 1958. This was at a time when America was gripped by anti-communist hysteria, whipped up by Senator Joe McCarthy who claimed to have lists of communist agents and sympathisers who had infiltrated the government. McCarthy was a charlatan who was eventually exposed in 1954, but the notion a government riddled with, or even under the control of, communists lived on in groups like the John Birch Society (named after a priest murdered by Chinese communists, the first American Cold War martyr). They even accused President Eisenhower of promoting communism, which they equated with any kind of social legislation, however mild. Illegal violence or any kind of authoritarian action was justified if it helped to preserve American values. At its height in the 1960s, the society was a massive organisation, but declined when the right captured the White House under Nixon and later Ronald Reagan. The ending of the Cold War rendered the 'Birchers' and similar groups largely redundant. However, the government seen as involved in some great alien conspiracy lived on in a different form.

Survivalists groups, such as the Christian Patriot Defence League (CPDL) and the Covenant, the Sword and the Arm of the Lord (CSA), believe not so much that America will be taken over by alien forces, as that economic and social forces are such that the country will sooner or later collapse into a predominantly racial civil war. It is a war they are determined to survive and thereby preserve the American way of life. Survivalists are mainly Christian, racist and para-military, stockpiling weapons and training against the day when Armageddon begins. The survivalists grew in the 1970s and 1980s, but have been rather overtaken by the new citizen militia movement of the 1990s.

Hostility to government and the citizen militias

The American tradition of dislike and suspicion towards central government, largely in abeyance from the 1930s to the 1960s, began to return with the advent of the New Right and its growing dominance of the Republican Party from the 1970s (see Chapter 9). But with the ending of the Cold War (1989–91) it has taken on virulent new forms in the 'patriot' or 'citizen' militia movement and the prevalence of anti-government conspiracy literature.

Before the 1990s the nearest thing to the new militias were a loose association of anti-government groups called the 'county movement' or Posse Comitatus (Latin = power of the county). Founded in 1969 it rejected the authority of both federal and state governments and saw legitimacy only at the lower county level. These armed vigilantes reacted violently to attempts by authority to make members obey the law (above all, paying taxes) attacking government officials who tried to force them to conform. By 1992 the county movement, which had been confined largely to the American central farm belt, was dying out. It was overtaken by the new anti-government movement of the militias. This was a much wider movement challenging the legitimacy of central and state government, but the issue was less paying taxes than keeping guns. Some modest gun control measures passed by Congress the previous year (the banning of assault weapons) was seen as the beginning of a government campaign to deprive Americans of their weapons and therefore their constitutional rights. It was soon whipped up into a general conspiracy centred on the United Nations to take over America with federal help.

In 1992 the FBI laid siege to the Idaho home of a white supremacist activist, Randy Weaver, and accidentally shot his wife and son. On a wave of right-wing outrage, groups began to form to defend themselves against the federal government. The following year a much worse incident occurred in Waco, Texas, where a religious sect called the Branch Davidians, who were stockpiling weapons in preparation for Armageddon, was besieged by the federal agency concerned with tobacco, alcohol and firearms. The siege ended in a fire in which eighty-two men, women and children died. It seems that the fire was started accidentally or else by the Branch Davidians themselves, but the anti-government far right portrayed it as a deliberate massacre and conclusive evidence of the intention of the federal government to deprive all Americans of their guns.

The Waco siege was an enormous boost to the militia movement, which attracted thousands of new members and became active in over forty states. Most are white males and many of the groups are racist, but some are not. Numbers of militiamen were calculated at about 10,000, but with supporters running into hundreds of thousands, calling themselves 'patriots'. They support a massive literature of conspiracy theories. Propagandists like Linda Thompson and others maintain a continuous stream of stories, films, videos and even radio broadcasts devoted to proving that the federal government is engaged in a conspiracy with foreigners to rob Americans of their rights, beginning with their right to own guns, and impose a totalitarian conspiracy. A sophisticated communication network using the latest technology keeps the groups in touch. Most militiamen believe that a United Nations invasion (with federal connivance) of America is imminent, and train to that end. Such conspiracy theories are not however, confined to a lunatic fringe, but have entered the mainstream. In 1991, the Reverend Pat Robertson (the most prominent leader of the New Christian Right and a very powerful figure in the Republican Party) published a book called *The New World Order* outlining just such a theory.

On 19 April 1995 a car bomb destroyed the Alfred P. Murrah Federal Building in Oklahoma City, killing 169 (including many children since a crèche for federal employees was close to the blast) and injuring 500. It was the worst domestic terrorist incident in American history, and was perpetrated by individuals on the fringes of the militia movement, who shared the same beliefs and were inspired by the same conspiracy propaganda. The attack was deliberately made to coincide with the anniversary of the Waco fire, and be some kind of revenge. Militia leaders rapidly distanced themselves from the bombers but affirmed their beliefs in conspiracy and determination to arm and train in preparation for what they believe to be the inevitable conflict to come.

There have been other incidents since, but nothing on such a dramatic scale. In 1996, federal agents arrested a militia group in Arizona apparently planning another bombing on the scale of Oklahoma City. In the meanwhile the conspiracy literature grows, including the much-promoted theory that it was the federal government who planned and executed the Oklahoma atrocity to discredit the militias.

9

The New Right

The New Right rose to prominence in the 1970s and reached a peak of influence in the 1980s, and while it suffered something of a decline in the 1990s, it is still influential, especially in America and Britain. Although it is among the newest of ideologies, there is not much about the New Right that is in fact new: it is really some very old left-wing ideas fused with some old right-wing ones. The New Right is a broad movement with a number of components that are more or less essential according to different points of view. However, the one unquestionably essential and the dynamic element is what is best characterised as 'neo-liberalism'. That is, a revival of the classical liberal thinking of the early nineteenth century (which in those days was a radical doctrine on the left of the spectrum).

As far as practical politics were concerned, that version of liberalism had long since died a death. Its second coming, full of vigour and confidence, captured a different space on the political spectrum. It was not Liberal parties that espoused this revival, but Conservative ones, and it was neo-liberal ideas that gave such parties their intellectual strength and electoral success. In terms of doctrine, therefore, the New Right may be characterised as neo-liberalism in various combinations older strands of conservatism. These do not always fit well together, but the internal conflicts arising from this have not diminished the doctrine's success.

From Swiss chalet to White House

Since the Second World War New Right ideas have risen from complete obscurity to world importance. The most important figure in the early development of these ideas was Friedrich von Hayek.

Hayek's influence

Hayek's *The Road to Serfdom* of 1944 was a book out of step with its time. The post-war world was going to be planned, and have a welfare state; and insofar as it was capitalist it would be a Keynesian-managed capitalism (see Chapter 2). But Hayek's book argued that any kind of socialism, however mild; any kind of economic planning or state welfare, however well-intentioned; or any kind of interference with the free market, however seemingly sensible, was profoundly wrong. It was a diminution of precious freedom and a step toward a new tyranny and a new serfdom for ordinary people.

Although widely read, *The Road to Serfdom* was widely dismissed as a hankering after a discredited Victorian ideal of *laissez-faire*. (A distinguished Oxford philosopher, Anthony Quinton, later referred to the book as a 'magnificent dinosaur'.) Although Austrian by birth, Hayek had been a professor of economics at the London School of Economics since the 1930s. He was also an activist who sought to promote his neo-liberal ideas on the widest scale. He found a rich patron to support his projects and he organised a conference in 1947 to launch a society devoted to the kind of free-market ideas he believed in. His patron happened to be Swiss and the conference was held in a Swiss hotel in the town of Mont Pelerin. Milton Friedman and Karl Popper were among those who attended.

It was from these rather humble beginnings that the New Right began as an international movement and from which its ideas spread slowly. In 1957 the Institute of Economic Affairs was established in London in order to promote free-market solutions to problems. Its work was much derided by orthodox economists and it did not make an impact until the 1970s. Other bodies were founded elsewhere. In 1959 Hayek moved from the LSE to Chicago to join another founder member of the Mont Pelerin Society, Milton Friedman. It is in America that New Right ideas first made a political impact.

The spread of New Right ideas

During most of the 1960s the policies of Kennedy and Johnson followed European models of state welfare and Keynesian economic management. During this period of the early and mid-1970s New Right ideas were developing, largely outside the Republican Party, against a background of general disillusionment and doubt. The economy was stagnant, the great social programmes of the 1960s had failed, America's failure in Vietnam seemed to reveal America's weakness in the face of the ever-growing communist threat, and Watergate and other scandals made Washington politics seem corrupt and without direction.

It was in the early 1970s, partly in reaction to the New Left ideas of the previous decade, that neo-conservative ideas began to flourish. Irving Kristol, Nathan Glazer, Daniel Bell and others, who were mostly former Democrats disillusioned with the 'liberalism'(see Chapter 2) of the Democratic Party and with the failures of the Great Society programmes and other left-wing causes, wanted a return to more traditional values of family and hard work and patriotism. They operated through journals such as *The Public Interest* and *Commentary*.

At this time also the religious fundamentalists began to take an active role in politics for the first time (see Chapter 11), with for example new organisations like the Moral Majority, campaigning against permissiveness, pornography and other moral causes. Religious leaders, such as Jerry Falwell and Pat Robertson, became national political figures through their campaigns to 'cleanse America' of the evil ideas of the 1960s and restore traditional Christian values. A number became famous as 'televagelists', mixing fundamentalist religion and right-wing politics and persuading their followers to campaign against politicians who supported 'liberal' causes like abortion and gay rights.

The early 1970s also saw the formation of the New Right think tanks such as the Heritage Foundation and the Free Enterprise Institute. Their principal stance was libertarian and neo-liberal. It was in 1974 that this kind of thinking received important philosophical support with the publication of Robert Nozick's *Anarchy, State and Utopia*. This revived Lockean ideas of natural rights, especially property rights, as the foundation of society, and the illegitimacy of government infringing those rights with high taxation, economic regulation and welfare policies. Nozick's writings gave intellectual weight to neo-liberal thinking just at the time when it was beginning to emerge as a political force in America and Britain. However, it was not theoretical developments that created political interest in neo-liberalism, but the course of events; and in particular the failure of Keynesian economics.

From the mid-1970s, the Western world was plagued by severe economic recession, triggered off by large and sudden increases in the price of oil. These difficulties were characterised by a new phenomenon of what was called 'stagflation', which was a combination of a lack of economic growth causing unemployment (stagnation) together with rapidly rising prices (inflation). According to current Keynesian orthodoxy, this was not supposed to happen: one could have one or the other, but not both at the same time. This led to disillusionment with Keynesianism and a search for economic alternatives. Neo-liberal ideas that had been developing in the US, but had also been advocated in Britain for some years by politicians such as Enoch Powell, seemed to offer an answer. These ideas captured the Conservative Party when Margaret Thatcher became leader in 1975. Initially, her New Right beliefs were a minority in the party, but during the 1980s came to dominate Conservative thinking.

Thatcherism

Mrs Thatcher came to power in 1979 with a clear and consistent neo-liberal programme, which was quite different from the consensus policies all parties had offered for the previous thirty years. Although there have been some modifications and compromises on individual policies, the programme as a whole was pursued with remarkable consistency through the subsequent decade. The central theme of this programme was the reversal of Britain's post-war decline and the restoration of the country's prosperity and economic health. To begin with, this involved a wholesale rejection of the post-war consensus.

The neo-liberal analysis of Britain's post-war failure put the blame on the consensus policies of the managed and mixed economy and the welfare state, that appeared at the time to give steadily growing prosperity combined with social progress. However, these policies had created massive government with high taxes, endless regulation, state ownership, state planning, state monopolies, state subsidies, incomes policy, regional policy and various other forms of state intervention. Nationalisation, the argument went on, directly diminished the private sector, putting in its place costly and inefficient state enterprises which were a burden on the taxpayer and soaked up investment funds that should have gone to private industry. At the same time, the free enterprise system was being strangled by bureaucracy, weighed down by excessive taxation, intimidated by over-powerful unions, and exploited by inefficient state monopolies.

Meanwhile the independent spirit of the people was being undermined by too much state provision of everything: health, pensions, houses, jobs and whatever else people thought they needed. The welfare state had created a 'dependency culture' where growing numbers of people simply lived off the state, and thought little of doing anything else, while many more depended on the state to fulfil their needs (what Mrs Thatcher called the 'nanny state').

All this regulation and provision had necessitated a massive civil service and local government bureaucracy with a vested interested in maintaining consensus policies and which made sure nothing ever changed. Consensus policies also created huge government borrowing, easy credit and printing of money in order to increase demand and maintain high employment, despite wages being too high and our industry uncompetitive. All this led to inflation, the great enemy of free enterprise, which ruined savings and investment. Thus, Britain had declined economically and was sinking into a condition of depending on the state for everything.

The overall aim of the Thatcher government's policies from 1979 was the restoration of the country's prosperity by following the classical liberal principles of relying on the free market, minimal government interference and individual liberty and responsibility. The government's strategy has been to create the conditions in which free enterprise can flourish by means of policies, which can be broadly grouped into four closely related areas:

• the conquest of inflation
• reducing the size and cost of the state
• providing incentives for hard work and enterprise
• removing restrictions on the operation of the free market.

Defeating inflation was the absolute priority, taking precedence over every-thing else, although the initial purely monetarist approach was abandoned. Great efforts were made to reduce government spending, although success really only amounted to slowing the rate of growth. The central incentives policy was the reduction of income tax, although other taxes had to compen-sate. Removing restrictions covered many things from reducing trade union power to allowing non-opticians to sell spectacles. But perhaps the most strik-ing policy of the Thatcher revolution was privatisation in its various forms. For neo-liberals it fulfilled all their ideals virtually at a stroke: reducing the role of the state, expanding the free market, providing more consumer choice, and for those who bought shares or council houses, greater freedom and responsibility. Whatever the criticisms of privatisation, it was the most characteristically neo-liberal and Thatcherite policy of all.

Ronald Reagan

Thatcherism was the fullest expression of neo-liberalism in action and was influential around the world (the privatisation programme in particular has been widely imitated). Yet in many ways neo-liberalism's greatest political triumph was to capture the government of the most powerful state in the world. This was the Reagan Presidency of 1981–89.

When the Nixon presidency ended in disgrace in 1976 over the Watergate scandal (his former vice president, Spiro Agnew, had resigned earlier over a different scandal), the Republican Party was demoralised and in disarray. It was at this point that the New Right began to take over the party. The old left wing of the party seemed to shrivel, and New Right thinking became dominant and has remained so since. The New Right soon found a champion in Ronald Reagan, who combined neo-liberal attitudes on economics and the minimal state, together with many of the traditional social and moral attitudes of the neo-conservatives and the religious right, and a fierce anti-communist stance common to them all.

As a neo-liberal, Reagan came to power determined to reduce welfare, reduce taxes, reduce bureaucracy and 'get government off the people's backs'. He did all of these things, though he managed only by massive government borrowing (in contrast to Mrs Thatcher who was more consistently neo-liberal in this respect) and leaving America with a very serious problem of govern-ment debt. This arose from Reagan's determination massively to increase expenditure on defence, which relates to the different New Right preoccupation of defeating communism. There were, therefore, conflicting priorities within Reagan's programme, and one of the features of his presidency was the tendency for different groups to be influential at different times and in different areas of policy.

But whatever the other right-wing elements of Thatcherite and Reaganite policies, underlying the analysis of what was wrong and the strategies for putting it right lay a strong foundation of neo-liberal theory derived from the writings of Hayek, Friedman and others, and the ideas of organisations like the Institute for Economic Affairs, the Adam Smith Institute and their American equivalents. It is these ideas that we must now examine more closely.

Updating classical liberalism

Neo-liberalism is a modernised version of classical or *laissez-faire* liberalism (see Chapter 2). It consists of the classical liberal themes of free market, minimal state and individualism (that is, individual freedom and responsibility) adapted to modern conditions. The world today is very different to that of the early nineteenth century, and neo-liberalism reflects the intervening experience and theoretical developments, as well as our present-day problems. Much of what makes revived classical liberalism different from the original is reflected in the work of the most influential figure in the neo-liberal movement, Friedrich von Hayek.

Hayek and Austrian economics

Hayek's economic ideas were strongly influenced by the intellectual traditions of his native Austria. There are a number of characteristics that distinguish Austrian theory from that of the English-speaking world. For one thing, Austrian economics is less abstract. Instead of explaining the economy in terms of the interaction of large-scale economic forces like overall demand, levels of investment, balance of payments, commodity prices and the like, Austrians tend to explain economic activity in terms of psychology and the roles of economic actors, such as consumers, entrepreneurs, capitalists or politicians. It is consequently less formal and mathematical, and also tends to see economics as a wider subject embracing the whole of society. Second, whereas English-speaking economists have tended to ignore the role of the entrepreneur (that is, the creative businessman who pioneers new products and starts new businesses), Austrians tend to emphasise their role as essential to the healthy workings of the system.

Finally, Austrian economics has concerned itself with the analysis of socialism and the role of the state in the economy. English-speaking economics never produced a clear refutation of Marx's economic thinking. It was simply ignored, for the good reason that Marxism had made very little impact in Britain or the USA or the rest of the English-speaking world. This is not true of continental Europe. Austrian economics produced a major critique of Marxism and of socialist economics in general, arguing that state control could not be beneficial for the economy or society as a whole.

Neo-liberal theory could be described as a synthesis of classical liberalism, Austrian economics and some later theoretical additions, mostly American.

Free markets and invisible hands

Neo-liberals share with classical liberals a limitless faith in the power and
benevolence of the free market. No other system, they insist, can satisfy human
wants so widely or so efficiently, while at the same time making maximum use
of whatever resources a society has and guaranteeing greatest possible prosperity. In a free market the consumer can always choose between rival products, and will always choose what is cheapest and best. Rival producers must
either improve their product or lower its price or find some new version that
people want, or else go out of business. All producers, whether of goods of services, are under constant pressure to improve. Competition ensures highest
quality at lowest prices, and also that new needs will be explored and new technologies will be developed to produce better and cheaper products.

The market develops an ever wider network in the drive to satisfy human
wants. Thus, we purchase objects made of many components and materials
produced in many parts of the world, and all brought together through innu-
merable means by the power of the market in a way that benefits all.

Everyone pursues their own interests, yet in doing so benefits the whole. In
a famous passage, Adam Smith wrote of the individual who

> intends only his own gain is led by and invisible hand to promote an end which
> was no part of his intention. Nor is it always the worse for society that it was no
> part of it. By pursuing his own interest he frequently promotes that of society
> more effectively than when he really intends to promote it.
>
> (*The Wealth of Nations*, 1776)

It would not be put in quite those terms today. Rather than somewhat mystical
talk of 'invisible hands', Hayek speaks of the market creating a 'spontaneous
order' which no-one has, or could, design or control. What makes it all possible
is the combination of two factors: the price mechanism and the entrepreneur.

The price mechanism is a vast information system which tells everyone
what materials, labour, borrowing and finished goods will cost, and therefore
their relative scarcity and value to those who might use or consume them. It is
the key indicator for those who would invest, providing both information and
incentive. Products commanding a high price and high profits will attract
investment, which will encourage extra production that will bring the price
down, making the product more widely available. In the meanwhile high
profits will be attract fresh investment elsewhere. However, this only works if
there is competition. It is vital, therefore, that consumers have choice, that they
can express their preferences; it is their choices that drive the system. Patterns
of consumption emerge, although these are not fixed. Needs change, fashions
change, technology changes, as does the availability of resources. The market
is, therefore, in a constant state of flux.

The key figure that thrives on the flux, that searches for new needs and new
means to satisfy them, is the entrepreneur or 'enterpriser'. Capitalists often

invest in standard goods that command a steady income, but some make riskier investments in the hope of higher profits. Capitalists themselves may be entrepreneurs, although more frequently the enterpriser is borrowing in the hope of profit over and above the lender's return.

English-speaking economists from Adam Smith to Keynes have tended set little store by the work of entrepreneurs, subsuming them within the general category of businessman or capitalist (Adam Smith wrote quite scathingly about businessmen). Indeed, the demise of the entrepreneur was much canvassed, for example, by Joseph Schumpeter, an Austrian-American economist, in *Capitalism, Socialism and Democracy* (1943); their role, it was said, had been taken over by the research and development departments of big corporations. It is one of the notable features of the neo-liberal revival that the role of the entrepreneur and small businessman has been emphasised (Mrs Thatcher called them 'these wonderful people').

Given that the market is in a state of constant change, it is not surprising that from time to time things can go badly: there is a dearth of investment, or overproduction, or unemployment, or whatever. The beauty of the free market is that it is a self-righting vessel, and given time will always solve its own problems. Interference only delays recovery. Once restored, the free market will continue its historic task of maximising prosperity for all.

Threats to the free market

Neo-liberals allow no criticism of the free market. All faults flow from the free market not being allowed to work properly, and there are various things that prevent it from doing so, including monopoly, inflation and government intervention. Monopoly is bad for the market because it denies competition and therefore distorts both consumer choice and the price mechanism. Monopolists can charge what they like and there is nothing the consumer can do about it, and if competition is impossible there is no incentive for anyone to try to provide a better or cheaper alternative.

Inflation distorts the price mechanism in a more comprehensive and damaging way. Prices do not go up evenly, but depend on varying wage settlements and a number of other factors. Prices cease to be an accurate indicator of demand, or of likely profit or good investment. The whole economy slows, people will not save, nor make risky investments. Worse still, inflation can get out of hand and destroy an economy, as it did in Germany in the 1920s. Neo-liberals see inflation as a great evil that must be overcome at all costs, and see this is the one crucial role of government in the economy.

However, though inflation is a great evil, government intervention is seen as the most potent threat. In fact some neo-liberals see government as the root cause of monopoly and inflation. They therefore see government, and government alone, as the ultimate enemy of economic freedom and consequently of freedom as such; and government intervention is identified with socialism.

Socialism and the dead hand of the state

Liberals have traditionally identified certain enemies of freedom. In the seventeenth and eighteenth centuries it was the tyranny of priest and king; J.S. Mill added the tyranny of the majority; while today's neo-liberals point to what might be called the 'tyranny of centralised benevolence'. That is, governments genuinely seeking to improve the lot of their people by such policies as interfering in the market to 'correct its faults', promoting equality, and trying to alleviate poverty, ignorance and other social problems. The result of these policies, neo-liberals insist, is invariable failure to achieve their objectives, or even to do as well as the outcome of doing nothing at all.

The growth of collectivism

Neo-liberals believe that in Britain a free society was created in the early nineteenth century, but in the latter part of the century there began a long retreat towards collectivism. It was all benign and with the best of intentions, but it was all a mistake. It began with social policies and proceeded to the economic. However, for the neo-liberal the economic always comes first.

During the long depression of inter-war years, especially after the Wall Street Crash of 1929, the old classical economic orthodoxy of allowing the economy to solve its own problems, without government interference, appeared to fail. The thinking behind this policy was challenged by J.M. Keynes, who argued that governments should intervene to prevent both booms and slumps by controlling the amount of demand in the economy (see Chapter 2). This became the orthodoxy of the post-war world, when governments spent freely to generate demand and avoid unemployment.

Monetarism

Neo-liberals maintain that this strategy was a mistake. Milton Friedman, for example, insists that many myths surround the Great Crash and its aftermath, and that in fact full recovery could have occurred if governments had kept their nerve. This is a highly controversial analysis. More importantly, he insists that the proposed Keynesian cure was in fact worse than the disease. This is because Keynesian policies inevitably lead to inflation, which is the real economic evil, not unemployment.

Friedman is renowned as an economist for his analysis of inflation. Many immediate causes are recognised, but what the most basic cause might be is a matter of dispute among economists. Keynesians argue that a certain amount of mild inflation is an inevitable accompaniment of economic growth (demand runs ahead of production creating shortages, extra demand for skilled labour pushes up wages, and so on), but this can be tolerated. Beyond this, in a situation of full employment unions are in a strong position to bid up wages, causing 'cost-push' inflation, which is more serious but can be controlled by government incomes policies. Friedman disagrees. He argues that unions are too well protected in two respects: by government policies of full employment and by legal immunities. That is, there is no consequence of unemployment if their demands are too high. Furthermore, unions will always strive to stay ahead of inflation.

However, Friedman's fame rests upon his analysis of inflation in terms of an excess of money in the economy. Either government prints too much or allows the creation of too much credit, often in pursuit of Keynesian policies to stimulate demand. In other words, it is government policies that cause inflation, and indeed it is government's sole economic function to control inflation through its control of money supply. His theory is called 'monetarism' and is widely held among neo-liberals (although some are sceptical including Hayek). It was a key part of early Thatcherism.

Even without monetarism, neo-liberals agree that inflation is the great economic evil and that government economic policy should be aimed at making the free market work as effectively as possible, with controlling inflation as the prime economic duty. Government intervening in the economy in other ways is condemned; this includes economic planning, state ownership, high taxation, incomes policy, minimum wage and regional policy. They all distort the market, and hinder rather than help in solving economic problems.

This general neo-liberal view of economic policy, of which monetarism is one rather extreme version, goes by the name of 'supply-side economics', to distinguish it from Keynesian economics which is about manipulating demand. It has even influenced, particularly in its milder versions, socialist parties in Britain and Europe (see Chapter 5).

The welfare state

Neo-liberals are similarly critical of the role of the state in the field of social policy. They argue that the attempt to intervene to make up for the deficiencies of the market are invariably counter-productive. Social security systems in Britain and elsewhere are under severe strain. They appear to create legions of dependent poor on permanent benefit because the problems they are designed to solve just get worse instead of better. For example, aid for one-parent families just creates more one-parent families because the social security system allows one partner to abandon their families more readily. Or again, unemployment benefit tends to create unemployment because people who can rely on unemployment benefit become more choosy about jobs they will accept. In short, social security institutionalises poverty rather than solves it.

However, neo-liberals disagree about the extent to which the system should be dismantled. Some say the break up should be total and its role left to private charity. Others would prefer to see the system greatly reduced, leaving only a last resort for the very few.

In the USA programmes to help the poor have also had little apparent success, particularly in respect of the blacks. One black neo-liberal writer, Walter Williams, has argued that they have made the situation of blacks positively worse. Handouts have made blacks dependent yet resentful, at the same time disinclining them to work. Many of the jobs they might have done – that is, jobs that employers will only provide if they can pay very low wages – have been ruled out by minimum-wage legislation that was designed to help them. Other policies like 'affirmative action' (that is, positive discrimination) and 'bussing' (bussing black students to white schools to ensure balance) are also deemed counter-productive.

Lack of government funds are usually cited as the reason for poor social services in Britain, but neo-liberals insists that this is never a sufficient answer. Other countries have better services, without necessarily spending more. These services are just not responsive to customer demands as they would be if run by private enterprise.

Public choice theory

Part of the problem with these services, from the neo-liberal's point of view, is that they are not considered part of the market, and market thinking is not applied to them. They are state monopolies where the consumer has little effective choice. As a consequence they are 'producer-led' rather than 'consumer-driven'. In other words, it is a combination of political decision and 'expert' advice (teachers, doctors and other professionals) that prevails and not that of the consumer. It is in the interests of all those on the producer side (politicians, bureaucrats and professionals) to ensure maximum and expanding provision, irrespective of demand. Hence, for example, until recently nobody in the NHS could say what an operation cost in different hospitals, whereas that is a very important guide to efficiency in the private sector. In the NHS efficiency was not a major concern.

It could be argued that the public sector is a different kind of animal from the private sector and that public service is a different motivation from profit. However, neo-liberals maintain that there is a public service mystique that ought to be dispelled. They point out that in America, and increasingly in Britain, there has grown up a body of theory and empirical analysis that makes sense of a great deal of otherwise inexplicable public sector phenomenon by assuming that agents in the public sector, whether politicians or officials or professionals, are as much motivated by self-interest as anyone in the private sector. This body of work goes under the general name of 'public choice theory'.

Of course public sector actors are not motivated by profit. Instead, so the theory goes, they have a number of different objectives according to their role. Put crudely, politicians seek votes, bureaucrats seek departmental expansion and a higher budget, while professionals want power and status. One of the abiding problems of democracy is the tendency of politicians to maximise votes by making expensive promises that require higher government spending and therefore more taxes and inflation which in the long run undermines the economy. Bureaucrats and professionals have a vested interest in encouraging the politicians in this. But whereas in the private sector there is the check of competition there is normally no such check on public sector services since they are normally monopolies; so it is producer decision and not consumer choice that decides the nature and level of service. There is, therefore, little incentive to be efficient and a good deal of incentive to be over-staffed and over-funded. Consequently, many neo-liberals see government agencies as necessarily inefficient and inferior to the private sector, and want to see them privatised or in some way made subject to private sector disciplines.

In all, then, modern state intervention is deemed inefficient to the point of being self-defeating. The most extreme example is the communist states which in recent decades have demonstrated the effectiveness of full state control by collapsing into poverty and economic chaos.

The neo-liberal free society

Neo-liberals believe that a society based on their principles will not only be the most efficient and prosperous possible society, but will also be morally superior to any other. This is because they believe that their kind of society will be the most free, and freedom is, they believe, the greatest value of all.

Hayek and freedom

The free market is, for Hayek, the engine of progress and civilisation. Freedom is the absolute value, and the freedom of the market is the guarantee of all other freedoms, both political and intellectual, as well as the best chance that freedom will spread elsewhere. The way in which economic freedoms underpin other freedoms tends to be argued and illustrated be neo-liberals in a negative way. It is asserted that in socialist societies civil liberties count for little, and that state planning and the effort to maintain equality and 'social justice' must involve stopping people from doing what they would otherwise do, which necessarily impinges on their liberties and is ultimately tyrannous. We only have to look at the experience of communist regimes in Eastern Europe and elsewhere to see the truth of this.

If freedom is the basic value, and economic freedom is the root of all other freedoms, then whatever interferes with economic freedom must be wrong in some fundamental sense. This is the basis of a moral criticism of economic intervention, of the welfare state, and of socialism in general. Hayek insists that state ownership, economic planning and a great deal of regulation and interference is basically immoral because it induces people to do what they would not otherwise do. The high taxes that go along with big government are also an infringement of property rights. Spending other people's money on what is not absolutely essential is intrinsically wrong, and especially so if taxes are used to redistribute wealth. Hence the welfare state is wrong.

In his first major work on social questions, *The Road to Serfdom* (1944), Hayek pictured the development of the welfare state as the unconscious first steps towards totalitarianism, a new serfdom. This was thought fanciful by many at the time and since. However, neo-liberals are given to radically simplifying opposing ideas regarding all political ideas advocating state intervention as merely varying gradations of socialism, the complete version being communism. Consequently, social liberalism, social democracy, communism and even fascism are indiscriminately lumped together as fundamentally the same thing. Thus, Mrs Thatcher once dismissed the Labour Party leader Neil Kinnock in the House of Commons as a 'crypto-communist', generating a great deal of both mirth and puzzlement on Opposition benches.

The point is that neo-liberals see the growth of the state as a threat to freedom, however limited or benign the initial motivation may be. Indeed, the threat is more insidious for being in the name of what appears to be laudable ideals, such as equality as the means to freedom and justice. In fact the attempt to enforce these things will be self-defeating. Only freedom matters and anyone who would limit it, for whatever reason, is to be condemned.

Hayek insisted that Adam Smith's 'invisible hand' works not just for the economy but for society as a whole. In other words, if people are left free to deal with each other without government interference, then they will always create a spontaneous order, a 'natural' order, that is both organisationally and morally superior to any that is artificially imposed. This is because the spontaneous order will not be based on any coercion but upon everyone's consent. Societies arrived at in this way will invariably be characterised by inequality, but Hayek will not countenance any suggestion that such a society could be unfair. The notion of fairness or justice, he thinks, cannot be ascribed to society as such but only to individual acts. If people cannot point to where they have suffered from some particular act of injustice for which some person is directly responsible, then they have no grounds for claiming that they are oppressed by 'the system'.

Hayek, however, is prepared to concede a certain bare minimum of welfare provision for the sake of social stability, and Milton Friedman slightly more (with his ideas for negative income tax and educational vouchers). But others are more radical, insisting that even this is completely illegitimate. We have seen that Nozick questions any function for government beyond providing law and order, while the anarcho-capitalists (see Chapter 6) believe the state has no legitimate functions at all, summed up by the slogan 'War is mass murder, taxation is theft'.

True liberalism and false

All liberals believe that freedom is the supreme value and human nature cannot flourish without it. However, neo-liberals insists upon a particular definition of freedom which many other modern liberals regard as too narrow. Hayek wrote his major works attacking government management of the economy and the welfare state at a time when these were regarded as a major extension of freedom.

For neo-liberals genuine freedom is 'negative freedom', meaning simply the absence of constraint. But this can mean that although a person will starve if they do not take a job, they are still free because they are able to refuse it. Many modern liberals hold the view that poverty, ignorance and other deprivations limit people's freedom, and that the state can and should step in to alleviate these through collective provision. This view is called 'social' or 'welfare liberalism' (see Chapter 2).

Hayek, Nozick and others reject social liberalism as a false liberalism, and notions of 'social justice' that go with it as so much nonsense. The government, they insist, has no duty to intervene in society to aid the disadvantaged. This would involve taking wealth from others (as taxes) which Nozick argues is an illegitimate violation of their natural rights. Moreover, it means interfering in the market, which is the guarantee of everyone's freedom; destroying freedom to make people free is self-contradictory.

The demands for state intervention to provide welfare services and other means of redistributing wealth in the name of social justice are seen as arising partly from the illegitimate demands of newly enfranchised classes in the late nineteenth century, but also partly from false conceptions that had become lodged in the liberal tradition in earlier periods. During the eighteenth century Enlightenment, the authentic tradition of Locke was continued by Adam Smith and the American Founding Fathers. This is a sceptical, empirical, limited liberalism that does not seek to change society, valued the individual and is suspicious of all power, especially political power. But another version developed in continental Europe, through Rousseau and the radicals of the French Revolution (see Chapter 2). This was a rationalistic liberalism that believed in popular sovereignty and equality. It sought to redesign society according to a preconceived rational theory by capturing political power and using it to create a perfect world.

This 'false' liberalism resulted in the disaster of the French Revolution, whereas 'authentic' liberalism created a great age of freedom and progress in Britain during the nineteenth century, and in America for even longer. Unfortunately, the neo-liberals argue, in Britain 'alien continental influences' and working-class socialism began to permeate and dilute the genuine liberal spirit. The result was social liberalism, which is really a mild form of socialism, culminating in the welfare state and the mixed and managed economy. As the neo-liberal writer David Green puts it:

By the First World War liberalism had lost its former sway, even to the extent that liberal ideas had been wholly abandoned by the Liberal Party. By the 1930's liberty was barely understood by British intellectuals, and even America had fallen under the influence of socialistic 'liberalism'.

(1987, p.32)

Hence the irony that Hayek felt when writing *The Road to Serfdom*: that the Allies were fighting a war in order to preserve freedom, while, because of a lack of understanding, they were preparing to abandon it voluntarily at home. It has taken the economic failures of the 1970s to show how mistaken was the social liberal path, and to stimulate the restoration of genuine liberalism.

We can see this neo-liberal version of liberal history as a variation on the traditional liberal theory of progress, which sees mankind proceeding through the development of freedom and reason towards an ever happier future. In this version we have an additional twist of the truth being lost and abandoned, and only now being rediscovered, but of course the truth must be acted upon if progress is to resume. We also have here the germ of a neo-liberal theory of ideology, which is also slightly different from the conventional liberal view.

Liberals normally define ideology in terms of social thinking that claims to be absolute truth, and which therefore despises toleration, pluralism and discussion as impeding the 'truth' being put into practice. Thus, ideology is the kind of thinking that leads to totalitarianism. The neo-liberal version (perhaps best exemplified by Kenneth Minogue's book *Alien Powers*, 1985) would include 'false' liberalism as well. Ideology is bound up with the false idea that the source of human unhappiness is 'the system' and that vigorous state action can reshape society in order to ensure human happiness. This means forcing people to behave in ways they would not otherwise behave, and this is the road to totalitarianism. It is an attitude neo-liberals particularly associate with socialism, and why they tend to lump together socialism, communism, social liberalism and fascism as though they were all the same thing.

Neo-liberalism therefore represents itself as 'true' liberalism, that is, liberalism that is above all individualist; that argues that while human beings may be selfish, they are nevertheless rational and therefore entitled to pursue their own interests and their own happiness in their own way, so long as they respect the same right in others. This releases people's intelligence and energy and talent, and their free interplay creates a spontaneous harmony that is natural and right.

Within this broad framework there are some variations among neo-liberals. Where the main variations and complexities come within the New Right is in the relationship with the more traditional right-wing beliefs.

The New Right spectrum in America and Britain

The New Right is not just neo-liberalism, but has a significant right-wing content as well. This has varied according to circumstances and tradition, as can be seen in the two major instances of the New Right in power: in America and Britain.

The American New Right spectrum

In America all major parties are liberal in the sense that they believe in individualism and free enterprise, and there has never been a significant political party that has not. Nevertheless, within this consensus there is a broad spectrum of left to right. Traditionally, both Republicans and Democrats had their left and right wings, although from the 1960s this traditional pattern has declined. Since then, the Republicans have become more predominantly the party of the right, and the Democrats of the left, although there are moderates on both sides.

The right of the American political spectrum is very different from the traditional European right. The latter was concerned with the maintenance of the rights and privileges of an aristocratic class. The American right is entirely different. 'Conservatives' on the right of the American political spectrum believe in pure *laissez-faire* liberalism: that is, the capitalist system should be given free reign; state welfare should be reduced or abolished, with individuals pulling themselves up by their own bootstraps; and government should be as small as possible. This outlook has always been strongest in the Republican Party.

This fitted with America's strong tradition of minimal government. However, from the 1930s the country was faced by a series of crises that seemed to demand a huge increase in central power. These were the Great Depression, followed by the Second World War and the Cold War. In these years the Democrats tended to be the main party of government, with its policy dominated by the party's left or 'liberal' wing. Those on the left of the American political spectrum are social liberals (see Chapter 2) advocating 'big government', who really came into their own in America during the New Deal period of the 1930s and dominated government up to the Kennedy-Johnson period. Rather confusingly, these are known in everyday American politics as 'liberals', and to those on the right they are little better than socialists.

In the 1960s the Democratic Party had embraced not only the Kennedy and Johnson anti-poverty programmes, but also black civil rights and causes of other minority groups. This offended the conservative wing of the Democratic Party, particularly in the much more conservative South, which resulted in many southern Democrats defecting to the Republicans. In addition, there were a number of intellectuals who had embraced the liberal causes of the Democrats, but had become disillusioned at the failure of the anti-poverty programmes, and worried by America's weakness, evident in the defeat in Vietnam and the spread of communism. Many of these 'neo-conservatives' switched their allegiance to the Republican Party.

At the same time the traditional right was reviving in the 1970s. The writings of Hayek, Friedman and Nozick brought intellectual weight and distinction to an American right that had been somewhat on the defensive since the 1930s. They brought a revised, updated neo-liberal version of *laissez-faire* liberalism, or neo-liberalism, with its emphasis on the free market, minimal government and individualism. The New Right were prepared to accept the necessity of big government, but only in respect of defending America in the Cold War and not in respect of providing welfare. They believe in otherwise reducing the state and cutting taxes. In addition various nationalists, isolationists and protectionists also found their place in the New Right spectrum.

They were joined by the growing 'Religious Right' or New Christian Right who shared their concerns for American weakness and were especially anxious to halt America's loss of traditional values. The Religious Right came together in the 1970s and began to campaign in a highly effective manner on issues such as abortion, feminism, homosexual rights, pornography, and school science that conflicts with the Bible (see Chapter 12).

These different groups constituted a considerable expansion of the right in America. Together they captured the Republican Party in the late 1970s, and (like the Thatcherite capture of the Conservative Party in Britain) turned it into much more of an ideological party than it had been in the past. Yet it was an umbrella ideology of varying views, such that after Ronald Reagan was elected president in 1980 he experienced considerable difficulties holding together the New Right coalition that made up his administration, which included both passionate free traders and protectionists, social libertarians, Christian fundamentalists, and others.

Conflicts within the New Right

The New Right thus represents an array of differing elements that are not always compatible. The most striking contrast is between the libertarians, who would include minimal statists, and anarcho-capitalists (see Chapter 6), and the Christian right. Libertarians think that everyone should be able to do just what they like, particularly in moral matters, so long as they do not harm others. Some even advocate the legalisation of drugs and allowing parents to auction off their unwanted children. Above all, they do not want the state interfering in people's lives. The more extreme libertarians, including the anarcho-capitalists, have their own small Libertarian Party (founded in 1971), but otherwise their natural home is among the Republicans. The Christian Right, on the other hand, is highly puritanical and would use the power of the state to enforce traditional Christian morality (see Chapter 11).

Another source of conflict lies in the attitude towards the state. While moral authoritarians are more inclined to see the need for a strong state, the New Right in general seeks to minimise the state. Right-wing hostility to central government, manifested in the Republican's 'Contract with America' manifesto of 1994, not only corresponded to New Right theory, emphasising the minimal state and the free market, but also to a more general disillusionment with government in America, and especially the federal government. Despite growing national prosperity through the 1990s there was none the less growing anger among the general public that America was failing, that there was economic insecurity, too high crime and immigration, and that government was corrupt and ineffective (see Esler, 1998).

The most startling manifestation of such hostility is in the citizen militia movement, which stockpiles guns and trains for combat because they see the federal government as engaged in a conspiracy to deprive Americans of their liberties, and culminated in the Oklahoma bombing of 1995 (see Chapter 8). The bombing was the worst act of terrorism in American history and rather discredited the more extreme Republicans. Nevertheless, there is a continuum between Republican conservatism and the more extreme anti-state activists.

The mood of hostility in fact is a modern manifestation of a strong American tradition of suspicion going back to the Founding Fathers and Thomas Jefferson, as well as the extensive anarchist tradition. For many the end of the Cold War in 1991 has removed the final justification for central government, and has been followed be an explosion of anti-state feeling that may not die down until substantial changes are made in the American political system.

New Right ideas in the 1990s and since

During the 1980s the Republican Party was the party of the New Right, while the Democratic Party was dominated by its left or 'liberal' wing. In the early 1990s, especially with the advent of President Bill Clinton (elected 1992), it was felt that perhaps conservatism was in retreat. But this was not the case. In the first place, Clinton was a 'New Democrat', meaning that he was only moderately left on social issues and to the right on economic issues, and was not tied to 'special interest groups' such as the unions. This centrist formula was very similar to that of Tony Blair's New Labour and many European social democratic parties (see Chapter 5). Indeed, Clinton and Blair participated together in seminars on the 'Third Way', designed to develop the centrist agenda.

Furthermore, the Republican conservatives had a remarkable revival in the Congressional elections of 1994 when the Speaker of the House, Newt Gingrich, led the Republicans to a position of dominance in both Houses of Congress for the first time in forty years with a strongly conservative manifesto.

This was called the 'Contract with America' designed to 'renew the American Dream' through commitments to reduce central government, reduce taxes, limit welfare, spend more on law and order and defence and make government more responsible to the electorate. The more skilful Clinton outmanoeuvred Gingrich and went on to be re-elected in 1996. Nevertheless, Republican domination of Congress limited what Clinton could accomplish in social policy.

The presidential election of 2000 was widely seen as a decisive election determining whether America would swing to the right or left. At the outset it seemed that the Democratic candidate, Vice President Al Gore, would continue the Clinton centrist legacy, but at the Democratic convention Gore moved the party more to the left with traditional 'liberal' rhetoric about protecting ordinary working people against the big corporations and increases in welfare. This was the kind of platform that Clinton had moved away from, and was regarded by some as Gore's mistake. The Republican winner, George W. Bush, presented a moderate conservatism, with modest tax cuts, reducing government and limiting America's commitments overseas. He also talked of 'compassionate conservatism', which seemed to mean little more than encouraging voluntary bodies, such as churches, to be more involved in providing welfare. The religious right maintained a low profile throughout the campaign.

However, far from being a watershed, the 2000 election proved to be probably the most indecisive in American history. The confusion over the much-disputed hairsbreadth result was compounded by the fact that the losing candidate won more votes across America and that Congress was divided equally between the two parties. Whether this election indicated a change of direction in American politics may take a long time to emerge.

Thatcherism after Thatcher

In Britain the New Right spectrum has never been as complex or extensive as in America. There is, for example, no British equivalent of the religious right. Nevertheless, Mrs Thatcher did combine her neo-liberalism with certain traditional right-wing features. She had little time for tradition for its own sake, yet she emphasised 'traditional values'. This sometimes led to tensions in her outlook. An example was broadcasting policy, where she believed that everything should be left to the market and consumer choice; except, that is, when it came to the portrayal of sex and violence, which needed to be subject to strict government control.

A more important traditional concern of the right that was combined with neo-liberalism was nationalism. This was chiefly manifested in Mrs Thatcher's growing hostility to the EU. Relations with Europe precipitated several crises during her period of office and were a factor in her rejection by her party in 1990. Under her successor, John Major, the neo-liberal programme was continued in seeking the reduction of government, privatisation and, whenever possible, reducing taxation. Despite this the party was riven by conflict over Europe, which was a major factor in the party's catastrophic defeat in 1997.

The scale of the defeat left the next Conservative leader, William Hague, with the difficult task of reconstructing the party's outlook and programme. This task was made hugely more difficult by the fact that the New Labour that won so massively in 1997 had appropriated a significant part of the Thatcher neo-liberal legacy. The Blair government pursued supply-side economics, privatisation and welfare reform, cut direct taxes and emphasised law and order. It has been difficult for William Hague to position the party to the right of Labour without appearing extreme and doctrinaire. The parliamentary party shifted to the right in the 1990s, and Thatcherism remained as dominant as ever.

Lower public expenditure and further reductions in taxation were promised, although the most striking difference between the parties was over Europe. Hague isolated the leading pro-Europeans in his party and united the party around opposition to joining the European Single Currency in the near future. The party as a whole has grown more hostile to Europe, although potential for conflict remains. There are still 'one-nation' pro-European conservatives, while at the other extreme there are those who would withdraw from Europe immediately. The right also has its own internal conflict. On the one hand, there are libertarians who would dismantle the welfare state and drastically diminish government altogether (see, for example, Duncan and Hobson, 1995), and who take a tolerant attitude towards different lifestyles. On the other, there are moral authoritarians who would pursue more interventionist policies in support of traditional standards and values.

Criticisms of the New Right

Much might be made of the relationship between the new free-market and libertarian ideas as against the old right ideas of authority and discipline. Certainly there are conflicts and contradictions here. However, the New Right stands or falls by its neo-liberal core.

Neo-liberalism is a vigorous, crusading ideology, and its critics attack it with corresponding vigour and passion. For many, a return to *laissez-faire* represents a return to barbarism, with society based on the law of the jungle in which the strong survive and the weak go to the wall. It would, so the argument goes, create a society where vast wealth would go side by side with great poverty, squalor and distress; where the lives of a great part of the population would be governed by fear and insecurity; and where greed and rapaciousness would rule and all would seek to exploit everyone else. More specifically, there are plenty of detailed theoretical criticisms to be found for individual aspects of neo-liberal thought.

The free market

Neo-liberals will brook no criticisms of the free market. They insist that the free market is the guarantee of maximum prosperity for all, of justice and fairness, and of all other freedoms. Critics point out that with unrestrained capital people are exploited and damaged, as was evident from the nineteenth-century industrial system with such horrors as children working in factories and mines. Misery was caused on a massive scale, particularly in conditions of slump. From the establishment of the free market there was a cycle of booms and slumps that culminated in the Great Depression of the 1930s which caused huge distress, dislocation, waste and political instability, which contributed to the rise of Hitler and the Second World War.

The present rush towards globalisation is creating its own tensions and instabilities. A growing free market always tends to be destructive of traditional ways of life and practices and values. This can and has created local tensions, with regions seeking independence, religious attacks on Westernisation and other conflicts (see, for example, the discussion of John Gray, a former New Right enthusiast, in *False Dawn: The Delusions of Global Capitalism*, 1998).

Adam Smith's benign 'invisible hand' is, critics argue, a myth. There is no compelling reason why the free operation of the market will result in the optimum benefit for all. It is more like a random distribution of gross wealth for the few and misery for the many. Furthermore, the notion that state intervention to influence the economy or distribute welfare only ruins the system is nowhere proven. The economic difficulties of the 1970s were due to the oil price rises, not government intervention. Besides, the most successful economies – Germany and Japan – are certainly not based on a complete absence of government intervention. The main neo-liberal argument against the managed economy – that it is the thin end of a totalitarian wedge – is simply based on prejudice and demonstrably not true.

The neo-liberal attack on the welfare state is also challenged on the grounds of weak evidence. Certainly there are administrative problems and schemes that do not work, but neo-liberals triumphantly represent these as the whole. All major organisations and administrative systems have their problems, and can be made to look foolish by generalising examples of failure, especially in times of economic stringency. In a similar way, socialists of various kinds have little difficulty, and take equal delight, in finding inefficiency, waste and absurdity in the workings of capitalism.

A narrow freedom

Critics also question neo-liberal notions of freedom and justice. Freedom in particular, they say, is defined far too narrowly. To say that someone is free when they only have formal liberties which they cannot possibly enjoy, relies on a definition of freedom that is quite arbitrary. Moreover, it is not at all clear that the neo-liberals have disposed of the social-liberal/socialist case that people who are deprived, exploited and denied education and adequate health and housing because of their poverty, are genuinely free just because they technically have civil liberties. Neo-liberals argue that a concept of freedom which says that people have a right to be free from these things is contradictory because ensuring such freedom would involve some people losing their liberty. But it is not that black and white. The rich would lose a tiny amount of freedom, of which they have a very great deal, in the interests of greater freedom for the majority. To say that this necessarily involves or leads to totalitarian tyranny is merely melodramatic.

Having defined freedom in an absurdly restricted way that suits the rich and successful and nobody else, the neo-liberals proceed, critics argue, illegitimately to elevate this freedom to be the supreme value, and the only one of any worth. Other values are either ignored altogether (as with notions of community) or else defined in terms of it. Thus, the just society is one where unrestricted freedom prevails, and where social outcomes are entirely determined by the market. Such a society is seen as necessarily just, quite irrespective of whether people are prosperous and happy or starving and exploited. A society where social justice is pursued in the name of a wider notion of freedom is deemed unjust, purely on the grounds that the market is interfered with. There is no reason to accept the insistence of Hayek and Nozick that 'social justice' is a meaningless phrase, or that a situation cannot be unfair if nobody planned it or acted to bring it about.

Natural rights and human nature

Nozick and a number of others who take an extremely narrow view of what government can legitimately do, rely ultimately upon a notion of natural rights, and especially a natural right to property. For Nozick this right is absolute and inviolable. But the idea that such rights exist is extremely difficult to demonstrate. John Locke, who was the first to argue that a natural right to property existed, insisted that these rights had been granted to mankind by God. But the existence of God is not something that can be proved, and by no means all who do have faith believe in a God-given right to property. If we do not rely on religious ideas, then it is not sufficient to merely assert that we have such rights. We need to be able to prove their existence to someone who denies they exist. But there would appear to be no such proof. Certainly Nozick does not supply one.

Another object of criticism is the notion that social liberalism, fascism and every variety of socialism all amount to the same thing. It is a crucial part of the neo-liberal case against wider notions of freedom, the welfare state, the mixed economy and other aspects of state activity in the modern world. But this lumping together, critics argue, is entirely illegitimate. One can draw a multitude of distinctions and point to a host of differences. Social liberals and social democrats are particularly resentful of being identified with communism and fascism. The notion that a welfare state like Britain's is a giant step on the road to totalitarianism is ridiculous. The point of all this lumping together is in order to promote the totally false suggestion that the only real alternative to the neo-liberal society is totalitarianism or proto-totalitarianism.

Finally, neo-liberals see human nature in terms of a selfishness and a competitiveness which when given free reign, thanks to some happy contrivance of nature or the divine, always ensures harmony and progress. Critics point out that such selfishness simply contradicts common experience, and that, mercifully, human beings have many other qualities. It is precisely these other qualities that make civilised life possible. If people were just selfish and competitive then we could hardly have a social life at all. Theories like public choice theory simply ignore all the other qualities that produced the public system and make it run; besides, if it were true, then it would not have taken political scientists so long to think it up. If anything, human nature has so many facets and characteristics that to pick out one and call it fundamental is to risk looking foolish.

Of course neo-liberals defend themselves against such criticisms, and they have managed to capture parties and governments in major states. On the other hand, these governments have had to be cautious about implementing many neo-liberal ideas. For neither President Reagan nor Mrs Thatcher was it politically possible to do away with state welfare. Both gave way to less committed successors, and while neo-liberal ideas have been influential in many parts of the world, the total commitment of Reaganites and Thatcherites has rarely characterised other governments. All of which gives rise to questions about the future of neo-liberalism. The New Right is still one of the most vigorous ideologies in today's world. Some see it as the last of the great universal ideologies, and perhaps, if we live in a postmodern world, it is doomed for that reason. On the other hand, there are features of neo-liberalism that fit in with postmodern ideas, such as the emphasis upon freedom and individuality and consumer choice. Indeed, the free market is just what is creating the present world at such an alarming pace, although what the consequences will ultimately be, no one can say.

10

Feminism and liberation ideology

Most of the ideological beliefs that influence politics in the world today belong to broad traditions of thought that began to take shape around the period of the French Revolution. However, in recent decades there have developed a number of ideological outlooks that stand somewhat apart from the main traditions, including animal rights, gay liberation and the ideas of the green movement. These new ideological developments have been associated with what political scientists have called 'new social movements' which since the 1960s have pursued political objectives outside the organisation and agendas of normal political parties, and have added a new dimension to democratic politics. Among the most important of these movements has been the women's movement. However, this movement, together with its feminist ideology, is unusual in that it can be said to be both a new movement and an old one.

Feminism, like most modern ideologies, dates its continuous life from the French Revolution, and by the middle of the twentieth century it had built up a substantial body of writings and theory. However, virtually all such expressions of feminism were linked to the values and ideas of other ideologies, principally liberalism and socialism. It was not until the late 1960s with the advent of 'women's liberation' or 'second wave' feminism that it could be said to have achieved emancipation. It virtually reinvented itself as a new ideology. As such it belongs to a group of the new ideologies associated with new social movements that are sometimes called 'liberation' ideologies. They include black liberation, gay liberation, animal liberation and liberation theology. These will be discussed later in the chapter. In the meanwhile, to understand contemporary feminism we need to look at the whole of its development.

Early feminism

In virtually every society in recorded history women have been accorded a subordinate role, principally confined to the home and excluded from the public affairs of society. From time to time the protest has been made that this is unfair and wasteful, and occasionally the possibility of an alternative has been articulated (for example in Plato's *Republic* where he argued that women were as fitted to be philosopher-rulers as men), but it was the advent of liberalism that provided the first vehicle for a sustained tradition of feminist writing and theorising to develop.

Early liberal ideology was based on the notion of natural rights to which all men are entitled by virtue of their reason. The term 'men' was being used generically (that is, meaning 'humanity'), yet for many the early theorists it was only the male part of humanity that was entitled to the full exercise of those rights which they deemed natural. Locke, for example, did not extend full civil and political rights to women, although he gave no reasons, while the far more egalitarian Rousseau insisted on women's 'sexual nature' fitting them for the role of pleasing men and looking after a husband and family. Only with the coming of the French Revolution was there a significant theoretical work to insist that natural rights applied as fully to women as to men.

Mary Wollstonecraft and liberal feminism

The publication of Edmund Burke's *Reflections on the Revolution in France* in 1790 provoked an array of radical responses; and these included the first major feminist work: Mary Wollstonecraft's *Vindication of the Rights of Women* (1792). In essence the work applies liberal values and arguments to the women's case. She rejected the view that women's inferior position was God-given and natural, insisting that women's nature was primarily human. Before anything else a woman was a rational being, and therefore entitled to the same rights of liberty and self-determination as a man.

If women often seemed little fit for wider responsibilities, it was because they were not educated and not had the opportunity to develop themselves, their talents or their character. They had been brought up to be dependent and submissive and emotional because of society's false conception of their true nature. If they could be properly educated, if they could enjoy full civil rights (Wollstonecraft was ambiguous about political rights), and if they could be legally independent of their husbands and exercise their talents in any occupation, then they would be full members of society and fit companions for men.

Wollstonecraft had little doubt that only a minority of exceptional women would pursue independent careers and that the majority would find fulfilment in the roles of wife and mother. Nevertheless, proper rigorous education, the end of legal dependence on the husband, and the demonstrated capacity of women for occupation, even if it is not pursued, would give women the independence and capacity to be effective wives and mothers, and through the exercise of reason and virtue in that role (though not exclusively in that role) to fulfil their nature as human beings.

In not challenging the family, or women's traditional responsibilities within it, Wollstonecraft was at one with most liberal thinkers, feminist and non-feminist. Similar arguments were put forward by a range of both male and female liberal theorists during the course of the nineteenth century (the most famous being John Stuart Mill). They fuelled a growing movement for the extension of women's rights which flourished from the middle of the century in Europe, America and parts of the British Empire. In America the movement for women's rights grew out of the movement to abolish slavery and began with a famous conference at Seneca Falls in 1848. The result of all this activism was a steady extension of women's civil rights in the late nineteenth century, including the right to hold property within marriage and have access to higher education and the professions. After a series of militant campaigns, such as the Suffragettes in Britain, this was extended to political rights, mostly after the First World War.

Charles Fourier and socialist feminism

In the meanwhile, the women's cause was taken up by ideologies on the left. From the beginning of the modern socialist tradition, most theorists have been enthusiastic feminists. This is perhaps partly because socialists (that is, what we have called 'classical socialists' who have sought the abolition of capitalism) have generally wanted to see the abolition of the existing family. One of the most interesting examples is the 'utopian' socialist, Charles Fourier (see Chapter 5). He saw history in terms of a series of progressive stages, and the status and treatment of women as the critical indicator of progress: the higher their status and greater their liberty, the more advanced the stage of civilisation. Ultimately, in the ideal society of co-operative communes that he envisaged, the restrictive family would be abolished and women would be able to develop themselves fully. When that happened, he believed, women would outshine men both in qualities of character and in the performance of any activity that did not depend on physical strength.

Fourier saw both the family and monogamous marriage as oppressive to women. In the future, women and men would choose partners as and when their inclination dictated. In his 'phalanstery' there would be a 'hotel system' with private accommodation and common services, for such as eating and cleaning, which would be undertaken by those for whom these were chosen occupations. Similarly, children would be cared for communally by those who specialise in the work, while still leaving room for the exercise of parental affection. This would free women for any occupation (or occupations) they chose on the same basis as men. However, Fourier is unusual objecting to monogamous marriage, since in most socialist thinking the abolition of the traditional family is not meant to imply the abolition of marriage. The more common argument has been that in capitalist society women may have a formal equality with their husbands, but the reality is of subordination because of the husband's economic power (that is, earning power and control over family property, and so on). In socialist society, these considerations would not arise and marriage would be a genuine partnership of equals.

There were various other socialists who developed feminist ideas in other directions. For example, Charlotte Perkins Gilman (1860–1937) was greatly influential in the USA after the publication of her *Women and Economics* in 1898, in which she developed a social Darwinist version of socialist feminism. She believed that the processes of social development, of differentiation and specialisation, were processes from which women were excluded, and this was simply because men had enslaved women and condemned them to a mindless domesticity. Women were thereby prevented from making their contribution to progress and to the fulfilment of human destiny. Gilman also wrote several feminist utopias of which *Herland* (1915), picturing a society composed entirely of women, is the most famous.

Marxist feminism

Like Fourier, Marx also believed that the status of women was an indicator of progress and that they would only develop to their full potential, equal with men, when released from the bourgeois family. However, Marx himself wrote little on the subject, leaving that to his collaborator Frederich Engels, who produced the major Marxist work on the position of women in class society, *The Origin of the Family, Private Property and the State* in 1884.

In this book, Engels set out to trace the development of the family and women's place in society through various stages of history. His account of the early stages was based on the speculations of the American anthropologist Lewis Morgan, and saw the early stages of society, before the rise of private property, as based on communal property, matriarchy, group marriage and descent through the female line. But with the development of private property came the dominance of the male, who wished to pass his property to his recognised heirs: hence monogamy (at least for females) and descent through the male line. It was, Engels declared, a world-historical defeat for the female sex, and was followed by millennia of domination and oppression of women by men in differing forms according to the historical form of society.

The modern bourgeois family, supposedly based on love, is in fact based on a form of prostitution in which a woman must sell herself into domestic slavery in order to live. The man has all the economic power, so that within the home he is, in a sense, the bourgeois while the wife is the proletarian. The family is an economic unit and its whole existence is bound up with property. The communist revolution, by abolishing private property, would remove the economic basis of the monogamous bourgeois family. Housekeeping and child-care would become matters of public provision, and marriage would become genuinely based on love and mutual respect. It was the family and not marriage that was the obstacle to women's emancipation and full entry into society.

Women's freedom and equality is, therefore, bound up with the emancipation of humanity and only fully realisable through a communist revolution (see Chapter 7).

The Bolshevic Revolution of 1917 provided an opportunity to put these ideas into practice. Led by Alexandra Kollontai, Commissar of Social Welfare and head of the Central Women's Department, the new Soviet state began to implement laws giving women a new status and new freedom from the family. However, within a few years the policy was changed and women were exhorted to be good mothers and maintain family life. In a sense they were worse off in that women were expected to be full-time workers and fulfil all their traditional family duties at the same time (although some changes were retained, such as easy divorce).

Achievement and disillusion

The practical movement to change the condition of women was dominated by the liberal feminists, who in the late nineteenth and early twentieth centuries secured many important rights for women in terms of the removal of legal disabilities, access to education and the professions and above all the right to vote. New Zealand was the first modern state to give women the vote in 1893. Women over the age of thirty were enfranchised in Britain in 1918, while all American women received the vote in 1920 (although earlier in some states of the Union).

As these gains were secured, feminism as an active movement went into a substantial period of quiescence, as though the gains had to be experienced and digested and evaluated. There were still women who, through what they did or what they wrote, challenged the prevailing norms. Nevertheless, feminism as a movement shrank to being the preoccupation of a few. Discussion among intellectuals continued and this flourished increasingly after the Second World War.

Although there was formal equality for women and, in the 1950s and 1960s, there was growing affluence for the overwhelming majority of people in the West, there was also a degree of disillusionment. Despite the gains, the world was overwhelmingly male-dominated and women were heavily discriminated against in almost every walk of life. Two writers in particular articulated these feelings and their books caught the imagination of a generation of women. The work of Simone de Beauvoir and Betty Friedan can be seen as precursors of the later feminist movement that exploded in the late 1960s.

In *The Second Sex* (1952) de Beauvoir gives a long and penetrating account of women's subjection. She argues that women have always been defined in terms of their feminine nature, and therefore in terms of their relationship with men. Men, on the other hand, are defined as free, independent beings, and not in terms of their relationship with women. This asymmetry both expresses and is part of men's domination of women. Since women are defined in terms of their sex and not their human rationality and freedom, they are being classified as incomplete human beings. Men subordinate women in order to guarantee their own freedom, but the price is unsatisfactory relationships.

There is a good deal of existentialist philosophy in de Beauvoir's analysis which reflects the influence of her lifetime partner, Jean-Paul Sartre; yet, unlike Sartre, she is not ultimately pessimistic about human relationships. She believes that, while the differences between men and women are more than merely physical, she does believe that women can assert their freedom and transform their lives, and can achieve satisfactory relationships with men on the basis of equality.

Betty Friedan's book, *The Feminine Mystique* (1963), was significant in changing the direction of liberal feminism, flatly rejecting the taken-for-granted assumption that women were different, had basic characteristics that especially fitted them for domesticity, and just needed formal equality of status. For Friedan this was just not good enough. She insisted that the differences, symbolised in the so-called 'feminine mystique', were overrated, and what women really wanted and needed was to get out in the world, have careers and compete equally with men.

However, despite the importance of de Beauvoir's and Friedan's work, it was in the late 1960s that modern feminism, what is sometimes called feminism's 'second wave', really took off. This happened when growing discontent felt by women, especially young women, began to be articulated in terms of the concepts and categories of the New Left.

Second wave feminism

The late 1960s 'second wave' of feminism, or 'women's liberation', amounted to virtually a new ideology. Previous feminist theory was always an extension or special case of more comprehensive ideologies; but with the development of radical feminism that was no longer the case. Radical feminism became a new strand of feminism in its own right, but also influenced other strands, so that, at least initially, the women's liberation movement had a certain unity of outlook. A number of radical writers, like Kate Millett and Germaine Greer, influenced feminism generally, while others, such as Shulamith Firestone, are more strictly confined to the movement's radical wing.

Kate Millett and patriarchy

Characteristic of the new thinking, and widely influential across the feminist spectrum, was Kate Millett's *Sexual Politics* (1970). Like much of the early women's liberation theory, it was much influenced by New Left ideas, with its notions of domination and repression and alienation, and the use of psychoanalytic concepts. Nevertheless, the problem she posed and the conclusions she reached struck a chord far beyond radical politics. She simply asked why it was that in a free society, where women have the full range of civil and political rights and all possible educational opportunities, that all important decisions in society are made by men, that women have to suffer a subordinate role that men had assigned to them.

It was Millett's book that developed the modern feminist's concept of 'patriarchy' to explain women's subordination and oppression. She said it worked by brainwashing women from childhood into accepting a role that was constructed for them by men, and reinforced by law, tradition, language, social 'science' and such aspects of popular culture as television and women's magazines. The main stereotype was the wife and mother: passive and caring, emotional rather than logical, and preoccupied with domestic matters and personal appearance. (The other common stereotype, though not socially approved, was of the whore and temptress. Women were here portrayed as a little more independent and dangerous, but still there for the benefit of men.)

Distinguished social scientists, such as Talcott Parsons who was the most influential sociologist of his day, described women's role in society as based on biology, while significantly giving men no such specific role. Women internalised these sex-role stereotypes and came to accept them as natural. In other words, differences of 'masculine' and 'feminine' were treated as sexual differences (that is, deriving from nature), instead of as what they really are, which is gender differences based on socially constructed roles. Those women who did not see their fundamental role as domestic and rejected the stereotype tended to be derided as 'unnatural'; in the Freudian view they are suffering from 'penis envy' (feminists think Freud has a lot to answer for). Thus, from all sides there was pressure on women to conform to the stereotype, and in this way women were kept in subjection with no overt coercion being employed.

Millett also developed the notion of 'sexual politics' by arguing that even in the most personal relations between men and women, it is men who control the sexual relations, take the initiative and define and restrict female sexuality in terms of their own needs, leaving women often unfulfilled. This is deemed 'political' in the sense that it is a power relationship, a relationship of domination and subordination, a dimension of the situation where the subordinate exists for the sake of the dominant; in other words it is a dimension of patriarchy. The traditional view of politics as belonging to the public sphere which is separate from the private sphere (a distinction particularly important in liberal thinking), is challenged and a distinctly feminist view of politics is seen as encompassing even the most intimate aspects of our lives. Hence the feminist slogan: 'The personal is the political'.

Aspects of patriarchy

Many other writers worked along the same lines and developed different aspects of the analysis of patriarchy, such as language and how women appear in history and literature and in social and political theory. Earlier thinkers discussed in previous chapters of this book (all male), for example, invariably talked in terms of 'man in society', the 'nature of man' and so on. Thus, the American *Declaration of Independence* talks of all *men* being equal, while even figures sympathetic to the women's cause, such as Karl Marx, always talked automatically of humanity in masculine terms, as in 'to each according to *his* need'. While some theorists like Locke and Rousseau did explicitly give women an inferior status, for the most part there was no deliberate denigration of women, it was merely taken for granted that 'man' stood for all human beings. But it was just this assumption to which feminists drew attention. The point being that in a multitude of small cultural ways – such as the generic use of 'man', God always being presented as male, heads of committees always being 'chair*man*', and so on – the male is always the standard, implying that the female is very much the 'second sex'. Women therefore demanded changes in the way we speak and write; although some of the changes demanded by the more radical are less convincing than others, such as 'herstory' instead of 'history'.

There was a general reaction against the notion of women as 'different', that they had different emotions, that they valued different things, that they had different ways of thinking, that they had different needs, including sexual needs. This question was addressed by Germaine Greer in her influential book, *The Female Eunuch* (1971). Greer argued that the traditional conception of female sexuality as being soft and passive was in fact a stereotype imposed by men, which satisfied them but left women unfulfilled. Women's true sexuality was distorted and repressed to the point of effectively rendering them 'castrated' and sexless, mere 'sex-objects'. Greer was influenced by Herbert Marcuse's analysis of contemporary society as repressive and in need of sexual liberation, applying the idea particularly to women. There was indeed something of a fashion in the late 1960s for aggressive heterosexuality and a rejection of the passive image. More generally, women insisted on being treated as 'persons' and not 'sex-objects'; they resented being patronised and put into categories and told that 'all women think like this'.

This general rejection of 'stereotyping', of how women ought to think or behave or look, was the origin of the notorious 'bra burning' which radical feminists were supposed to go in for, that became part of the popular press image of feminists as bra-burning lesbians. Insofar as any feminists did do such things, it was a comprehensible symbolic act that rejected the stereotyped image of the ideal of woman as being of a certain shape which all women were supposed to try to achieve in order to please men. It went along with attacks on pornography and beauty contests.

Lesbianism was also deemed as something that was artificially classified as 'unnatural'. Its condemnation by society was interpreted as part of a general denigration of any female behaviour that did not conform to the male-imposed stereotype, the mould constructed by men into which women's behaviour is forced in order to keep them subservient. In this respect all feminists recognised a common cause with gay men, who are also engaged in challenging the sexual stereotype of their own sex.

The initial second wave feminist ideal was not just a society with no discrimination on grounds of sex, but a society that was 'androgynous'. This would be a society where men and women were not expected to behave differently and have different roles; a society where a woman's 'masculine' characteristics (such as ambition and aggression) and a man's 'feminine' characteristics (such as gentleness and caring) are not suppressed. Men and women can therefore be themselves, be 'natural' instead of trying to conform to some socially constructed stereotype.

Liberals and socialists

Much of this radical analysis became common across three main types of feminist thought. There were theorists and groups recognisably liberal in their outlook, other recognisably socialist, and now a new category of radical feminists. These broad divisions still remain, although they exist as neat categories more in the minds of those trying to describe feminism than in practice. There is great variety and considerable overlapping, and at the grass roots of the feminist movement a good deal of eclecticism, taking from different theories and traditions whatever seems useful. Nevertheless, these divisions have some use in gaining an initial understanding of a complex field.

Post-1968, liberal and socialist feminism continued to flourish. The liberal preoccupation with rights has been extended to making those rights a reality. That is, not merely the right of women to enter the professions, politics, and other traditional male preserves, but also to see women in senior positions. In America, the National Organisation for Women (NOW) is the biggest women's organisation, whose major campaign is for an amendment to the US Constitution that would ban discrimination on grounds of sex. Such campaigns are characteristic of liberal feminism.

Socialist feminists often support these campaigns, but often campaign in addition for working women's and black women's causes. The vital difference, however, is that while liberal feminists seek a change in women's situation within an accepted liberal-capitalist framework, socialist feminists see women's liberation as part of a more general liberation following the abolition of capitalism. Theoretically, they have been principally concerned with integrating new developments in feminist thought into socialist theory. As a result, they put less emphasis on the traditional notion that female oppression is part of the mechanism by which the capitalist class keeps the working class divided and therefore less revolutionary, and more on developing the view that women suffer a double oppression, of men and the capitalist combined. It is a view that rejects the traditional Marxist-feminist belief that the overthrow of capitalism is itself sufficient for emancipation.

Socialist feminists are usually associated with groups and parties on the far left generally, whereas radicals have gone in more for small group structures, 'consciousness raising', sharing experiences, more anarchist in the sense of preferring leaderless, grass roots, federal organisations, without formal national structures. Some, especially the 'anarcha-feminists', insisting that conventional state and party power structures are essentially masculine. But as well as organisationally, it is the radicals who have been the most innovative and interesting theoretically.

Shulamith Firestone and the primacy of sexual oppression

Although often sympathetic and theoretically close to the socialists, radicals are uncompromising in their insistence that the cause of women's oppression is not class or socialisation or any other social structure or process, but simply and emphatically *men*. Men are the enemy. It is, therefore, just not enough to give women more of the important jobs or facilities for easing the burdens of child care, or to change the social structure. Women's oppression goes much deeper and its ending requires more drastic change. This argument is an important aspect of feminism's emancipation from other doctrines.

For socialists who follow Engels, women's oppression, like racial oppression, is a special case of class oppression. But radicals argue that, on the contrary, it is the oppression of women by men that is the most fundamental, and that other oppressions, of class or race or whatever, are special cases or extensions of the basic sexual oppression. The most sophisticated expression of this view is that of Shulamith Firestone in her book *The Dialectic of Sex* (1970).

Firestone argues that Marxism's historical materialism is correct in form but incorrect in substance, in that it does not recognise that the root inequality and therefore the root oppression is that of women by men. Class domination and exploitation begins with 'sex class', economic class comes later. The origin is biological. Because of women's role in reproduction, and their consequent dependence on men, they are vulnerable and exploited. Women's oppression is, therefore, built into the biological family.

Consequently, the key to revolution is sexual revolution. It is not the overthrow of bourgeois capitalism that is the key to human emancipation:

> unless revolution uproots the basic, social organisation, the biological family ... the tapeworm of exploitation can never be annihilated. We shall need a sexual revolution much larger than – inclusive of – a socialist one to truly eradicate all class systems.
>
> (Firestone, 1970)

The obvious question arises as to how this is possible. Firestone puts her faith in science. By means of 'artificial reproduction', and by socialising childcare (that is, sharing the work among all members of society), women's physical and psychological responsibility for reproduction would be eliminated, and their liberation possible.

Although not all radicals accept Firestone's analysis in full (and still less her prescriptions), they do share the belief that the basic problem is men and not society, that sexual oppression is the most basic oppression and that the emancipation of women is the necessary condition of the emancipation of humanity from other forms of oppression. However, beyond this common outlook there is much controversy over a wide range of issues.

Controversies within radical feminism

Some radicals still hold to the Engels view of a matriarchal golden age, and it is a convenient morale-raising myth, but few sophisticated feminists now take it seriously. The more common view is that, whatever the historical origins, what is important is that women's oppression is now being reaffirmed and reproduced day after day and generation after generation. The nature of the oppression is made up of various kinds: economic, legal, psychological and so on; but there is some controversy over what is basic, what is the root. For some it is physical violence. For example, Susan Brownmiller, in her book *Against Our Will* (1976), insists that it is the ultimate threat of rape that keeps women in subjection, and that every time a man rapes a women he is doing so on behalf of his whole sex, reinforcing the fear of violence and violation that keeps them submissive.

Another source of difference and controversy within the feminist movement is the question of the nature and importance of 'feminine characteristics'. In the first flush of 1960s feminism the tendency was to regard supposed feminine characteristics as a myth, a set of submissive and domestic qualities imposed upon women as a means of oppressing them. They were just part of the 'stereotyping process'. Consequently, women who had opted for domesticity were seen as somehow betraying their 'sisters'. But since then there has been something of a change of heart among feminists of all varieties. Many women felt that the early denigration of the family, the insistence on competing with men on equal terms and the ideal of the androgynous society, in fact denigrated and denied the value of the experience of most women; while the ideal of a career and public role smacked too much of having to 'be like men'.

It was argued that while 'women's characteristics' may have been the result of stereotyping and an immensely long period of subordination, they are nevertheless the stuff of women's experience and are the source of values and of a moral vision that could be the foundation of a better world. In response to such arguments there has been much more of a tendency to celebrate women's experience and women's culture and therefore 'feminine qualities' like caring and co-operation, whatever the origins may be. This in turn has led to an impetus to recover women's history and achievements, which had initially tended to be ignored. The view of 'women's qualities' that gained ground was that while they may have been artificially emphasised in women through socialisation and women's situation, they are nevertheless characteristic of women and provide an alternative approach to the world which is at least as valid and arguably superior to the approach that stems from 'masculine characteristics'.

An important minority of feminists have, however, taken this view much further. They have revived the old view that masculine and feminine characteristics are not the result of socialisation, but are natural and inherent and have some kind of biological origin; in so doing they have rejected one of the central tenets of the modern feminist movement. However, in contrast to the older advocates of this belief, they insist upon the superiority of feminine characteristics, women's values and the female sex in general. Women, they believe, are morally superior to men and the world will only be safe and civilised when women rule it. Feminist theorists of this kind may be called 'supremacists' and include such as Mary Daly, Andrea Dworkin and Dale Spender (see, for example, Daly's *Gyn/Ecology*, 1979, or Spender's *Women of Ideas (and What Men Have Done to Them)*, 1982) . Although in a minority, their ideas, because extreme, do attract much attention and controversy.

The supremacist issue has some connection with the more practical issue of the nature of the feminist movement. Supremacists, as might be expected, abjure dealings with men. Some are lesbians, or 'political lesbians'. Political lesbianism is the view that women should strive to fulfil all their needs, including emotional and sexual, from among themselves, and that, whatever a woman's personal preference may be, a man is not essential for such fulfilment. Any woman may therefore choose to be a lesbian as a political act. Radicals who argue in this way are inclined to see women who choose to have male partners as necessarily incomplete women. They are 'man-identified', in the sense of allowing themselves to be defined in terms of a man, instead of being 'woman-identified' and therefore autonomous and complete.

But lesbianism, of whatever kind, is not a necessary condition of such a supremacist or an isolationist approach. Some argue that women's psyche is so damaged by millennia of male domination that women have to live apart for some time until recovered, before again having dealings with men. This has given rise, at the extreme, to all-women communes (especially in the USA) which try to live as apart from men and male-dominated society as possible.

Less extreme and much more common is the building of women's organisations from which various categories are excluded. Some exclude women in a permanent relationship with a man, others just exclude men however sympathetic to the cause. In fact small groups of women sharing experiences and giving each other support are a notable feature of the women's movement in general. Liberal feminists tend to be the least impressed by these arguments and least likely to exclude men from their political campaigns.

Although in total a considerable movement around the world, national or international organisation is limited. Women's political parties, for example, are almost unknown (in marked contrast to such as the greens). This would seem to be because, compared with the green movement, feminism is much more diffuse and intangible in its goals and priorities, and some at least are firmly locked into pre-existing ideological outlooks with their accompanying antipathies. Different trends within feminism have developed their own networks of groups, often at odds with each other. Some have argued that these conflicts are now redundant and we are now in a situation of 'postfeminism'. This is a complex and controversial term that needs some discussion.

Postfeminism, postmodernism and the future
of the women's movement

The term 'postfeminism' has become fashionable, but tends to mean a number of different things. Initially it was used, especially in France, by continental feminists, who were influenced by structuralism and post-structuralism. They rejected contemporary American and British feminism as based on a too-shallow analysis which theirs went beyond (hence 'post'). This meaning remains, but the term is now more commonly used in a quite different sense to refer to an attitude among many women of disillusionment with feminism as too strident and unappreciative of women's success. This change of mood has implications for the future of the women's movement.

French postfeminism and postmodern feminism

The origins of early postfeminist thought lay in French structuralist and post-structuralist thinking of the 1960s onwards (see Chapter 13). Structuralism and poststructuralism are based on the idea that our language does not in fact reflect the world (as common sense would suggest) but creates the world in the sense that the way we divide up the world so we can understand it is determined by the structure of our language. It was thought to follow that our assumed independence as free autonomous individuals who generate meaning is something of an illusion; language determines most of what we think and therefore behave. Jacques Lacan applied these ideas to psychoanalysis and reinterpreted Freud so that our inner psychology reflects the structure of language. In particular our sexual identity develops around the binary oppositions of language, such as male/female, mind/body, culture/nature, and in a way that always privileges the male. Thus, our language and thought processes are 'phallocentric', built around the superiority of maleness.

Following Freud, Lacan saw male sexuality and sense of self as basic, with female sexuality interpreted as derivative and secondary. The female sense of self is derived from the sense of the lack of maleness or 'penis envy' (the feeling of 'anatomical lack' ultimately translating into the desire for children). French postfeminists, such as Hélène Cixous, Luce Irigaray and Julia Kristeva accepted male-centredness as built into our language and thinking, but argued that female sexuality and identity is not derivative from male but distorted and suppressed by male power that is embodied in language.

Using post-structuralist techniques of 'deconstruction' they seek to expose and challenge the male-dominatedness of language, and indeed to develop female, or at least neutral, ways of writing and thinking, known as *écriture féminine* (developed initially by Cixous in the 1970s). Changing the language was the key to changing the world. The term 'postfeminism' came from their initial rejection of earlier feminism as being concerned exclusively with the assertion of women's rights. While these thinkers actively supported campaigns for these rights, they believed this was not enough and that a much deeper transformation of culture and society was necessary. This version of the term 'postfeminism' is therefore somewhat misleading, and its ideas can be understood as one version of feminism amongst others.

Structuralism and post-structuralism found little favour in Britain or the anglophone world generally. It was only as postmodern ideas, which incorporated a good deal of post-structuralism, became gradually more acceptable through the 1980s and 1990s that this version of feminism became more influential. The postmodernist dimension (evident in Kristeva and others) involves a challenging of the idea of 'woman' as a universal category. Postmodernists are anti-essentialist and suspicious of universal categories in general. The notion of essential human nature for example, with specific human attributes and needs, as a source of political ideal society is rejected because it inevitably marginalises somebody who does not fit the stereotype and may be ignored or forced to fit it. In contrast postmodernism asserts and celebrates difference and variety. Similarly, insisting on a universal notion of woman, with universal characteristics and needs, may well lead to the playing down of difference and certain groups suffering unjustly because they do not conform. Postmodern feminism, therefore, emphasises the differences among women, due to such factors as class, race and sexuality.

Postfeminism and the women's movement today

Post-structural and postmodern feminism add to the variety, but also the fragmentation of feminism. In the 1980s and especially the 1990s and since, feminist thinking has run into a bewildering number of channels. Apart from the varieties already mentioned, there a multiplicity of theories, perspectives and methodologies, often not consistent with each other. There is green feminism, black feminism, post-colonial feminism, anarcha-feminism and cyber-feminism, not to mention feminist theology, feminist geography, feminist art criticism, and many others.

At the same time, feminism as a political movement has somewhat declined in vigour. There are still political campaigns and internal conflicts between feminist groups, such as the Campaign for an Equal Rights Amendment to the American Constitution and conflicts over campaigns for abortion rights. But there has been a loss of more general support. As one writer observed in the early 1990s: 'it sometimes seems as though feminism's recent arrival within the academy has coincided with the demise of that once powerful network of grass-roots organisations which, certainly in the seventies and early eighties, constituted the heart of the women's movement' (Kemp and Squires, 1997, p.5).

This decline may be partly a result of success. There has been an extraordinary transformation of the position of women in Western societies since the 1970s. Young women today are in a far stronger position and have more confidence to assert their rights than would have been thought possible in the 1950s. Indeed, many young women today shun the feminist movement, objecting to its assumptions about how women ought to think and feel, its theoretical obscurity, and resenting the continual insistence on women as victims of male oppression that many no longer feel. It is this view that is now most commonly called 'postfeminism', and is perhaps most spectacularly articulated by the American critic Camille Paglia. Other writers, such as Naomi Wolf in America (especially *Fire with Fire*, 1993) and Natasha Walter in Britain (*The New Feminism*, 1999) have argued along similar lines, if a little less stridently. In popular culture, the term has been associated with artists such as the Spice Girls and Madonna, who insist on independence and 'girl power' but without hostility to men.

Postfeminism in the more recent and general sense is increasingly appealing as it is more positive and assertive of women's possibilities than many other versions of conventional feminism. Not surprisingly, however, some traditional feminists have attacked it as a betrayal of the feminist cause, induced by a male-dominated media (including Germaine Greer, *The Whole Woman*, 1999). Some feminists have sought to address some of the criticisms of traditional feminism while fashioning a new agenda for feminist activism. This movement has been developing in America and calls itself 'third wave feminism'. It accepts variety and even contradiction in theory and outlook, though without rejecting theory. Indeed, it has much in common with postmodern feminism in that it speaks to the variety of women's experiences, and supports different kinds of activism according to differing needs.

Feminist theory, whether or not that is seen to include postfeminist thinking, is still growing vigorously and with bewildering variety, although as a political movement feminism has less momentum than in the recent past. But perhaps this is only temporary.

Other liberation movements and ideologies

In the late 1960s and early 1970s feminism virtually reinvented itself as a new and fully independent ideology that was known, particularly in its early stages, as 'women's liberation'. The term 'liberation' and much of the general theoretical approach of the new feminism was inspired by the New Left, which was the most dynamic and influential radicalism of the time (see Chapter 7). New Left ideas similarly influenced other groups, generating a series of 'liberation ideologies', including not only women's liberation, but black liberation, gay liberation, liberation theology and animal liberation. To understand the development of these ideas we need to understand the influence of the New Left.

The New Left and 'liberation'

The New Left of the late 1960s was a departure from the fixed positions of the Cold War. Although broadly Marxist in inspiration, it was a highly eclectic movement that brought in new ideas which generated a Marxism that was very different from any previous orthodoxy. Economics was abandoned in favour of changing society immediately through a transformation of consciousness.

As a vast, sprawling, inchoate movement, the New Left was doomed to failure. Yet the New Left did develop a distinctive style of thinking that could be, and has been, applied to other things. The result has been an array of 'liberation' movements on behalf of various 'oppressed' groups, often giving new life and a sharper edge to old causes. They have demanded more than just formal equality in the recognition of rights, but insisted on an equality that necessitates, to a greater or lesser extent, a new or changed society.

The New Left style of thinking originally saw workers oppressed by capitalists in the traditional Marxist manner, but this was adapted to blacks oppressed by whites, women by men, homosexuals by heterosexuals, and so on. What was especially new about the New Left approach was the notion, derived from Marxian ideas of ideology and alienation, that the oppressed participate in their own oppression through the absorption of their oppressor's conception and evaluation of the world; that is, their oppressor's ideology, beliefs, values and language. Thus, where the workers saw the system as fair and just, and therefore their own position in it as fair and just, so blacks see themselves as naturally inferior; women accept their inferior position as normal and natural and right; homosexuals accept their feelings as 'unnatural', and so on.

A further feature of the New Left approach is that just as the oppressed are seen as participating in their own oppression, so the oppressed must participate in their own emancipation. An essential first step in this process is a 'raising of consciousness', which means to 'confront, criticise and overcome' the alien ideology which is seen as damaging the victim's psyche and from which they must be released. Finally, the oppressors themselves must be seen as alienated and as much in need of liberation as the victims; they too need a change of consciousness, involving seeing the oppressed as fellow and equal human beings. All this fits in with the New Left theme of liberation through the transformation of consciousness. Much psychological and psychiatric theorising (much of it unorthodox and speculative) went into the elaboration of this theory with the aim of establishing a 'psychology of oppression' and the means of overcoming it. Thus, the oppressed self is seen as internally divided, because of feelings of inferiority and even self-hatred induced by the prevailing ideology. Antidotes are seen in terms of techniques whereby the oppressed are able to throw off their feelings of inferiority and build their self-esteem.

Oppressions and political correctness

The first area, beyond the conventional 'class struggle', to which these ideas were applied was that of black rights (see Chapter 8). Indeed, the black struggle for civil rights in America was a powerful contemporary issue at the height of the New Left, so that black liberation was seen as part of the New Left movement.

As the first such movement, black liberation became the model for subsequent liberation movements, especially women and gays, but aspects of it have also used by other groups. We have, therefore, equivalents of racism such as sexism, heterosexism, speciesism, ageism, and so on. Some groups have applied the analysis of self-hate to their own situation and have developed their own techniques of 'consciousness raising' to overcome it. The strategy has been used by a variety of groups seeing themselves or seen by others as oppressed and in need of liberation. The best known are women and gays, but we might also add to this list a variety of disadvantaged groups who feel discriminated against, including the old and the disabled; and others who have sought to make a case on behalf of animals and children and the mentally ill. There is also 'liberation theology', a movement among Catholic priests, especially in South America who have applied some of these ideas to the position of the poor in this area.

These various liberation movements were largely responsible for a controversy in American higher education over cultural supremacy that still reverberates. The argument is that what is taught in American colleges is male and Eurocentric, so that white European male culture is elevated to the detriment of other cultures (black African, Asian or women's) implying that they are less important. The slogan is 'No more DWEMs', that is, no more 'Dead White European Males', such as Plato and Kant and Shakespeare and Beethoven and the rest. Presenting these as the pinnacle of human achievement is seen as a subtle form of oppression of anyone not white and male. Another aspect of this movement is an insistence on everyone being 'politically correct' (PC), which especially applies to language. Thus, to use the word 'mankind' is seen as an offence to women and should in all circumstances be substituted by the PC word 'humankind'; the word 'disabled' is not PC, while the phrase 'differently abled' is; and so on.

The PC controversy has often been very bitter, with accusations of censorship and intimidation, but no doubt it will all die down in time. To some extent the controversy may be seen as a symptom of Western society coming to understand itself in a new way. That is, as a much more pluralist, multicultural society. A number of liberation movements are, however, of more lasting political importance and need to be looked at in further detail.

Animal rights

The ideas of animal liberation have as much theoretical connection with green thinking (see Chapter 11) as with liberation movements. Both greens and animal liberationists see humanity as out of harmony with nature and both see the roots of this in the Western tradition of thought, in contrast to other important traditions. Both point to Biblical passages that elevate humanity above the rest of creation. The Ancient Greeks are also held responsible, particularly Aristotle, whose view of a hierarchy of nature with inferior species existing for the benefit of the higher ones (and above all human beings) was standard Western thinking until the nineteenth century. Animal liberationists regard the Western tradition in this respect as intellectually inadequate and, more importantly, morally flawed.

The animal rights case is almost exclusively a moral one. The practical aspect of the ideology, in terms of social or economic improvement of human existence, is of little importance. The world needs to be changed because it is right, and for no other reason. Such moral concern for the welfare of animals goes back to the nineteenth century, and was most significant in Britain. Early reformers campaigned against 'unnecessary cruelty' to animals (which led to the founding of the RSPCA in 1824), although for most of them there was no serious objection to vivisection, hunting, or killing animals for food or fur. Only occasionally was there a voice that suggested that the moral case was much deeper and that there was no such thing as 'necessary cruelty'. The most distinguished precursor of modern animal rights thinking was the utilitarian philosopher, Jeremy Bentham, who, when discussing slavery, wrote 'The day may come when the rest of the animal creation may acquire those rights which never could have been withholden from them but by the hand of tyranny' (quoted in Peter Singer, 1993, p.49). A fuller case was put by Henry Salt in his *Animal Rights* (1892), as part of a moral justification for vegetarianism.

However, it is only recently that such thinking has been sufficiently widespread and influential to have inspired a political movement. There have been a number of contributing thinkers, although the most important has been the Australian philosopher Peter Singer. Among his arguments is the questioning of the justification we have for eating other creatures. The usual argument is that we have reason and speech and they do not. But there are, sadly, some human beings who lack reason and speech; do we therefore have a right to eat them? Singer agrees with Jeremy Bentham when he wrote 'The question is not, Can they reason? nor Can they talk? but, Can they suffer?' (*ibid.*, p.50)

Singer has argued that we have no moral right to regard other species as simply there to do with as we please; that animals have rights just as we have; and that the many uses we make of animals without regard to these rights is morally indefensible.

It is undoubtedly true that animal rights thinking has had an impact on popular attitudes. This is not just those such as greens and vegetarians and others with related interests, but the general public and especially the young. There is a growing moral repugnance at such practices as vivisection (particularly where experiments are to improve, for example, cosmetics rather than medical research), hunting for sport, the use of animal furs for expensive clothes, the killing of animals for use in dissection in schools, and so on. While it seems unlikely that this will result in human beings ceasing to be carnivores, the movement may well achieve further success in the future.

All these changes in attitude and behaviour could be said to be the positive side of the animal liberation movement, but there is also what is widely regarded as a negative side. This is the resort, by some followers of the movement, to violence and terrorism. The argument is that since animals cannot liberate themselves then humans must do it for them. Hence laboratories are raided, shops attacked, fur warehouses set afire, goods in shops poisoned, and even individuals attacked. In some places (most notably in parts of Manchester) butchers have had their shops damaged and their businesses ruined by members of the activist group the Animal Liberation Front. Many people sympathetic to the cause are angered by such activity. It is perhaps one thing to release animals from where they would otherwise suffer, but quite another to threaten people's lives and legitimate livelihoods. The activists may well do their movement more harm than good.

Animal rights is an unusual member of the liberation ideology family in that the 'oppressed group' is not going to have its consciousness raised or participate in its own liberation. But it does fit in other respects. The oppressors do themselves have to be liberated and overcome their alienation, in the form of 'speciesism' (the belief that human beings are superior and that this entitles them to treat other animals in any way they choose). On the other hand, if an ideology always offers a key to human salvation, the overcoming of speciesism is not a very convincing candidate. It is perhaps most convincing as making a contribution to a wider world-view, such as that of the greens.

Gay liberation

Something similar might be said of gay liberation, which needs to be part of a wider set of ideas to be convincing as the key to human salvation. This is a more conventional liberation ideology. In this case, those deemed victims of the oppression are human and can rethink the world and participate in their own emancipation.

Homosexuals have long been discriminated against in Western and other societies on the grounds that homosexuality is 'unnatural' and 'perverted', arising from some kind of sickness or malfunction, and provoking a natural repugnance. Gay liberationists insist that it is an unjust oppression, which has nothing to do with what is 'natural' but is based, like racial discrimination, on ignorance and prejudice that has long roots in Western thought. In this case, it is not the Greeks who were at fault (as they are for animal liberationists, greens and feminists), for while not as liberal towards homosexuality as is often supposed, Ancient Greek culture was not what gay liberationists call 'homophobic'.

The source of Western homophobia lies in religion. Jewish and Christian thought has always been virulently hostile to homosexuality, and insistent that it is unnatural, sinful and an offence to God. (This is also true of Islam. The Islamic Fundamentalist regime of Ayatollah Khomeini in Iran executed homosexuals until quite recently.) In the West, this religious view was standard until the twentieth century. Today, although there has been some easing of legal disabilities, homosexuals are still widely discriminated against in the West, including Europe and North America.

As with black and women's liberation, gay liberation is concerned not just with the assertion of gay rights but with giving gays a sense of worth and self-belief. Hence the emphasis on 'gay pride' and 'coming out', the assertion of gay's contribution to history and culture and of working together to overcome the psychological 'damage' of society's prejudices. The internalisation of society's hostility produces the same kind of destructive 'self-hate' that is found among blacks.

The gay movement is also concerned with 'liberating the oppressors' in the sense of combating the common prejudices of a 'heterosexist' society', that is, beliefs about gays being unnatural, promiscuous, sick or whatever. The situation has not been helped by the advent of AIDS. Gay liberationists campaign to end legal discrimination, and this open campaigning as gays is itself deemed a 'therapy' and source of confidence.

In terms of theory, gay liberation echoes some of the divisions of feminism. There are liberals who see the issue in terms of right and prejudice. There are also socialists and Marxists who see gay liberation as largely the divisions of society – male/female, black/white, proletarian/bourgeois, heterosexual/homosexual – and as functional to the operation of capitalism, and that ending capitalism is the key to ending discrimination against gays. Other theories question the whole nature of human sexuality, seeing its divisions as an artificial construct (see Butler, 1990). This 'queer theory', as it now likes to be called, draws some of its inspiration from post-structuralist thinkers such as Michel Foucault. But like animal rights, gay liberation cannot alone sustain a world-view that can claim to hold the key to mankind's ideal future. It needs to be part of a wider vision, such as feminism. Indeed, there are close links between the two, if only because the lesbian cause overlaps both.

Liberation theology

The 1962–63 Second Vatican Council of the Roman Catholic Church made a bold move away from its traditional conservatism and urged the church to involve itself to a greater extent in the lives of ordinary people. Theologians in Latin America responded to this by developing a new theology of liberation, which incorporated social criticism and criticism of the traditional role of the church in South America where there was mass poverty, exploitation and state brutality among a deeply Catholic population. Traditionally the church supported, and indeed was part of, the ruling class.

The theologians varied in the analysis, but all insisted that poverty was not something that was natural and simply to be endured, but the consequence of greed and other sins. A number used Marxist analysis, although this was less true of probably the most important figure, the Peruvian theologian, Gustavo Gutierrez, whose *A Theology of Liberation* (1971) was a critical text. The need was to raise the consciousness of the poor and help them overcome their poverty, but also to raise that of the rich to make them recognise their role and take action. In 1968 a meeting of a number of Latin American bishops in the Columbian city of Medellin endorsed these views and insisted that the church cease neglecting the poor in favour of the rich. A few priests went so far as to take up arms in support of revolutionary movements.

The Vatican, particularly under Pope John Paul II, has roundly condemned liberation theology, but its influence has spread beyond Latin America and indeed beyond the Catholic church.

11

Green politics and ecologism

Alongside the student movement and the liberation movements of the 1960s and 1970s grew the green movement. Like traditional ideologies, radical green theory, or ecologism, is a universal theory that embraces all humanity, yet it has much in common with the new ideologies of liberation and identity. As a political movement green activism operates in the world of protest and pressure groups and frequently shuns the conventions and trappings of traditional party politics, often taking common cause with the new radicalisms of the age. It was, and remains, a major part of the 'new social movements' that have changed Western democratic politics in recent decades.

The green movement

It was the Industrial Revolution, and the huge growth in population and urbanisation that went with it, that provoked the first concerns about the destructive impact of human activity on the environment. Victorian social critics contrasted the healthy natural countryside with the ugliness and squalor of the new industrial towns. Pressure and action to protect the countryside began to develop. One example was the movement in America to create national parks, to prevent the ruination of unspoiled areas of wilderness for commercial purposes. The Yellowstone Park in California was the first of its kind created in 1872, since which time the concept has been adopted around the world.

British national parks are based on a different principle, of protecting a human-created working landscape of great beauty. They grew out of a movement to introduce planning and stop the spread of urban sprawl that was beginning to threaten the countryside in the inter-war years. It was a period of growing awareness of the countryside and the need for outdoor recreation. Nazi Germany was a leader in the field of environmental awareness and progressive policies. After the Second World War such concerns led to comprehensive planning systems in Britain and elsewhere. But within a decade or so it was becoming increasingly clear that the problems of the environment were more than the threat to beautiful countryside.

Environmentalism and ecologism

In the second half of the twentieth century, overpopulation, depletion of resources, destruction of the world's forests, the extinction of species, the poisoning of land, sea and air, acid rain, the thinning of the ozone layer and global warming, not to mention the threat of nuclear annihilation of the planet, all pointed to the likelihood of some global catastrophe engulfing mankind. Such fears prompted the development of an environmental movement in the 1960s right across the developed world, to put pressure on governments for preventative action to diminish the risks.

The movement encompasses an enormous variety of organisations and campaigns, ranging from small local groups to international ones with massive memberships. The achievements of this movement have been considerable in putting the environment on the political agenda, yet the threats to the environment are as great as ever. Indeed, new threats regularly emerge, such as genetically modified crops, which environmentalists perceive as fraught with potential danger.

However, for some it is simply too late to deal with the problems individually; they believe that mankind can only be saved from catastrophe by a total transformation of human society and consciousness. Consequently, the green movement tends to divide into two branches. The first, known as 'environmentalism', assumes that environmental problems can be dealt with within existing political and social frameworks. In this sense we can understand environmentalism as a set of principles (sustainability, preservation of biodiversity, and the like) that are compatible with existing major ideologies. The second branch, that demands a new kind of society for humanity as a whole and is not compatible with the major ideologies, is called 'political ecology' or 'ecologism'. The difference between the two branches is sometimes referred to in terms of 'light green' and 'dark green'. It is the latter, the more radical version that only really came together in the early 1970s, which can be seen to be a complete ideology in itself, and to which the rest of this chapter is devoted.

Green politics

Ecology is one of the biological sciences that studies how living things interact and live together in a given environment. The political ecology movement is not a movement of biologists, but of those who take the idea of ecology to have profound social and political implications for how people live and think about reality. The political ecology or radical green movement began as small groups and local parties in several countries. The first national political party, significantly called the Values Party, was formed in New Zealand in 1972. Britain's was formed the following year. It was initially called PEOPLE, then changed to the Ecology Party and finally, in 1985, the Green Party.

It was the German ecologists who started to call themselves 'Greens' (*Die Grünen*) and the name has now been almost universally adopted. The green movement is now worldwide, with parties in just about every country. The most politically successful have been the German Greens. Although only founded in 1981, the party astonished Europe in 1983 by winning twenty-eight seats in the Buderstag, as well holding seats in many provincial and local assemblies. The party thus became a major force in Germany, Europe's most powerful economic nation, virtually overnight; it went on to win 8.3 per cent of the vote and forty-two seats in the 1987 general election. This success has, however, created problems of how to relate to other parties, which parties elsewhere have yet to experience. After deep internal divisions and conflict in the 1990s, the Greens did well in the general election of 1997 and entered a coalition government with the Social Democrats. Among their successes has been the securing of a commitment to the eventual phasing out of the entire civil nuclear power programme (the sixth largest in the world, supplying 30 per cent of Germany's electricity).

Many countries in Europe and elsewhere now have Green MPs. Britain does not have any, although there are some Green local councillors, and members of the Welsh Assembly and Scottish Parliament. In the 1989 British elections for the European Parliament the Greens gained a remarkable 15 per cent of the vote, but no seats. Support is nothing like this in general elections, but the result did show the potential support for Green policies; and there might be more support in general elections if Britain's electoral system did not penalise small parties. It would be wrong to say that the Greens are now a major factor in world politics, but it is true that the environmental movement as a whole, of which they are part, has put the environment firmly on the agenda of world politics.

Radical connections

Many came into the green movement from the New Left in the early 1970s, attracted by the radicalism of the cause. Indeed, many felt that green ideas were a natural extension of New Left ideas (see Chapter 7) that rejected both capitalism and communism; that was suspicious of all bureaucracy and large-scale organisation; that strove to transform modern consciousness; and that experimented with alternative ways of living in communes and small anarchist groups, based on sharing and without domination or alienation. These ideas and attitudes are shared by many greens who have no interest in the New Left's Marxist origins, together with ideas from other movements that grew out of the New Left, such as feminism, gay liberation, animal liberation, the defence of soft drugs and so on.

Not all of the early greens came from the New Left, but some of the leading thinkers did, such as the German former-Marxist radical, Rudolph Bahro, and the American anarchist, Murray Bookchin (see Chapter 6). Bookchin has argued that 'authentic' green thinking is the culmination of all the radical movements of the 1960s and 1970s, although this is a rather extreme claim. It is perhaps more accurate to say that political ecology grew out of the more general environmental movement, but that the influence of the New Left gave it a more radical and anti-authoritarian edge.

Some of the most vigorous direct action political activity of recent years in many parts of the world has been green inspired, often with links with the anarchist movement. In Britain there is the anti-roads movement, in Germany the anti-nuclear movement, in America action to prevent logging in ancient forests of the north west, and so on. American radicals are among the most extreme, the most notorious being Earth First!, founded in 1980 by disaffected environmentalists who felt that their movement had been drawn into the establishment and was ignored as a result. Earth First!'s notoriety comes partly from their actions sabotaging logging companies and developers with such 'ecoterrorist' acts as driving metal into ancient trees about to be logged, which makes the use of saws extremely dangerous, and indeed causing some serious injuries. Their activities have created massive controversy, not least within the ecologist movement itself.

More recently, radical greens played a major part in the anti-capitalist protests in London, Seattle, Prague and elsewhere that began in 1999. There are, therefore, multiple levels or 'shades of green' ranging from international direct-action groups to political parties in government to local people trying to protect a local natural amenity. However, at least the greater part of the spectrum would subscribe to some form of green ideology.

Green ideas

The radical green movement quickly developed a substantial body of thought so that there is already a tradition of green ideology with many branches and variants. Nevertheless, there is also much that is common to various groups and strands.

Traditional attitudes to nature

Although the newest of ideologies, green thinking claims to be discovering an ancient wisdom concerning the human being's place in nature. Philosophies of ancient India, China and elsewhere have emphasised the need to live in harmony with all natural things. It is implicit in a famous passage (much quoted by green writers) in the reply purportedly made by the Red Indian, Chief Seattle, to the request of the US government to be allowed to purchase some of his tribe's traditional lands:

How can you buy or sell the sky? We do not own the freshness of the air or the sparkle of the water. How then can you buy them from us? Every part of the earth is sacred to my people, holy in their memory and experience. We know that the white man does not understand our ways. He is a stranger who comes in the night, and takes from the land whatever he needs. The Earth is not his friend, but his enemy, and when he's conquered it, he moves on. He kidnaps the earth from his children. His appetite will devour the Earth and leave behind a desert. If all the beasts were gone we would die from a great loneliness of the spirit, for whatever happens to the beasts happens also to us. All things are connected. Whatever befalls the Earth befalls the children of the Earth.

(1855, quoted in Dobson 2000, p.36)

What is important here is the sense of humanity as not separate from nature but merely one part among others, as contrasted with the characteristic Western attitudes which it rejects. It is in understanding this contrast that greens insist is the beginnings of genuine wisdom.

In contrast to the words of Chief Seattle are those of the Bible on the question of how human beings relate to nature:

And God said, Let us make man in our image, after our likeness: and let them have dominion over the fish of the sea, and over the foul of the air, and over the cattle, and over all the earth ...

(*Genesis* I.26)

This sets humanity apart and above nature, giving it dominion over nature and conceiving the natural world as being there solely for human benefit. It was a view reinforced by Aristotle, who saw all natural forms in terms of a great hierarchy culminating in the human being, with lower forms existing for the benefit of those above them. It was the conception of the natural world that largely dominated Western thinking until the nineteenth century. However, no great evil consequences for the environment could flow from this attitude until humanity had vastly increased its power over nature. In all parts of the world and in all kinds of habitats, people adapted to their physical environment and of necessity lived in some kind of balance. It was when Western civilisation acquired unprecedented powers over nature that the balance became lost.

The impact of modernity

The process began with the development of physical science and accompanying materialistic outlook, the eventual outcome of which was the Industrial Revolution. This gave human beings the potential to destroy nature as never before, and there was, in the West at least, no religious or ideological restraints on the process. Greater production, greater exploitation of resources and greater profits all became gods of the new age, and have continued to be so.

The outcome is today's consumer society with its conspicuous consumption, massive waste and appalling consequences for the environment. Capitalism bears much of the blame, with its profits at any cost. But the communist world had been no better in its attitude to production and indifference to environmental damage. The Third World has been bullied or persuaded to participate, industrialise and compete in world markets. Yet despite the fact that the world is beset by social ills of poverty, starvation, unemployment and urban decay, even to the extent that some think that modern industrial society is breaking down, nevertheless, the solution of all contemporary ideologies of those in power, is the panacea of economic growth, which is, greens insist, the root cause of all the problems. Humanity is rushing towards an abyss and all the world's politicians can suggest is that we rush ever faster.

The super-ideology of industrialism

Although greens are perfectly aware of the differences between the main ideologies, they are more impressed by what they have in common. Conservatives, liberals, social democrats, democratic socialists and communists, are all and everywhere preoccupied with economic growth and technology and what they like to term 'progress'. For this reason greens are inclined to see them as differing manifestations of the same 'super-ideology' which they call 'industrialism'. The main features of this industrialism are:

- a devotion to economic growth and industrial expansion and continuous technical innovation
- a belief in the overriding importance of satisfying people's material needs
- large-scale centralised bureaucratic control
- scientific rationality the only kind of reasoning that matters
- large-scale units – as in industry, administration, etc. – are most efficient ('Big is beautiful')
- a predominance of patriarchy and an emphasis on 'masculine' values of competition, aggression and assertiveness
- an anthropocentric view that sees the earth and all that lives on it as simply there to be exploited for any human purpose
- a hierarchical social structure where power and wealth is concentrated at the top
- economic considerations predominating in society and moral, social and artistic values being of lesser importance.

(based on Porritt, 1988)

Within this common framework, the predominant systems of East and West have their own horrors. Communism suppresses human freedom in the name of an inhuman system. And although communism has almost disappeared, rivalry between the two systems has left the legacy of a vast stock of nuclear weapons that could destroy the planet many times over.

Western capitalist democracy has become triumphant within this 'super-ideology'. But while, compared with communism, it has much to commend it in terms of liberty, it is even more ruthless in its destruction of the environment. On top of the 'industrialist' feature it shares with communism it adds its own destructive characteristics. It is an outlook that favours aggressive individualism, competition and selfishness, that finds expression in a free-market economy that is given free reign to make profit irrespective of the damage it causes. Profit is given priority over all things. The modern consumerism that the free market has created positively encourages people to buy what they do not need and throw things away as soon as possible. Continuous consumption is deemed desirable, as good for the economy, no matter what resources it wastes. Free-market capitalism has also created a world market, within which encouragement has been given to the Third World to industrialise and compete, despite their severe disadvantages and the destruction of their traditional ways of life.

The most basic assumption – that economic growth, with ever greater production and consumption, is the solution to all ills – is the most destructive. We are so imbued with these assumptions, greens claim, that it requires a considerable feat of imagination to break free of them. But break free we must if disaster is to be avoided.

The green alternative

The first step is to realise that there is an alternative. The green perspective is not just a set of solutions to environmental problems but a complete theory of the human and the social. There are variations, but most greens would subscribe to the following.

First of all, human beings are part of nature and must live in harmony with nature or risk destruction. Green thinking is not anthropocentric but biocentric. What is good is not what is good for humankind in isolation, but what is good for the earth and all that live on it. Consequently, protection of the biosphere and the conservation of finite resources are central priorities; and to achieve this, international co-operation must replace competition and aggression between nation-states. There must be an end to both economic growth and population growth. Economic systems that recklessly exploit the earth's resources as though they were infinite are inherently wrong. We must recognise that there are limits to growth and that we have to develop economies which do not diminish the earth; that is, economies that are 'sustainable'. This includes the number of people the environment can sustain without damage. The Norwegian, Arne Naess, who was one of the founders of 'deep green' thinking (the phrase is his) has argued that the optimum human population of the earth was 100 million (at present it is 6,000 million and rising).

The giving up of such wasteful systems will necessitate a lower standard of living, with less growth and, for example, fewer cars and other consumer goods. Industrial society is breaking down, as is evidenced by such symptoms as chronic unemployment, inner-city decay and general alienation. It needs to be replaced by a simpler and more satisfying way of life, one based upon more spiritual values rather than the material ones that dominate our world at present.

The majority of greens would add the following principles reflecting further the preoccupations of contemporary radicalism. Patriarchal characteristics and values of aggression and competition must become much less important beside 'feminine' values such as co-operation and caring. In green writing nature is often portrayed as 'female', from which it is an easy step to the assumption that feminine values are superior to masculine. There must be a massive redistribution of wealth; and not just between rich and poor within a society, but between continents and between generations (that is, we must not use up the earth's resources that future generations could benefit from). The greens are not against private property as such, but against excessive wealth and power. Greens insist that any kind of decent society must be characterised by 'social justice', and be without discrimination or inequality. A world built upon such principles, it is argued, would be free, safe, humane and just.

Green controversies

However, it must be said the while there is a good deal of consensus about what greens are against, there is much less agreement about what greens are for. There are considerable differences over detailed policies, strategy and tactics, and also over deeper theoretical matters.

The human relationship to nature

Greens differ a good deal among themselves as to the exact place humanity has in nature and its ideal relationship with the natural world. For most, green thinking must involve a spiritual element, and the salvation of mankind must involve some kind of spiritual renewal (see, for example, Jonathon Porritt's or Sara Parkin's writings). For some, indeed, ecologism is a new religion. The earth is a goddess, Gaia, with whom we must be in tune, and so on. The most famous exponent of this view in Britain is David Icke, a former television presenter and leading spokesman for the Green Party. He astonished the world in 1990 by announcing his religious beliefs (about him being the son of God and having a mission to save the world and so forth) which most people found eccentric to put it mildly. However strange Icke's beliefs may be, there is a large background to this kind of thinking in New Age religion (see Chapter 12), and his claims would not be considered unduly outlandish in parts of America.

Other greens see the need only for a greater reverence for nature, and greater humility in its presence, without any need for spirituality. Others still dismiss all this as dubious metaphysics and emotionalism, and see nothing beyond the science of ecology as needed for a green vision of the world.

A major controversy concerns just how far biocentrism should go. The American group, Earth First!, as suggested above, is notorious for its direct-action politics, but is also notorious for some of its expressed opinions. The seeming indifference to human life and limb characteristic of its actions is also expressed in many of its pronouncements. The most infamous was an article in its journal under the name of 'Miss Ann Thropy' which extolled the benefits of AIDS:

> If radical environmentalists were to invent a disease to bring human population back to sanity, it would be probably something like AIDS ... the possible benefits of this to the environment are staggering ... just as the Plague contributed to the demise of feudalism, AIDS has the potential to end industrialism.
>
> (quoted in Reed, 1988, p.21)

The editor of the same journal subsequently expressed indifference to the survival of the human race, believing that all species, including deadly bacteria, had an equal right to flourish. He thought aid to starving people should be stopped and that perhaps some deadly bacteria, such as smallpox might be reintroduced, so that nature would find its natural balance.

The nature of 'ecotopia'

There are other disagreements about what kind of world might be possible if and when humanity comes to its senses. What, for example, should be the role of technology? Some see our faith in science and technology as the root of our present crisis. Salvation lies, it is argued, in rejecting high technology and developing 'low-tech' solutions to practical problems that everyone can under-stand and operate. Yet others see modern information technology as the key to a decentralised social life where people can live at home and live in small communities.

Another source of controversy concerns the macro-organisation of a green society. Positions range from the need for a centralised state to anarchist visions of various kinds. One of the most interesting is the intermediate position of the bio-regionalists. This is a view associated with Arne Naess and others which sees the world as naturally divided into ecological regions, and insists that we should learn the ways and the ecology of the region we occupy, or rather re-learn those ways that sustained human existence before industrialisation. The implication of this is a virtual end to international trade, and a general retreat into self-enclosed eco-geographical units. A picture of what life might be like in such a bio-region, cut off from the rest of the world is given in Ernest

Callenbach's utopian novel, *Ecotopia* (1975). Ecologism is one of the few major ideologies today in which inspires utopian writing.

Relation to other ideologies

A major source of division in the green movement is the development of various hybrids that synthesise green ideas with older ideologies. Some have reworked traditional Marxist ideas to argue that capitalism is inherently the enemy of the environment, and that some form of communism is the only solution. Others have argued that feminist categories are the key to understanding the situation. Thus, male competitiveness and aggression are the source of the problem, which is essentially a side effect of patriarchy; while it is female qualities of care and co-operation that must be the basis of a solution.

In many ways it is anarchism that is seen to have most affinity with green ideas. The trend of green thinking towards smaller, self-sufficient communities, as against large-scale modern industry, organisation and urban life is an inevitable consequence of any kind of green approach, yet is strongly reminiscent of older anarchist ideas of federations of small communities in the writings of such as Prouhdon, Kropotkin and William Morris, as well as of the more recent anarchism of the of the 1960s (see Chapter 6).

On the other hand, it is undoubtedly true that the rise of green movement coincided with the era of the New Left, and in consequence green ideas take on many of the features of what was the fashionable radicalism of the time, sometimes to the extent of promoting causes that are not very relevant, such as the legalisation of cannabis. However, green ideas do not necessarily preclude quite different ideas that involve hierarchy and authority. What for some may be a desire to create a viable post-industrial society, may for another be a desire to recreate a pre-industrial society based on social hierarchy and discipline. Writers like Edward Goldsmith, in *Blueprint for Survival* (1972), see a green programme in terms of preserving an essence of traditional Englishness in its rural purity. Then again, green ideas can be consistent with fascism. One dimension of Nazi ideology was its emphasis on a mystical relationship between the Germanic peoples and the land of Germany, summed up in the slogan 'blood and soil'. This was more than a nostalgia for a rural past of sturdy peasant life; the Nazis also pioneered early policies designed to preserve the natural environment.

Greens have an ambiguous attitude to political power. Once they come close to it, differences tend to come to the fore. This has happened in Germany, where the Greens' electoral success has put them in a position of influence, with the consequent necessity of making hard political choices about who they can support. There were rows and splits within the party during the 1980s and early 1990s. Green parties have deliberately pursued a policy of trying not to behave like other parties, to be an 'an anti-party party'. Often they do not have a single leader, while party conferences are a series of seminars, and so on. But some greens feel such tactics are counter-productive. In Britain, considerable recrimination and acrimony followed the party's poor showing in the 1992 general election, following which the party split.

Criticisms of green ideas

Green ideology comes in many forms; however, the main criticism levelled against the Greens is not so much their variety and eclecticism, as their other-worldliness. The idea that we can simply dismantle the industrialised world and create some rural idyll, borne of nostalgia and a romantic imagination is, so it is claimed, a fantasy. We cannot forget science and disinvent industry. Greens counter this by insisting that we either do something drastic along these lines or we destroy ourselves. Besides, greens insist that there is no desire on their part to recreate some mythical bucolic past. New technology is fine in its place – although not all greens agree.

Apart from the overwhelming problems of persuading today's consumerist humanity to abandon much of its prosperous lifestyle, there are serious theoretical problems with the whole green way of thinking. Greens commonly look to nature as the source of the values we should live by. Thus, the diversity and interdependence that scientific ecologists observe in nature is taken by political ecologists as underpinning the human need for tolerance, equality and democracy (see Dobson, 2000, p.21 ff.). Further values are drawn from the frequent characterising of nature as essentially female, implying the inferiority of typical male characteristics. This jump from facts of nature to human values has long been recognised as an illegitimate one. The current green version is no more valid than when earlier thinkers used Darwinian evolution to justify the competitive capitalist society or totalitarian authoritarianism and race war.

Greens are almost universally committed to liberal democracy, tolerance, freedom and equality. This is entirely in keeping with the spirit of the present age, but it does present them with peculiar problems. One such problem lies in reconciling the freedom and equality that greens insist upon with the drastic transformation of society that they insist upon even more strongly. What if people do not want to live in small communities or change their lifestyle or co-operate with their neighbour? Will they have to conform? Will they be forced to be free? This is a particular problem with the anarchistic character of many green visions of an ideal future.

Will there not need to be severe restrictions on people's economic activity? And who will enforce them? Many greens reject the modern state. Yet it is possibly only a strong state that could enforce green policies; it would certainly have a better chance of doing so than a network of self-governing communes. Greens often talk as though it is only necessary for people to understand the environmental dangers to stop them wanting to make money by polluting rivers or destroying forests, or to stop them wanting cars or other goods. But the idea that all will be well once everyone sees things the right way is one of the oldest of political illusions. How to stop people behaving in ways deemed undesirable is a particular problem for greens who reject authoritarianism.

Whatever answers to these problems greens come up with, it seems likely that green ideas will become more important in the future. Although whether the future of green parties will be one of greater strength and political success it is difficult to say. It may turn on whether the greens can agree sufficiently on their ideas and learn to play the political game successfully, or whether ideas and energies will be dispersed among other parties and beliefs: green socialists, green liberals, green conservatives, green Marxists, green Christians, and the rest. Either way, green ideas seem likely to make a major impact across the ideological spectrum.

Looked at another way, it could be argued that of all major ideologies, ecologism potentially has the greatest future. But then it may well be that only some great catastrophe will enable humanity as a whole to recognise its importance, by which time it may be too late.

12

Religious fundamentalism

The rise of modern industrial society in the West during the nineteenth and twentieth centuries was accompanied by a general decline in religious belief and observance. Secularisation seemed to be an inevitable part of what social scientists called 'modernisation', along with industrialisation, urbanisation and the growing influence of science. In the Western world, even in countries where levels of belief remained relatively high, religion was increasingly marginalised in public affairs and confined to the private sphere. As the communist world developed there was official condemnation and repression of religion as part of the effort to modernise and catch up with the West. In the emerging post-colonial 'Third World', covering large parts of Asia, Africa and South America, the priority was invariably 'modernisation' on the Western model. This was usually pushed through by elites, educated and deriving their ideologies from the West, who regarded their countries as backward, and saw religion as part of that backwardness. In the push for modernisation, religion, once central to social life, would be left behind, a matter of private belief. Not surprisingly, many predicted the steady disappearance of religion as modernisation advanced around the globe.

However, developments in the last quarter of the twentieth century turned much of this conventional wisdom on its head. Since the 1970s there has been a remarkable revival of religion which has not only embraced the Third World, but the Western world and the former communist world as well. It has involved all of the world's 'great religions', and drawn each of them into the political arena in defence of their values. Islam, which has become a major force in world politics since the Iranian Revolution of 1979, is the most striking case, and the one to which most of this chapter is devoted. But Jewish, Hindu and Christian fundamentalists, as well as Sikh and Buddhist revivalist movements, have also had a significant political impact in particular countries. Often such revivals have occurred at the same time as more conventional and established expressions of the faith have continued to decline.

'Religious fundamentalism' is something of an umbrella term, often used to cover religious revivals of all kinds. But it will be taken here to mean political activism inspired by traditional religious belief that is aimed at a radical transformation of society that is at odds with the norms of the modern world, such as turning a secular state into a religious one. This chapter will also include the growth of new religions, the cults and sects that are often brought together under the term 'New Age religion'. Although not usually directly political, these movements do have implications for society and social thought.

The growth of religious fundamentalism around the world has occurred in so many different circumstances and taken so many different forms, from the affluent suburbs of America to the desperate slums of Beirut, that it may not be appropriate to look for common features or common causes. However, there is one connecting theme which these disparate phenomena would seem to share. This is some kind of rejection of modernity and a harking back to past certainties, past values and past authority. This is certainly true of Islamic fundamentalism, which has made by far the greatest impact on world events.

Islamic fundamentalism

Islamic fundamentalism is the oldest of fundamentalisms. As a modern political movement it dates back to the 1920s, although Islam has always been the most political of the world religions from its very beginning.

The origins of Islam

The Prophet Muhammad (670–732 AD) founded the first Islamic state and led its early expansion. He was, therefore, a political and military, as well as a religious, leader. This is in striking contrast to the founder of Christianity who was not a political leader, and still less a military one. Christ left no guidance on political matters beyond the injunction to 'render unto Caesar the things that are Caesar's and unto God the things that are God's', which implies a clear separation between church and state. The Islamic ideal has always been the unity of political and religious authority. It has always been a conquering, proselytising faith, and within a couple of centuries of its foundation possessed an empire stretching from Spain to India. Towards the end of the Middle Ages the leadership of Islam passed from the Arabs to the Turks, who for a time threatened the conquest of much of Europe.

Islamic thought on politics did not centre on the state but around the idea of the community of all Muslims led by the *caliph*, or successor of the Prophet, who was a political and religious ruler to whom the entire Islamic community owed allegiance. The caliph would rule with the advice of the *ulama*, the body of religious scholars who were experts on the *sharia*, or divine law found in the Koran (conceived, like the Bible, as the direct word of God) and in the sayings and deeds of the Prophet.

When the Ottoman Turks came to dominate the Islamic world, the Turkish ruler, the Sultan, also became Caliph and claimed the loyalty of all Muslims in the world (from Morocco to southern China). Arab Muslims did not have much choice since the Turks had conquered their lands, but Muslims of India and beyond also came to look upon the Turkish Sultan for leadership as they became increasingly subject to European control. After the heyday of Turkish power in the sixteenth and seventeenth centuries it was Europe which came to dominate the world with its sheer economic and military power. This was resented by many Muslims who regarded their civilisation as greatly superior to the European.

On the whole, Islamic political thinking under Turkish leadership was extremely conservative, traditionalist and quietistic. While Europe had been swept by major intellectual movements, like the Renaissance, the Enlightenment and the democratic and nationalist ideas of the French Revolution, these had all passed the Islamic world by and its thinking had changed little for a thousand years. But the European conquest of large parts of Islamic Asia, and then North Africa, with Turkey itself becoming weak and vulnerable as the 'sick man of Europe', provoked fresh thought which began to appear in the late nineteenth century.

Broadly there were two main responses to the success of the Europeans. One was to say that the Islamic world had fallen behind, and that it needed to learn from Europe and modernise its thinking and its way of life. The other response was to say that the Europeans had only succeeded because the Islamic world had become lazy and slack and neglectful of religion. Only by restoring the true faith to the centre of life would the Islamic world restore its former eminence.

Fundamentalism and the state

It is the second of these responses that belongs to the Islamic fundamentalists. However, there was one aspect of the modern world which fundamentalists accepted as much as the modernists – the nation-state. The fundamentalists have not sought to recreate the worldwide Islamic community as a single political entity led by a caliph (although for some this may be an ultimate ideal). Their energies have been directed at turning existing national states into Islamic states. That is, to restore the unity of religion and politics, but within a modern political framework.

The question of whether to Islamicise or Westernise is a dilemma facing all Islamic societies in the modern world. Yet in some ways it is a modern form of a long-standing tension within Islamic thought and practice as to the proper relationship between religious and political authority. The Prophet and his immediate successors are deemed to have held them in perfect balance, but historically the political has usually predominated and the religious authorities have been subservient to it. Modernising nationalism would keep it that way and learn from the non-Islamic world. Fundamentalism is about 'restoring the balance', although in practice it means subordinating the political to the religious. (Islamic fundamentalism is not about asserting the literal truth of the Holy Book, as it is for Christian and Jewish fundamentalists, for all Muslims believe this as a matter of course.) However, the choice between these two alternatives, to Westernise or Islamicise, remained largely academic before the fall of the Ottoman Empire.

The collapse of the Turkish empire in the First World War marks the beginning of modern Islamic politics to a considerable degree. Under Kemal Atatürk (1881–1938), the Turks themselves moved decisively towards the creation of a modern Western nation-state. This involved the overthrow and abolition of the sultanate and caliphate (ending the traditional fusion of political and religious authority), along with the introduction of Western law, the emancipation of women, and the suppression of traditionalist Islamic opposition.

Among the Arab peoples newly independent of Turkish control, the Turkish model of modernisation was favoured by nationalists. For the more traditionalist, the end of the nominal religious leadership of the caliph left the way open to develop the idea of the Islamic state, that is, a modern territorial, centralised nation-state, but one inspired by Islamic ideals and based upon the divine law. It is this latter view that has been the particular province of Islamic fundamentalism, which first appeared as a modern political movement, in the sense of a political party seeking power, in the late 1920s in Egypt. Oddly enough, the first Islamic fundamentalist state was being founded around the same time, not through modern political methods, but more in a manner characteristic of the Middle Ages and the methods of the Prophet himself.

The creation of Saudi Arabia

Abdul Ibn Saud was the hereditary leader of one of the tribes of the Arabian peninsular, which since the eighteenth century was also the home of a particularly puritanical version of (Sunni) Islam. The Turkish withdrawal left a vacuum in the area that needed to be filled. Like the Prophet, Ibn Saud was a charismatic leader who united some of the tribes around him, and, by a mixture of political manoeuvring and force of arms, conquered the Arabian peninsula and made himself king. His new kingdom included the two most holy sites of Islam, Mecca and Medina, which enabled him to claim a religious significance for the whole of the Islamic world as the guardian of the Holy Places. They also brought great wealth because of the religious duty of all Muslims to go on a pilgrimage (the *haj*) to the holy places at least once during their lifetime. However, the 1930s, being a period of world depression, was also low on pilgrimages and Ibn Saud signed an agreement with Standard Oil of California for the exploration and exploitation of oil reserves. The combination of oil and pilgrimages has made the Saudis immensely rich ever since.

Nevertheless, Saudi Arabia is a deeply religious country where Islamic practices are strictly observed. The *ulama* (the body of religious-legal scholars) controls a religious police who enforce the prohibition on alcohol, the wearing of traditional female dress and much else. Saudi society is extremely conservative. When the introduction of television was proposed in the 1960s, the *ulama* was opposed on the grounds that it clearly involved magic and was therefore the work of the devil. Only when the king arranged for an experiment in which passages from the Koran were transmitted did religious objections cease, on the grounds that the devil would not allow the transmission of the Koran. Saudi Arabia is still an absolute monarchy (although the *ulama* is consulted on legislation) with no political parties. One might say that the extremely large royal family amounts to a party on its own; Ibn Saud, the founder of the dynasty, had nearly 300 children of his own.

However, despite its adherence to Islamic codes, its religious standing and its generous patronage of Islamic causes, the Saudi royal family has been subject to criticism by fundamentalists. The major objects of criticism have been the close alliance with the USA and the lifestyle of the royal family, especially since the 1970s oil-price crisis, as a result of which the Saudis became even richer. The idea of royal princes living a high life in the fleshpots of the West, while avoiding their religious duties at home (such as fasting for the month of Ramadan) have been very damaging.

Saudi royalty has been vilified for being corrupt and un-Islamic by the Iranians since their 1979 revolution and this has led to conflict with Iranian pilgrims to Mecca. But much the most serious trouble has been home grown. In 1979 a group of fundamentalists captured the Great Mosque at Mecca and were only removed with considerable difficulty. They had believed (mistakenly) that the king would be there; but in any case they hoped that their action would inspire a general uprising against the ruling family. This did not happen, but their removal took several days and a great deal of bloodshed. Those captured alive were subsequently beheaded in various public squares around Saudi Arabia, as a lesson to all. Yet the incident was a serious blow to the prestige of the royal family. It was not enhanced by its need to rely on the Americans and their Western allies to protect Saudi Arabia against the threat of invasion by Iraq in 1990–91.

The dependence on America (seen by many fundamentalists as the main source of evil in the modern world) was reinforced by the 1991 Gulf War. Iraq had invaded Kuwait the previous year and Saddam Hussein was widely believed to be bent on capturing the Saudi oil fields next. Saudi Arabia was protected from Iraqi invasion by American bases and missiles. The world's most successful and formidable Islamic fundamentalist leader, the former Saudi businessman, Osama bin Laden (see below), began his terrorist career after being expelled from Saudi Arabia in 1991 for criticising the Saudi government for allowing 'armed infidels' on to Saudi soil.

The Islamic Brotherhood

The entry of Islamic fundamentalism into conventional political activity came with the formation of the Islamic Brotherhood in Egypt in 1928. Egypt at the time was firmly under British control, with a subservient king and establishment. It was the most Westernised of Arab countries and Western dominance was much resented. This expressed itself in two forms. There were the modernising nationalists and there were the traditionalists. It was one of the latter who founded the youth movement, the Islamic Brotherhood, which in the 1930s became the first fully fledged fundamentalist political party.

The founder of the Brotherhood, Hassan al Banna, believed that the Islamic world had become corrupted by Western ideas and needed to be purified. A restored faith must then be placed at the centre of the nation's life. The *sharia* (divine law) must resume its central authority, and Islamic principles applied to all aspects of social and economic life. The result would be an Islamic society that was neither socialist nor capitalist. This would come about as the result of a *jihad* or holy war, which would destroy the colonial power and liberate Egypt and then the rest of the Islamic world.

The post-war years were characterised by increasing political instability and violence in which the Brotherhood had a leading part. It culminated in the overthrow of the monarchy by a group of colonels, one of whom, Gamal Abdel Nasser, eventually took control. Initially the Brotherhood co-operated with Nasser's modernising nationalist government, but eventually went into opposition. Nasser cracked down severely and many went into exile, spreading Islamic fundamentalist ideas throughout the Arab world. However, the catastrophic defeat of Egypt by the Israelis in the Six Day War of 1967 forced Nasser to compromise, attempt to appear as a good Muslim and allow the Brotherhood more scope, and enabled many to return from exile.

There seemed more likelihood of closer ties with Nasser's successor, Anwar Sadat, who appeared to be a more genuinely religious man than Nasser, and who was initially hailed as the 'believer president'. However, his decision to ally himself with the Americans and allow a considerable commercialisation of Cairo in the attempt to attract American investment outraged the fundamentalists. They took to rioting and an orgy of destruction in Cairo's nightclub district in January 1977. But what incensed them even more was Sadat's peace with Israel, signed in 1979. Islamic fundamentalism grew rapidly with many more extreme groups than the Brotherhood, one of which assassinated President Sadat in 1981.

Sadat's successor, Hosnay Mubarak, has had to tread a difficult course trying to prevent the flair up of fundamentalism, including making a number of concessions to religious sentiment while at the same time seeking to stamp out the radicals who wanted to overthrow the regime and establish an Islamic state. After a period of suppression the militant fundamentalist re-emerged in 1992 to declare war on the Egyptian state. Supported by the Islamic regime in neighbouring Sudan, they almost assassinated Mubarak while on a state visit to Ethiopia in 1995. They have also killed numbers of government officials and Coptic Christians. Their greatest success has been in trying to cripple the Egyptian tourist industry which for them has the double advantage of stemming a potent source of Western influence and of undermining the government economically. Attacks on tourists culminated in a massacre of fifty-six of them outside the temple of Hatshepsut near Luxor in 1997. Tourism, which is vital to the Egyptian economy, is still trying to recover.

The spread of fundamentalism

The Brotherhood and its offshoots are to be found in many countries. In Syria, for example, fundamentalists formed the only significant opposition to the otherwise absolute rule of President Assad. On several occasions during his rule, fundamentalist uprisings have been put down with considerable bloodshed. He too (and now his son), despite leading a secular Ba'ath Party, has made concessions to religious sentiment and must be wary of provoking fundamentalist action.

Fundamentalism is strong in several countries and has challenged secular authority, with sometimes tragic consequences. The most dramatic recent case in the Arab world is Algeria, which illustrates a pattern of involvement with the West that has led to the growth of fundamentalism in many Third World countries. Algeria became free of French rule in 1962 under the leadership of the National Liberation Front (FLN), who went on to rule the country as a one-party state. This was a nationalist party devoted to modernisation, Westernisation, industrialisation and socialism. Like similar regimes, it became part of the Western economic system and suffered badly in the recessions in the West in the 1970s and 1980s. Furthermore, nationalisation and other modern ideas simply did not work, while attempts at the creation of a modern industrial economy produced a new urban working class who suffered particularly from economic failure. Bad times produced much poverty and disillusionment and an excellent recruiting ground for the fundamentalists. Western pressure to democratise then gives the fundamentalists the opportunity for power. Failed attempts at the creation of a modern industrial economy produced a massive pool of urban poor, amongst whom the fundamentalists have recruited large numbers.

At the end of 1991, the first democratic election since independence produced a huge vote for the fundamentalists, leading to the cancellation of the second round and an army takeover. This led to a savage and as yet unresolved civil war of atrocity and counter-atrocity. During the rest of the 1990s over 60,000 died as a result. The conflict is viewed with anxiety by surrounding regimes, including Morocco and Tunisia, all of whom fear their own Islamic fundamentalists. In Libya Colonel Gadafy has suppressed the fundamentalists with great ferocity, while claiming, rather doubtfully, to be one himself.

Other Islamic countries vary in the degree of fundamentalist influence and their relationship to the regime. In Turkey it is a growing phenomenon which worries many Westernised Turks. In Pakistan a strong influence is accepted as appropriate given the country's creation as an Islamic state. In Sudan fundamentalists dominate the government and are a threat to the Christian population in the south.

However, the most complete examples of Islamic fundamentalism in power are to be found further east, in Afghanistan and Iran. Although these are neighbours and have both undergone Islamic revolutions, they nevertheless represent different kinds of Islam and their respective revolutions arose from very different circumstances. Feeling its influence to be threatened by a new government, the Soviet Union invaded Afghanistan in December 1979 in order to restore a sympathetic regime. This provoked a reaction among the strongly Islamic population and resistance was organised by the *mujahidin* who led a holy war against the atheistic Soviets. Backed covertly by the West, the Soviets suffered serious losses and eventually withdrew in 1989; the regime it sponsored was defeated in 1992.

Civil war followed among the various armed Islamic factions and their warlord leaders in which tens of thousands were killed. But in 1994 a new force emerged that was to sweep the country. This was known as the 'Taliban', coming from the Persian word for student. The Taliban were Islamic fighters largely recruited from the religious schools set up among refugees in exile in Pakistan, and consequently they were the most religiously fervent and uncompromising, and strictly under the control of religious leaders. As they gradually took control of the country they imposed Islamic law in its most extreme and traditional form. There were public amputations and executions, women were forbidden to work outside the home, girl's schools were closed and a woman could not leave her home unless covered from head to foot and accompanied by a male relative.

The Taliban government has also been at odds with international opinion over denial of human rights, and UN agencies were withdrawn. A continuing conflict exists with America over the government's refusal to do anything about the Saudi terrorist leader Osama bin Laden. There has also been conflict (almost leading to war) with the neighbouring Islamic regime of Iran. The Taliban are Sunni Muslims, while the Iranians are Shias and support the Shia Muslim minority in Afghanistan who were being persecuted. The different kinds of Islam need to be understood.

Shia fundamentalism

All the versions of fundamentalism touched upon so far have belonged to one of the two main branches of Islam, the Sunni branch. Sunnis do in fact constitute about 85 per cent of the world's one billion Muslims. The other

15 per cent are Shias. Yet it is Shia fundamentalism that has produced the most spectacular and aggressive version of fundamentalism, that of Iran and its admirers. To understand the particular nature of this fundamentalism we need to see something of the difference between the Sunni and the Shia versions of Islam.

Sunni and Shia Islam

Muslims are divided among a number of different sects, but the two most important are the Sunnis and the Shias. These two branches of Islam parted company at an early stage over the succession to the Prophet. Shias were the followers ('shia' means 'follower') of Ali, the son-in-law of the Prophet, who was pious and idealistic and who refused to become caliph on the terms offered him, although he did eventually become caliph on his own terms. One of Ali's sons, also revered by the Shias, chose to suffer martyrdom rather than renounce his claim to the caliphate. This self-sacrifice and standing on principle is characteristic of Shiaism. Shi'ites tend to be more puritanical, more fundamentalist and more devoted to martyrdom, to holy war and to the fusion of religion and state than the Sunnis. Although by no means without their fundamentalists and puritans, the Sunnis on the whole tend to be more pragmatic, and supportive of established authority. They have also been more ready to adapt to the modern world and to accept the secular state.

Shiaism tends to be the more emotional and inspirational, and also the more anti-establishment form of Islam, putting greater emphasis on social justice. As such it is often found as a minority sect which appeals strongly to the poor and dispossessed. Sunnis are followers of the *Sunna*, the Beaten Path or Tradition, and Sunnism is usually the establishment religion, although there are periodic eruptions of radicalism. In most Sunni states the religious leadership is part of the establishment: the law, education and preaching are all done under the aegis of the state and the *ulama* receive state salaries. The Sunni clergy have often acted as the mouthpiece of the state. The Shia clergy, even in Shia states, have a separate organisation from the state and have traditionally had a more critical role.

Furthermore, Shiaism has a messianic dimension that Sunnism lacks. Sunnism sees human history in terms of a perpetual tendency of the Islamic community towards corruption, and needing a periodic restoration of purity by a charismatic religious leader; but beyond this, history has no overall direction. For Shias history does have a final end. Sunnis believe a caliph to be merely a fallible interpreter of the Koran, whereas Shias believe a 'true caliph' is an *Imam*, a divinely inspired and therefore infallible religious leader in true descent from the Prophet and Ali. The true descent of the Prophet has been lost, but, Shias believe, will eventually be found again. Ultimately, there will be a restoration of the rule of the Prophet with the return of the 'hidden Imam' who will one day lead the Islamic community to a final paradise, when all injustice will be banished and the oppressed will inherit the earth.

In most Islamic states Shiaism is a minority sect. Iran is the most important of the few places where this is not so.

The Iranian Revolution

Hostility between the state and the Islamic leadership has a long history in Iran. The recent history goes back to the period after the First World War when a new Shah, who had seized power and was establishing a new dynasty, proceeded to strip the religious leadership of much of its power, financial, legal and educational, and began a vigorous programme of Westernisation backed by Britain. Everyone had to acquire a Western-style surname, and Western dress was required. The Shah forbade Shia religious rituals, such as self-flagellation, and even forbade the pilgrimage to Mecca.

His son pushed ahead with Westernisation and developed close links with the USA. This alienated even the most moderate clerics. The Shah's actions were fiercely attacked in public by Ruhollah Khomeini, a junior cleric, who became the hero of the more religious part of the population, while the more affluent and Westernised supported the increasingly autocratic Shah. When Khomeini was arrested in 1963 there were massive riots all over Iran, which were put down with great violence and up to 10,000 demonstrators were killed. But Khomeini continued to attack the Shah fearlessly, especially over Iran's increasing dependence on America, and was eventually sent into exile.

From his base in Iraq, Khomeini launched bitter and vituperative attacks on the Shah and the whole concept of monarchy. He argued that the *ulama* should not just give advice on laws and government actions, as is their traditional function, but should actively participate in the overthrow of repressive governments and lead the regimes that replace them. The modern state, he argued, had taken over the secular powers and authority originally held by the Prophet, but sovereignty could lay with a senior cleric who could supervise the state, ensure that the *sharia* was adhered to, and be the ultimate 'guardian of the nation'. The ideal Islamic state was, therefore, a theocratic state with which hereditary monarchy was incompatible.

As economic difficulties added to the regime's problems in the 1970s, there was an increasing gulf between the Shah and the people, and an increasing reliance on the armed forces and on American support. This gradually alienated the Westernised middle class. All groups looked to Khomeini for support, and he was careful to play down aspects of his thought that offended educated groups (such as his theocratic ideas and his traditional beliefs about the role of women). He stressed his fierce nationalism, and the need to abolish the monarchy (despite its boast of a continuous existence for over 2,000 years) which tended to bring all together. The regime became increasingly oppressive, so that 'Death to the Shah' became a popular cry and riots and bloodshed became common. Eventually the army became discontented and the situation could no longer be controlled. In January 1979, the Shah fled into exile and the Ayatollah Khomeini returned in triumph.

The Iranian Revolutionary state

Immediately upon his return to Iran, Ayatollah Khomeini established his legitimacy by holding a referendum on the creation of an Islamic republic. The new constitution put the ultimate authority in the state in the hands of a Leader of the Islamic Republic. The Leader must be a senior cleric who (pending the ultimate return of the Messiah, Hidden Imman or Mahdi, who would lead the faithful to Paradise) had to be a distinguished religious scholar and jurist who would be head of state and officially appoint the elected president, as well as control the judiciary to ensure that divine law prevailed. Khomeini was give this position of Leader for life. The president (who must be a male Shia Muslim), aided by a prime minister, would be in charge of the day-to-day running of the country, implementing the constitution and executing the laws passed by parliament.

The system is democratic, although within limits. The parliament and the president are both elected, along with, when necessary, the council of 'experts' whose task is to choose a successor to the Leader. However, there are also means of ensuring that whatever the Islamic Republic does is 'in conformity with the will of God'. In the first place, the *sharia* or divine law is incorporated into the constitution. Second, the Leader appoints a Council of Guardians, composed of religious scholars, to make sure that no law passed by parliament is in conflict with divine law. Thus, the people are sovereign within the wider 'sovereignty of God' as interpreted by the religious leadership.

Initially, Khomeini's leadership and the aspiration towards an Islamic Republic was acceptable to most parts of Iranian society that were not fundamentalist. Khomeini swept to power on a wave of enthusiasm that was at least as much anti-Shah, nationalistic and anti-imperialist as it was Islamic. Khomeini sought to bring along others, who were not his immediate supporters, but who thought that an accommodation would be possible with the new order. As time went on, however, Khomeini's supporters became more and more dominant and others felt undermined. The regime became more clerical, more intolerant and totalitarian. Enforcement of Islamic law became more vigorous. Women were harassed for not wearing Islamic dress, forced out of occupations and education. Not only enemies of the regime were executed in large numbers, but also drug dealers, adulterers and homosexuals.

Iran became isolated, even within the Islamic world. Having created an Islamic Republic, Khomeini assumed that Iran was now the leader of not only Shia Muslims, but all Muslims. It condemned other regimes and encouraged Muslims to overthrow their leaders. In particular, Khomeini insisted that hereditary kingship was incompatible with Islam, and that the monarchies of such as Saudi Arabia and Kuwait were corrupt, tyrannical and in the pocket of the hated America, which he called 'the Great Satan', in other words, the great source of corruption in the world.

Such sentiments did not endear the Iranians to their neighbours. Saudi Arabia was particularly resentful of the regime's pretensions to leadership, a position it had tended to assume by right. Relations reached rock bottom with the *haj* (pilgrimage to Mecca) of 1987, when a large number of Iranian pilgrims chanted political slogans and waved pictures of the Ayatollah. The confrontation with Saudi police provoked a riot and stampede in which over 400 people were killed, mostly Iranians. Khomeini insisted that it was a deliberate Saudi massacre inspired by the Americans. Khomeini also offended many in the West with his *fatwa* ('judgement') in 1989 condemning to death the British writer Salman Rushdie for allegedly making offensive references to the Prophet in his novel *The Satanic Verses*. The Ayatollah died the same year, but such was his stature that it was extremely difficult to modify his decision and the unfortunate Rushdie had to live in hiding under police protection for the best part of a decade.

Only with the death of Khomeini in 1989 and the advent of a more moderate leadership under President Rafsanjani and concern to rebuild Iran following a long destructive war with Iraq, was there a change of mood. Rafsanjani and his successor, President Khatami (another moderate cleric) have had to move cautiously, since the radicals are still a major force. The radicals retain a tight hold on the judicial system and the forces of law and order. In 1999 these forces were used against students and other supporters of the moderate president, provoking the worst riots since 1979. Nevertheless, there has been a restoration of relations with the West to some degree, and this was helped by the role Iran played in restraining its followers in Lebanon.

Iranian influence

Shia influence outside Iran is relatively small. However, it does occur in a number of important trouble spots. There is an important Shia presence in the southern republics of what was formerly the Soviet Union; there is a Shia majority in Iraq, although the Sunnis have always ruled; but the most important influence has been in Lebanon.

After 1975 Lebanon collapsed into civil war among its different religious and ethnic groups. Among these, the Shias have always been the poorest and least well represented community. It had long looked to Iran for inspiration, but following the 1979 revolution the fundamentalists became especially strong, and have seen their community as engaged in a holy war against the Israelis, encouraged by Iran. With the Israeli invasion of 1982 the Shi'ite militias came to the fore. Their suicide attacks on the Israelis and against the peace-keeping forces of the Americans and French shocked the world. (Three hundred US marines were killed in one incident in 1983.) Even more shocking to the West was the capture of Western hostages, who were ill-treated and kept prisoner for up to six years.

The Shia militias saw the West and Israel as all the same, and their activities were blessed by the Ayatollah Khomeini as contributing to a holy crusade to liberate the Islamic holy city of Jerusalem from the Zionists. Death in this struggle was martyrdom and ensured instant access to heaven. It was only in 1991, after the death of Khomeini, and when the Iranian regime wanted better relations with the West, that it was able to persuade the Lebanese Shias (the Hezbollah and other groups) to release the Western hostages. The Shias are still, however, an important factor in the politics of the area, and a crucial part of the opposition to the Middle East 'peace process'.

The importance of Islam

There are more than one billion Muslims, about one in five of the world's population. Islam is important for that reason alone. But also, the centre of the Islamic world is the Middle East, which is the most tangled, fraught and dangerous of the world's trouble spots. The inherent conflicts of the area are complicated by the fact that the rest of the world has a profound interest in the region's oil supplies. The industrial world is heavily dependent on oil, and more than half the world's oil reserves are to be found in the states surrounding the Persian Gulf: Saudi Arabia, Kuwait, Iraq and Iran, all of which have been involved in major wars in the region over the past decade. It was because of the West's interest in oil that America, Britain and France engaged in war with Iraq in 1991 to liberate Kuwait (an American politician cynically remarked that if Kuwait had produced carrots instead of oil nobody would have given a damn).

Conflict with Israel

However, the most potent source of conflict in the region is not between Islamic states, but between the Arabs and Israel. All Arabs believe that Israel was artificially created out of land that belonged, and still rightfully belongs, to an Arab people, the Palestinians. In addition, all Muslims believe that the Palestinian cause is a cause for the whole Islamic world, since Jerusalem is the third most holy place for Muslims after Mecca and Medina. To complicate matters, the USA (the most powerful country in the world) is both dependent on the Middle East oil that is entirely under Arab control and is the main supporter of Israel, which could not survive without American support.

The situation is, to say the least of it, difficult. Conflict in the area always threatens the West. The Yom Kippur War of 1973 and the oil price rise that followed it was responsible for the recession and mass unemployment in the West in the mid-1970s. Something similar happened in the early 1980s following the Iranian Revolution, a situation exacerbated by the Iran–Iraq war of 1980–88. There was yet another threat to the West's prosperity in 1991 when Iraq invaded Kuwait, and only averted by the speed with which the allied powers forced defeat upon Iraq. Before the collapse of the Soviet Union, it was often said that if a third world war were going to start anywhere it would be in the Middle East, where a local conflict would suck in the 'superpowers'. With the end of the Cold War this is now unlikely, but the area remains extremely dangerous. The 'peace process' is a hopeful development, if it can be sustained (see Chapter 8), but dangers remain. These dangers are increased with the continuing spread of Islamic fundamentalism.

Anti-Western terrorism

In recent years, Islamic fundamentalism has taken over from Palestinian nationalism as the major source (or so perceived in the West) of international terrorism. With the portrayal of the West, and particularly the United States, as the source of evil and corruption in the world, inevitably some of the more extreme fundamentalists have seen attacking the USA and its allies as a religious duty. In the 1980s attacks on Western interests were largely confined to existing trouble spots, such as the killing of over 300 US marines in a suicide bombing in Beirut in 1983. But the 1990s saw a spreading of attacks to the United States itself and across the world.

In February 1993 followers of the Egyptian religious leader Sheikh Omar Abdel-Rahman bombed the World Trade Centre in New York, killing six and injuring many more. The perpetrators were quickly rounded up and a series of planned atrocities prevented. But already a far more formidable adversary of the West was operating. This was Osama bin Laden. A former Saudi business-man, he has devoted his energies and considerable wealth to waging a Holy War against the West in general and the United States in particular. Since 1992 Bin Laden has been credited with organising lethal attacks on American armed forces in Saudi Arabia, Yemen and Somalia in 1996–97. He has also been linked with the assassination attempt on Hosnay Mubarak and the massacre of tourists at Luxor in 1997. In February 1998 Bin Laden called upon all Muslims to kill Americans anywhere in the world. This was soon followed by the bomb-ings of the American embassies in Dar es Salaam and Nairobi in August when 263 were killed and over 5,000 injured. After the embassy atrocities the American government targeted Bin Laden personally. American warships in the Arabian Sea fired cruise missiles at his base and guerrilla training camp in the Hindu Kush mountains in southern Afghanistan. Around twenty were killed, but Bin Laden escaped. The breakdown of the peace process in 2000 was followed by an attack on an American warship in the Yemen killing sixteen sailors and attributed to Bin Laden. Even if this particular leader is stopped, the problem of such terrorism seems likely to be with us for some time to come.

Rejection of liberal values

Some have suggested that the Cold War between the communist bloc and the liberal democracies was really a local family conflict, and that the really significant conflict, between the West and Islam, is just about to begin. This may be unlikely, but it is certainly true that communism and liberal democracy, despite drastic differences in practice, have shared ideals and aspirations, and common roots in Western thought going back to the Enlightenment and even to Ancient Greece.

It is also true that, while it may embrace a form of democracy, as in Iran, fundamentalist Islam is the most significant alternative to Western liberal values, which are the values we associate with modernity. In this sense there are a number of ways that pure Islam could be said to be in conflict with the modern world. Examples include the role of religion in the state, the position of women, sexual morality, punishment for crime, the problem of usury and relations with the non-Muslim world.

Women are accorded great respect in Islam, more than was the case in the West when it was dominated by Christian ideas (in such matters as, for example, the ownership of property). But Islamic society is none the less highly patriarchal. Men may have several wives. Contraception is strictly forbidden. Women's role is largely confined to the home, and the traditional education of girls accords with this. To the traditionalists, it is not appropriate that women should have the same education as men, or follow careers. Neither should they adopt Western dress, but should be covered from head to toe in the traditional manner. Westernised women have been attacked and intimidated and female university students harassed.

Sexual morality in Islamic law is strict and inflexible. Extra-marital sex is strictly forbidden, as are homosexual acts. In some fundamentalist countries, such as Iran, adulterers and homosexuals have been executed. There are also severe punishments for the drinking of alcohol. The traditional punishment for thieves is the amputation of the hand.

To many modern Muslims much of this is mediaeval and barbaric; they see no reason why the morality of sixth-century Arabia should be imposed on people today. Like modern Christians, they see the need to interpret the teachings of their religion in a modern context. To fundamentalists, however, this is a dangerous attitude. Modernity tends to mean Westernisation, corruption and the undermining of Islam. Western influence and decadence is deplored and there is a tendency to isolationism. Modernists see this as absurd in today's world, and see the necessity of at least learning from the West, if only to stop being left behind and vulnerable as the Islamic world was in the past. A strong Islamic world needs modern technology and other modern products and techniques. An interesting conflict between Islamic traditionalism and modernity is in the question of usury. As in mediaeval Christianity, it is banned by Islamic divine law. Strictly interpreted, this would forbid the existence of a banking system, which is one of the essential ingredients of a modern economy.

There are, however, more basic differences of value. Liberal societies are founded on the freedom of the individual, based on civil liberties that are protected by the constitution. Thus, we largely take for granted freedom of speech, freedom of association, freedom of religion and related civil liberties, and underlying all them is the liberal value of toleration, the willingness to respect views different from our own. Islamic fundamentalists (and indeed other religious fundamentalists) see no virtue in such values and liberties. They conceive of themselves as possessing the truth and see no reason to give opportunities for falsehoods to flourish by allowing people to say what they like, nor to triumph through democracy. Indeed they point to Western problems such as crime, pornography and family and community breakdown as consequences of tolerance. Truth must prevail above all, and only when that is secure can democracy be permitted to contribute to decisions that do not involve that truth.

There is, therefore, a profound gulf between the values and attitudes of the Islamic fundamentalists and those of the West, many of which are shared by modern Muslims. Conflicts between Islamic traditionalism and modernity are to be found throughout the Islamic world.

Other religious fundamentalisms

Islam has not been the only one of the world religions to see a revival that has had political importance; it has also been true of others, including Judaism, Hinduism, Christianity, Sikhism and even Buddhism. However, these have had less impact than Islam since in each case their influence has been confined to a single country. Jewish fundamentalism is significant only in terms of Israeli politics (although Israeli politics does have a wider international significance) and Hindu fundamentalism in terms of the politics of India. In both cases there is a strong link with nationalism. In the case of Christianity, there is a long and complicated relationship between various Christian churches and the political order that is still significant in some parts of the world, including Europe, South America and elsewhere. But in terms of fundamentalism it really only the USA where it could be said to be a significant political force.

Christian fundamentalism

Christian fundamentalism in the USA shares with other religious fundamentalisms a common rejection of 'liberal attitudes' to morality, lifestyles and politics, in favour of traditional values of social morality, social order and old-fashioned nationalistic patriotism. For American fundamentalists 'liberal attitudes' had led to the anarchy, atheism and moral degeneracy of the New Left and permissive society of the 1960s. This outlook put the fundamentalists firmly on the right of the political spectrum, as one of the major strands of the New Right that emerged in the 1970s.

The fundamentalists are on the evangelical wing of American Protestantism, and often call themselves 'born-again Christians'. They believe in the literal truth of the Bible, reject Darwinian evolution, uphold traditional religious values in personal and social matters, and bitterly oppose communism as an atheistical system opposed to everything Christianity and America stands for. In many ways their outlook is authoritarian and is in direct conflict with the libertarian wing of the New Right (see Chapter 9).

Although levels of religious belief and observance are much higher in the USA than in Britain, there has nevertheless been a general decline in religious commitment in America since the Second World War. The great exception to this has been among the various fundamentalist churches whose following has grown. Churches, and federations of churches, such as the Southern Baptists, Seventh Day Adventists, Mormons, Assemblies of God, Jehovah's Witnesses and Pentacostalists, have all grown substantially since the 1950s, so that by 1980 they had some thirty million followers, or roughly one-third of all American churchgoers. This is partly, no doubt, because the fundamentalists offer simplicity and certainty in a complex and uncertain world. They are also zealous and proselytising in their approach, embracing radio, television and the latest communications technology. But it is only since the 1970s that some of their crusading zeal has been applied to politics. Hitherto these groups had traditionally stood aloof from political activity and even from voting.

What occasioned this changed was a reaction to the age of permissiveness and the general rejection of traditional values by American youth of the 1960s, and what they saw as the continuing abominations of feminism and the gay movement. These challenged the traditional family and its values, and what they understood to be the natural patriarchal order of things. For many the culminating event of America's spiritual decline was in the Supreme Court decision of *Roe versus Wade* of January 1973 which gave American women limited rights to abortion. The fundamentalists felt that their values had to be defended politically and that America had to be 'cleansed'.

This led to the creation of a multitude of crusading organisations led by Protestant ministers and pastors, campaigning on a variety of issues such as 'pro-life', ending sex education in schools, and against homosexual rights and pornography. Organisations like the Moral Majority, the Christian Coalition and Christian Voice were religious-inspired general campaigning groups, created to persuade voters to rid Congress of all who supported 'liberal' causes. The introduction of Christian fundamentalism has given the political scene a harsher and more uncompromising tone, making compromise difficult if not impossible. The Christian fundamentalists in Congress were behind the unsuccessful attempt to impeach Bill Clinton, despite lack of popular support, and pursued him relentlessly as an 'immoral president'.

The concentration on family values chimed with other elements of the New

Right, such as the neo-conservatives, and indeed seemed to speak to many people not of their religious persuasion. This even included the Catholics, against whom Protestant fundamentalists were traditionally hostile, and who had been traditional supporters of the Democrats. In the early 1970s Catholics and extreme Protestants found common cause on many moral issues, especially abortion, and a common enemy in 'liberals' who believed in such things. The fundamentalists ideas fitted less well with the New Right libertarians on moral issues, but did find common ground in other areas, such as hostility to communism and a passionate defence of American capitalism. Thus the Reverend Jerry Falwell, the leader of Moral Majority, wrote:

> The free enterprise system is clearly outlined in the Book of Proverbs in the Bible. Jesus Christ made it clear that the work ethic was a part of His plan for man. Ownership of property is biblical. Competition in business is biblical. Ambitious and successful business management is clearly outlined as part of God's plan for His people.
>
> (*Listen America*, 1981)

The fundamentalists also shared with the conservative belief in individual responsibility and hostility to state welfare.

The fundamentalists thus became part of a wider New Right spectrum that found its champion in 1980 in Ronald Reagan, who openly declared himself to be a born-again Christian, spoke of the USSR as the 'evil empire', talked of 'family values', and opposed the feminist campaign for equal rights to be written into the US Constitution. Reagan in office did not, perhaps inevitably, deliver much that the religious right wanted, but they none the less campaigned vigorously for him in 1984 and, with a little less conviction, for his successor, George Bush. They were particularly influential in the 1992 Republican campaign, when 'family values' and related issues were a major part of the Republican platform.

George Bush was heavily defeated in 1992 and it was widely held among analysts that the influence of the religious right was more a hindrance than a help. This was also said in 1996, though less so in the presidential election of 2000, when the Christian right kept a low profile for the sake of getting the Republican candidate elected. This does not indicate a return to the more traditional fundamentalist stance of non-participation. On the contrary, they have built up an infrastructure of organisations, journals and institutions, as well as a following that has become experienced in political campaigning, and if anything have a stronger grip on the Republican Party than ever before. The leading figure has been the Reverend Pat Robertson who founded and is leader of the Christian Coalition (estimated membership of 1.7 million in 1995) and is one of the most powerful figures in the Republican Party, courted by potential candidates and other leaders of the party. Robertson is the most successful of a number of 'televangelists' who use television programmes to promote their religious and political message. Robertson, who claims to be in direct contact with God, owns his own channel, the Christian Broadcasting Network or CBN (55 million viewers in 1999), which is now the centre of a vast business empire worth $200 million. It is difficult for a potential presidential candidate to succeed in the Republican Party without the endorsement of the religious right.

The religious right is even stronger in the politics of many individual states, where they have scored victories in respect of the same feminist, gay and 'family' issues that have come to figure in national politics, but also over issues confined to the state level, such as sex education and, perhaps most surprisingly from a European perspective, the question of the origin on the universe. Christian fundamentalists insist on the literal truth of the Bible, and in particular God's creation of the world in seven days (around 4000 BC). Fossils are explained as left over from Noah's flood, dinosaurs were in the ark, but were subsequently hunted to extinction by man. Fundamentalists believe this should be taught in schools as 'creation science' instead of Darwin's theory of evolution. There is, however, a strong tradition in the USA of separating church and state, one of the consequences of which is that religion is not taught in public (i.e. state-funded) schools. In 1987 the Supreme Court ruled that supposed 'creation science' was not scientific but just religion by another name and could therefore not be taught in public schools. Since then the fundamentalists have striven to have the teaching of Darwinian evolution, and any other theory they deem in conflict with the Bible, banned. In August 1999 the Kansas School Board decided to remove Darwinian evolution from the school curriculum; later the Big Bang theory was similarly removed. Leading academics in Kansas and across America condemned the decision. Despite this there is strong religious pressure in states such as Arizona, Alabama, Georgia, Illinois, New Mexico, Texas and Nebraska to follow the Kansas example.

Although highly organised and united in most of their campaigns, there is one major cleavage within the religious right. Some see their central role as defending and promoting their way of life and vision of a better America, whereas others see the ultimate task as the creation of a theocratic state, a Christian fundamentalist America firmly committed to their religious world view.

Jewish fundamentalism

There have always been those in Israel who have insisted upon a strict observance of traditional Jewish codes, and there have always been political parties to cater for this. These parties have grown in importance since the 1970s, partly because of the nature of the Israeli electoral system and party balance, where governments have needed their support to remain in office.

What has grown in recent years is the demand for the annexation of the West Bank on the grounds that it is the part of the Ancient Israel that is Judea and Samaria. Fundamentalists insist that this land is the historic land given to the Jews by God, and that they thus have a religious duty to settle it, defend it and make it fertile. They see the founding of Israel and the collapse of communism as part of God's plan for the return of the Jews to their homeland. But Jews must play their part and fight for what is theirs. There must be no compromise with the Arabs. Indeed, some fundamentalists believe that it is religious duty to recover the site of Solomon's temple, which would mean destroying the Al Aqsa mosque – one of Islam's most holy shrines. Jewish fundamentalism is, therefore, aggressive and nationalistic.

Since the creation of a Palestinian state is the only conceivable basis for a peace settlement between Arabs and Jews, the fundamentalists are making demands of greatest importance to peace in the region and the world (see Chapter 8). Their determination to create new settlements in the 'Occupied Territories' (which infuriates the Arab states) has been a major stumbling block in the peace process. Despite small numbers (only about 10,000 in all) the Jewish fundamentalist have had a big impact on Israeli and world politics.

Hindu fundamentalism

Aggressive nationalism is also characteristic of India's Hindu fundamentalists, whose growth has been one of the most significant developments in India in recent years. The movement is associated with the Bharatiya Janata Party (BJP) or Hindu Revivalist Party. This is an authoritarian, right-wing party which believes that Hindus need to assert themselves against non-Hindus (especially Muslims), and that the state should be overtly Hindu and should have a more aggressive foreign policy.

The BJP's most infamous cause was the demand that an ancient mosque in Ayodhya in Uttah Pradesh should be demolished to make way for a Hindu temple to the god Ram, who, they believe, was born on the spot. The result of this provocative demand was months of rioting in late 1990 and early 1991 in which more than 1,000 people died and over 4,000 were injured. The following year Hindu extremists demolished the mosque, provoking further riots.

Although it insists that it is dedicated to reviving traditional Indian culture many see the BJP as distorting Indian tradition and has more in common with a fascist party. For one thing, the god Ram is a minor deity in the Hindu pantheon. He is given such emphasis by the BJP because he was a warrior god who, in the mythical past, helped to drive alien invaders out of India, and can therefore be presented as a nationalist god. Furthermore, although it has fought wars in recent times (against Pakistan and China), modern India has conceived of itself as possessed of a particular vocation for peace and tolerance. In the Cold War, for example, it was a powerful advocate of non-alignment. This is partly the legacy of Mahatma Ghandi who was dedicated to bringing about change by peaceful methods, and to tolerance (he was assassinated by a

Hindu fanatic just as India became independent). But also there is a strong strand of pacifism in Indian culture (see Chapter 4).

The BJP is not traditionalist in that it has no such commitment to peace and tolerance. Nevertheless, it has gained considerable electoral success. In the general election of May–June 1991 (during which the Indian prime minister, Rajiv Ghandi, was assassinated), it ended as the second biggest party and the main opposition. In 1996 it emerged as the biggest single party in parliament and two years later assumed power at the head of a coalition government. Among its first acts was to order India's first nuclear weapons tests. This caused consternation around the world that was increased when Pakistan immediately conducted its own tests and the two countries came close to war over the disputed territory of Kashmir. An aggressively nationalistic India threatens the stability of the whole region and beyond.

Sikh radicalism

India's constitutional commitment to the maintenance of a secular state has been undermined by Hindu nationalism. But perhaps this has been inevitable in a country where religion is so important to people personally and as a source of communal identity. A further example was the rise of Sikh nationalism in the 1970s, which aimed at the creation of a separate Sikh state of Khalistan. The conflict came to ahead in 1983 when the prime minister, Indira Ghandi, ordered troops into the Golden Temple, the Sikh's holiest shrine in Amritsar, in order to oust its extremist occupiers. This act of desecration led to Mrs Ghandi's assassination by her Sikh guards and to more than a decade of violence in the Punjab.

Postmodernity and new religious movements

The religious revival of the late twentieth century contradicted the widespread belief that modernisation would reduce it to social insignificance. However, many today would prefer to put this a different way and say that modernity in fact failed and came to an end, and the various religious revivals, along with the growth of what social theorists call 'new religious movements', are manifestations of postmodernity.

Religion and postmodernity

If we accept the widely held view that we now live in a postmodern age, where we have become disillusioned with, and sceptical of, the certainties of modernity – progress, faith in science, Western materialism, modernisation – then the religious revival may be seen as part of the postmodernising process, the process of replacing the certainties and universalities of modernity with variety and the principle that truth is multiple and local. If anything links the diverse expressions of religious fundamentalism it is the rejection of modernity and its effects. It rejects the secularisation, the uniformity of thought, the materialist metaphysics and the easy tolerance that are characteristic of modernity. It asserts quite different truths, quite different ways of looking at the world from those that the liberal, capitalist, scientific West has until recently taken for granted as progressive and true.

The religious revival, and particularly the fundamentalist forms, can be seen as postmodern phenomena. However, any account of late twentieth-century religion would be incomplete without mention of the religious developments and beliefs that go under the general heading of 'new religious movements'. These beliefs often have only a tenuous relationship to politics, but are none the less an important feature of what is claimed to be the postmodern nature of contemporary society, that will directly and indirectly influence the political and ideological future.

New religious movements

The last quarter of the twentieth century has seen a continued decline in orthodox religion but a burgeoning growth in less orthodox forms, of which fundamentalism is one example. Within orthodox Christianity, for example in Britain, it is the charismatic, evangelical Protestantism that is the one area that is thriving, as in the USA. The emphasis is upon more intense religious experience and more commitment to allowing that experience to pervade life in general. But more important have been the growth of new non-Christian or semi-Christian religious movements. The cults, sects and general beliefs, often of Eastern origin, that have proliferated, similarly offer a greater intensity of experience and commitment that orthodoxy fails to provide.

The evangelicals live life more intensely irrespective of the sphere in which the individual finds themselves. Some groups reject the world altogether as irredeemably corrupt. A notorious example is the Unity Church or 'Moonies', who encourage their recruits to cut themselves off from family, friends and other ties and to devote themselves totally to the faith. Others embrace the world positively and maintain that life itself can be lived more intensely, like the followers of the Maharishi Yogi, Hari Krishna and the Mahara Ji. Yoga and other Eastern techniques are the secret of more intense and successful living. These latter cults tend to be more open and eclectic. They have millions of followers, as does the American 'church' of Scientology that combines Eastern philosophy with psychotherapy and the occult. This mixing of religious elements from different sources relates these cults to the wide spectrum of belief that has come to be called 'New Age'.

New Age religion and belief

New Age is an umbrella term covering a great range of non-orthodox beliefs in the supernatural of varying degrees of coherence and spirituality, from reincarnation to feng shui. There is a long history of such beliefs in Europe going back at least to the Renaissance revivals of Ancient occultism and the nineteenth-century interest in spiritualism and exotic religions. However, what is of particular interest here is the upsurge of this kind of thinking from the 1960s and 1970s onwards, when it became known as the New Age or Age of Aquarius movement and was part of the youth and counter-culture movements that rejected contemporary society. They were part also of the 'new social movements' which were the legacy of this period.

The term New Age refers to a belief that humanity is on the edge of a massive transformation to an expanded consciousness and greater powers and wisdom. The idea partly comes from Eastern religious notions of historical cycles and sequences, but also borrows from the apocalyptic visions of fundamentalist Christianity (who are none the less deeply hostile to New Age thinking for reintroducing the occult and therefore Satanic thinking). The nature of the apocalypse varies, from war and terror to great natural cataclysms. Either way, only a proportion of mankind will survive to the New Age of wisdom and light, known as the Age of Aquarius, when humanity (such of it as survives) will make a quantum leap in evolution. These ideas are supplemented by all kinds of beliefs and ideas from all the religious and philosophical traditions of the world. They are also joined by all kinds of theories and beliefs, from the prophecies of Nostradamus to the healing power of crystals, to UFO and inter-galactic communication, to various conspiracy theories, belief that Ancient civilisations were founded by spacemen. Indeed virtually any kind of theory or belief rejected by the mainstream seems to become part of the 'cultic milieu'. However, the full apocalyptic belief is only for the fully committed. They share features of the great penumbra of belief now associated with the New Age.

One of the most distinctive characteristics of New Age religion, and of new religious movements generally, is the centrality of what is essentially an Eastern notion of spirituality that is quite different from the one common to Western and Middle Eastern religions, principally Christianity, Judaism and Islam. In these later faiths, belief revolves around the relationship between human beings on the one hand, and an all-knowing, all-seeing, all-powerful God on the other. In Eastern religions, such as Hinduism and Buddhism, God is not conceived of as a remote and external being, but within each of us. The emphasis is thus upon realising the divine within us and becoming our true selves.

As a consequence of this conception, there is much less emphasis upon divine authority, or the authority of churches that mediate between God and the individual believer. Instead of stressing the truth of a Holy Book, or the sanctity of traditional forms of worship, the emphasis is all on personal experience. Notions of orthodoxy and conformity do not make much sense in this context. Nobody is in a position to deny any other individual's personal experience of spirituality, or question what that experience leads them to believe. Furthermore, divorced from Eastern communities, where there are traditions of authentic experience and interpretations, New Age believers are free to believe whatever they like, however bizarre. What more often happens is that individuals select what appeals to them from the various major religions, as well as a variety of other cults and sects, together with any number of metaphysical belief, from the complexities of witchcraft to a simple faith in the power of crystals. Such mixing is underpinned by a general belief that all religions are different roads to the same God, doctrinal conflicts being simply ignored.

The result may be an incoherent mish-mash, but what matters is individual belief. It is this stress on the authority of the individual believer and their inner development, and the variety of belief that this engenders, which tends to distance New Age belief from social and political ideas and movements. However, the association with the counter-culture of the 1960s and 1970s has in turn associated it with many of the movements of the time. In consequence there are New Age greens, feminists, animal rights supporters and anarchists, including activists in these fields. They are also associated with the commune movement, for example New Age travellers who reject contemporary society, travel about and often are the focus of conflict when the converge on sites they see as religious, such as Stonehenge.

Although there may be political activists in new social movements, the new cults and sects do not usually pose any serious threat to society (although sometimes to themselves as with the Solar Temple and other suicide cults). But there are exceptions. The most frightening was the Aum Supreme Truth sect of Japan, which stockpiled weapons during the 1990s in preparation for Armageddon, from which they would emerge to dominate the world. In 1997 the leader, the self-styled His Holiness the Master Shoko Asahara, ordered the beginning of the destruction of Japanese society with nerve gas attacks on the Tokyo subway, killing dozens of people. The leaders were rounded up and put on trial for mass murder. Nevertheless, the cult continues to grow.

However, it would be wrong to portray New Age believers as characteristically at odds with society. Such beliefs have spread among the general population. A recent example was the fate of the England football manager, Glen Hoddle, who was forced to resign after protests at the revelation of his beliefs that disabled people were suffering the consequences of bad behaviour in a previous life (a fairly common New Age belief). By no means all have such strong religious convictions as Hoddle. Such beliefs are even commercially exploited in self-development courses and books ('Release the power of the inner you!' and so forth).

The significance of New Age belief lies not in the political sphere so much as in what it represents in the general trends of society (which ultimately has an impact on politics and ideology). As with fundamentalist movement in the established religions, New Age beliefs can be seen as a manifestation of post-modernity. But where fundamentalism can be seen as embodying some features of the postmodern (in their rejection of universalism, globalisation, materialism, cultural uniformity, in the name of communal particularism and identity) New Age belief represents other features. Instead of communal assertion of difference, New Age belief can be highly individualistic, with the individual choosing from an almost infinite range of possibility, mixing and matching what appeals from what already exists or making up something new. One might call it a consumerist approach to religion. It is an assertion of personal identity, an identity which is self-created and subject to change. Such belief might be seen as a substitute for political ideology.

This discussion leads to a consideration of where society, whether we conceive it as postmodern or not, is going and what role ideology will play in the future. This is the subject of the final chapter.

13

Globalisation, postmodernity and the future of ideology

We live in an age of rapid and accelerating change the outcome of which nobody can tell. Nevertheless, we can look at current trends and come to some provisional conclusions as to where they might be taking us. In politics there would seem to be two major trends of greatest importance that contradict each other, and the future of politics and ideology to a great extent may turn on the ways in which these contrary trends interact. One trend is that of making the world ever smaller, ever more integrated, ever more compelled towards standardisation, and consequently ever more homogenised and ever more the same. The other and opposite trend is towards fragmentation, the assertion of difference and insistence on variety. The first of these trends is associated with the process of globalisation and the second with the more controversial idea of postmodernity, although both can be complex and ambiguous in their implications.

These trends tend to undermine the nation-state, which is the most basic unit of modern politics. They have also played their part in the modifying or erasing of hitherto taken-for-granted features of the political landscape. The Cold War, the party system, the left–right political spectrum and many institutions and relationships have gone or have changed, while new forms of political participation have altered the parameters as well as the form of politics in Western states. These in turn have had an impact on the ideological climate, to such an extent that we have arguably entered a new age of ideology.

Cold War to globalisation

The origins of this present age of change lie in the social, economic, political and intellectual developments of the late twentieth century. But if we seek a starting point, some watershed event to mark the transition from old to new, then the end of the Cold War and collapse of the Soviet empire (1989–91) is an obvious candidate.

Cold War endings

Globalisation could clearly not be fully global while the communist world was excluded. The ending of this exclusion left the forces of globalisation free to develop. But equally important, the Cold War managed to enshrine and perpetuate the politics of class division that had been the feature of modernity since the French and Industrial Revolutions. From at least the 1960s, society and (more slowly) politics had been changing, but in a sense the Cold War seem to freeze politics and ideology in the old categories of left and right, artificially sustaining this polarisation beyond its natural lifespan. Since the end of the Cold War a new society and new politics, sometimes called postmodern, have had greater freedom to grow and evolve.

The distinguished historian, Eric Hobsbawm, has identified the end of the Cold War as the end of the twentieth century as an historical unit (Hobsbawm, 1994). More dramatically the American theorist Francis Fukuyama declared that it signified the end of history as such (Fukuyama, 1989). He argues that if we understand history in terms of humanity's search for the optimum form of society, then the end of the Cold War must mark the end of history since, having seen off all serious rivals, including fascism and communism, free-market liberal democracy had proved itself to be the only possible candidate.

The Fukuyama thesis provoked considerable controversy (Adams, 1990), but is now generally seen as dated and simplistic. His analysis belongs to the age whose passing it marked. Some say that the age that passed with the end of the Cold War was in fact the modern age, and that we now live in the age of 'postmodernity'. Whatever we call this new period of change, globalisation and postmodern ideas are important features of it. We need to look at each in turn.

Globalisation

Undoubtedly the most important agent of transformation in recent decades has been the growth of the global economy and its political impact. What is meant here by economic globalisation is not merely the further growth of the international economy, but a qualitative change. 'International economy' implies economic relations between sovereign states, whereas the term 'global economy' is meant to suggest a network of economic relationships and processes beyond the responsibility or control of any state. The power of multinational corporations, able to switch production from one country to another at will, has long been known. But the explosive growth of global communications has opened up global financial markets of enormous power.

In the late 1970s, before international money markets were as powerful as they later became, the Labour government in Britain was forced to change its more radical policies in the face of a loss of confidence in the pound in international markets. A similar fate befell President Mitterand's socialist policies in France in the early 1980s. A more recent example of this power was Britain's withdrawal from the European Exchange Rate Mechanism (ERM) in 1992 because the markets thought the pound was overvalued. Billions were lost trying to prop up the pound to no avail.

International markets are now immensely powerful, and there is an increasing tendency for international financial opinion to impose a kind of uniformity on states in terms of economic policies. This, of course tends to restrict what other policies a state can have, what levels of public expenditure and taxation and therefore what social policies can be pursued. Such constraints have profound implications for parties and their ideologies as well as for national sovereignty. The days when a government that is involved in the international economy could choose its own economic policies, and set levels of taxation and welfare independently of international economic considerations seem to be over. Hence the claim that the nation-state has, so to speak, been undermined from above.

Regional groupings, such as the European Union, may give some degree of collective autonomy, but in the end no economic grouping or superpower can be immune to global imperatives. All must live with the new global order, and are subject to both its benefits and its drawbacks. Globalisation and economic liberalisation (that is, deregulation of markets) have increased economic insecurity. Whatever the horrors of totalitarianism, security under communism was a major bonus for ordinary people. In the West, social democracy, which included Keynesian economic management (the leading economic wisdom of the post-war West up to the 1970s) and high welfare spending, also provided levels of economic security unknown to previous generations. But not only has communism been largely swept away, so too has Keynesian social democracy.

Keynesian economics involved government intervention to prevent unemployment. Such intervention is now no longer an option because one effect of globalisation is that it is no longer possible to treat a single economy in isolation. All over the world there has been a liberalising of markets, and a consequent growth in economic insecurity. More deregulated markets inevitably mean some become very rich; but such markets also inevitably produce higher levels of poverty and unemployment, increasing the effects of trade cycles and creating pressure to reduce welfare. The effects of these changes are felt across the social spectrum.

Another aspect of global communications is the internet and other devices whereby international communications between citizens are possible in ways difficult for governments to regulate. It would seem that it is quite technically feasible for someone living in Barnsley to work from home for a firm in, say, Buenos Aires or Brisbane.

The pressure to conform even extends to the political sphere, as seen in the interventions of the international community, once hamstrung by Cold War rivalries. In the Gulf War of 1991an international force waged war on Iraq in order to reverse its illegal conquest of neighbouring Kuwait. More significantly, NATO went to war in 1998 against Serbia because it disapproved of its *internal* policies in Kosovo. These and other examples require states to conform to international standards of behaviour (although this discipline is not consistently applied).

Forces of fragmentation: nation and faith

At the same time as there are forces of unity and conformity in the global economy diminishing the state from above, there are also contrary forces of fragmentation working from below.

One of the first and most obvious consequences of the end of the Cold War and removal of the discipline of superpower rivalry has been the disintegration or weakening of multinational states, particularly under the force of revived nationalism. The Soviet Union began to break up almost immediately, with outlying republics seeking independence and reviving old conflicts. The Russian Federation itself has come under strain and may yet fragment. Yugoslavia also disintegrated and wars broke out with a viciousness not seen since 1945. Czechoslovakia split into two states, though peacefully. But states in quite different circumstances have also suffered threats of disintegration. India has suffered from Sikh and Tamil extremism; and even Canada, modern, prosperous and seemingly stable, has seen an upsurge of Quebec nationalism that has threatened and continues to threaten the unity of the federation.

Such strains have been felt in Western Europe. France (in Corsica), Spain (in Catalonia and the Basque areas) and Italy (with its separatist Northern League) are among those effected, while Flemish nationalism threatens the breakup of Belgium. The list also includes Britain. Irish nationalism has threatened the Union by unconstitutional means while Scottish and Welsh nationalism does so by conventional politics. Britain since 1997 has embarked on a major experiment in devolution which some hope and some fear will lead to independence, while others have thought a measure of devolution necessary merely to preserve the United Kingdom.

But it is not only the end of the Cold War that has released suppressed nationalism. Globalisation and its attendant insecurities has also been influential. The response to economic insecurity in the past tended to be a rise in support for socialist parties and ideas, but this seems no longer the case (at least for the present). The alternative in many cases is a growth of nationalism. We see this in former communist areas, the former Soviet Union and Yugoslavia and Eastern Europe; but also in the West, where in particular regional entities that have suffered economic distress have seen autonomy or independence as the answer to their difficulties. This occurs when, for example, the demands of international economy oblige governments to cut public expenditure and neglect distressed regions. There is an important element of this in Scottish and Welsh nationalism, but also in other parts of the world.

However, it is not only national identity that has been asserted, but also religious and racial identity. There is an established and obvious link between authoritarian and racist anti-immigration politics and economic distress. This is true in Western Europe, particularly France and Germany, but also in Russia and the East, where such parties recruit among the unemployed. Another dimension is religion. Islamic fundamentalism is also partly a response to economic insecurity: in Algeria, Iran, Egypt and elsewhere, the disaffected urban poor, who are in a very different situation from traditional rural poor, are a major recruiting ground for extremist movements. This is also true of other fundamentalisms (although it is the cultural threats that stem from globalisation that are more important than economic ones). A major upsurge of nationalism, racism and religious fundamentalism, and the assertion of ethnic identity, around the world in the closing decades of the twentieth century, has put strains upon the nation-state in many regions.

Curiously, a factor in this move towards the assertion of regional identity and aspiration towards independence is the European Union. It suggests a framework within which smaller states may comfortably survive in a way not possible outside the EU. In addition to independence movements there is a more general move to more devolution to lower levels and a demand for more regional autonomy, which again diminishes to some degree the nation-state.

Undermining culture and tradition

Other forces of fragmentation are more subtle, although in the longer term perhaps more destructive. These are cultural forces that undermine the sense of nation as a cultural unity, a shared way of life. Global communication and economy have great potential to undermine any cultural identity that a government or religion may wish to preserve. Islamic fundamentalists rail at the Americanisation of Islamic youth with pop music and television and consumer goods. The aim of the Hindu revivalist party that came to power in India in 1998 is to 'remain anchored to our roots as we modernise so we don't lose ourselves in a tidal wave of modernisation' (quoted in Haynes, 1998, p.170).

More generally, non-Western nations may have little hope of quelling popular demand for goods that are seen by their citizens whether they want them to or not. It is a perhaps a sad but significant fact that the biggest factor in the fall of East European communism was not the desperate striving for political freedom so much as a desire for a Western standard of living seen on Western television which East Europeans could pick up, a standard of living that communist governments could not deliver. The loss of much economic sovereignty, and the limited capacity of governments to control what happens within their borders, has diminished the nation-state.

The striving for economic growth and entry into the world economy has also undermined traditional cultures all over the non-Western world. In many areas it has involved urbanisation and the Western lifestyle that goes with it.

In more rural communities an economy may be replaced by the comm-ercial growing of early vegetables for the Western market, or exotic cultural practices in a remote region may be turned into a sanitised spectacle for rich tourists.

In Western countries we are all aware of how modern media and commer-cialisation erase local differences in dialects, customs and ways of life generally. Much of what used to be determined by the traditions of community, family, class and country has become a matter of consumer choice. It is part of a general trend away from the communal and collective and towards the individual. There has been a general growth of a kind of individualism that sees human beings as essentially creatures bent upon pursuing their own interests and satisfactions with little reference to others or the community generally. This is a 'new individualism' that is both a cause and effect of a decline of tradition.

However, the more important point in the present context is the effect of a self-regarding individualism upon social solidarity and national solidarity. It was the traditions of family and class and local community that had deter-mined our identity, who we are; this now is much more subject to choice, with inevitably deleterious effects on our general sense of community. It also tends to undermines the nation-state, in the sense that the overriding allegiance of the citizen to the state comes under strain. There are too many other links, and too many other identities in the modern world, for one to override all others. The idea that identities are multiple and in flux, and to some degree subject to choice, is related to the notion that we are now in a new kind of society, if not in a new phase of human history, both of which may be desig-nated 'postmodern'.

Modernity to postmodernity?

Globalisation and the communications revolution are only part of a much wider picture of change. The late twentieth century saw the beginning of a transformation of human society that is still going on. These changes used to be discussed under the heading of 'post-industrial society', but the more fash-ionable term today is 'postmodern society'. However, the term postmodern is a contentious one since it implies that the transformation we are live living through is so great that we have left the age of modernity behind and now live in a completely new age of human history and consciousness. This is the theory of postmodernism. The postmodernists who hold this view argue that the new world of postmodernity we have entered involves an entirely new kind of society, as well as new ways of understanding reality and ourselves, that would have been unthinkable a few decades ago.

Postmodern society and individuality

What *post*modern society is supposed to have passed beyond is modern industrial society, generated by the Industrial Revolution, with its the mass production, mass workforces, standardised goods, and with a class-based society and class politics. Since the Second World War we have moved steadily towards a society based on consumerism, where former standardised goods now come with countless variations, service industries are as important as manufacturing, and there is an abundance of consumer choice in everything. It is a world driven by advertising, where products are often less important in themselves than for what they represent in terms of image and lifestyle.

The whole trend of late twentieth-century consumerism is towards ever greater choice and variety. People choose their lifestyles and to some degree thereby choose who they are. We live in a media-drenched world. Television bombards us with images from around the world and advertisements from around the world, while the internet is increasingly making it possible to shop around the world. In much of the things we watch and read, the clothes we wear, the motor cars we drive, and even what we eat and drink we share with countless other people in countless other countries. Our cosmopolitanism has become such that anyone can choose to fashion their homes to have, say, a Roman-style bathroom, Japanese-style bedroom, Moroccan-style living room and Italian-style kitchen, and be ready to change them again according to the next fashion. Or we may prepare Chinese food one evening, Italian the next, Indian the next and so on. The familial, communal, class and national traditions that largely determined these things for us a generation ago have limited meaning today.

It is clearly the case that economic and media developments threaten the distinctiveness of local and national cultures. Some would go further and argue that the effect of mass media and communications and consumerism is now not merely to undermine local cultures but to undermine culture generally, in the sense of reducing everything to a common denominator. In watching television we are subjected to a stream of images, serious and comic, real and fictional, high art and low entertainment, so that the boundaries are blurred and these distinctions are undermined in life generally. Television, so the postmodernist argument goes, reduces everything to the same level, turning everything into a commodity and undermining tradition, all distinctions between cultures, between high and low culture, all local and regional differences. The fragmentation, mixing of styles and general shallowness and lack of seriousness in postmodern art are said to reflect this post-industrial/postmodern cultural world.

One consequence of a decline in a sense of national and local culture is a loss of common standards of morality, which is replaced by a generalised belief that everyone should be more or less free to 'do their own thing' so long as others are not harmed. Good and bad, right and wrong, are increasingly seen as matters for each individual. This individualism is reinforced by consumer culture, which is in turn reinforced by the kind of free-market beliefs prevalent since the 1980s, with their emphasis of freedom of choice and above all consumer choice. What was regarded as national culture has to a considerable degree in post-industrial/postmodern society become commercialised, so that intangible cultural objects such as images, stories, labels, information, ideas and fashions become traded as commodities like any other. In fact they are more valuable and more profitable than physical goods.

These features of a post-industrial economy have implications for a post-industrial society. Employment is much more variegated, fragmented and insecure. Great industrial armies in coal and steel and manufacturing are a thing of the past, while a secure job for life is ceasing to be a reality across the whole range of employment. Until at least the 1960s we could speak confidently of different and clearly distinguishable social classes, differing not merely in type of occupation, but also in dress, lifestyle attitudes, beliefs and much else. These distinctions have been steadily eroding under the impact of television and consumerism. There has been a general decline in class awareness and the idea of distinctive class cultures. What used to be thought of as solid class blocks are criss-crossed with a multitude of equally important divisions of age and ethnicity, sex and sexuality, locality and economic sector and others. We now live in a pluralist, multicultural society where it is no longer acceptable to pressure minority cultures to conform to the dominant culture in ways that were commonplace a generation ago.

Politics in postmodern society

Politics in industrial society revolved around major political parties broadly reflecting class divisions. These were conventionally arranged along a left–right spectrum, with parties of property on the right, expressing a conservative or liberal pro-capitalist ideology, and parties of the propertyless espousing some kind of socialism on the left. With American parties concentrated on the middle to right of the spectrum (relative to Western Europe) and the communist states to the left, the Cold War projected this spectrum on to world politics.

However, the fragmentation and decline of the working class and the rise of individualist consumer society has gradually changed traditional political concerns and allegiances. From the 1950s support for major mass parties, in terms of both voting and membership, gradually began to decline across the Western world, as did the strength of party allegiance. Electorates have become more volatile and fickle and major parties can no longer take mass support for granted as they once did.

Perhaps it goes with the kind of 'individual-as-consumer' picture particularly associated with the dominance of free-market thinking in the 1980s, which both reflected and encouraged a trend away from more traditional forms of thought and action. In its political aspect, this outlook depicts the citizen as a consumer of government goods (policies and services) in a political market place where parties offer competing wares, and where what is on offer is based upon market research and has little ideological content. Some argue that we are reaching this stage in British politics, and that the Labour Party won the 1997 general election partly because it understood the new political reality better than the Conservatives.

This decline in automatic support for the traditional parties, and the development of a more consumerist politics was accompanied by a corresponding growth of smaller parties and what social theorists call 'new social movements' (NSMs), which have altered the political landscape sufficiently for some to talk of the 'new politics'.

New social movements

NSMs began to appear in the 1960s with the student movement in Europe and the USA, the black civil rights movement, the peace movement and others. In due course we had the women's movement, gay movement, animal rights, the environmental movement, as well as, in some areas, movements relating to minority nationalisms, indigenous peoples and religious groups. At the same time, there was a growth of smaller parties, even where, as in Britain, such parties were disadvantaged by the electoral system. These parties often brought to prominence new issues and concerns.

The earliest of the new social movements, the student and civil rights movements, were political movements, although not in any conventional sense. They were not political parties, they raised issues not on the normal political agenda, they were concerned with changing society and the way people think, and their methods were not those of conventional politics. Organisation was often based on loose networks of the like-minded rather than centralised bureaucratic organisations like conventional parties or trade unions. All of these features have been characteristic of the movements that followed. Even in the case of the green movement, which has taken the apparently conventional route of forming political parties, it has prided itself upon creating parties of a distinctly unconventional kind, 'anti-party parties', as they like to characterise themselves.

Characteristically these movements are concerned with issues to do with 'lifestyle and identity'. What is meant here is issues concerning how people choose to live their personal lives, their quality of life and how individuals relate in personal relations, with the community and with the environment generally; things that in the past that were often taken for granted and left to tradition and culture. They include issues from sexual orientation to the things we eat – not merely its safety (a long-time concern of government) but whether it is ethical (treatment of animals) or scientifically dubious (GM foods). Questions of lifestyle are also bound up with questions of identity: that is, of belonging and status and citizenship. This covers race and ethnicity and religion, but also sex and sexual orientation. Social attitudes are the main target, but the state and law are also important with issues over whether minority groups have the same rights as the majority (gays in the military, gay marriage, laws of blasphemy applying to religions other than the state religion), issues that reflect multicultural, plural nature of contemporary society where all demand equality of treatment and respect.

In focussing on such issues, new social movements have extended the range and scope of what we understand as politics. As we saw with liberation ideologies in Chapter 9, they are often about changing attitudes, through consciousness raising and trying to change the outlook of the general public. Perhaps the most striking example is the feminist claim that 'the personal is the political'. The ideologies of these new social movements are also unconventional in the sense of being neither universal nor 'exclusive' in the sense that they are often concerned with a particular group rather than humanity as a whole. It is also possible to have commitments to the beliefs of many such groups, instead of one comprehensive commitment as the major ideologies normally demand. This fits in with postmodern theory about how we now see politics and society. We need, therefore, to look at postmodernism before assessing the significance of these new ideological forms.

The theory of postmodernism

The idea that humanity has passed beyond modernity and has moved into a new age of postmodernity was first suggested by the French philosopher, Jean François Lyotard, in 1979. Lyotard's argument built on earlier French poststructuralist thought, found in various works that are notoriously difficult and obscure, and was subsequently developed largely in France. In consequence, postmodernism was long regarded by English-speaking thinkers as a French eccentricity, and dismissed as the radicalism of disillusioned and incomprehensible French ex-Marxists. But, far from being a passing fashion of no importance, postmodern ideas persisted and became more widely influential in mainstream thinking in the 1990s. We need to understand something of the debates surrounding postmodernism if we are to make an assessment of how politics and ideology may develop in the future.

Postmodernists see a deep connection between the economic and social developments just described and postmodernism in the arts, characterised by a mixing of styles and multiple points of view, which they believe reflects and expresses the nature of the present age, as other contemporary artistic movements and fashions do not. More importantly, postmodernists make the crucial and much more controversial connection between all these developments and the intellectual movement known as post-structuralism. It is in their acceptance and use of post-structuralist analysis that postmodernist thinkers are most at odds with their critics.

Post-structuralism and the crisis in Western reason

Post-structuralism is principally concerned with the nature of language and its relation to reality. It denies that language has any fixed meaning and argues that any 'text' (which includes anything we can interpret in different ways, even physical objects) is open to any number of meanings, none of which is better than any other. The most famous exponent of this view, the French thinker Jacques Derrida, has used a technique known as 'deconstruction' to analyse philosophical texts in such a way as to show them to be full of contradictions and ambiguities, hidden assumptions and rhetorical tricks and therefore not capable of demonstrating anything. He seems to undermine the possibility of all objective reasoning, including philosophy and science (although critics claim that this must include post-structuralism itself). Objectivity, or truth in the conventional sense, is an illusion. There is no universal absolute truth, only local and relative truth. Since Western thought is built on ideas of universal truth, post-structuralists see Western rationality as in crisis.

Postmodernists have developed the historical implications of this idea. They argue that the modern age began with, and has been shaped by, the Enlightenment movement of the eighteenth century, which believed that life and society should no longer be based on tradition but on reason (see Chapter 2). Enlightenment thinkers invented the idea of progress, and believed that through the application of universal reason to every human problem, humanity could move steadily towards the fully rational society in which there would be freedom, prosperity and happiness for all. This is what postmodernists call the 'Enlightenment project', which they believe *defines* the modern age. Since they believe that this project has clearly failed and we no longer believe in social progress, then, they insist, the modern age must be over and we now live in a new age, an age of *post*modernity.

How, then, has the Enlightenment project failed? In the first place, there is no doubt that the appalling wars, genocides, pollution, threats of nuclear annihilation and other horrors of the twentieth century have undermined our faith in progress. War, poverty, exploitation and injustice are still commonplace in the world. We are no longer confident (as we were until recently) that the Western path of 'modernisation' through industrialisation and urbanisation and their consequences, are the correct path of 'progress' for the rest of humanity.

Of course, there are different versions of the rational society. Enlightenment thinkers came to understand a rationally organised society in liberal terms of constitutionalism and natural rights, and a rational economy as capitalist, while others, such as socialists, conservatives and nationalists, later argued that their kind of society was the most rational for all mankind. Thus, postmodernists see modern ideologies as expressing different versions of the Enlightenment project. But all have failed to deliver the freedom, prosperity and happiness for all that the project promised.

The postmodern belief that in some sense Western rationality has failed, does not mean that we can no longer use our reason to solve social or scientific problems. What postmodernists object to is not reason as such but the notion of universal reason, that there is one rational way of doing things that is the same for every human being. Postmodernists are relativists: what is rational or true for one group at one time may not be rational or true for another group at another time. It is the failure to understand this that accounts for the failure of progress. The problem with modern ideologies, postmodernists believe, is their claim to universal validity, which has been used to justify all kinds of infamy. What is wrong in principle, they argue, is one part of humanity imposing its ideas and values and control over other parts, one nation imposing on another, one group in society imposing its values on other groups.

Jean François Lyotard, in the first major work of postmodern theory, *The Postmodern Condition: A Report on Knowledge* (1979, translated into English 1984) argued that the most basic feature of the postmodern world was an 'incredulity towards metanarratives' (p.xxiv). By metanarratives he means the stories or myths that are used to justify our activities. To begin with, he has in mind science. That is, the belief that science is progressive and all for the human good. But he wishes to go further, and suggest that all social and political activities justified by apparently universal truths no longer have any hold on us. We have, he is suggesting, rejected grand theory, with its accompanying notions of universal human nature and universally human needs, and therefore a universally ideal form of society. This whole way of thinking is wrong. This of course principally applies to modern universalistic ideologies. Lyotard goes so far as to say that any attempt to impose one universal vision on anyone, not just Marxist or fascist, but liberal or nationalist, is totalitarian and 'terroristic'.

Thus, postmodernism can be seen as a rejection of universal truth, the idea that there are truths that apply to everyone everywhere. This is also associated with Western dominance and the idea that Western ideas are superior because they are universal. Postmodernists argue that we now live in a world of shifting truths, of multiple points of view, where there is no means of determining who is right and who wrong. All is relativism and subjectivity. Our beliefs have no solid foundations in universal human nature or anything else. Truth is always 'local truth'; that is, only valid within the group or community which generated it. Thus, there is no one truth but multiple truths, no one reality but multiple realities. This calls into question all kinds of authorities – political, scientific, intellectual, social – along with the hierarchies and justifications that go with them.

Postmodern politics and identity

This might suggest modern society has to be pluralist and tolerant with a multitude of differing viewpoints from a multitude of groups, sections, social groups and individuals. In these circumstances, it is argued, it becomes impossible to impose, and morally wrong to try to impose, an ideology or any kind of mass identity, including class, nation or ethnicity. Indeed, we are now in a world of shifting identities, where we acknowledge or choose many identities and may change our minds. The individual, so the theory goes, is recognised as having multiple identities and resents ideological claims that one – be it class or nation or sex or whatever – must be overriding. There is no fixed universal human identity, only the specific identities that come from historical accident.

But what does this mean as a practical doctrine? Different postmodernists have different views and can be broadly categorised as optimists and pessimists. Jean Baudrillard, for example, argues that modernity was the era of production, but now we are in an era of reproduction. We drift around in an endless stream of media images that refer to nothing beyond themselves, with little capacity for ordering them in a meaningful way. These images have become far more real to us than real life: 'TV is the world.' What has not been recorded on film or video, cannot have happened. Our sense of reality has collapsed, and we have lost all sense of history. We can no longer distinguish between image and reality, the real and the unreal; and consequently we are simply lost in a world of images with no escape. Political action to change things is futile. Baudrillard is the gloomiest and most extreme of the pessimists.

However, others are more optimistic. For some the postmodern world is a liberating one, freeing us from traditional authorities, hierarchies and ideologies; a much more egalitarian world. They see a more fragmented and various society, no longer divided by simple and ideologically charged divisions like social class, and with much more of the politics of social groups and associations based on age, gender, locality, nationality, ethnicity, sexual orientation, occupation, and so on. Politics of this kind is a matter of pressure groups and social movements, such as the women's movement, gay rights, environmentalism, and so on. The base of mass parties is eroding anyway. However, the postmodernist thinkers who have seen things this way, such as Foucault and Lyotard, have insisted on resistance to authority in all its forms and in all circumstances. There is no overall theory of government or social organisation. Their politics is purely a politics of protest and resistance, in which the other major force shaping the world, globalisation, is the enemy. It is questionable how far this represents any kind of realistic politics.

Postmodernism's weaknesses and strengths

Apart from its limited practicality, postmodern theory has been subject to many criticisms and of different kinds. It may be argued that it is self-contradictory and self-defeating, in that it uses general forms of reasoning that is says are no longer valid and claims truth and objectivity while at the same time claiming that truth and objectivity are impossible.

Indeed, one can see postmodernism is precisely the kind of 'metanarrative' or universal ideology it condemns. Thus, human beings have such a nature that they generate cultures and ways of understanding themselves and their world which, because of their different circumstances, are various and incompatible. It is invalid and wrong for one such culture to impose itself upon any other. There is, therefore, an ethical imperative to create a world in which all cultures and points of view may be respected and allowed to flourish. This is a classical ideological form of a universal kind. As with all such ideologies there is a denigration of rivals and a simplification of history. An example is postmodernism's simplistic identification of modernity with the Enlightenment. Scepticism about Enlightenment ideas and ideals is as much a part of modernity as the Enlightenment itself. One does not have to be a postmodernist to be sceptical of science and rational organisation in the light of twentieth-century experience.

A further major problem with the idea of postmodernity is that all its features and ideals grow out of modernity. The major forces shaping the world today are capitalism and new technology, the very same forces that shaped modernity. Similarly, in the field of political ideas, the aspiration of the postmodernists are their own versions of greater freedom, equality and democracy, and again these are the ideals of modernity. Postmodernity could therefore be interpreted as much as an acceleration of modernity as its demise.

Given these problems, and there are many others, it may be wondered just what the appeal of postmodernism is, why it has persisted and continues to be influential. The answer is perhaps that these ideas, despite their weaknesses, seem to chime with much in contemporary experience. In the first place, themes of fluidity and fragmentation and shifting meanings that undermine established structures, hierarchies and authorities, seems to reflect much of the fluid, changing world of today, including disillusionment with progress. Second, we need to live in multicultural societies and insensitivity to the needs and aspirations of minority groups is no longer acceptable. But in doing so we often need to redefine our identity and perhaps modify our Western prejudices, which many find difficult and disorientating.

The need for self-redefinition is part of a wider phenomenon of the decline of tradition. This has been a major theme of the whole of modernity, but postmodernity has seen an acceleration of this process for reasons of consumerism, globalisation and high technology that we have discussed. The world is changing at dizzying speed, all is fluid and melting, structures are fragmenting, all we thought solid seems fragile and contrived, meanings shift. This loss of traditions and the sense of loss and insecurity that go with it have fuelled much of the politics of postmodernity. This the politics of identity, which may be expressed in minor nationalist movements, or parties bemoaning the loss of national identity in organisations like the European movement, or in religious fundamentalisms of various sorts. What are we to believe in a world where nothing seems fixed and we no longer seem to have tradition to fall back on as we did in the past?

Postmodern or late modern?

Nevertheless, this may be a mood that will change. We might see the world in transformation but things could be interpreted differently and less apocalyptically. It may well be that in a decade or so (or less) we may look back and see postmodern theory as a product of an age of flux and that a more measured response to these changes is to see them as a new phase of modernism. The leading sociologist Anthony Giddens has suggested that we have moved into 'late modernity', in which globalisation, technology and our capacity to free ourselves from tradition and choose who we are can all be seen as an intensification of modernity rather than its transcendence.

Whether we deem the present age postmodern or late modern in the end hardly matters, for ultimately it is for historians to judge. But on the simple judgement as to whether our current transformation is as great as that between classical and mediaeval, or mediaeval and modern, it does not seem that revolutionary (although it is something about which we might yet wish to change our minds). Nevertheless, there are huge changes in progress and it is an important and interesting question as to how politics and ideology will respond.

A new age of ideology?

From this and previous chapters a picture emerges that suggests that the great age of competing universal ideologies, what might be called the 'age of the French Revolution', is over and that a new age of small-scale, non-universal, non-exclusive ideologies has begun. While there is an element of truth in this picture, it is problematic for at least two reasons. The first is the case of liberalism. While some versions of it may be in decline, liberal ideas and values show no sign of disappearing. Indeed, as we saw at the beginning of this chapter, there is a case for arguing that liberalism is triumphant and the only serious ideology left. Second, the small-scale ideologies of limited groups and special interests are all very well, but they cannot be the basis of coherent government, or of major parties competing for power. We need to consider these two questions before attempting to assess what the future of ideology might be.

Liberalism's triumph and decline

Fukuyama has a point when he argues that liberalism triumphed with the fall of communism, having seen off its last serious rival and would be the main form of government henceforward. Ignoring his questionable assertion that this would now be for ever, there is some truth in the idea that capitalist liberal democracy is spreading and there is no serious alternative in terms of practical politics. On the other hand, without the simplicities of the Cold War, where there appeared to be a clear contrast with an aggressive enemy, liberalism is not the self-confident, universally agreed doctrine one might expect from Fukuyama's analysis.

One way to understand this paradoxical situation is to see that liberal democracy and capitalism simply became the 'given' for much of the world and the inevitable future for much of the rest. They have merged in to the background. Liberal ideals – freedom, equality, constitutional government and democracy – can be understood as the ideals of modernity itself. The rise of political liberalism (supplemented subsequently by economic liberalism and democracy) was part of the transformation from mediaeval to modern, and taken up in many doctrines of various forms and in various combinations in various ideologies. One might argue that we are left with the ideals while the doctrines have declined or fragmented, rather like Christianity.

Insofar as it is an active political doctrine, liberalism is not monolithic, but is deeply divided into different and in some ways hostile forms. In Western states, like Britain and the USA, politics revolves around different versions or hybrids of liberalism, broadly New Right versus social liberalism, which have very different agendas, very different notions of freedom and equality, and very different conceptions of how society ought to be. On a more philosophical level there is a huge range of liberal positions between Rawls and Nozick and others. All of which stretch the notion of liberalism in different directions and challenge the simplistic universalism of Fukuyama.

At the same time, liberalism is assailed by doubts resulting from attacks from within and without, by communitarians and multiculturalists and postmodernists. And this has induced a certain loss of confidence. Some may wallow in the triumph of a supposed post-Cold War dominance, but some of the most distinguished liberal thinkers, such as Rawls and Rorty, have abandoned its traditional claims to a universality appropriate for all (see Chapter 2).

Liberal ideals have to a considerable extent become absorbed into the fabric of contemporary life, while as an active political doctrine liberalism is fragmented and beleaguered (partly for not living up to its own ideals). What is left is a kind of generalised belief in freedom, equality and their achievement through democracy. It is less accurate to say with Fukuyama that liberal ideology rules the world than to say that the political and social values of modernity have prevailed and been expressed in various divergent forms of liberal ideology, as well as suffused through various other ideologies, and to a considerable extent have merged into the taken-for-granted constitutional background.

The universal and the particular

Beyond liberalism, it has been a major feature of late twentieth-century politics in general that most of the major ideologies of modernity have been in serious decline: Marxism, socialism, fascism, conservatism, anarchism and so on. At the same time the ideologies that have spread and flourished have been the smaller-scale ideologies associated with new social movements and the politics of identity and lifestyle, including political religious movements and small-scale nationalisms, which address a smaller following rather than humanity as such.

There are, however, a variety of ambiguous cases. There is nationalism, for example, which has always had both its universalist versions (such as the view that all peoples have an equal right to independence and autonomy) and its narrow particularistic versions which express a national self-assertion that cares little for the rights of others. It is the latter that most flourishes today. Feminism too can have its universalist and particularist sides. Then there is the green movement, which undoubtedly has a universalist ideology, yet belongs in the new social movements. It is made up to a considerable degree of small single-issue groups often with different outlooks, its ideas tend to be non-exclusive and it belongs in the 'lifestyle and identity' group in term of origins and organisation and connections.

But these ambiguous cases apart, the move from modernity to post/late modernity in ideological terms would seem to be in terms of a change from universal, exclusive ideologies to predominantly small-scale ideologies to do with identity and lifestyle, and which are not exclusive in the sense that one can support the greens and black rights and be a feminist and nationalist all at the same time. This suggest two different types of ideology: the universal and exclusive on the one hand, and the particular and non-exclusive on the other.

The source of the universality and exclusivity of modernist ideologies lies in their foundations: that is, in their theories of human nature. The opening chapter of this book defined ideology in terms of universality and exclusivity, and the means by which this was achieved was that every ideology, or rather ideological position, had a particular view of human nature (as only capable of flourishing in conditions of freedom or equality or when racial differences were observed or when in the right relationship with nature or whatever). It is precisely this insistence that human nature is all the same and that from it the same prescriptions can be deduced that apply to human beings everywhere that postmodernists object to, and which, quite independently, we seem to have become sceptical about, if not disillusioned with, in our present age. Smaller-scale ideologies seem less concerned with such absolutes than with a particular identity, as female, gay, black, nation, ethnic minority, and so on. More often than not that identity can be taken for granted.

Put another way, universal ideologies are concerned to establish people's essential human identity and this often involves elaborate theory to establish what that is and link with some particular cause. Marxism's identifying the cause of the proletariat with the cause of humanity is a good example. But with particular identities, people know who they are to start with and that they are oppressed: blacks, gays, women and so on. In the case of ethnic nationalism, very little theory is needed. More usually myth is involved more, since elaborate theory not necessary. Myth is an element in all ideologies, but more explicit in small ones, with stories of past oppression and atrocity which help to define the nation.

This is consistent with the post/late modern preoccupation with identity and multiple identity. Because they are not concerned with one's essential identity as a human being but with lower-level identities, one can hold several small-scale, particularist ideologies at the same time, and even change them from time to time.

Political reality and an ideological mixed economy

All this might support the earlier suggestion of a new, post-French Revolution, age of ideology, where all the universal ideologies have faded or merged into the background and the ideological future is in terms of smaller, non-exclusive non-universal ideologies of identity and lifestyle. But that would be politically unrealistic.

For one thing, while the nation-state and the mass political party have both been diminished by globalisation and other developments, neither are dead and neither are likely to disappear in the foreseeable future. There is a permanent need for parties of government, even if they are more constrained than in the past. There is still room for conflict and debate – perhaps between the New Right and social liberalism, with an admixture of new social movement policies and ideologies. This is what parties are about today, with their search for consensus, reliance on focus groups, appeal beyond traditional class boundaries, and minimal (though not non-existent) appeal to ideology.

The world is in flux. When the pace of change dies down and we can see the outlines of the new political landscape there may be a new surge of ideological creativity of a universal kind. Old ideologies may revive, in perhaps new versions, or there may be new ones altogether. Perhaps there may be a new polarisation between ideologies of world government and ideologies of resistance to such universality (of which postmodernism may be seen as a precursor).

In any case it would seem that the future lies in a 'mixed economy' of universal, small-scale, and perhaps even personal ideologies: the big, the small and the even smaller. It will be a complex age, which as yet it would be foolish to try to name.

References and further reading

1 Introduction and general

Adams, I., *The Logic of Political Belief: A Philosophical Analysis of Ideology*, Harvester-Wheatsheaf, 1989.

Adams, I., *Politics and Ideology in Britain Today*, Manchester University Press, 1998.

Adams, I., 'The inevitability of political metaphysics', *Journal of Political Ideologies*, 4:3, October, 1999, 269–88.

Ball, T. and Dagger, R., *Ideals and Ideologies: A Reader*, 2nd edn, HarperCollins, 1995.

Ball, T. and Dagger, R., *Political Ideologies and the Democratic Ideal*, 3rd edn, HarperCollins, 1999.

Barker, R., *Political Ideas in Modern Britain: In and After the 20th Century*, 2nd edn, Routledge, 1997.

Bell, D., *The End of Ideology: On the Exhaustion of Political Ideas in the Fifties*, 2nd edn, Free Press, 1962.

Best, G. (ed.), *The Permanent Revolution: The French Revolution and its Legacy 1789–1989*, Fontana, 1988.

Eccleshall, R., *et al.*, *Political Ideologies: An Introduction*, 2nd edn, Routledge, 1994.

Freeden, M., *Ideologies and Political Theory: A Conceptual Approach*, Oxford University Press, 1996.

Gamble, A., *An Introduction to Modern Social and Political Thought*, Macmillan, 1981.

Heywood, A., *Political Ideologies: An Introduction*, 2nd edn, Macmillan, 1998.

Journal of Political Ideologies, Carfax, 1996 to present.

Kamenka, W., *Contemporary Political Philosophy: An Introduction*, Oxford University Press, 1990.

Leach, R., *British Political Ideologies*, 2nd edn, Prentice Hall, 1996.

Lent, A. (ed.), *New Political Thought: An Introduction*, Lawrence & Wishart, 1998.

McLellan, D., *Ideology*, 2nd edn, Open University Press, 1995.

Miller, D., *et al.* (eds), *The Blackwell Encyclopaedia of Political Thought*, Blackwell, 1991.

Riff, M.A. (ed.), *Dictionary of Modern Political Ideologies*, Manchester University Press, 1987.

Schama, S., *Citizens: A Chronicle of the French Revolution*, Penguin, 1989.

Scruton, R., *A Dictionary of Political Thought*, 2nd edn, Macmillan, 1996.
Vincent, A., *Modern Political Ideologies*, 2nd edn, Blackwell, 1995.

2 Liberalism and democracy

Arblaster, A., *The Rise and Decline of Western Liberalism*, Blackwell, 1984.
Beveridge, W. (chairman), *Social Insurance and Allied Services*, Cmd 6404, HMSO, 1942.
Bramsted, E.K. and Melhuish, K.J., *Western Liberalism*, Longman, 1978.
de Condorcet, A-N., *Sketch for a Historical Picture of the Progress of the Human Mind*, The Noonday Press, 1955 [1795].
Darwin, C., *The Origin of Species*, Oxford University Press, 1902 [1859].
Dewey, J., *Individualism Old and New*, Allen & Unwin, 1931.
Dewey, J., *Liberalism and Social Action*, Putnam, 1935.
Eccleshall, R. (ed.), *British Liberalism: Liberal Thought from the 1640s to 1980s*, Longman, 1986.
Etzioni, A., *The Spirit of Community*, Fontana, 1995.
Foley, M., *American Political Ideas: Traditions and Usages*, Manchester University Press, 1991.
Freeden, M., *The New Liberalism: An Ideology of Social Reform*, Oxford University Press, 1986.
Fukuyama, F., 'The end of history?', *The National Interest*, Summer, 1989, 3–18.
Gaus, G., 'Liberalism at the end of the century', *Journal of Political Ideologies*, 5:2, 2000, 179–99.
Gray, J., *Liberalism*, 2nd edn, Open University Press, 1994.
Gray, J., *Enlightenment's Wake*, Routledge, 1995.
Green, T.H., *Lectures on the Principles of Political Obligation*, Longman, 1941 [1882].
Hartz, L., *The Liberal Tradition in America*, Harcourt, Brace & World, 1955.
Hamilton, A. *et al.*, *The Federalist Papers*, Mentor Books, 1961 [1788].
Held, D., *Models of Democracy*, Polity, 1987.
Hielbroner, R., *The Worldly Philosophers*, 5th edn, Penguin, 1980.
Hobhouse, L.T., *Liberalism*, Cambridge University Press, 1994 [1911].
Hobson, H.J., *The Crisis of Liberalism*, Harvester-Wheatsheaf, 1974 [1909].
Hofstadter, R., *The American Political Tradition*, Cape, 1967.
Holden, B., *The Nature of Democracy*, Nelson, 1974.
von Humboldt, W., *The Limits of State Action*, Cambridge University Press, 1969 [1792].
Ions, E. (ed.), *Political and Social Thought in America 1870–1970*, Weidenfeld and Nicholson, 1970.
Jefferson, T., *Jefferson: Political Writings*, Cambridge University Press, 1999 [1776].
Jones, H., *Victorian Political Thought*, Macmillan, 2000.
Keynes, J.M., *The General Theory of Employment, Interest and Money, Vol V. Collected Writings*, Macmillan, 1973.
Locke, J., *A Letter Concerning Toleration*, Bobbs Merril, 1955 [1689]
Locke, J., *Two Treatise of Government*, Mentor, 1965 [1690].
Mill, J.S., *Utilitarianism, Liberty, Representative Government*, Dent, 1910.
Mullhall, S. and Swift, A., *Liberals and Communitarians*, 2nd edn, Blackwell, 1996.
Nicholas, H.G., *The United Nations as a Political Institution*, Oxford University Press, 1971.

Nozick, R., *Anarchy, State and Utopia*, Blackwell, 1974.
Nozick, R., *The Examined Life*, Simon & Schuster, 1989.
Paine, T, *The Rights of Man*, Penguin, 1969 [1791–2].
Parekh, B. (ed.), *Bentham's Political Thought*, Croom Helm, 1973.
Plamenatz, J., *Readings from Liberal Writers: English and French*, Allen & Unwin, 1965.
Rawls, J., *A Theory of Justice*, Oxford University Press, 1971.
Rawls, J., *Political Liberalism*, Columbia University Press, 1996.
Rousseau, J-J., *The Social Contract*, Dent, 1973 [1762].
Sandel, M., *Liberalism and the Limits of Justice*, Cambridge University Press, 1982.
Sharp, A. (ed.), *Political Ideas of the English Civil Wars 1641–1649*, Longman, 1983.
Smith, A., *The Wealth of Nations*, Pemguin, 1976 [1776].
Spencer, H., *Man Versus the State*, Penguin, 1969 [1884].
Talmon, J.L., *The Origins of Totalitarian Democracy*, Secker & Warburg, 1952.
Taylor, C., *Sources of the Self*, Cambridge University Press, 1980.
de Tocqueville, A., *Democracy in America*, 2 vols., Fontana, 1968 [1835–40].
Vansittart, P. (ed.), *Voices of the Revolution*, Collins, 1989.
Unesco, *Democracy in a World of Tensions*, UNESCO, 1951.
United Nations, *Universal Declaration of Human Rights: adopted and proclaimed by the General Assembly of the United Nations on the tenth day of December 1948*, United Nations Department of Public Information, 1949.

3 Conservatism and the right

Burke, E., *Reflections on the Revolution in France*, Penguin, 1969 [1792].
Eatwell, R. and O'Sullivan, N. (eds.), *The Nature of the Right*, Pinter, 1989.
Eccleshall, R. (ed.), *English Conservatism Since the Restoration*, Unwin Hyman, 1990.
Gilmour, I., *Inside Right: A study of Conservatism*, Quartet, 1978.
Gilmour, I., *Whatever Happened to the Tories?*, Fourth Estate, 1997.
Gray, J. and Willets, D., *Is Conservatism Dead?*, Profile Books, 1997.
Ludlam, S. and Smith, M., *Contemporary British Conservatism*, Macmillan, 1996.
McClelland, J.S. (ed.), *The French Right: From de Maistre to Maurras*, Cape, 1970.
O'Gorman, F. (ed.), *British Conservatism: Conservative Thought from Burke to Thatcher*, Longman, 1986.
O'Sullivan, N., *Conservatism*, Dent, 1976.
Quinton, A., *The Politics of Imperfection*, Faber, 1978.
Reiss, H.S. (ed.), *The Political Thought of the German Romantics 1793–1815*, Blackwell, 1955.
Scruton, R., *The Meaning of Conservatism*, Penguin, 1980.
Weiss, J., *Conservatism in Europe*, Thames and Hudson, 1977.

4 Nationalism and internationalism

Alter, P., *Nationalism*, Edward Arnold, 1985.
Calhoun, C., *Nationalism*, Open University Press, 1997.
Darwin, C., *The Origin of Species*, Oxford University Press, 1902 [1859].

Hobsbawm, E.J., *Nations and Nationalism Since 1780*, Cambridge University Press, 1990.
Hutchinson, J. and Smith, A. (eds), *Nationalism*, Oxford University Press., 1994.
Hutchinson, J. and Smith, A. (eds), *Ethnicity*, Oxford University Press, 1996.
Kedourie, E., *Nationalism*, 3rd edn, Hutchinson, 1966.
Mazzini, J., *The Duties of Man and Other Essays*, Dent, 1907.
Minogue, K., *Nationalism*, Methuen, 1967.
Sieyes, E.J., *What is the Third Estate?*, Pall Mall, 1963 [1789].
Smith, A., *National Identity*, Penguin, 1991.

5 Varieties of socialism

Anderson, P. and Mann, N., *Safety First: The Making of New Labour*, Granta, 1997.
Benn, T., *Arguments for Socialism*, Penguin, 1980.
Berki, R.N., *Socialism*, Dent, 1975.
Bernstein, E., *The Preconditions of Socialism*, Cambridge University Press., 1993 [1899].
Crick, B., *Socialism*, Open University Press, 1987.
Crossland, C.A.R., *The Future of Socialism*, rev. edn, Cape, 1964 [1956].
Foote, G., *The Labour Party's Political Thought: A History* (3rd ed.), Macmillan, 1997.
Fourier, C., *The Theory of the Four Movements*, Cambridge University Press, 1996 [1808].
Gamble, A. and Wright, A., *The New Social Democracy*, Blackwell, 1999.
Giddens, A., *The Third Way*, Polity, 1998.
Giddens, A., *The Third Way and its Critics*, Polity, 2000.
Hyndman, H.M., *England for All*, E.W. Allen, 1881.
Kelly, G., *The New European Left*, Fabian Society, 1999.
Lichtheim, G., *The Origins of Socialism*, Weidenfeld & Nicholson, 1968.
Ramsay Macdonald, J., *The Socialist Movement*, Williams andNorgate, 1911.
McLellan, D. (ed), *Karl Marx: Selected Writings*, Oxford University Press, 1977.
MacKenzie, N. and MacKenzie, J., *The First Fabians*, Quartet, 1977.
Sassoon, D., *One Hundred Years of Socialism: The West European Left in the Twentieth Century*, Fontana Press, 1997.
Sassoon, D. (ed.), *Looking Left: European Socialism After the Cold War*, I.B. Taurus, 1997.
Taylor, K., *The Political Ideas of the Utopian Socialists*, Frank Cass, 1982.
Webb, B., *Our Partnership*, Cambridge University Press, 1975 [1948].
Wright, A. (ed.), *British Socialism: Socialist Thought from the 1880s to 1960s*, Longman, 1983.
Wright, A., *Socialisms: Theories and Practices*, Oxford University Press, 1986.

6 Anarchism

Apter, D. and Joll, J. (eds), *Anarchism Today*, Macmillan, 1971.
Bakunin, M., *Bakunin on Anarchism*, ed. S. Dolgoff, Black Rose Books, 1980.
Bakunin, M., *Statism and Anarchy*, Cambridge University Press, 1990.
Bookchin, M., *Post-Scarcity Anarchism*, Wildwood House, 1974.
Bowen, J. and Purkis, J. *Twenty-first Century Anarchism*, Cassell, 1997.
Carter, A., *The Political Theory of Anarchism*, Routledge and Kegan Paul, 1971.

Edwards, S. (ed.), *Selected Writings of Pierre-Joseph Proudhon*, Macmillan, 1969.
Friedman, D., *The Machinery of Freedom*, Harper, 1973.
Godwin, W., *An Enquiry Concerning Political Justice*, Penguin, 1976.
Hamilton, A. *et al.*, *The Federalist Papers*, Mentor Books, 1961 [1788].
Illich, I., *Deschooling Society*, Penguin, 1970.
Kropotkin, P., *Mutual Aid*, Heinemann, 1910.
Marshall, P., *Demanding the Impossible: A History of Anarchism*, Fontana, 1993.
Miller, D., *Anarchism*, Dent, 1984.
Nozick, R., *Anarchy, State and Utopia*, Blackwell, 1974.
Porritt, J. and Winner, D., *The Coming of the Greens*, Fontana, 1988.
Proudhon, P-J., *General Idea of the Revolution in the Nineteenth Century*, Freedom Press, 1923.
Rothbart, M.N., *For a New Liberty: The Libertarian Manifesto*, Collier, 1978 [1973].
Stirner, M., *The Ego and His Own*, Cape, 1921 [1844].
Thoreau, H.D., *The Duty of Civil Disobedience*, Signet, 1960 [1849].
Ward, C., *Anarchy in Action*, Freedom Press, 1982.
Warren, J., *Equitable Commerce*, Fowler & Wells, 1852.
Woodcock, G., *Anarchism*, Penguin, 1963.
Woodcock, G. (ed.), *The Anarchist Reader*, Fontana, 1977.

7 Marxism

Avineri, S., *Karl Marx: Social and Political Thought*, Cambridge University Press, 1968.
Berlin, I., *Karl Marx*, 3rd edn, Oxford University Press, 1963.
Bernstein, E., *The Preconditions of Socialism*, Cambridge University Press, 1993 [1899].
Bottomore, T. *et al.* (eds), *A Dictionary of Marxist Thought*, Blackwell, 1983.
Caute, D., *'68: The Year of the Barracades*, Paladin, 1988.
Cullenberg, S. and Magnus, B., *Whither Marxism?*, Routledge, 1995.
Deutscher, I. (ed.), *The Age of Permanent Revolution: A Trotsky Anthology*, Del, 1964.
Engels, F., *The Condition of the Working Class in England*, Panther, 1969 [1844].
Evans, M., *Karl Marx*, Allen & Unwin, 1975.
Held, D., *Introduction to Critical Theory: Horkheimer to Habermas*, Hutchinson, 1980.
Laclau, E. and Mouffe, C., *Hegemony and Socialist Strategy*, Verso, 1985.
Kolakowski, L., *Main Currents of Marxism*, 3 vols., Oxford University Press, 1978.
Lenin, V.I., *Selected Works*, Lawrence & Wishart, 1968.
Lenin, V.I., *Imperialism, the Highest Stage of Capitalism*, Foreign Language Press, Peking, 1973 [1916].
Lenin, V.I., *What Is To Be Done?*, Oxford University Press, 1993.
Lichtheim, G., *Marxism* , 2nd edn, Routledge and Kegan Paul, 1964.
McLellan, D. (ed.), *Karl Marx: Selected Writings*, Oxford University Press, 1977.
McLellan, D., *Marxism after Marx*, 2nd edn, Macmillan, 1979.
McLellan, D., *The Thought of Karl Marx*, 2nd edn, Macmillan, 1980.
Marcuse, H., *One Dimensional Man*, Sphere Books, 1964.
Schram, S. (ed.), *The Political thought of Mao Tse Tung*, 2nd edn, Praeger, 1969.
Teodori, M., *The New Left: A Documentary History*, Jonathan Cape, 1970.
Weber, M., *The Theory of Social and Economic Organisation*, The Free Press, 1964 [1922–3].

8 Racism and fascism

Benewick, R., *The Fascist Movement in Britain*, 2nd edn, Allen Lane, 1972.
Biddis, M.D., *Gobineau: Selected Political Writings*, Cape, 1970.
Blinkhorn, M. (ed.), *Fascists and Conservatives*, Unwin Hyman, 1990.
Bulmer, M. and Solomos, J., *Racism*, Oxford University Press., 1999.
Carmichael, S. and Hamilton, C.V., *Black Power: The Politics of Liberation in America*, Random House, 1967.
Cheles, L. *et al.* (eds), *Neo-Fascism in Europe*, Longman, 1991.
Eatwell, R., *Fascism: A History*, Vintage, 1996.
Fanon, F., *Black Skin, White Masks*, Grove Press, 1982.
Griffin, R., *The Nature of Fascism*, Routledge, 1993.
Griffin, R. (ed.), *Fascism*, Oxford University Press, 1995.
Hainsworth, P. (ed.), *The Extreme right in Europe and the USA*, St Martins Press, 1992.
Hainsworth, P. (ed.), *The Politics of the Extreme Right: From the Margins to the Mainstream*, Pinter, 2000.
Harris, G., *The Dark Side of Europe: The Extreme Right Today*, Edinburgh University Press, 1990.
Hitler, A., *Mein Kampf*, Hutchinson, 1969.
Jäckel, E., *Hitler's World View*, Harvard University Press, 1972.
Lyttleton, A., *Italian Fascisms: From Pareto to Gentile*, Cape, 1973.
Nolte, E., *Three Faces of Fascism*, Mentor, 1965.
O'Sullivan, N., *Fascism*, Dent, 1983.
Paine, T., *The Rights of Man*, Penguin, 1969.
Robertson, P., *The New World Order*, Word Publishing, 1991.
Snyder, L.L., *The Idea of Racism*, Van Nostrand, 1962.
Thompson, L., *The Political Mythology of Apartheid*, Yale University Press, 1985.
Wilkinson, P., *The New Fascists*, 2nd edn, Pan, 1983.
X, M., *The Autobiography of Malcolm X*, Grove Press, 1966.

9 The New Right

Clarke, P. and Graham, G., *The New Enlightenment: The Rebirth of Liberalism*, Macmillan/Channel 4, 1986.
Duncan, A. and Hobson, D., *Saturn's Children: How the State Devours Liberty, Prosperity and Virtue*, Sinclair-Stevenson, 1995.
Esler, G., *The United States of Anger*, Penguin, 1998.
Friedman, M. and Friedman, R., *Free to Choose*, Penguin, 1980.
Gamble, A., *The Free Economy and the Strong State: The Politics of Thatcherism*, Macmillan, 1988.
Gillespie, E. and Schellhas, R. (eds), *Contract with America*, Random House, 1994.
Gray, J., *False Dawn: The Delusions of Global Capitalism*, Granta, 1998.
Green, D.G., *The New Right: The Counter Revolution in Political,Social and Economic Thought*, Wheatsheaf, 1987.
Hayek, F.A., *The Road to Serfdom*, Routledge and Kegan Paul, 1944.
Keegan, W., *Mrs Thatcher's Economic Experiment*, Penguin, 1985.
King, D.S., *The New Right: Politics, Markets and Citizenship*, Macmillan, 1987.

Levitas, R., *The Ideology of the New Right*, Polity, 1986.

Minogue, K., *Alien Powers: The Pure Theory of Ideology*, Weidenfeld & Nicholson, 1985.

Nozick, R., *Anarchy, State and Utopia*, Blackwell, 1974.

Peele, G., *Revival and Reaction: The Right in Contemporary America*, Oxford University Press, 1984.

Sampson, G., *An End to Allegiance: Individual Freedom and the New Politics*, Temple Smith, 1984.

Schumpeter, J., *Capitalism, Socialism and Democracy*, Harper & Bros., 1947 [1943].

Smith, A., *The Wealth of Nations*, Penguin, 1976 [1776].

10 Feminism and liberation ideology

de Beauvoir, S., *The Second Sex*, Penguin, 1972 [1952].

Bouchier, D., *The Feminist Challenge: The Movement for Women's Liberation in Britain and the United States*, Macmillan, 1983.

Brownmiller, S., *Against Our Will: Men, Women and Rape*, Penguin, 1976.

Butler, J., *Gender Trouble*, Routledge, Chapman & Hall, 1990.

Charvet, J., *Feminism*, Dent, 1982.

Clarke, P. and Linzey, A., *Political Theory and Animal Rights*, Pluto Press, 1990.

Coward, R., *Sacred Cows: Is Feminism Relevant to the New Millennium?*, HarperCollins, 1999.

Cruikshank. M., *The Gay and Lesbian Liberation Movement*, Routledge, 1992.

Daly, M., *Gyn/Ecology: The Metaethics of Radical Feminism*, Beacon Press, 19978.

Engels, F., *The Origin of the Family, Private Property and the State*, Lawrence & Wishart, 1972 [1884].

Firestone, S., *The Dialectic of Sex: the Case for Feminist Revolution*, Paladin, 1970.

Friedan, B., *The Feminine Mystique*, Penguin, 1965 [1963].

Gamble, S., *The Icon Critical Dictionary of Feminism and Postfeminism*, Icon Books, 1999.

Gilman, C.P., *Herland*, The Women's Press, 1979 [1915].

Greer, G., *The Female Eunuch*, Paladin, 1971.

Greer, G., *The Whole Woman*, Anchor, 1999.

Gutierrez, G., *A Theology of Liberation: History, Politics and Salvation*, Orbis Books, 1973 [1971].

Henshaw, D., *Animal Warfare: The Story of the Animal Liberation Front*, Fontana, 1989.

Humm, M. (ed.), *Feminisms: A Reader*, Harvester-Wheatsheaf,1992.

Kemp, S. and Squires, J., *Feminisms*, Oxford University Press,1997.

Millett, K., *Sexual Politics*, Virago, 1977 [1970].

Mohr, R., *Gays/Justice*, Columbia University Press, 1988.

Singer, P., *Animal Liberation: Towards and End to Man's Inhumanity to Animals*, Thorsons, 1983.

Singer, P., *Practical Ethics*,2nd edn, Cambridge University Press, 1993.

Spender, D., *Women of Ideas (and What Men Have Done to Them)*, Ark, 1983.

Tong, R., *Feminist Thought: A Comprehensive Introduction*, Routledge, 1992.

Weeks, J., *Coming Out: Homosexual Politics in Britain, from the Nineteenth Century to the Present*, Quartet, 1977.

Walter, N., *The New Feminism*, Little, John & Co, 1999.

Wolf, N., *Fire with Fire*, Vintage, 1993.
Wollstonecraft, M., *Vindication of the Rights of Women*, Penguin, 1975 [1792].

11 Green politics and ecologism

Bahro, R., *From Red to Green*, Verso, 1984.
Bookchin, M., *Post-Scarcity Anarchism*, Wildwood House, 1974.
Callenbach, E., *Ecotopia*, Banyan Tree Books, 1975.
Dobson, A., *Green Political Thought* (3rd ed.), Routledge, 2000.
Parkin, S., *Green Parties: An International Guide*, Heretic Books, 1989.
Porritt, J., *Seeing Green: The Politics of Ecology Explained*, Blackwell, 1984.
Reed, C., 'Wild men of the woods', *Guardian*, 13 July, 1988, 21.
Smith, M., *Ecologism: Towards Ecological Citizenship*, Open University Press, 1998.
Goldsmith, E., *A Blueprint for Survival*, Tom Stacey, 1972.

12 Religious fundamentalism

Bruce, S., *The Rise and Fall of the New Christian Right: Conservative Protestant Politics in America 1978–1988*, Oxford University Press, 1988.
Choueiri, Y.M., *Islamic Fundamentalism*, Pinter, 1990.
Enayat, H. *Modern Islamic Political Thought*, Macmillan, 1982.
Holden, P., *The New Age Movement*, Blackwell, 1996.
Hiro, D., *Islamic Fundamentalism*, Paladin, 1988.
Icke, D., *The Truth Vibrations*, HarperCollins, 1991.
Katz, D. and Popkin, R., *Messianic Revolution: Radical Religious Politics to the End of the Second Millennium*, Allen Lane, 1998.
Ruthven, M., *Islam in the World*, 2nd ed., Penguin, 1991.
Thompson, D., *The End of Time: Faith and Fear in the Shadow of the Millennium*, Sinclair-Stevenson, 1996.

13 Globalisation and postmodernity

Adams, I., 'Can history be finished?', *Politics*, 11:2, October, 1991, 3–8.
Fukuyama, F., 'The end of history?', *The National Interest*, Summer, 1989, 3–18.
Fukuyama, F., *The End of History and the Last Man*, Hamish Hamilton, 1992.
Giddens, A., *Modernity and Self-Identity: Self and Society in the Late Modern Age*, Polity, 1991.
Giddens, A., *The Runaway World: How Globalisation is Reshaping Our Lives*, Profile Books, 1999.
Gray, J., *Endgames: Questions in Late Modern Political Thought*, Polity, 1997.
Hobsbawm, E., *The Age of Extremes: The Short Twentieth Century 1914–1991*, Abacus, 1994.
Haynes, J., *Religion in Global Politics*, Longman, 1998.

Kumar, K., *From Post-Industrial to Post-Modern Society: New Theories of the Contemporary World*, Blackwell, 1995.

Lyon, D., *Postmodernity*, 2nd edn, Open University Press, 1999.

Lyotard, J-F., *The Postmodern Condition: A Report on Knowledge*, Manchester University Press, 1984.

White, S., *Political Theory and Postmodernism*, Cambridge University Press, 1991.

Index